Astrology and the Lives of People

Finding Compassion, Character, and Heroism in the Horoscope

Astrology and the Lives of People

Finding Compassion, Character, and Heroism in the Horoscope

Joseph Crane

THE WESSEX ASTROLOGER

Published in 2023 by
The Wessex Astrologer Ltd
PO Box 9307
Swanage
BH19 9BF

For a full list of our titles go to www.wessexastrologer.com

© Joseph Crane 2023
Joseph Crane asserts his moral right to be
recognised as the author of this work

ISBN 9781910531846

Cover design by Fiona Bowring at Bowring Creative
Astrology charts created using Solar Fire v9.0.29 Astrolabe Inc (alabe.com)
Typeset by Kevin Moore

A catalogue record for this book is available at The British Library

No part of this book may be reproduced or used in any form or
by any means without the written permission of the publisher.
A reviewer may quote brief passages.

Table of Contents

Acknowledgements	viii
Introduction: Origins and Purposes	ix
Our Connected and Singular Lives	xii
Some Conventions and What Is Ahead	xiii
Chapter One: Astrology's Many Voices	1
Natal Astrology, Newer and Older	1
We All Want to Be Happy – But What is That?	3
Astrology's Polyphony	10
Astrological Applications	15
Part One: Living The Luminaries	**25**
Chapter Two: Soul and Will, After-Life and In-Life	27
Lunar and Solar Souls	27
The "I Will", "I Won't", and "I Can't"	31
Survival and Possibility: Two Examples	38
Calling and Being Called	43
Addiction: Paths of Misery and Redemption	46
Changes of Life: Spiritual Tranformations	49
Chapter Three: The Moon's Many Appearances	53
Astrology's Traditional Moon	53
The Body Moon	55
What Is Happening Right Now	61
The Rhythm (and Adaptation) Section	67
Moon and Saturn – Other Possibilities	69
Envy, Resentment, and the Lunar Side of Bigotry	70
Lunar Values and Heroics	72
Chapter Four: Astrology's Sun, Its Shadows, and the Stories We Tell	77
The Traditional Sun	77
How to Recognize a Solar Person	82

The Solar Luminary Develops Within Us	88
Pride Before, During, After the Fall	89
Identity and the Stories We Tell	92
The Imprint of History, Personal and Cultural	95
Chapter Five: Twelve Ways to Be Heroic	101
Solar and Lunar Heroes	100
Heracles as Solar-Hero and Everybody	102
Zodiacal Identity and Solar Heroism	105
Part Two: Planetary Excellence and Not So Much	**115**
Chapter Six: Planetary Character	117
Planets Dignified and Disposing	118
Who is in Charge Around Here?	126
Chapter Seven: The Wit and Wisdom of Mercury	131
Mercury's Households and a Tall Tale	132
Mercury and *Realpolitik*	*134*
The Excellences and Corruptions of Mercury	138
Great Things Come from Debilitated Planets	143
Mercury in Decline, Saturn as Remedy	148
Chapter Eight: Venus, For a Good Time	155
A Glittering Example	155
"The Fair Planet that Inclines Us to Love"	158
Venus in Contrast	159
The Sensory and the Sublime	161
Music and Love	163
Transcendent and Practical: Music and Marriage	166
Power and Sociability	170
Sex and Being Funny	173
The Life of The Rose	175
Venus and "Obscenity"	178
Chapter Nine: Mars: Good-Doer and No-Good Doer	183
Medieval Literary Elemental Mars	183
Quality, Sect and Dignity	184
Mars as People	186
My Favorite "Martian"	187
Mars with Other Purposes	189
Adversarial Mars	195

Table of Contents

Mars in Action	198
Mars-Mercury: Lifetimes of Fabrications	199
Sexualized or Sexually Abusive Mars	202
Affliction: Another Dark Side of the Red Planet	208
Transcendent Mars	210

Chapter Ten: Big and Vast Jupiter   213
    What They Said   214
    Jupiter: Solar and Lunar   217
    Joviality   218
    Interlude: Jupiter and Hierarchy   232
    Nonpolitical Jupiter   234
    Limiting Jupiter   238

Chapter Eleven: Saturn's Solitary Realm   242
    Jove's Executioner   242
    Finding Some Balance   245
    What Tradition Also Says   246
    Saturn and Grit   248
    Many-Splendored Saturn   249
    More Titans of Saturn   251
    Roman Nonholiday   260
    Oppression: Internal and External   265
    Standing Apart, Saturn Style   274

Part Three: The Connected and Well-Tempered Life   **279**
    Astrology's Surroundings   280

Chapter Twelve: Virtues and Intelligences: The Luminaries   283
    Virtue and Excellence   283
    Luminaries and Character Strengths   288
    Ways of Knowing: Intelligence and The Luminaries   291

Chapter Thirteen: Virtue's Components and Its Neighbors   303
    Virtues and Character Strengths   303
    Friends, Colleagues, and Lovers   310

Chapter Fourteen: Beyond the Planets and Beneath the Stars   319

Bibliography   329

Acknowledgements

Many people have contributed to completing this book. For their encouragement I thank Vanessa Lundborg, a fellow astrologer, and Judy Raiffa, a fellow traveler along different paths. Enid Newberg, my co-teacher at Kepler College, helped me develop much of this material over the last ten years, and she has been a steady friend throughout my writing. Alec Senese read through earlier chapters and offered helpful advice. Closer to home, my wife Penny read through the completed work very carefully and helped make many changes. A special debt of gratitude goes to mercurial Kimberly Ryan, who read the work from a beginning student's perspective – she knows more than she thinks – whose close reading yielded encouragement, advice, and many corrections to make. Now as in the past, Margaret Cahill of The Wessex Astrologer has offered me her confidence in my work, patience with my process, and close attention to both structure and detail. Adding in my clients and students over the years, it has taken not a village but a large community to make this book. Hopefully what I offer in return will be of some value.

Introduction

Origins and Purposes

When does something like a new book truly begin? Judging from its eventual result, I can trace this project to about twenty years ago, to a large-scale astrology conference I attended.

On the first morning there was a plenary presentation on ethics in astrology. I then sat through many hours of proposed rules and regulations that were clearly based on similar documents by psychotherapy organizations. I may have had some quibbles with certain portions of this presentation, but more immediate in my mind were, "instead of all these rules, what character strengths make for an ethical astrologer? What are the assumptions about people that underly these rules and would it not be better to discuss them directly, especially since they unconsciously inform our consulting practices?" I was probably the only attendee who did not respond to the presentation with wild applause: I knew that astrology needed a different voice.

For many years afterwards, my work was taken up with exploring Hellenistic and medieval astrology. I took particular interest in how the luminaries and the five visible planets were depicted, noting some important differences from their modern representations: some of their original attributes had been moved over to the modern outer planets. Some of my observations found their way into my book on Hellenistic astrology.[1]

Later, as I was revamping my astrology programs, I realized that *taken together, the luminaries and five planets express a totality of human nature: our failings and deceptions, the changing conditions of our lives, and our possibilities*

---

1 See *Astrological Roots: The Hellenistic Legacy*

for living abundantly. Each planet makes its own contribution but the luminaries most of all.

I recalled that early in my teaching career I had said to my new students, "Planetary symbolism, especially the inner planets, is the easiest thing in astrology to learn – they express who we are. You already know this stuff from your own lives." These seven planetary bodies have been with us all along. Sign placement and aspects from outer planets modify the action of the inner planets but do not change them: if the inner planets are the keys on the piano, sign placement and outer aspects are the pedals below.

I began to look around the cultures that supported traditional astrology and a new insight occurred to me. *Alongside the development of astrology were wisdom traditions that continue to apply to people and their life situations.* Too much modern astrological work has over-emphasized the intrapsychic or inner world – spiritual and otherwise – at the expense of attending to present conditions that drive people to talk with astrologers – vicissitudes of love and work that connect one to the larger world, also travel, friendships, and health. Much more than in modern times, there were cultures and schools of thought that addressed these issues. I returned to Plato, Aristotle, and the Stoics, not for their metaphysical speculations but for their psychological and ethical teachings. Astrology's spiritual side brought me to the medieval era and to Dante's *Commedia* that features a sustained use of planetary symbolism to depict the heights and depths of human nature.[2]

To my surprise, I found that some current trends in the fields of philosophy and psychology returned to these cultures, particularly virtue ethics in philosophy and in positive psychology. One need not force-fit astrology into a procrustean bed of modern psychological or spiritual principles, because our traditional astrological symbolism already contains

---

2   See *Between Fortune and Providence: Astrology and the Universe in Dante's* Divine Comedy

features that continue to be relevant in our lives. Since the field of astrology always reflects the culture in which it operates, I was heartened to see that some trends in our contemporary world mirror the value systems inherent in the original depictions of the luminaries and five planets.

These explorations informed my work with clients that had become more focused and, I believe, more helpful to them. Their ordinary and sometimes extraordinary lives helped me understand and appreciate traditional planetary symbolism and the value systems that go with their symbolism.

Over the past decade, I wrote many reviews of current astrology books. I liked some more than others, but found that most promoted specific astrological techniques, interpretations or reinterpretations of new planetary bodies, or engaged in metaphysical or spiritual speculations. I slowly realized that if I wrote about the wider and deeper implications of the seven visible planetary bodies, it was inevitable that I would be writing about people, their problems, and their possibilities.

Over the many years of political and cultural upheaval and to balance my own discouragement during this time in history, I researched and composed astrological profiles of historical people who I consider exemplary in some way. I found that their lives and often their writings clearly expressed basic planetary symbolism that easily applies to ordinary people like you and me. You will meet many extraordinary people here; their ethical and political orientations continue to be important now.

I finally began writing this book one month after the beginning of the COVID lockdown in the United States and the draft was completed as Russian tanks were getting stuck around Kyiv. Since then, we've had more record high temperatures, other extremes of climate, and continued global political and financial uncertainty. Ongoing work on this book has occurred as popular protests in Iran, China, and even in Russia seek to reorder their national political and cultural structures.

Given these difficult times, I recognized that this work would reflect and respond to them unknowingly or unconsciously. To some extent this is inevitable, but it also implies that we are not isolated from but are part of the larger world, and our lives express the concerns and values of our times. Yet within this membership of the larger world, our own lives are unique and significant. *Considerations of larger context as well as personal uniqueness are both important when we apply astrology to the lives of people.*

Our Connected and Singular Lives

Consider these wise words from Hannah Arendt, renowned political philosopher from the previous century.

> "The birth and death of human beings are not simple natural occurrences but are related to a world in which single individuals, unique, unexchangable, and unrepeatable entities, appear and from which they depart. Birth and death presuppose a world which is not in constant movement, but whose durability and relative permanence make appearance and disappearance possible, which existed before any one individual appeared into it and will survive his eventual departure."[3]

Arendt highlights two considerations important to any astrological consultant. Each person is singular – Walt Whitman writes "untranslatable" – and as such defies stereotyping, astrological or otherwise. Our clients' lives humble decades of professional astrological practice. We also have our places within larger horizons – societal, cultural, historical – that were present before our birth and will outlast us, but also change within our lifetimes. These horizons form a personal background that is often left unexamined.

---

3   Arendt, Hannah, The Human Condition (1958/1998). p. 96-7

How do we best capture all this richness in our lives? It is not by increasing the number of astrological factors to consider but instead focusing on what is most basic. *What are the capabilities of these seven celestial bodies that are insufficiently emphasized in today's astrology? Their manifestations are both concrete and flexible, relating directly to particular situations, possibilities, and outcomes – and to our common nature.*

Who is this book for? Hopefully my students and clients will note how much I learned from all of them. The student of astrology will have less use for keywords to understand planets and will approach them personally and with an eye toward what we all have in common. There are also some considerations of technique they may find very useful. Professional astrologers will be introduced to new resources for applying astrological symbolism to the lives of people. Those of my friends and family who are alien to astrology will read great stories about those whose lives and works matter to our common world.

Some Conventions and What Is Ahead

This book is not strictly about astrological technique although some presentation of technique is unavoidable. I have some preferences, such as using Whole Sign Houses and aversion to the Twelve Letter Zodiac and outer planets being cast as sign rulers. The first chapter will attend to most of the astrological practices used throughout this book; others will be discussed as we go along.

You may find my some of my non-astrological sources unusual. Alongside ancient philosophy, particularly its treatment of ethical issues, you will find illustrations from the western literary canon and occasional Asian sources. In the field of psychology and psychotherapy, I stress current developments that are relational and focus not on individual pathology but a positive approach of building from strength. My sources, astrological and non-astrological, do not exhaust what is valuable to this inquiry, and much remains for you to discover and use, based on your own background and inclinations. I aim for extensiveness, not exhaustiveness.

The first chapter, "Astrology's Many Voices", begins our discussion with thoughts on current astrological schools, ingredients of happiness, and natal analysis guidelines. This work then divides into Part One, *Living the Luminaries*, and Part Two, *Planetary Excellence and Not so Much* that takes on Mercury through Saturn. These parts also apply our field of astrology to concepts of soul, will, and heroism (lunar and solar). Part Three, *The Connected and Well-Tempered Life*, considers virtues and intelligences, strengths of character, friendship and spiritual transcendence, along with their relationships to the luminaries and five planets.

Chapter One

Astrology's Many Voices

Natal Astrology, Newer and Older

Astrology has always expressed its surrounding culture, whether it is with the religious outlook from Mesopotamia, the stoicism of late antiquity, the monotheistic belief systems of the medieval era, the platonic assumptions that underlie traditional spiritual astrology, or the theosophical views that have given rise to modern spiritual astrology.

When I began learning natal astrology in the mid-1980s, there were two prevailing influences symbolized by two men born in the 1800s. *Alan Leo* in the early twentieth century and *Dane Rudhyar* in mid-century helped bring natal astrology into a modern era.

Alan Leo, who adopted the adage "character is destiny," popularized an astrology based on character types focused on the signs of the zodiac. Dane Rudhyar endeavored to bring a psychodynamic approach to astrology. This intrapsychic dimension of the person had been prevalent in our culture for decades previously, and natal astrology continues to be influenced by Carl Jung with assists from various humanistic psychologists of the past century.

Dane Rudhyar, Alan Leo, and others also helped pioneer spiritual applications to astrology. From the theosophical movement in the nineteenth century to Alice Bailey's esoteric astrology in the mid twentieth century, features of the spiritual life have been applied to astrological interpretation. According to these newer traditions, astrology can help us determine a "higher purpose" in this lifetime, maybe linked with past and future lifetimes, providing direction on the road toward spiritual transformation.

Over the past few decades many astrologers have combined psychology's recent emphasis on past trauma with spiritual trajectories attained over many lifetimes. Evolutionary astrologers have discerned traumatic events that may have occurred in a previous lifetime and persist in this one. They have used astrological factors to set up a narrative to disclose past trauma and evolutionary intent, a trajectory of attainment of higher purpose over lifetimes.

When astrologers first added the three outer planets, then asteroids, and more recently Chiron and the centaurs and other planetary bodies, this widened our astrological toolbox, but we paid a price. Our depictions of the lives of people increasingly emphasized the eccentric and uncanny to the expense of our usual life concerns.

Since 1985, beginning with the republication of William Lilly's *Christian Astrology*, many astrologers, including me, have been strongly influenced by practices and concepts prior to the modern era. This movement gathered strength through many translation and commentary projects that made ancient and medieval astrology accessible to non-specialists. My understanding and practice of astrology has benefited enormously from those who have undertaken this often thankless and poorly compensated work.

The strength of traditional astrology has been its emphasis on the dynamics of ordinary life and finding insights and remedies that are immediately available. Its weakness so far is that it has not included the value systems that underlay its application to the lives of people.

There are other difficulties with an exclusively traditional approach. There are gaps in our understanding of the development of ancient and early medieval astrology, and we often do not have a full range of astrological practices. We must also reckon with astrology's role in sustaining class dominance or patriarchy – call it what you will. Throughout our history, astrology has been a resource for people with higher status and more comfortable lives than most. Traditional astrological techniques are well disposed to deal with the actual lived world of a client, but this must be supplemented by recognizing a person's social, cultural, economic, and political environments and supporting one's life within these environments. Ptolemy and Lilly said this as well.

Then there is the criticism of traditional astrology being fatalistic or deterministic. This has resulted in a "gloom and doom" image for traditional astrological interpretations, yet modern spiritual or psychological astrology can also have these tendencies. Astrology, past and present, has always been concerned with the interplay of freedom and necessity, and need not be subject to fatalistic stereotypes.

Let's establish a baseline and begin a discussion about you and me and everybody else we know.

We All Want to Be Happy – But What is That?

One can tie oneself in knots on the simple issue of what people want. We're wrong to think that we all want one thing, or that our criteria for happiness do not change over our lifetimes – or from one month to another. This fluidity is captured nicely by the centuries of tradition, whether east and west, psychological, spiritual, or economic, that have attempted to ponder this ever-present problem in different ways. This book looks at several possibilities these traditions provide to us.

Early in his popular book *Flourish* (2011), psychologist Martin Seligman cites five factors that people want for their own sake, that could be ingredients for life satisfaction: Positive Emotion, Engagement, Meaning, Accomplishment or Achievement, and Positive Relationships. One or more major components are missing in many lives, and happiness is sought and achieved elsewhere. These five factors cover much territory but lack a coherent picture that might apply to choices we make. Astrology's luminaries help give his picture greater clarity.

Happiness as Contentment: One Luminary

Remember that *happy* is close to our words *happen* and *happenstance*, implying a kind of randomness, and contrasting *hapless* is unlucky. This kind of happiness is, of course, fragile and dependent on a largely cooperative world. Its goal is not those times of joyful intensity "we can tell our grandchildren about", but an enduring low-key contentment. Seemingly futile in its pursuit and fleeting in its accomplishment, our quest for contentment is a bedrock motivation of our existence.

We all want ease and stability in our physical and emotional health. We want our relationships to be pleasing and nurturing without unnecessary complication and discomfort. For work we want predictability, naturalness, and clear distinctions among the roles people have – and for our work to be meaningful. If we are having a bad day, we want to be able to coast a little, for others to give us some slack. None of us like being kept up at night by financial worries, nor do we like seeing shut-off notices taped to our front doors, or hearing "the boss needs to see you right now" at the tail end of a work week. We look forward to the dull visits with doctors and dentists, financial advisors and tax preparers, not the exciting ones.

Many draw a little circle around their respective zone of contentment and ignore all that lies outside that circle – usually this does not work very well. We are all vulnerable to reversals of fortune, to many insecurities, since we are corporeal creatures with a need for resources (material and emotional) and a limited lifespan. Our shared vulnerability gives us the capacity for empathy for those close to us and for compassion for those we happen to not know. Often this does not happen.

On important occasions we wish those we care for "all the happiness in the world" and when departing we may say "farewell" or "best wishes". Conventional happiness is so flimsy that the desire for us and others to be merely content is a powerful aspiration – Buddhists call it loving kindness or *maitri*. Think of this kind of happiness as *lunar* in nature.

Happiness as Flourishing: The Other Luminary

On the *solar* side is *flourishing*, of the same origin as our word *flower*: a living thing fulfilling its purpose, or at least presenting its greatest beauty and richness. There is also the implication of fertility, of abundance that extends beyond the self into a larger sphere of activity and into the future. This concept captures what it feels like to be fully alive and present and need not accompany happiness in the sense of contentment – often it does not. Instead, on occasion we have moments punctuated by great joy, and then we're on to the next thing.

We all want opportunities for creativity and agency. I want to be "master of my fate, captain of my soul" with the ability to think and act from my own inspiration, to think and do things never thought or done before, and to have some impact on the world around us. All of us at least sometimes would like to be famous, even historical.

As we become older, we may think back, noting previous difficult and challenging times during which we were firing on all cylinders. We now say to ourselves, "that was a really good time", despite the anxiety or self-doubt or contentiousness we may have felt then. We wax nostalgic for those times, even when we were conventionally unhappy.

Aristotle's *Nichomachean Ethics*, maybe the first systematic human potential discourse in the West, is a resource that I have relied upon in my astrological and counseling work. Aristotle speaks of *eudaimonia*, a good spirit, the sense of completeness for a life well-lived, including the joy that accompanies the skills for doing things well.

According to this ancient philosopher, flourishing fulfills one's innate human potential as rational beings who have developed habits and dispositions of virtue (that is, those appropriate to a non-slave male living comfortably in the Greek *polis*). Aristotle's social and political work spoke, from our point of view, from the solar side.

What of the Five Starry Planets?

How do Mercury, Venus, Mars, Jupiter, and even Saturn bring contentment and flourishing?

Mercury: The satisfaction we all feel in solving problems, cleverly moving the parts of our environment so they cooperate with our needs or desires, the satisfaction we get in puzzles, games of strategy, seeing one's progress in learning a new language or fixing a broken toilet or learning a craft. This includes learning motor tasks like playing a musical instrument or driving a truck. And in a clever scheme, to spread misinformation or defraud.

Venus: Pleasure is known to us all in the form of romantic desire, sexual arousal and satisfaction, friendship, and companionship especially in pursuit of leisure activity – like parties, nightclubs or pubs, and nights at a sports bar with friends. It is also the pleasure we take from whatever we consider sublime – in different forms of music, art, or literature.

Mars: The joy of competitiveness and of leaving nothing on the field, even if the outcome is that the other guy wins. We give our all and endeavor to make an impact around us. Mars is the joy of flexing our intellectual or physical muscles, of resistance training of all kinds, the pleasure of endurance especially when we're done enduring.

Jupiter: Less personal and more tribal or even planetary, this is for gathering and participating in community. Jupiter brings us to concerts and sporting events or just a walk in the park with others on a beautiful day. Jupiter is the joy of seeing wider, like being on a mountain and seeing the great distances around us. It's what makes rich people want to go into space, fund renovations of damaged medieval cathedrals, or why we sing along at a rock concert.

Saturn: The joy of simplifying our modern lives with all its inconveniences. It is the joy we take in throwing out what is unnecessary, whether they are worn-out clothes or outmoded ideas. Some of us have moved to smaller places, donated an automobile to an adult child or to a worthy cause. This is often accompanied by a sense of relief, even liberation. We even enjoy living on a budget and having fewer choices about spending money, or, in a monogamous relationship, who we are attracted to. Even weight-reduction/exercise programs have their austere joy. All these activities help us maintain ourselves on this good earth.

These are some joys of the five starry planets, but what are their miseries? They also tell us much about the planets' intrinsic natures, operations, and difficulties. These are easy to understand, for we have all encountered these problems.

Mercury carries numbness, being stuck, feeling stupid when our thinking leads us nowhere or we find ourselves clueless and without resources. We easily forget that before we know something we don't know it, and consequently the act of learning can feel like an uphill climb.

Venus carries the hunger of thwarted romantic, sexual, affiliative, or aesthetic passion that often results in frustration, coldness and even hatred toward our former object of desire.

Mars encounters futility and helplessness in its many forms, resulting in frustrated lashing-out or self-pitying depression, in cruelty and aggression toward oneself or others.

Jupiter presents us with all kinds of excuses for numb conformity and sectarianism as we feel increasingly alienated from ourselves and what gives our lives its uniqueness. If Jupiter brings us into a larger world, it may also signal disharmony with that world.

Saturn afflictions carry a sense of being pushed around by outside factors outside our control. We may admire people who choose austerity, frugality, discipline, and renunciation. Yet when these conditions are involuntary, we have confinement, romantic or sexual frustration, bankruptcy and poverty, and the simplicity of the prison cell or hospital bed. We find none of these circumstances pleasing.

Life at the Extremes

Aristotle tells us that there is a floor to flourishing: we need to meet our biological needs first. It is not a happy life if our energy is consumed in a daily search for security or if we are ailing physically or mentally. Yet, in discussing happiness or eudaimonia in the light of fortune's down turnings, and in a solar fashion, he gives us the picture of *nobility in the face of adversity*:

> "If [life's events] turn out ill they crush and maim happiness; for they both bring pain with them and hinder many activities. Yet even in these nobility shines through, not through insensitivity to pain but through nobility and greatness of soul."[1]

The centuries after Aristotle gave us the image of the Stoic sage. For example, Epictetus, born into slavery, and limp of gait, taught that we can live contentedly under difficult external circumstances – if we let go of what we have no control over, i.e., the seemingly wayward turnings of fortune.

We know from history that some people have voluntarily reduced their lives below common necessities to serve a higher calling, like the medieval Francis of Assisi or the Tibetan sage Milarepa and their respective close followers. Those who live in spiritual communities or as spiritual hermits pledge to live austerely without the comforts most of us take for granted. We also know of many who have lain down their lives for what they conceived to be a larger purpose: political prisoners, those who perished in war or those risking their deaths to thwart mass violence.

---

1 Translated W.D. Ross, *Basic Works of Aristotle, p. 948*, 1100.27-33. Another translation by R. Hackman appears in *Loeb Classical Library*, Bk. I.10.12-13.

All these people have put aside ordinary concerns for creature comforts and securities – their lunar selves. They may inspire and instruct us but many of us consider their lifestyles and achievements beyond our reach. Or, thinking of those who have risked their lives in quick reaction to an emergency, we wonder whether we would or could be as selfless and heroic as they were.

From the *lunar* side of things, we consider those compassionate and generous spirits who have operated out of the limelight, seemingly renouncing a need to stand out and be noticed for their kindness and generosity. I think of the *hidden benefactor*, the person who causes benefit but does not stand around for the applause – and sometimes suffers for their quiet generosity. This often takes place in families when one sacrifices one's own happiness to promote that of another. Sometimes we find these qualities illustrated in movies, from Chaplin's *City Lights* to Kurosawa's *Ikiru*, to the excellent German film *The Lives of Others*.

How often in life does one "take one for the team" or lets oneself suffer for the benefit of others? In daily life this happens all the time, especially in family life. In public we hardly ever see it, yet it is often there just under the surface, and it serves to bind us together.

At the other extreme, can we truly flourish, can we be happy while sinking into moral depravity? We would all like to believe that moral depravity cannot happen to us, yet we also learn that we can feel strong when dominating, ripping off, or even endangering the lives of innocent people. Isn't it better to be a "winner" and not a "loser"? But must this imply defeating others, that others must be the losers? Can you truly flourish but at the same time diminish those around you?

In my view, Western philosophy never came up with an adequate solution to this problem. Much of Plato's *Republic* is an elaborate attempt to account for the idea that the virtuous life is the happy life – unsuccessfully. Nor do Aristotle or the Stoics address this issue adequately, although both try mightily. The Christian solution was to send evildoers to eternal punishment after they have died. The Buddhist idea of karma maintains that consequences of evil activity may occur within a lifetime and beyond.

Many of us have learned, and maybe life has taught us over and over, that diminishing others and degrading our world coarsens our minds and makes us fearful. Somebody who habitually lies, or cheats, divides himself or herself from others and are no longer trusted by them. If your idea of "winning" is to make losers of others, you become overly protective of yourself, for you fear others could turn the tables on you sooner or later. If you damage your environment – human or natural – you isolate yourself from that environment. The result of "winning" is often a kind of anxious narcissism, one that pervades but does not yet dominate our current culture.

I and you and the rest of us – and most of our astrology clients – are of a mixed character, virtuous except when we have something to lose, having noble ideals and aspirations that often diminish in the face of bitter reality. All of us aspire toward *both* contentment and flourishing. We all wish to "live long *and* prosper."

How do we apply all this to astrology? We begin with the poet Walt Whitman. If he was writing an astrology book, he might start by quoting his own words: "Do I contradict myself? Very well then I contradict myself, (I am large, I contain multitudes.)"

Astrology's Polyphony

If we look past one day's news stories in our lives, our lives have many dimensions. Although we see ourselves as continuous and we do look strikingly similar from day to day, our lives do not come together in one way only. Our lives are richer and more ambiguous than can be broken down into one major theme.

Ongoing personal integration is not only unnecessary, but it is impossible. As we get on in years, what is foreground and what is background will also change and in many ways. The conditions of our lives and our worlds necessitate different responses from what is habitual. Astrology allows us to see this multi-dimensionality of our lives, to explore its variability over time. I think of our lives as continual movements of asymmetries.

From ancient times up into the modern era, a natal chart was broken down into issues pertaining to development across the lifespan (Ptolemy) or the sequence of the Twelve Houses (Guido Bonatti, William Lilly, and many others). None of these styles endeavor to reduce a chart to a theme but uses specific indicators to answer questions about different life issues. This seems to be a very reasonable and practical approach.

How do we depict the multiplicity but also the coherence of our lives within our astrological charts? I settled on the musical notion on *polyphony*. The word comes from "many" and "voice". As in our music, different melodies or sequences in our lives appear over time – sometimes successively, sometimes concurrently – and are only finished when our lives are finished.

Musical *polyphony* requires two or more musical expressions, discrete but connected in some way, within one piece of music. If they are completely dissimilar the result can be mush. Themes can also contrast and harmonize as they weave and interweave. Musically they provide moments of sublimity. They can give forth creative responses but sometimes mush, what we call "confusion".

Much natal astrology is about recognizing patterns of similarity and contrast that can make life confusing, can cause one to be misread by others and even oneself, or can be beautifully polyphonic. Much astrological polyphony involves separate configurations involving the two luminaries separately, expressing their different ways of developing and being in the world – but not always between luminaries, as we will see with our first example chart.

Astrology and the Lives of People

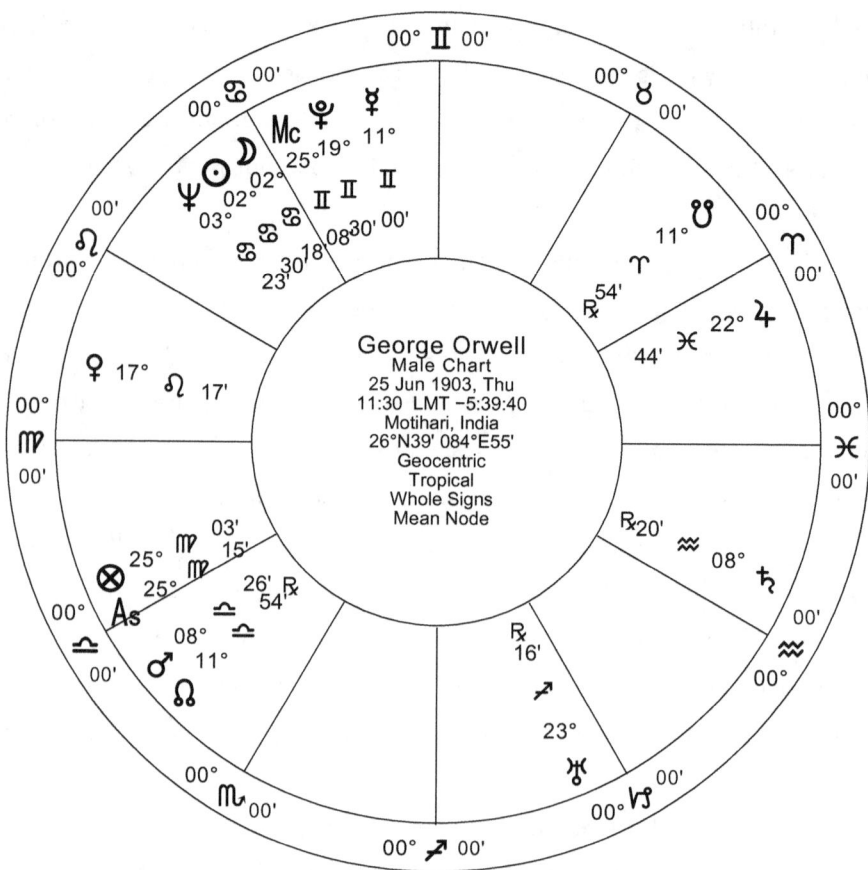

George Orwell was one of the great literary figures and political prophets of the twentieth century.[2] The Sun-Moon-Neptune configuration in Cancer speaks to his nostalgia for the English countryside and a gentlemanly lifestyle and, in his case, empathy with all kinds of oppressed peoples and cultures. This allowed him to learn first-hand the human cost of colonialism and authoritarianism. And he also loved his home and garden, which were properly cared for.

Co-existing and contrasting is Orwell's strongly mercurial nature, symbolized by this planet strongly in dignity and well-placed in the tenth

---

2   An alternate time given for Orwell is 2:30 PM that gives early Scorpio rising. This chart here is most commonly used for Orwell.

Astrology's Many Voices

house. Additionally, Mercury is oriental to the Sun, in sect, also configured with Mars in Libra and Saturn in Aquarius. Orwell showed an ability to observe and articulate life from the smallest detail to the largest scope; he was also a strong critic of the corruption of language to establish and maintain political control.

These contrasting themes of travel and intellectual adventure and of rural loyalty could have led Orwell to a life of confused purposes in conflict with one another, but for him they did not. In his years of maturity, sometimes these two configurations alternated, sometimes they worked together and so brought us his classic work. Orwell's life shows neither conflict nor unification but polyphony.

Margaret Sanger was the controversial and successful advocate for birth control availability for women in the United States. It is difficult not to notice this chart's strong angularity, with the Moon in the first house in Leo in close square to Mars and Pluto.[3]

Around the turn of the nineteenth century Sanger was employed as a nurse, treating immigrant women in some of the poorest places in New York City. Her life work began when she encountered the damage done to many of her clients by lack of information and resources on birth control, as opposed to its relative availability to women of greater privilege.

In line with her Moon and the squares from Mars and Pluto, Sanger's interest in the practical welfare of women kept company with a tenacity of purpose in a public spotlight that also cost her in personal and familial relationships.

It took more than this configuration to make Sanger successful over time. The Sun in Virgo contains more adaptability than her angular Leo-Taurus planets, and this is enhanced by Mercury in Virgo that applies to a close Uranus-Jupiter opposition. Sanger separated her cause from other liberal causes of her day, like women's suffrage, and worked the medical

---

3   This birth time is the only one available for Sanger.

Astrology and the Lives of People

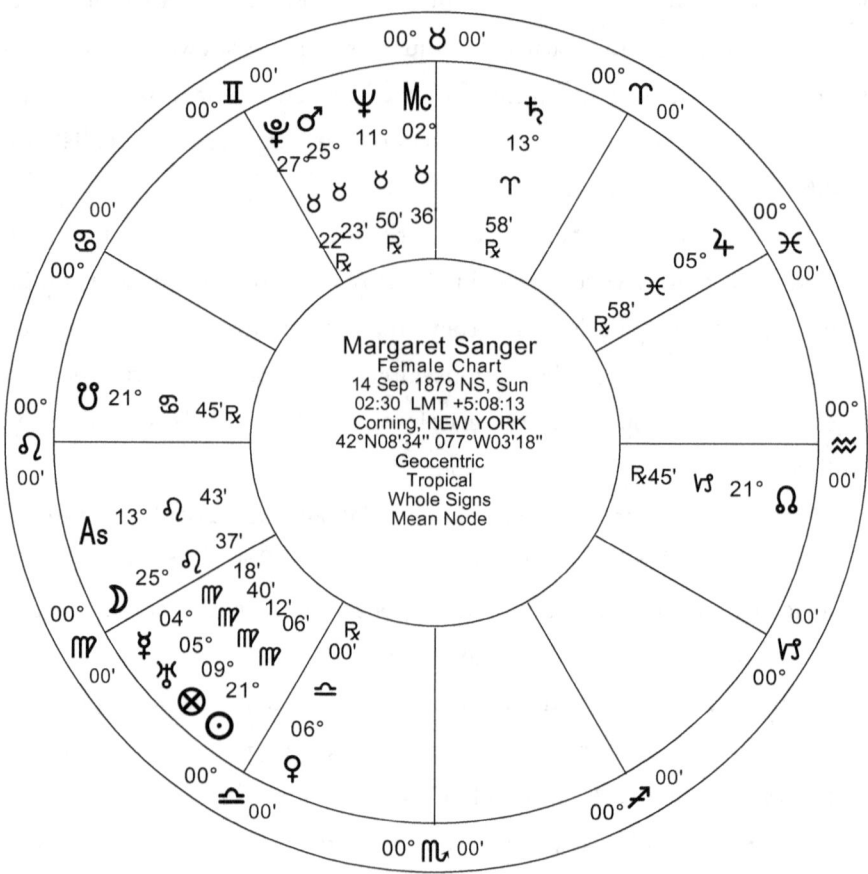

angle instead, finding her way into the medical establishment to gain mainstream support.

Sanger's chart contains one motif having a lunar nature, the other a solar one, and this is not uncommon. They speak to how the astrologer might interpret different realms of life. Even famous and driven solar individuals may have personal lives of chaos, the otherwise virtuous may have impossible relationships with family members and romantic partners, the "slacker" falls in love or becomes a solar hero (dramatically) or a lunar hero (more quietly). These motifs of our lives, although distinct, change places and connect in different ways over a day, over a year, over a lifetime.

Sometimes the same melody appears but in a polyphonic manner and our lives are like the "same damn thing" happens over and over but with variations, like a traditional canon. Sometimes our lives are more like variations of a fugue subject that has stability but can contain surprises and all kinds of creative excursions. Sometimes our lives are like different melodies occurring simultaneously and there are fleeting moments when things seem as one, but that moment passes into the next thing that asks for a different resolution. Looking from a distance there is much beauty to behold.

Astrological Applications

Some astrological conventions will persist throughout this work. Since modern astrologers may vary considerably in what they see in a natal chart, it may be helpful to the reader that I mention technical features that may be unfamiliar.[4]

For example, you may not be familiar with Whole Sign Houses, planetary sect, calculating and using the Lots of Fortune and Spirit, triplicity or trigons as a planetary dignity, and symmetries of two planets to the cardinal axes. Additionally, will we use Uranus, Neptune, and Pluto, the modern planets? Following chapters will cite house joys and paranatella. We'll survey Abraham Lincoln's astrological chart to illustrate some of astrological conventions I will use throughout this book.

Did Abraham Lincoln *flourish* during the Civil War? If on any given day past March 1861, if you asked Lincoln if he was "happy" in the sense of contentment, the answer would have been a clear "no" – yet no one doubts that his life was abundant during his final years. We could say that he was fulfilling his purpose, but that sounds a bit too abstract and does not measure up to the suffering this man also experienced at this time.

---

[4] For more information on these features, see Crane, J. *Astrological Roots* (2007) The Wessex Astrologer

I begin with what is most glaring to the modern astrologer, accustomed to using the four angles of the natal chart to determine the houses. Instead, Whole Sign Houses cast the entire sign of the Ascendant degree as the entire first house, and the others follow in the order of the zodiac. Lincoln was born "around sunup" and the Sun and Ascendant are very close.[5]

Using Whole Sign Houses means that aspect relationships between houses and between signs are the same: the sign of the eleventh house always sextiles the first as Sagittarius always sextiles Aquarius. Nor does one muddy the interpretative waters trying to figure out "intercepted" houses where more than one sign (and planetary ruler) is present.

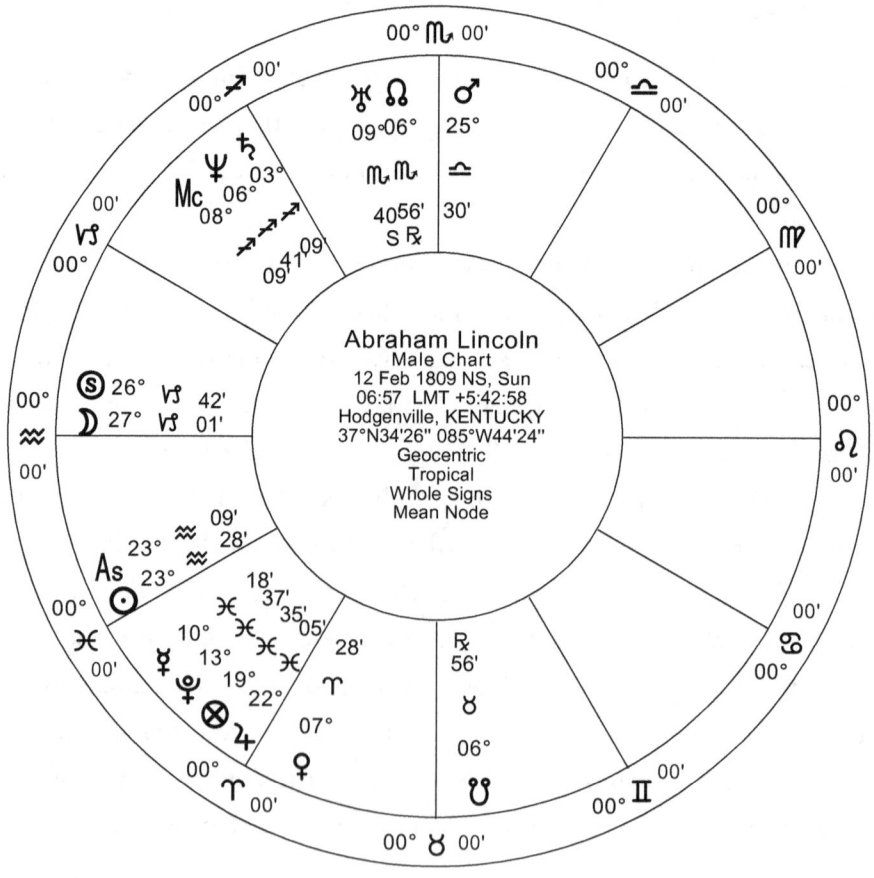

---

5   Rodden "B" – from biography

Since Lincoln was born at "sunup", it is unclear whether an accurate chart for him would be diurnal or nocturnal: this chart, with the Sun slightly below the horizon, is nocturnal. Planets in the "diurnal sect" are the Sun (of course), Jupiter and Saturn; those in the "nocturnal sect" are the Moon (of course), Venus, and Mars. Mercury can be either diurnal or nocturnal, depending on whether this planet precedes the Sun (diurnal) or follows the Sun (nocturnal). Planetary sect helps determine whether a planet is in a compatible or incompatible environment.

Whether Lincoln's chart is diurnal or nocturnal makes a big difference when one casts his Lot of Fortune and Spirit along traditional lines.

The Lot of Fortune, otherwise known as the Lot of the Moon, is more about luck and those features of life over which we have less control. Lot of Spirit, or the Lot of the Sun, is more our general attitude and the decisions we make and the initiative we take. Being practical, these two Lots form more a continuity than a contest.

One can often "eyeball" the Lots of Fortune and Spirit from a chart. What is the distance between the Sun and the Moon? Take that distance from the degree of the Ascendant. For the Lot of Fortune we'll use the distance from the Sun to the Moon in a day chart, from the Moon to the Sun in a night chart, the other way around for the Lot of Spirit. For nocturnal charts, use the distance from the Moon to the Sun for the Lot of Fortune, and on the other side of the Ascendant, using the distance from the Sun to the Moon, is the Lot of Spirit.

We can apply it to Lincoln's nocturnal chart:
- Lincoln's Moon is in the twenty-eighth degree of Capricorn, his Sun the twenty-fourth degree of Aquarius, placing the distance of twenty-six degrees between the Moon and the Sun.
- Starting from the Moon, the luminary of the nocturnal sect, and casting these twenty-six degrees from the Ascendant, one arrives at a Lot of Fortune at 20 degrees of Pisces,

governed by Jupiter in its own sign. The glyph should be familiar.
- Lot of Spirit takes the same number of degrees but from the Sun to the Moon, here all the way around the zodiac, from the luminary that is not of sect to the one that is. Taking the same number of degrees from his Ascendant, Lot of Spirit lands one degree from Lincoln's Moon.

These two Lots that use the Sun, Moon, and Ascendant are always symmetrical to the Ascendant. Lincoln's melancholic temperament is supported by the Lot of Spirit conjunct the Moon in Capricorn, and his place among politicians signified by the placement of his Lot of Fortune in Pisces with Jupiter. If Lincoln was born around sunup with a diurnal chart, Fortune would be in Capricorn and Spirit in Pisces. Lincoln might have had a more idealistic temperament but continued wandering the Illinois countryside as a travelling lawyer, not as a wartime and visionary American President.

Before things begin to look too bleak for our American President, we need to add his triplicity or trigon lords. This is a traditional category of dignity, used in addition to our standard categories of domicile or sign ruler and exaltation. (Later we'll use these lords for purposes of *disposition*, what planet governs a zodiacal placement.) Triplicities or trigons combines the diurnal/nocturnal distinction and the signs when divided into their elements.

First, we consider whether a chart is diurnal or nocturnal, with the Sun above or below the horizon. Then we divide the signs of the zodiac into their elements, each one of the four elements having its own ruler if the chart is diurnal or nocturnal. Triplicity rulers have the advantage of being easy to memorize and use on the spot.
- For planets in the *fire* signs by day, the Sun is the triplicity ruler; by night it is Jupiter.

- For planets in the *earth* signs by day look to Venus and by night look to the Moon.
- For planets in *air* signs, Saturn is the triplicity ruler; by night it is Mercury.
- For planets in the *water* signs, it is more confusing. Everybody agrees on Mars for nocturnal charts; for those who are diurnal, I and most sources look to Venus.

The Moon in Capricorn in Lincoln's nocturnal chart is in its own triplicity and so has dignity in this sign. (If he was born during the day, the triplicity ruler would be Venus.) As with Venus in Virgo in a day chart, placement in its own triplicity reduces the difficulty of a planet placed in detriment or fall.

Lincoln's Moon has a further complexity. Throughout this book we will be considering symmetries to the cardinal axes, Aries-Libra and Cancer-Capricorn. In Lincoln's chart Saturn and the Moon are equidistant from the Cancer-Capricorn axis and Jupiter and Venus are equidistant from Aries-Libra, both within one degree. These symmetries can bring planets together that are not in aspect; for planets in aspect *and* in symmetry (planets in square in fixed signs), their partnership becomes even closer. This book abounds with examples that illustrate the power of symmetrical configurations.

Symmetries to the Cancer/Capricorn axis have come down to us as "antiscia" and those of the Aries/Libra axis as "contra-antiscia" – here I follow the more modern practice of considering them equivalent. To an ancient astrologer, both are concerned with speed and visibility of given degrees of the zodiac at a given latitude. For the modern astrologer, two positions would have as midpoints the 0° Aries-Libra axis or the 0° Cancer-Capricorn axis.

First one learns the signs that are in symmetry, then simply look at their degree numbers. *If the degree numbers add up to 29-31 degrees*, they yield symmetries within one degree.

- Signs of antiscia, symmetrical to 0° Cancer-Capricorn, are Cancer/Gemini, Leo/Taurus, Virgo/Aries, Libra/Pisces, Scorpio/Aquarius, and Sagittarius/Capricorn.
- Signs of contra-antiscia, symmetrical to 0° Aries-Libra, are Aries/Pisces, Taurus/Aquarius, Gemini/Capricorn, Cancer/Sagittarius, Leo/Scorpio, and Virgo/Libra.

If one uses antiscia and contra-antiscia as equivalent, the position opposing one symmetry is the other one. For example, my Ascendant at 07° Libra would be symmetrical to 23° Virgo along with Aries/Libra axis and 23° Pisces along Cancer/Capricorn.

For our American President, symmetries between the Moon and Saturn and between Jupiter and Venus bring these planets together, even if not linked by aspect or disposition. From these considerations you may begin to view Mr. Lincoln as a rather saturnine person inwardly (Moon-Saturn) but with more outgoing and sociable characteristics of Jupiter and Venus in his overall presence.

Outer planets modify the activity of the seven visible planets that are our primary focus. Lincoln's Saturn placement in Sagittarius includes the influence of Neptune since Saturn is conjunct Neptune. Mercury's influences include a trine from Uranus and a conjunction to Pluto. (Mercury in Pisces has Jupiter, not Neptune, as dispositor and Jupiter is nearby in its own domicile or sign: Lincoln's Mercury has a strong Jupiterian influence.)

Digressing on Planetary Dignity and Character
Lincoln's chart also gives us an opportunity to think through essential debilities of the planets. You will notice that his Sun, Moon, Mercury,

Venus, and Mars are all in detriment, with only the Moon relieved by being in its own triplicity. Mercury is also in fall in Pisces.

From the time of Claudius Ptolemy to that of William Lilly, from the "Quality of the Soul" in the *Tetrabiblos* from the second century CE to the "Manners of the Native" in *Christian Astrology* in the seventeenth, astrologers have depicted a planet's positive or negative characteristics from whether that planet was well- or ill-situated in a natal chart.

In *Christian Astrology,* Lilly depicts the manners of a well-situated Mercury as "Being well dignified, he represents a man of a subtle and politic brain, intellect, and cogitation; an excellent disputant or logician, arguing with learning and discretion, and using much eloquence in his speech, a searcher into all kinds of mysteries and learning, sharp and witty."

On the other hand, a poorly placed Mercury is "A troublesome wit, a kind of phrenetic man, his tongue and pen against every man, wholly bent to fool his estate and time in prating and trying nice conclusions to no purpose; a great liar, boaster, prattler, busybody, false, a tale-carrier, given to wicked arts..."[6]

Abraham Lincoln, with natal Mercury in detriment and fall, did not conform to Lilly's depiction at all. Yet these distinctions are central to any astrological interpretation.

The difference between a planet being well- or ill-situated is most helpful with electional and horary astrology. If you ask your horary astrologer a question about a person you are meeting for a blind date, and the chart looks positive for making a connection but the ruler of the seventh house of the "other" is poorly placed by sign or house, your astrologer may tell you that the date will go okay but that the person may disappoint. If the ruler of the other is Mercury in Pisces or Sagittarius, indeed you may find this person a "troublesome wit" or somebody who lies and boasts and tries to con you.

---

6   Lilly, *Christian Astrology* facsimile edition, p. 77-8

For natal astrology, however, we need to reframe planetary dignity and debility. Because a person will have a lifetime with the same planetary placements, the planets will express their activity in different ways over time. Life circumstances change, we all go through different phases.

One possibility is that a planet in "essential" (sign placement) dignity manifests itself more straightforwardly because it has a more supportive zodiacal environment. There may be a natural talent here, as you may consider the capacity for empathy implied in Lincoln's Jupiter in Pisces. The native may (or may not) work to make a natural talent greater, and that may have to do with the physical and interpersonal environment around the native.

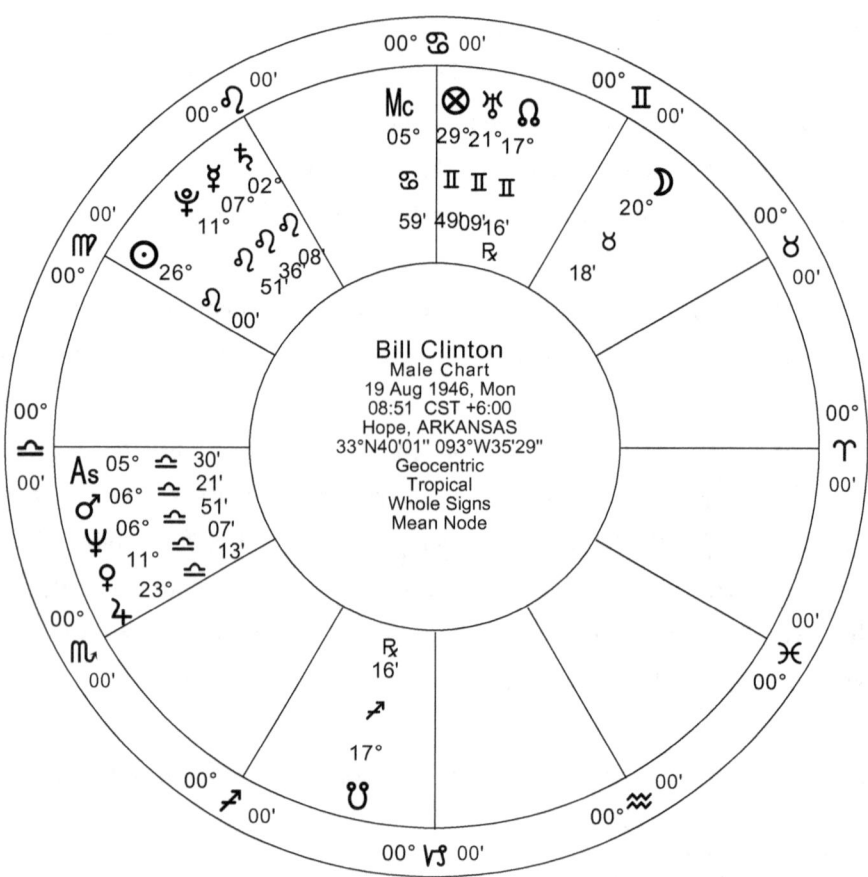

A well-placed planet may not always work to the benefit of oneself or others. Astrologers all know of people with a Mars or Saturn that is placed well but they take on too many of the malefic qualities assigned to those planets. This can also be the case with benefics – a positive placement may lead to a disappointing outcome.

The chart of a more recent American president provides an example. Many of us would envy a Venus placement like that of Mr. Clinton – in dignity, governing the Ascendant and the Moon, in the first house or place.[7] Certainly, there were positive features that manifested in his charm and ability to connect with others. Yet his political accomplishments are dwarfed by his history of sexual indiscretions through his earlier life and as President.

This chapter has summarized a general approach an astrological chart and some features that may be not well known to some modern astrologers and students of our art. Before examining a range of the Moon and Sun symbolism, we first explore two concepts dear to many modern astrologers, "soul" and "will", and their relationship to the luminaries.

---

7   Rated "B" – birth information from memory

Part One

Living The Luminaries

Chapter Two

Soul and Will, After-Life and In-Life

The Sun and Moon represent two different sets of concerns that are intrinsic to our lives. The Moon leans toward the physical, practical, and connected areas; the Sun is sense of identity, our identification and expression. How do the luminaries depict who we are and how we are, and how do they manifest in the critical realms of "soul" and "will"? Their histories go back far and broadly, over a vast realm of human experience, and show their universality and modern relevance.

Lunar and Solar Souls

Ancient burial practices and tomb treasures have been with us since paleolithic times – to the delight of grave-robbers past and present, writers of movie scripts, historians, and anthropologists. We all know about Egyptian pyramids and mummies; fewer of us know about paleolithic gravesites containing items from everyday life, Mycenean burial treasures, or Etruscan Cities of the Dead.

In 1974 farmers in China chanced upon a gigantic burial site that became one of the greatest archeological finds ever. Ying Zheng, emperor of the short-lived Qin dynasty of the third century BCE, was entombed with a fully equipped army of seven thousand individually rendered terracotta figures. This man meant to be as formidable after life as he was in life.

The later Han dynasty had complex burial practices but not on such a grand scale. Visiting an art exhibit from this historical period, I was struck by an elaborate jade garment woven for a deceased princess' burial. It was beautiful, but it was meant to be hidden from view eternally.

Astrology and the Lives of People

Why all this? The ancient Chinese had two concepts of soul: one like astrology's Moon, the other like the Sun.

The soul called *po* was thought to connect with the deceased person's corpse. Interestingly, in Chinese, the word *po* is related to the "moon's brightness," is a principle of physical growth, has some material substantiality, and is of a *yin* nature. This soul required maintenance, sometimes a ritual of nourishment by family descendants, or former subjects in the case of a deceased ruler. Ying Zheng, who thirsted for a corporeal immortality, wanted to meet death as intact and as well-defended as he was in life. For the Han dynasty woman, jade was used to delay the body's decomposition and so was a way of caring for the *po*.

We see this elsewhere. The entombment practices of the ancient Egyptians, Myceneans, and Etruscans also attempted to preserve remnants of the life formerly lived, and to offer an environment familiar to the deceased. In this way the person was to continue beyond physical death – although nothing new or interesting could ever happen again. And for those who were truly noble – by virtue or social status – the Etruscans promised an afterlife with comfort and enjoyment without a cloud in the sky. (This is captured in the Sixth Book of Virgil's *Aeneid*, in the "deep green valley" where Anchises, the hero's deceased father, resides.)

Different from the lunar-like *po* was the *hun*, the "cloud soul", sometimes rendered as "spirit," and with some of the same range of meaning. *Hun* was the human personality or psyche of the deceased, partaking of subtler nourishment than the earthly *po*. In some accounts the *hun* lives after death in a world of shadows; in other accounts it travels to heaven after death. Of the nature of *yang*, the *hun* comes close to astrology's conception of the Sun as an ongoing identity that could also transcend death's boundaries.

The ancient Egyptians had a complex rendition of soul, for they had many versions of soul that seem to form a continuum more than be a duality. If you were once or currently are a fan of Grade-B mummy movies,

Soul and Will, After-Life and In-Life

consider the range of depictions, from the monstrous to the tragically noble, of these formerly living beings.

Originally all these souls would apply only to Egypt's ruler, the Pharaoh. Ancient Egypt's entombment practices seem to have assumed a lunar human nature and divided specialized solar functions into several entities that extended a personal identity after life. The early monarchs' monumental endeavors were meant to bring together the individual, the kingdom, and the cosmos.

To the ancient Egyptians, identity was included in your real *name* that would be different from that name known by others. (This real name was kept hidden, for it would be useful for magical practice, or for somebody to use to put a curse you.) There was also a physically energetic force, perhaps like the *psyche* of the ancient Greeks. Additionally, the *ka*, another lunar-like soul, separated from the body at death but continued to reside in the tomb and could receive offerings of food and everyday items.

Now we move closer to astrology's Sun symbolism. The *ba*, a human-headed bird at the side of the deceased, could travel between worlds of the living and the dead but also required offerings of food. Importantly, the *ba* accompanied the Sun-god Re in its nightly journey through the underworld. The *ib*, the "heart", was a source of motivational force and moral awareness and this is what is judged in the afterlife. You are judged on whether you are worthy of a continued existence.

Likely you know this story – presiding over the soul's trial is Osiris, the King of the Afterlife, accompanied by forty-two other judges. First comes the Negative Confession, where the deceased denies killing, lying, stealing, causing others to be afraid, or making anybody hungry, and more. Probably you know what is purported to happen next: a ritual of weighing the soul, with a scale that has on one side an ostrich feather and the other the heart weighed down by a person's previous misdeeds. It is thus determined whether the individual will exist everlastingly or whether the soul will be cast out and destroyed. Having been judged worthy, what may survive into immortality is the *akhu*, the purified intellect and will, that may ascend to the heavens and can live with the gods.

Those who think these doctrines are far-fetched need look no further than a particular Catholic doctrine that is shared by some other Christian faiths. At the Last Judgment, our souls in the afterlife will be reunited with our former physical nature yet in a purified and eternal state. Eternal bliss is enhanced by this unification. In this tradition, some efforts are made to keep a body intact. In contrast, consider the tradition from south Asia of bringing corpses to a charnel ground for the birds and wildlife to devour. The body of the deceased is simply tossed aside, the lunar self is annihilated and one's nonmaterial soul or previous karmic propensities depart for places unknown.

When we move to the realm of folklore, we find worldwide traditions of ghosts who visit the living. Ghosts may have more solar characteristics of agency beyond the grave. Often a ghost appears when something is unfinished from the previous lifetime. Later, with the task complete, the ghost can go to a place of final rest. Ghosts (think of the German word for spirit, *Geist*) can also manifest more benignly as *spirits* to commune with their former loved ones through a medium.

Think of the modern imagined entities at the boundary of life and death, like zombies and vampires. Considering these various beings is like engaging in different thought experiments about our human nature. For example, what are *zombies* but lunar souls deprived of solar consciousness and will, rendered destructively?

Does a *vampire* symbolize a solar soul in reverse? These beings, for whom immortality is a curse, must avoid the sunlight and live in the shadows, and must get "life" from the blood of living beings. (In *Odyssey* Bk. 11, the inhabitants of the underworld must take the blood of sacrificed animals to talk with Odysseus). Vampires' dark attire, pale features, and their imperviousness to most causes of death qualify them as negative-solar without compensating lunar features (i.e., physicality, empathy, and an emotional life.) However, over time vampires have become more commonly depicted as having a full range of emotions including love; they have sex appeal and are quite approachable even if a bit vicious toward their competition.

The "I Will", "I Won't", and "I Can't"

> He who Doubts from what he sees
> Will neer Believe do what you please
> If the Sun & Moon should Doubt
> Theyd immediately go out.

These lines are from William Blake's "Auguries of Innocence" and help ground our understanding of the Sun and Moon and our tendencies toward hesitancy or confidence – as lunar and as solar beings.

The poet depicts an experience we all have had – when we doubt our abilities to deal with life as it is and ourselves as we are. This is when we step on our own sunshine (or moonshine?). Although related to the word for questioning, doubting here includes uncertainty, wavering, and the many ways we do not rise to an occasion.

William Blake, a poet and artist who received scant recognition during his lifetime but subsequently was considered a literary and artistic giant, did not suffer from lack of confidence in himself or his calling.

One finds Sun conjunct Jupiter in Sagittarius, both planets also in Jupiter's triplicity.[8] Jupiter also appears as related to the Ascendant degree by being symmetrical to the Aries/Libra axis. Blake seemed unbothered that expressing his vast vision resulted in inadequate sales of his work.

The Moon in its own sign of Cancer, in the first house, points to emotional sensitivity and interpersonal empathy that we see in much of

---
8   Rating A – from memory

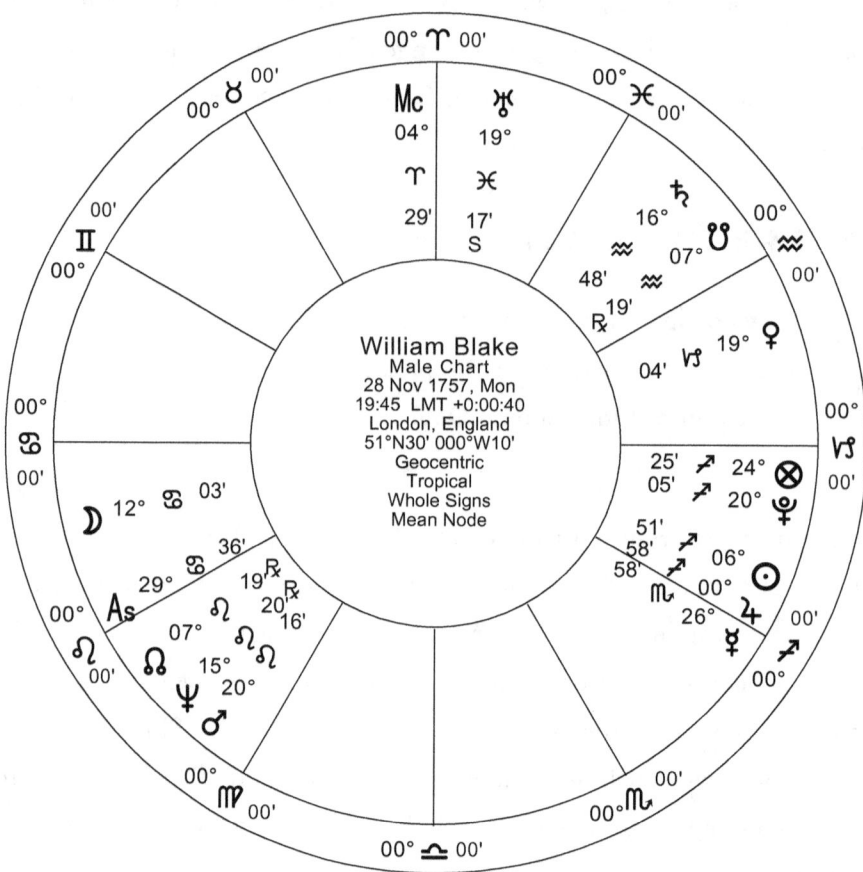

his poetry.[9] Aided by a strong marriage, indicated by Venus in Capricorn in the seventh house, Blake also had the lunar quality of *self-support* from the Moon in the first house, not succumbing to anxiety or dejection in the light of bad reviews and his work otherwise being ignored. Jupiter is not only the domicile of the Sun and in conjunction but also the exaltation lord of the sign Cancer that is his Moon placement.

---

9   This is a test of faith for those of us who use Whole Sign House systems: moving Blake's birth time a few minutes forward yields a Leo Ascendant; all planets would have different house positions. In my understanding of the native, I would think his birth time might be a little earlier.

William Blake's Jupiter served the function of maintaining both a lunar will to survive and a solar will to develop and express his large vision. Most of the rest of us are not that lucky.

How do the Sun and Moon recover from doubt? From the Sun: we learn to question ourselves and our worlds anew, we ponder those experiences and concepts and patterns of self-talk that debilitate us. From the Moon: we wake up to our physical and instinctive natures, our capacity for empathy and for love, and especially our desire to survive and grow stronger. As the luminary of the day, Sun usually operates within the scope of intention and awareness; the Moon often operates in more automatic ways, often outside our awareness: it is a body that moves more quickly than our brains.

The difference between stress or distress, between a sense of purpose or feeling adrift, begin and end with our sense of agency, our ability to take positive action, to initiate change around us. Different traditions call this capacity *volition*, *intention*, or *will*. Depicting this human function has had a long history with many psychological, philosophical, and existential lineages.

If somebody already does something naturally and without effort, like making a sandwich for lunch today, this is no act of will but doing something routine, spurred on by appetite and scheduling. On the other hand, if something is highly unlikely to occur, like winning a lottery jackpot or making a million dollars or pounds or euros as an astrologer, steps toward this goal are more indulgence in fantasy than moving toward something that would happen. To act upon will and desire, we need possibility and friction, opposition, or obstacle – factors that counter our willed intention -- to mobilize ourselves into creative action.

Lunar Burdens of Necessity
Astrology's Moon symbolizes exertions of will, but not much of what we call "free will". Here we endeavor for *survival* in the face of physical,

emotional, financial, or collective adversity and necessity. *Survival* has here many layers of meaning, manifesting in the light of physical and emotional ailments and limitations, family and personal crises, company lay-offs, legal and immigration problems, eviction notices and social ostracism as well as collective matters like climate change and social and political instability. What mobilizes Moon is anxiety, the shadow of powerlessness over factors we cannot control; Moon aims to restore normal – and "normal" means different things to different people.

Much of a consulting astrologer's practice works with a client's adversity and conditions of necessity. These situations unfortunately carry opportunities for astrological malpractice: by invoking calming platitudes, promoting new-age guilt by blaming the victim's bad karma for current difficulties, and fatalism. Our client needs to survive or endure, however broadly one interprets this; the astrologer needs to be creative to help a client see things clearly and make whatever productive choices can be made.

The Moon's modality and planetary contacts point to styles of enacting lunar will. In a fixed sign, the Moon may patiently persevere in a response long past its effectiveness. If in a mutable sign, the Moon can change erratically. Influenced by Mercury the Moon may go for the clever solution or the con-job for self-protection; the Moon influenced by Saturn may go for resignation, but influenced by Mars may "rage against the dying of the light."

For the Moon, what is a successful result of prevailing against experiences of sexual abuse, against cancer or other chronic ailments, or not having the money to pay rent? From a lunar point of view, it is a return to *normal*, the status quo. Back to normal may take effort of will, imagination, and intelligence, and the successful emotional result is relief, quieted anxiety, and re-establishing homeostasis. If we get through these problems reasonably intact, there is much to learn from them.

How might a Moon placement point to coping strategies and returning to normalcy? The Moon in Gemini might throw a post-divorce party for friends; in Sagittarius it may write a book while at home outlasting a pandemic –if Mars is in aspect to the Moon, keep up that exercise routine. The Moon in the fourth or fifth house may take on a baking challenge: either to feed the household or just for fun.

An ordinary but negative alternative is to tally up and stretch out our *resentments*. To counter being diminished by life's circumstances and by others, we passively fantasize superiority and a future come-uppance. Resentment is weirdly pleasing in the short run but costly over time. This response, when made habitual, increases self-loathing, futility, and a sense of powerlessness. This tendency toward resentment may be seen with difficult Moon placements or difficult aspects or current transits to natal Moon. Nonetheless, we astrologers should try to persuade our clients that resentment usually leads to poor outcomes and that there are always alternatives.

Ignoring the Moon's imperatives is perilous. Conjunct Neptune, one may ignore physical limitations – this is not a path I recommend to my clients. Both Simone Weil and George Orwell, two important twentieth-century writers who we will also consider later, had Moon conjunct Neptune in Cancer. Weil ignored her frail constitution and chronic migraines and eventually died of complications of malnutrition at the age of thirty-four; Orwell endured lung ailments his entire adult life and continued to take risks to his health in pursuit of what he thought was important. Orwell also died too young, soon after *1984* was published. Both, however, also exhibited positive qualities of their respective Moon placements.

The Solar Burdens of Possibility

The solar will emerges not from necessity and survival or endurance but from *self-definition* and *self-expression* that often desires to bring us into larger worlds. This feature of will belongs to the Sun and can be our sense of purpose which we may call a *calling* or *vocation*.

The Sun's placement, with planetary rulership and aspects from other planets, says much about processes of developing, changing, and dropping self-defining occupations and activities. Do our ambitions for ourselves materialize by accident, do they suddenly happen? (Sun conjunct Uranus?) Does being inspired lead to doing the hard work, or do we resist the inconveniences of fulfilling our desires? Do we skirt along surfaces, not willing to take the risks that commitments entail? (Too much domination by Mercury?)

Since we all exist in multiple ways, our choices cancel, postpone, or limit others that we could just as easily have made. Since making a choice implies proceeding on a specific course of action that often brings unanticipated results, we cannot "take it back" so easily once we have begun to act, for we may have begun a new karmic chain that may alter our lives and those around us.

Much of my work as a consulting astrologer is to help clients grapple with their desires, hesitations, and difficulties when making choices, committing to specific courses of action, tolerating the uncertainty of unknowable consequences, and doing damage control when the results are unfavorable. The astrologer need not be a psychologist or trained clinician – being one can limit one's range of communication with a client. Along with a practical knowledge of astrology, experience, maturity, and listening well can go a long way.

The solar will has a wider range of opposition than does the lunar will. For example, let's pretend that my heart is set on completing a marathon (something very difficult but not impossible at this time). To accomplish this, I would begin a multi-week training program that requires sacrifices and obstacles to confront. If I go ahead, there are many activities I would need to forgo. Consciously or not, narratives of previous accomplishments and nonaccomplishments emerge.

Any endeavor that takes effort – one could even use the infelicitous phrase "will power" – could bring great joy upon completion, or, if not wholly successful, at least the pride of having done ones best. If, however, I become discouraged early and toss the project aside, I may be reinforcing a pattern of giving up easily, and the eventual outcome is that I lose faith in myself.

Maybe after I somehow finish the marathon I define myself as a "marathon runner". (I doubt that would last very long.) If, during this process, I become injured or other events in life take priority, I may redefine myself as an "aspiring marathon runner." If, however, I give up because of lethargy or because l become discouraged, I may redefine myself as a "failure."

Although exertions of solar will come from us, we may easily discount the importance of outer (lunar) support. Our friends and partners may not take our aspirations seriously or prefer that we take up our time and energy with other things. When exploring the lives of highly accomplished people, we can see that significant others have supported their accomplishments by cheering them on, challenging their flagging spirits and distractions, and helping them pick themselves up after setbacks. Success in accomplishing solar purposes often depends on these supports attributed to astrology's Moon.

Natal placements of Sun may provide larger meaning to one's ambitions and achievements, but Mars may contribute passion and energy, Saturn provide discipline and endurance. Indications from secondary progressions, like Mercury completing an aspect to Mars or Jupiter, may excite competitive or cooperative urges respectively.

Transits to these planets can modify their activities in important ways. Transiting Saturn on the Ascendant may provoke an astrologer's reaction like "prepare for obstacles, acknowledge your limitations and apply yourself patiently – and don't assume success." A transit of Neptune on Mars would require the astrologer to caution about the results of ignoring physical needs or becoming discouraged too easily. A transit of Jupiter or Uranus onto Mercury may suggest that one use the experience as a learning opportunity, perhaps approach it scientifically, psychologically, or spiritually.

But even upon accomplishing the goal there are further discoveries to be made. We may find out that our goal has covered up an even greater challenge, like going to graduate school, or separating from one's partner, or running for elective office. Perhaps there's a problem with going from ambition to ambition. We can entertain ourselves through small accomplishments and ignore the major challenge that's in our face. There can be much uncovering to do.

Survival and Possibility: Two Examples

Man at the Beach

Here is the chart of Antonio Siciliano, an Italian immigrant to America who made fame and fortune as "Charles Atlas," bodybuilder and successful marketer of body-building programs and education.[10]

Mirroring events from his own life, he used the scenario of the "97-pound weakling" who had sand kicked in his face by some bullies. Humiliated and angry about the incident – especially because he is usually shown with a young woman - this so-called weakling begins to work on his conditioning, and years later he has his revenge. This weakling developed an image and training program that became a marketing juggernaut and established him as a body-building celebrity.

Siciliano's mythic response to early humiliation seems perfectly in tune with his planetary resources. A persistent and driven desire for revenge is your stereotypical Sun in Scorpio. Uranus with the Sun brings out even more determination, together with an independent spirit.

Mars, the planet of competitiveness and aggression, is not only the dispositor for Atlas's Sun in Scorpio but is also conjunct the Moon in

---

10 AA. From birth certificate (provided in 2017)

Soul and Will, After-Life and In-Life

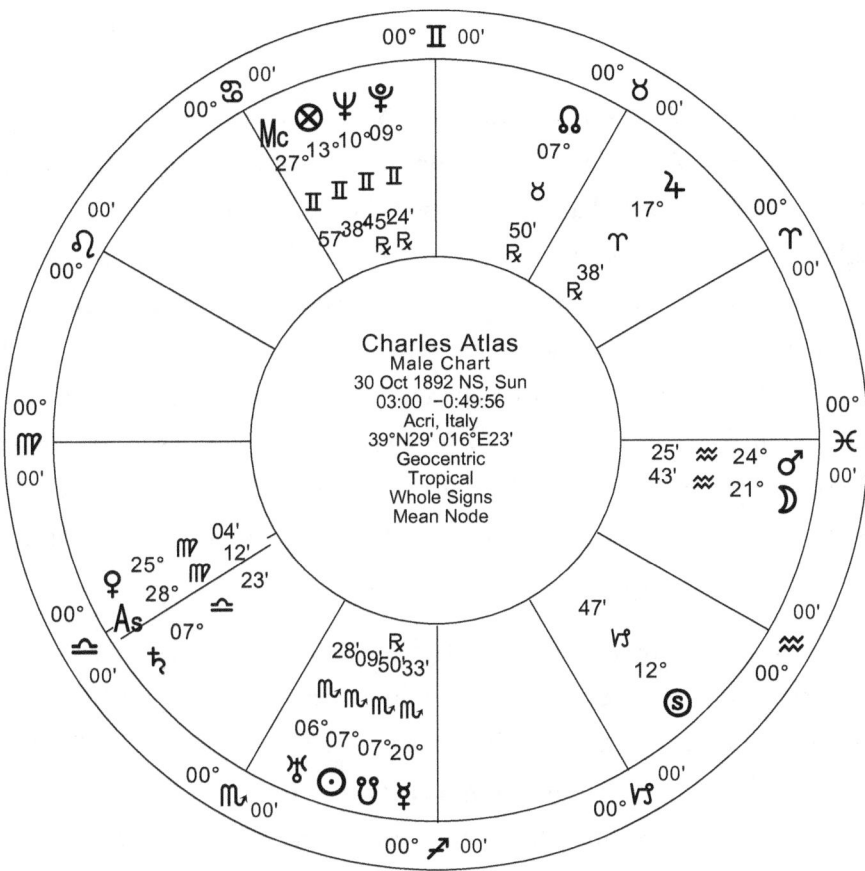

Aquarius. An athletic response seems to have been natural for this man, one that enabled him to pick himself up, and take an active role in his physical development and to bring it to others – at a profit. We must also note Saturn's role as the dispositor for his Moon-Mars conjunction but also allied with two outer planets in his tenth house of career. Physical conditioning requires sustained effort over time that brings Mars and Saturn together in a positive way.

Atlas's Venus in Virgo, so close to his Ascendant degree, and in sextile to Mercury, the ruler of his first and tenth houses, provides more information. The Virgo part reminds me of the very conditional narcissism that often accompanies men who revel in their musculature – why do so many gyms have wall mirrors facing their customers? The Venus-Mercury sextile adds precision and technique.

Not every "97-pound weakling" becomes Charles Atlas. With a more difficult Moon placement – like Moon in Scorpio or in the twelfth house – or a less developed character, the scrawny kid at the beach would not fight the bullies but *adapt* to them, most likely with a dollop of seething resentment. Maybe he works on his non-muscular areas of talent, but most likely he never goes to that beach or sees that woman again. Although our weakling may achieve other successes in life, malevolence against his former bullies may linger, so that later he secretly rejoices when bad things happen to them and even to his former female friend. This *lunar* choice is the safer but more passive and cowardly path, incurring less risk in the short term but a greater handicap later in life.

A Digression on House Joys

Charles Atlas's astrological chart contains a significant planet in its "house joy" – Mars in the sixth house. Over the centuries there have been different correspondences given to the seven planets and the twelve houses.

You may learned that there is a correspondence of the first house with Mars, the second house with Venus, the third with Mercury, following the order of domicile rulers. The Twelve Letter Alphabet casts the first house as similar Aries, the second like Taurus, etc. Over the years I have found this system to be wanting.[11] Here's a much better one:

House joys are a traditional system that aligns well with older depictions of the twelve houses. The planets in the solar sect are in their joy in houses above the horizon: Sun in the ninth, the place of the *Sun God*, Saturn in the twelfth house, that of the *Bad Spirit*, and Jupiter in the eleventh house, that of the *Good Spirit*. Below the horizon is nocturnal Moon in the third place of the *Moon Goddess*, Venus in the fifth house of

---

11   https://www.astrologyinstitute.com/articleprofile/articles/2016/untying-the-knots-of-the-twelve-letter-alphabet

Good Fortune, and Mars in the sixth of *Bad Fortune*. Mercury, as variable, is placed in the first house that is either diurnal or nocturnal.[12] Along with house joys, I have found these older designations for the astrological houses to be valuable.

Returning to our friend at the beach, Siciliano's Mars is in Pisces, in its own triplicity and in its house joy in the sixth house. This watery Mars would not pick a fight on the beach but could quietly build up his strength and later emerge the winner, if one goes beyond resentment. His square from Neptune to Mars may also point to successful glamorizing of the body-building endeavor.

Some readers may find that depiction of solar will makes too much of typical male revenge fantasy. The following chart captures a similarly strong will but a different story.

A Victorious Personality

Later renowned as author (*I Know Why the Caged Bird Sings*) and poet (well known for "Still I Rise"), musician and civil rights advocate, Maya Angelou was a survivor of childhood trauma.[13] Her response was a quiet rebellion that eventually became redemptive for her.

At the age of eight, while living with her mother in St. Louis, Marguerite (her name when young) was molested and later raped by her mother's boyfriend. After this was discovered, the assailant was tried, Marguerite was forced to testify in court, the perpetrator was found guilty but was released after only one day in jail. Shortly afterwards he was murdered, probably by Marguerite's relatives.

Convinced that her voice had killed her assailant when she testified against him, Marguerite stopped speaking for almost five years. Shutting down her speech, signified in her astrological chart by the square from Saturn to Mercury in Pisces, was a recourse that allowed her some autonomy

---

12 For more information see Crane, J. *Astrological Roots*, p. 132-138
13 AA rating: birth record quoted

Astrology and the Lives of People

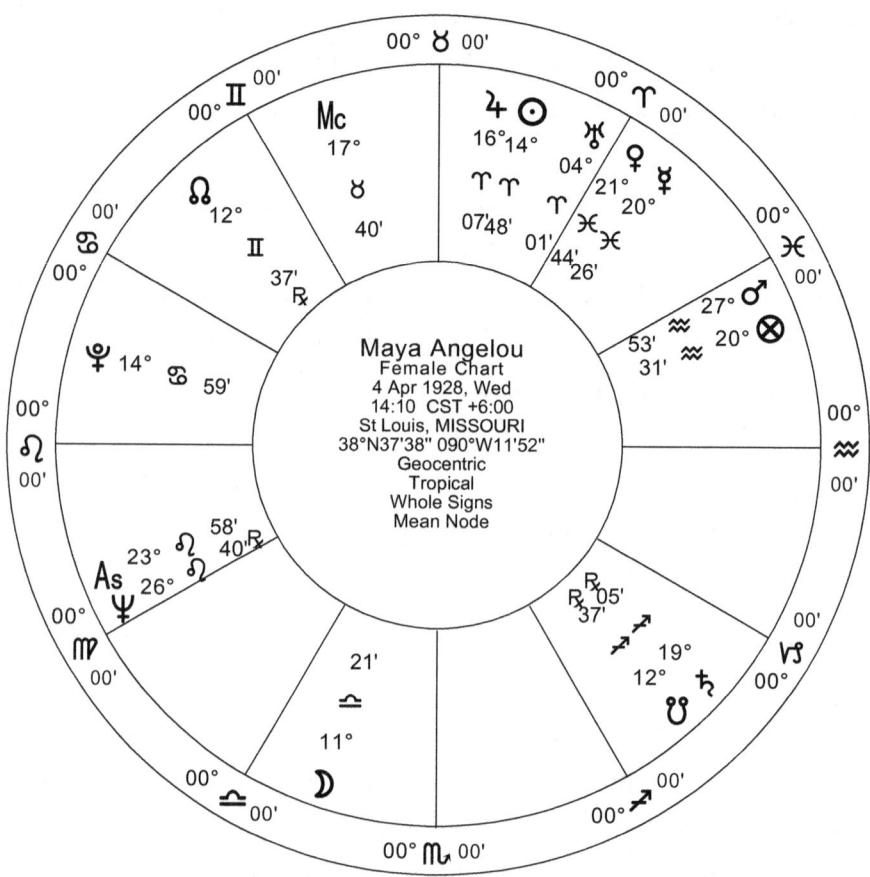

when so much was outside of her control. To be silent, she recounts, she had to "attach leechlike to sound"[14], and she immersed herself in literature and memorizing poetry.

How did a Libra Moon contribute to her survival? It seems to have been the planetary company it kept. We notice its square from Pluto in the twelfth house: in this case, what didn't kill her did make her stronger. Moon also opposes a Sun-Jupiter conjunction in Aries.[15] One could hardly

---

14 Angelou, *I Know Why the Caged Bird Sings*, Random House 2009, p.87
15 Using the modern designated "T-Square" aspect configuration, here with Pluto as an "apex planet", seems to make astrological application too abstract; better to consider each planet on its own.

Soul and Will, After-Life and In-Life

think of a Sun position being stronger than hers. Angelou would find ways to take matters into her own hands and restore solar agency from trauma.

Although convinced she would go straight to hell, and although she was punished by those around her for not speaking, Marguerite's choice to not talk gave her a chance to reorganize her social interactions and develop an inner independence. She survived to live a full and triumphant life, although not without other difficulties along the way.

Calling and Being Called

Many astrology clients, wavering between divergent interests and practical necessities, wonder whether there's a calling for them, whether their natal chart can say what "God" or "the Universe" wants from them in this lifetime, and how we may get stuck or turn to excuses.

Both our concepts of "soul" and "will" display themselves. Here we can find our identity, our role in the world, an endeavor promptly set aside when emergencies or life necessities come upon us; later we try to retrieve our original intention. We also find that pursuing our passion is soul-enhancing and, at the first sign of discouragement or boredom, our energies easily go elsewhere.

A strong example of calling and perseverance despite everything is the life and work of post-impressionist artist Vincent Van Gogh. As the reader surely knows, Van Gogh's work was hardly known outside a small circle of like-minded artists during his ten-year endeavor as an artist. He had mental illness (probably bipolar depression), famously cut off an ear, and died from a self-inflicted gunshot wound. After his death his work began to influence later generations of artists, museums containing his works are tourist destinations, and his paintings can fetch millions of dollars on the art market.

One sees a strong fire element represented in his astrological chart, especially for both luminaries.[16]

---

16 AA rating: birth record available

Astrology and the Lives of People

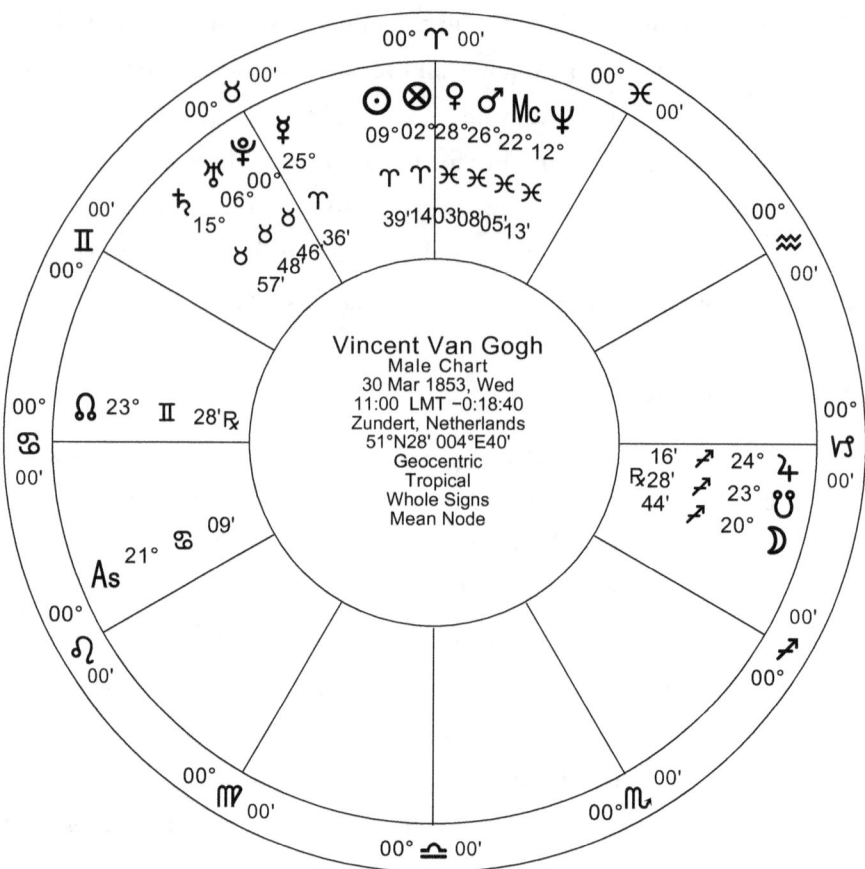

The Sun, exalted in Aries, is disposed by Mars in Pisces accompanied by Venus. Here we see an aesthetic and passionate nature – and a few disastrous relationships or would-be relationships.

The ninth house, representing spirituality and religion in part, has the Venus-Mars conjunction aspected by its sign ruler Jupiter in its own sign Sagittarius. If the ninth house tells of a religious or spiritual inclination in his art, Jupiter in the sixth shows an ability to work hard, keep his head up, and not get too discouraged that his paintings weren't selling.

From the Moon in Sagittarius in an applying trine to Mercury in Aries in the tenth house of career, we see an intense person looking for interest and excitement and unwilling to settle for some of the normal jobs he had as a young adult. As a young adult, Van Gogh had wanted to serve the poor in the ministry, but after a year his assignment was not renewed – he was just too intense. Then he decided – or he was called – to be a painter.

Vincent van Gogh was a difficult person up close: argumentative, opinionated, abrasive. He was no conventionally saintly person, although he was moved by the plight of the lower classes and converted humanitarian and religious sensibility into great art.

The artist also had some advantages that perhaps are not available to others. His brother Theo encouraged and bankrolled Vincent's artistic pursuits. This eliminated a problem most of us have had following a calling, but this situation also rendered Vincent guilt-ridden that his brother had to care for him financially. Making this slightly easier was that the artist had few material requirements; putting aside lunar desires to live a comfortably normal life, he applied himself completely to his creative pursuits. Guided by the strong fire element and an artistically inclined Venus/Mars conjunction, Van Gogh had a life focus that was unusually strong.

Most of us are not like Vincent van Gogh. Many of us – astrologers and clients – regret having missed previous opportunities, some of have felt we took some wrong road in life. We would have liked to have Vincent van Gogh's singleness of purpose, a reorganization of psyche so that our lesser desires and distractions naturally subordinate themselves to some higher calling. Most of us are inspired by the *idea* of becoming a vehicle of a higher purpose, yet we have many purposes, not just one, and we also like the status quo more than we admit.

Many of us have undergone personal transformations of different kinds, realignments of will and new discoveries of purpose. We have unfolded new aspects of ourselves with new areas of concern and activity. Often, the work of the astrologer is to discern and encourage these possibilities for our clients and give insight about timing.

Often these transformations result not from abstract longing but personal emergency, when the alternative to transformation is a diminished lifestyle, harmed caused to loved ones, or, all too often, an early death. It is to processes of addiction and recovery that we must now turn our attention. We move from a sense of purpose – an enlargement of solar soul and will – to the divided soul and divided will.

Addiction: Paths of Misery and Redemption

Many of us have seen occasions where a substance or behavior that once upon a time was fulfilling gradually became an addiction. Quickly or slowly, the substance or behavior becomes necessary to get through the day or night, to return to normal, to restore homeostasis.[17] In this way a switched-on Sun becomes a craving Moon. Craving is different from wanting, desiring, or wishing, because craving endeavors to bring back the normal, not to move toward something better. When the addictive process is in full-swing, one has the strong sense of not being who one is anymore – from an astrological perspective, this is not the darkened but the lost Sun. Recovery occurs not from self-mastery or self-control but a relaxation of will into a broader horizon.

When afflicted by addiction and consumed with the need to satisfy cravings, we sometimes take on a grim determination to resist the craving by force of will, and many struggle with these opposing tendencies and lose the battle. The exercise of personal will to combat addictive activity often results in short-term success and a deeper plunge afterwards. "Pulling yourself up by your own bootstraps" or "white-knuckle sobriety" usually fails in the long run.

Paradoxically, recovery from addiction – like that of many other types of conversion – often takes the form of surrender or deciding, in some

---

17 Addiction to painkillers begins with the desire to feel normal and not in physical pain, and our requirements for feeling normal become increasingly costly.

Soul and Will, After-Life and In-Life

way, to "turn over one's will" and so step aside from a collision of will and addictive instinct. This may sound bizarre to those who have never struggled with addiction. "Turning it over", a kind of relaxation response, may take a spiritual or an interpersonal form, as one may rely on a spiritual deity or a collective endeavor respectively. This process gives over the defensive autonomy that has served the addictive substance or behavior and opens oneself to new possibilities.

That's not the end of the matter. The source of difficulty becomes *self-will* that the "convert" manifests in the form of arrogance or complacency. One becomes bored and longs for some excitement to return, and later may regret this desire. A defiant reassertion of autonomy re-establishes pseudo-autonomy, and this can lead to returning to the addiction, or being a miserable person to be around.

By confronting self-will directly, the recovering addict can begin a new life, enforced by the remaining power of the addictive process and an immanent possibility of back-sliding into addiction. This contrast between "turning it over" and "taking it back" helps effect the transition from lunar will to survive toward solar creativity, to a less self-centered form of agency.

Here's one prominent example of this process. In 1935 Bill Wilson turned from a Wall Street speculator and spectacular drunk to co-found Alcoholics Anonymous. You see tendencies toward grandiosity in his Sun-Jupiter mutual reception but also, with Moon in Pisces and three visible planets in Scorpio, a sensitive but intense emotional nature.[18] (Uranus, in its relationship to both the Moon and Mercury, adds the possibility of sudden discovery.)

Previously, Wilson had heard from his doctor about the hopelessness of his condition. He also heard from a former patient of Carl Jung about the possibility of a religious solution; he then tried it and it failed. In June 1935, attempting to battle temptation during an unsuccessful business trip,

---
18 Chart rated B – from biographies

Astrology and the Lives of People

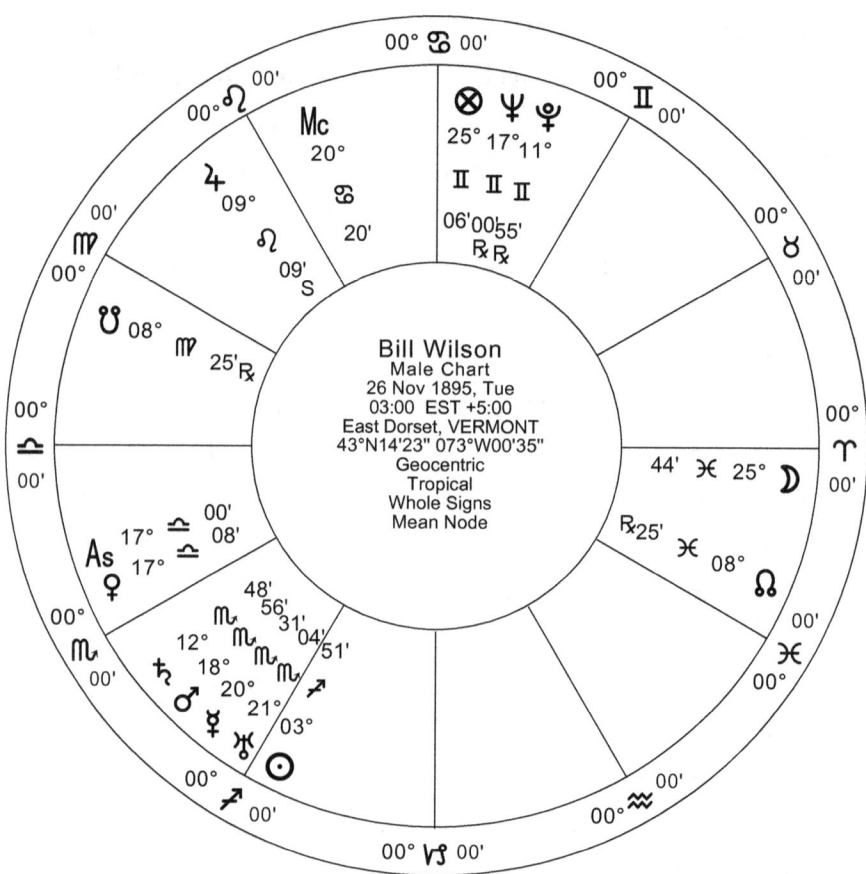

he found himself across the table from another person similarly afflicted. After their meeting neither Wilson nor "Doctor Bob" drank again; to sustain their sobriety they felt compelled to reach out to other alcoholics, and the rest is history.

You may recognize this as similar to a path undertaken by many spiritual seekers whose addiction, in their view, is to worldliness or habitual patterns of ego. Except for the rare spiritual genius among us, usually it is after previous exertions have failed that some form of surrender allows for transformation. We may find the same process in those individuals who find their "calling" that allows for singleness of purpose and the direction of soul and will.

Soul and Will, After-Life and In-Life

Changes of Life: Spiritual Tranformations

"Come to Jesus" moments, rare as they are, take a variety of forms. In his classic study *Varieties of Religious Experience,* William James states this directly:

> "The process of remedying inner incompleteness and reducing inner discord is a general psychological process, which may take place with any sort of mental material, and need not necessarily assume the religious form...For example, the new birth may be away from religion into incredulity; or it may be from moral scrupulosity into freedom and license; or it may be produced by the irruption into the individual's life of some new stimulus or passion, such as love, cupidity, revenge, or patriotic devotion." [19]

Augustine of Hippo of late antiquity was no friend to astrology – as he understood it. However, his *Confessions* narrates the stages and supports to a transformation into the new person he became when he adopted the Christian faith, and its aftermath. To what extent did he become such a new person?

Book Eight of the *Confessions* sequences his conversion. It contains a justly famous passage about his being of two minds: wanting a Christian life but also governed by his worldly sexual desires. In the throes of his confusion, he thought back to his adolescence:

> "I had been extremely miserable in adolescence, miserable from the very onset, as I prayed to you [God] for the gift of chastity I had even pleaded: 'Grant me chastity and self-control, but please not yet.' I was afraid that you might hear me

---
19 James. W. *Varieties of Religious Experience.* Penguin Classics Edition, p. 175-6

immediately and heal me forthwith of the morbid lust which I was more anxious to satisfy than to snuff out." [20]

It is hard not to love this passage – did he want chastity, or did he not want chastity? Most of us (and the overwhelming proportion of my astrology clients) have no interest in becoming less worldly, especially where romantic relationships are involved. Yet Augustine's passage captures well the frequent battles we have in other areas of temptation, willfulness, and resistance.

Equally of note is Augustine's passive stance – "God grant me chastity..." that says something about a process of reorganizing oneself: it is accomplished not by one's effort alone but coordinated with something perceived outside oneself, like the Christian "grace of God."

Yet responsibility for change cannot not lie with a Deity alone, for other factors are also involved. Augustine had an encouraging environment, from his Christian mother and from an increasing number of close friends who encouraged him. Nonetheless, he did have a miserable self-confrontation in the garden and the tears flowed. At some point, he was distracted by a voice in the distance. For a moment when his self-will relaxed just a bit, he heard the phrase "take up and read," perhaps from a children's game nearby. Thinking it was a message from God, Augustine randomly opened his nearby Bible and read a passage from an epistle of St. Paul, and he "read no further." Done – sort of.

In our daily lives finding a solution happens in small ways, as when we try to remember something or work out a problem, at some point we give up or something distracts us and a little while later the solution comes to us, seemingly from nowhere. Our attention may have gone elsewhere but the mind has not stopped working on the matter behind the scenes. This happens also when our lives change decisively, when we become a new person.

---

20 Translated by Maria Boulding, *New City Press*, Book 8, Chap. 17 p. 198

Soul and Will, After-Life and In-Life

From the point of view of astrological symbolism, when the solar will has exhausted itself with effort and lunar cruise control takes over, an authentic re-arrangement of the will might then begin. One cannot anticipate this nor manufacture it and sometimes it comes through the back door of coincidence, and for some it never happens at all.

Bill Wilson's transits are unimpressive for the middle of 1935 when he met "Dr. Bob". Wilson had previously completed one pass of Saturn in Aquarius transiting his Sun in Scorpio; later that year Saturn's retrograde station returned to that place. The walls of his addiction were closing in.

Transiting Jupiter was in Scorpio during the spring and the autumn of 1935. This is positive but not determinative for a major change in life. Wilson's secondary progressions give progressed Mercury in conjunction with progressed Uranus, another positive development for developing a new conceptual paradigm. Instead of one "road to Damascus" conversion event, we see a gradual development for Wilson that surfaced only when a specific event brought it forth, like a business trip gone bad and some activity from Jupiter by transit and Uranus by secondary progression.

Neither Augustine's nor Wilson's transformative experiences meant that their problems all went away. At the end of Book 10 of the *Confessions*, Augustine prays for God's help to overcome his shortcomings. His attraction to women was now subdued during the daytime but reappeared while he slept; then he felt captured by the pleasures of his senses. Additionally, pride and pleasure in the praise of others continued to afflict him. Wilson's urges, hesitations, and complacencies were there just as before but were now subordinate to his new paradigm. The urge to drink was lifted but not the accompanying afflictions of pride and grandiosity.

For both men, the totality of their psyche, including their personal limitations, became part of a larger paradigm when they "converted". Their new configurations suborned self-will and reduced the intensity of their inner conflicts. Both had more growing up to do and a long time remaining in which to do so.

Astrology and the Lives of People

From the astrologer's point of view, a client's path of transformation can be difficult to track. The client often applies great effort and then becomes indifferent when results do not occur. There can be bursts of progress alternating with periods of uncertainty, unpredictable coincidences ("God's way of remaining anonymous"), false starts and setbacks. The main event is usually a long-awaited final step.

Many decades ago and many years before I became interested in astrology, a similar thing happened to me. Looking back at it with astrology, there was a stunning configuration by secondary progression that coincided at one of the most painful times, occasions from which I began to make some progress, although no seeming breakthrough occurred until much time afterwards. Finally, almost two years after that, transits of Jupiter and Saturn to my Ascendant completed the process. When did my initial dissatisfaction begin that would someday bear positive results? About four years before, if memory serves.

Although the course of true change is unpredictable, an astrologer can point to trends that indicate intense activity and those that promote relaxing or "letting go". We may even suspect that an upcoming astrological configuration may finally be transformative. Noting upcoming configurations by secondary progression or transit (or decennials, solar returns, or solar arc directions) we can suggest outcomes from contexts given by the client. As confusing and frustrating as this may be, allying with a client in the process of real change is one of the joys of being a consulting astrologer.

In this chapter we've been looking at the Sun and Moon considering the key concepts of soul and will and processes of survival and transformation. By now the reader's appetite for a direct discussion of luminaries must be at its peak. The next chapters look at the Moon and Sun with their respective developmental arcs, standards, values, means of expression, and limitations.

Chapter Three

The Moon's Many Appearances

Our Moon is by far our quickest body, moving through the zodiac six times more swiftly than Mercury at that planet's fastest speed. The Moon's appearance is always on the move, always changing, appearing predictably through its phases in different sizes and shapes and in different parts of the sky. Astrology's Moon carries our corporeal nature, normal routines, and our ordinary sense of time. The Moon comprises much of our lives.

Astrology's Traditional Moon

The hierarchical and patriarchal nature of Western astrology's traditional culture displays itself in its depiction of the Moon. Yet their depictions also contain much we can use, including but not limited to our usual modern keywords "nurturing" and "feelings."

Al-Biruni was an eleventh-century polymath from the Islamic Golden Age. His *Book of Instructions in the Elements of the Art of Astrology* contains categories for each planet. He gives us buildings and countries, ores and metals, birds and animals, parts of head and face, finally "Disposition and Manners" and "Activities, Instincts, and Morals."

> "Simple, adaptable, a king among kings, a servant among servants, good-hearted, forgetful, loquacious, timid, reveals secrets, a lover of elegance, respected by people, cheerful, a lover of women, too anxious, not intellectually strong, much thought and talk." [21]

---
21 Ramsay Wright translation (1934), p. 250

Astrology and the Lives of People

It is striking how often the word *timid* is used to describe the traditional Moon. In part this goes along with the Moon's adaptability – being situationally responsive, the Moon looks before it leaps, does not try to impose itself on the world. Timidity is also related to *too anxious*: Moon in our lives has a defensive function, for it is also in tune with our vulnerabilities as physical and interconnected beings.

We see *simple* and not *intellectually strong* as limitations, but they have positive implications: the Moon does not complicate or conceptualize; it is straightforward, responding to what is immediately present. The Moon, as situationally adaptable, can be "a servant among servants and a king among kings." Whoever you are, you are with your familiars. In this context the Moon is personable and trusting and can also be accused of naivety.

The Moon is associated with the feminine – mothers and sisters (especially older sisters), other female relatives and in-laws. These are the people who kept up the home and raised the children. Mostly it was women who provided us with early practical and emotional maintenance, and the connections we carry with us as adults.

Johannes Schoener, from the sixteenth century, gives this description of lunar "Conditions and Peoples":

> "Thoughtful people, unstable, vagabond, timid, pusillanimous, worthless or whispering persons, sponsors of new things, prodigal persons, messengers, sailors, queens, noblewomen commanding the common people, millers, fishermen, and all those who work on the water." [22]

If the Sun is the king or aristocrat, the Moon is the commoner, the ordinary person. It stands for those features of us that are ordinary – the physical and habitual natures we share with others. Note Schoener's Moon-like occupations include many whose work sets them in continual motion.

---

22 Schoener, Johannes. *Opusculum Astrologicum* trans. R. Hand p. 29

The Body Moon

Astrology's lunar contributions to our activity and sense of self include our bodily sense, and the body's changes, rhythms, and cycles. This includes our changes in mood and emotion, our daily life and its supports, our habits, and our ability to dance with changing circumstances. In addition, the Moon contributes to most of our closest relationships over time and to our ability to identify with others – their suffering and their joy.

"Commodius Vicus of Recirculation"

The first word of James Joyce's hardly intelligible classic *Finnegans Wake* begins in mid-sentence with the word "riverrun", an archaicism that refers to a body of water flowing in a definite course. His first line continues and soon emphasizes "recirculation" or recurrence, alluding to the tidal flow between the Bay of Dublin and the River Liffey that also mirrors the rhythms of the Moon. "Recirculation" takes the reader on a broad path that brings together flowing history, human life and family, and an evening's dreamscape – having a particular lunar emphasis throughout. This line helps our focus on the universal domains of astrology's Moon, for there are many ways in which recirculation manifests.

Let us begin with recirculation in our physical lives. When are we "born"? This is an important issue for natal astrologers and is usually thought of as our first breath. After this moment, our urgent need for oxygenation accompanies us throughout our lives. Breath also accompanies many of our physical changes: excitement, fear, and relaxation. Breath is our moment-by-moment support in life, proceeding rhythmically while its pace and depth change as we move through the day and night. Not only do many physical/spiritual practices use breath control but, according to some traditions, our bodies keep time by the number of breaths we take, approximately fifteen per minute.

Primary ancient concepts of "soul" – the Greek *psyche* and Latin *anima* – were related to aliveness and the breath that begins at birth and ends at death.[23] Eventually we die and our breathing stops – then where does our breath go?

We also recirculate water. As we've been breathing molecules constituting the same air, the same water circulates over a long period of time. At normal temperatures, neither air nor water carries shape but changes its shape to fill different forms. Think of air in a balloon or expanding your lungs upon an inbreath, or water filling various containers, and they flow on. Air and moisture are principles of circulation that constitute many dimensions of astrology's Moon.

Radical Moisture, Vital Spirit

We can look at the interplay between cosmic pneuma (or prana) that is larger air or wind and the heat or "vital spirit" or "spark of life" that brings us through life. From the time of our first breath to our last, we are participating in the pneuma of the world, in its "world breath", and we have our pneuma as part of the whole.

The "vital spirit" that we perceive as body heat – is this a manifestation of lunar-like pneuma or is more a solar principle? In traditional medicine and traditional medical astrology, the "vital spirit" was associated with the Sun that maintains the body's heat. This is different from the "radical moisture", more the nature of the Moon. Yes, once upon a time the vital spirit was affiliated with the father and more spiritual or intellectual Sun and the radical moisture with the mother and more physical Moon.[24]

For more on the relationships between astrology's symbols and the human body, see Graeme Tobyn's groundbreaking *Culpepper's Astrology*.

---

[23] One translation of Homer's *Iliad* (Barry Powell, Oxford Press) renders the Greek *psyche* as "breath-soul".
[24] See Tobyn, Graeme, *Culpepper's Medicine* (1997), p. 108-114

The Moon's Many Appearances

Beyond Standard Divisions

It has been the Western tradition to divide our human nature into the lower, the corporeal, and the higher, the spiritual. As modern heirs to this tradition it is only natural for us to be guided, consciously or unconsciously, by these assumptions. The physical and common nature of the Moon, exacerbated by stereotypes of femininity, has placed this planet lower in importance to the Sun.

One proclamation of the equal status of the common and physical to the extraordinary and metaphysical is from the verse of the nineteenth century American poet Walt Whitman whose chart is included here. [25]

Whitman's verse, primarily captured in *Leaves of Grass* which he revised several times during his career, emphasized the non-hierarchical nature of the human spirit. This work delights in openness and nonchalance toward authority. The grand poem that opens this work, "Song of Myself", from which the verse accompanying his chart appears, applies to everyone, corporeally and spiritually.

In Whitman's chart, the Moon is at the end of the sign Leo in the positive fifth house with aspects from many planets. Neptune and more distantly Uranus in the ninth house in trine to the Moon, gives this luminary a more universal coloring; and an expressive and active Mars in Aries is in trine from the other side. Here is Whitman's desire to question conventional boundaries placed around the physical, sensual, and common - with a dash of cayenne from Mars.

Whitman's Moon is also close to the fixed star Regulus, the Heart of the Lion, the star of royalty. This is not by zodiacal degree, for their positions in the zodiac are more than a degree and a half apart; their contact is by *paranatella* or co-rising. Put differently: at the latitude and day at which Whitman was born, the Moon and Regulus rose at the same

---

25 A rating: from memory

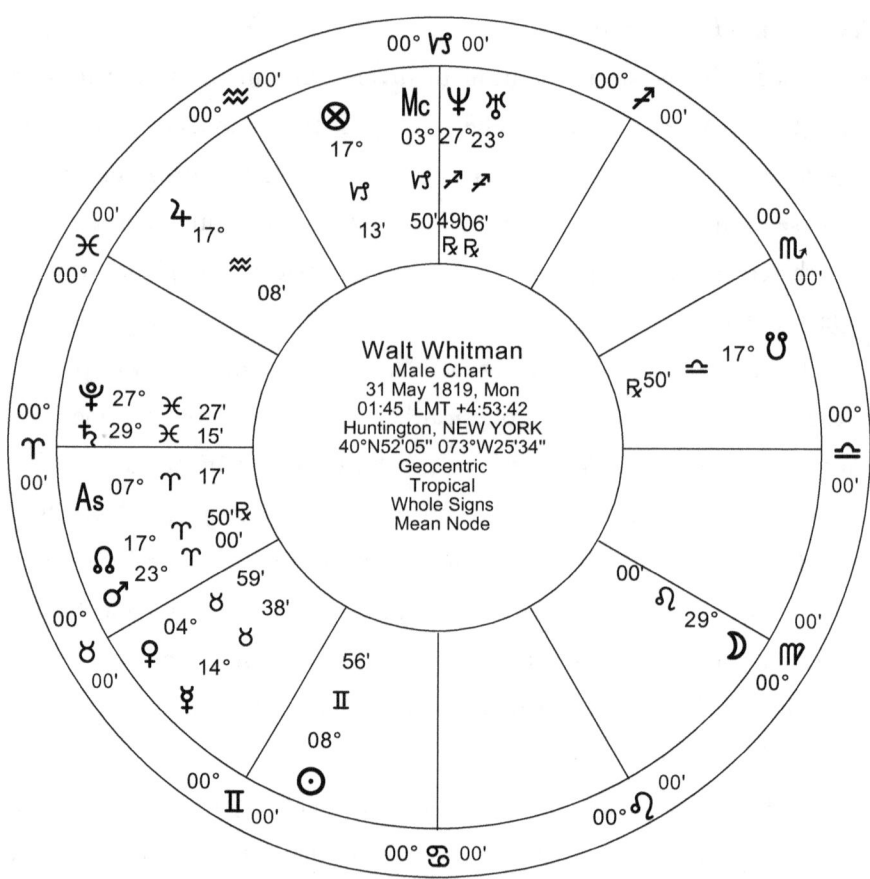

Having pried through the strata, analyzed to a hair,
counsel'd with doctors and calculated close,
I find no sweeter fat than sticks to my own bones.

time in slightly different parts of the sky [26]. For Whitman, his body, soul, and mind, had regal importance such that his verse extends to all of us.

Whitman's Moon is also the dispositor for his fourth house of home and family. Despite situational chaos, modest means, and his self-proclaimed independent spirit, he remained loyal to family commitments

---

26 For further information on paranatella see *Astrological Roots*, p. 222-225. For an exhaustive presentation, see Brady, B. *Brady's Book of Fixed Stars* (1998)

through much of his life, and his family network was a source of strength for him, perhaps compensating for a lifestyle that was unconventional for his time.

Here is the first stanza of a Whitman poem best known for its first line. He again blurs any distinctions between the physical and ordinary and the sublime or spiritual.

> I sing the body electric,
> The armies of those I love engirth me and I engirth them,
> They will not let me off till I go with them, respond to them,
> And discorrupt them, and charge them full with the charge of the soul.
> Was it doubted that those who corrupt their own bodies conceal themselves?
> And if those who defile the living are as bad as they who defile the dead?
> And if the body does not do fully as much as the soul?
> And if the body were not the soul, what is the soul?

Our Psychophysical development

In the second century of the common era, Claudius Ptolemy assigned seven phases of our lives to seven planets, with the first four years of our lives being governed by the Moon. These first years set the stage for our subsequent physical and emotional activities, all our feelings and interactions, all governed by astrology's Moon.

> "[The Moon produces] the pliancy and lack of solidity of the body and the rapidity of its growth, makes its nourishment, on the whole, moist, and finishes off that which is mutable in the body and that which is imperfect and inarticulate in the soul." [27]

---

27 Schmidt trans, Ptolemy IV, p. 43

As we start moving and controlling our new bodies, we begin the process of self-regulation, the gradual establishments of rhythms and routines that require both stability and flexibility. The care for our bodies begins at this early age and endures until the end.

Our first months and years also begin our social and interdependent selves. In the first year of our lives, we begin to sustain eye-contact and to experience the vicissitudes of early attachment that form the template for our personal relationships. Moments of joy and frustration – usually mirrored in the reactions of others to us – form the basis for being alone with ourselves and for being with others.

We imitate behavior and attempt to communicate with others however we can. Patterns of personal interaction begin to set up the development of language. Much of this is pre-programmed and is within a parental environment that is also, to some extent, pre-programmed. This process begins in a lunar way, then proceeds to the Mercurial.

Early in our lives we learn to read the moods, feelings, and emotions of others that help us in learning to discern our own. These experiences form the basis of empathy that will eventually introduce us to larger worlds and become a feature of the Moon's values.

Developing Love

Our early and ongoing experiences with dependence give us working models for adult relationships of all kinds. Relationships of dependence also fit in with our lunar needs for regulation and self-regulation, for the caretaker helps reduces anxiety through physical soothing. There is a causal relationship between the reliability of attachment and ability to explore an increasingly larger world. One's attachment style endures although it is subject to modification as we go through life.

We see this when an exciting Venusian romantic connection becomes the familiarity of a partnership in which people share their lives together. If left to Venus alone, we humans would be far less monogamous than we are, yet over time love takes on newer but more primary dimensions. Venus may add the ingredient of the other but Moon rests in an intuition of sameness.

Our Psychosomatic Self
When do we perceive ourselves *having* a body versus when we *are* our body? Aristotle and many others have observed that the soul cannot be a material part of the body, yet when we have strong localized pain from a toothache, the pain takes over our awareness. In some ways, the pain becomes us, but and at the same time remains an object for us. However, if we have flu or a heart condition or severe migraine, we become our entire afflicted body. We easily descend from Walt Whitman's somatic spirituality to the last time our inner hypochondriac expressed itself, convinced that each body ache, loss of energy, or shortness of breath must indicate that the current deadly virus is coming for us next.

When experiencing physical pleasure, from the jubilance of emotional joy to the pleasures of food, music, or sexual encounters, we are more likely to forget ourselves for a moment. We enjoy the body's mastery: it is at our disposal to provide pleasure and happiness, yet when we stub our toe or cut ourselves in the kitchen, suddenly we *are* our bodies.

This is different from being a dancer, soldier, an athlete, or even a casual runner like me: these bodies have become instruments or tools of goal achievement. However, even the dancer gets the flu before a performance and the brave soldier becomes terrified when in combat's danger; then their bodies are no longer instrumental but front and center. Moon's need for survival and maintenance has taken over from solar heroic ambitions.

What Is Happening Right Now

For most modern astrologers, the Moon is about moods and feelings, and the Moon certainly plays a role for them. In its ever-changing and immediate nature, the Moon depicts these quickly changing conditions.

These lightning-quick responses are halfway around the world before our discerning mind knows what is going on with us. This conforms with the speed of this planetary body compared to the others.

Moods and feelings are states of mind that appear to have lives of their own, yet we grab onto them as they arise, and when they turn into other moods and feelings – we grab onto those too. Even though our mind's weather patterns change continually, each time it rains or is sunny it feels like this is forever. Our quickly changing responses are antennae through which we encounter our world and respond to it, how we orient ourselves to life's situations, inner and outer.

Mood often forms the undercurrent of our state of mind. If you notice somebody attractive giving you a second look or pointedly looking past you, or you meet with unexpected criticism or praise, you may be in a good or bad mood for a time; other associated positive or negative feeling and emotions will be enhanced or diminished. For some of us, changes in mood are quiet and escape the notice of others – ask your partner if this is so for you. For others, everybody around notices the atmosphere you emit.

Feelings are a quick way of adapting and orienting ourselves to experiences, and they often leave us at the mercy of our surrounding circumstances. Although with practice – like affirmations or good habits of mind – we can attempt to manage our feelings, usually we are only partly successful, for they are spontaneous and resist programming.

Emotions are experienced and expressed by varying degrees of intensity and variability. We have different emotional inclinations – for some of us, anger or depression or cheerfulness come more naturally and more often. We're all aware that stronger emotional moments manifest physically, and we can induce emotional responses physically – if you let your body manifest angry or sad or happy behavior, that emotion can arise. How does an actor or actress access sadness or anger or love just before stepping onto the stage?

Emotions, as more physically involved, are more pronounced and enduring than feelings.

Many of us habitually ignore the bodily messages that our emotions can disclose, preferring to recognize our overt or hidden hopes and fears, projections, and preconceptions. For others, it's too easy to indulge and solidify our emotions, to prevent them from going away on us, regardless of how painful the emotion appears to be.

Astrology helps us identify potential difficulties and suggest remedies. It is helpful to look at the Moon in mutable, cardinal, or fixed modes – for variability or steadiness. For consistent emotional states, one starts with the Moon but then glances at Mars, Jupiter, or Saturn: problems include rashness, a desire to bypass what is ugly or painful, or rigidly repress or flee into melancholy.

There is some overlap between the Moon and the Ascendant, planets in the first house, and the domicile ruler of the Ascendant. Here we may encounter the distinction between our psycho-somatic body (Moon) and that which encounters others and that which we display to others (Ascendant, etc.). The following chart provides an excellent example.

Dorothy Parker was a noted twentieth-century theatre critic, short story writer and poet, a sage conversationalist, liberal activist, and creator of elegant jokes and of short ditties about sex, alcohol, and suicide.[28]

Celebrated for her brilliant writing and enduring witticisms, Dorothy Parker's Moon in Capricorn (with square to Saturn) could indicate her melancholy outlook, unsatisfying relationships, and lifelong alcohol dependency.

Parker's Moon at 10° of Capricorn has strong square from Saturn from 10° of Libra. The Moon is in sect, in detriment in Capricorn but in her own triplicity, and in square from sign ruler Saturn that is exalted in Libra. Usually, astrologers equate natal Moon in Capricorn with bitter

---
28 Rated B: from biography

Astrology and the Lives of People

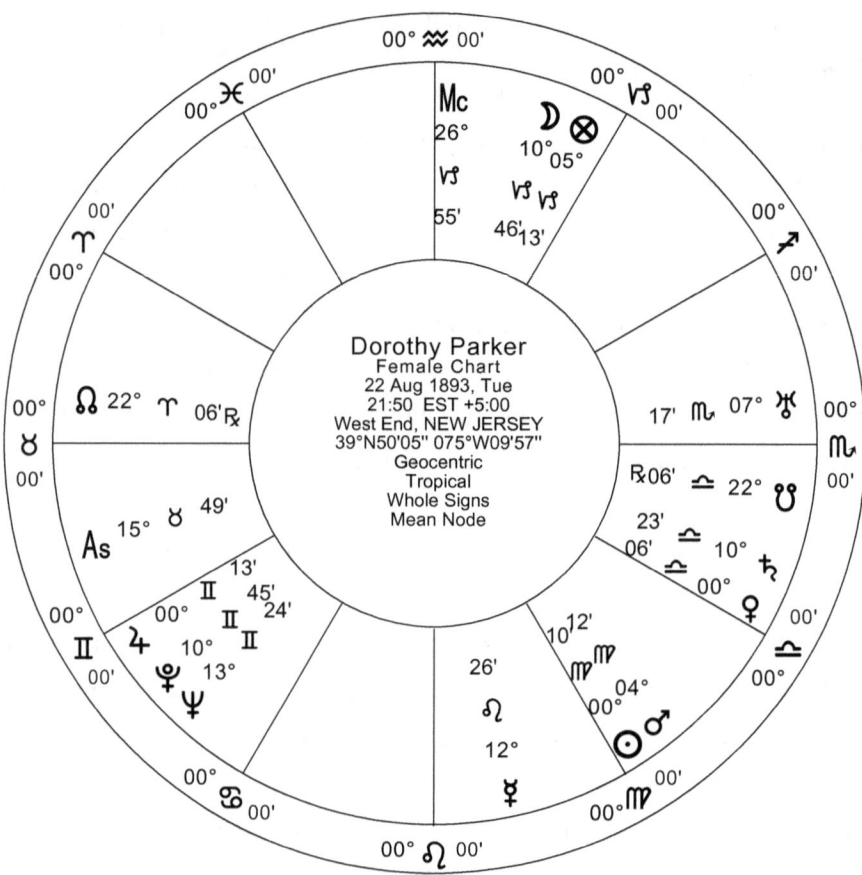

self-appraisal and a stunted emotional life. Yet this is a mixed Moon with intestinal fortitude but also harshness toward her own vulnerability and neediness.

The square to Saturn in Libra brings out some positive features of Parker's Moon placement: emotional clarity, a sense of limitation that is not self-indulgent, and, more positively, a recognition of the emotional limitations of herself and others.

Contrast this with her Ascendant in Taurus, governed by Venus in its own sign of Libra with an partile (exact to the degree) trine from Jupiter and we have the picture of an appealing and attractive personality – with a melancholy temperament just below the surface.

"Emotional Styles" and Lunar Brains

Richard Davidson's *Emotional Life of Your Brain* (2012) examines how specific brain circuits correlate with a wide spectrum of emotional functioning, circuits that engage so quickly that they are usually beneath conscious intention. Combining recent discoveries on the brain's plasticity and an interest in mindfulness meditation, Davidson offers interventions grounded in daily life. They may suggest to the counseling astrologer some practical ways to help our clients solve their lunar problems.

For example, if our responses lean toward the rigid and predictable, we lose a lot of our adaptability. Alternatively, we may err on the other side, sliding into over-sensitivity and being at the mercy of whatever temporary internal or external situations arise. This manifests over the six "emotional styles" marked out by Davidson*: Resilience, Outlook, Social Intuition, Self-Awareness, Sensitivity to Context,* and *Attention*. Extremes of these six styles also show how astrology's Moon can veer off course.

The most straightforward of the six is *Outlook* that ranges from the steadfastly optimistic and cheerful to the routinely downbeat. Whether it is disclosed by astrology's Moon or by a brain scan, tendencies toward positive or negative outlook can change over time, or at least modify and possibly rebalance.

Jupiter or Saturn placements, in relation to the Moon, can provide additional information and fine-tune standard remedies of a purely psychological approach. For those too jovial who need to be a little more realistic, one can practice delaying gratification and work to envision negative outcomes of situations or one's actions. For those overly saturnine, one can mentally focus on positive features of oneself, those in your life, and contemplate and express gratitude.

Resilience is another of the Moon's self-regulating capacities. Resilience is about our speed of recovery from a sudden occurrence, like the short-term irritation of being cut in line or in traffic, to the longer-term grief processes that accompany loss. Recovering too slowly from these setbacks, we become stuck in self-perpetuating negative states. Being too fast to recover means we do not stay with discomfort long enough to perceive what is happening around us or be able to process a setback fully. To assess these states, I look to whether the Moon is in a cardinal, fixed, or mutable sign, and its relationship – by aspect or disposition -- to fast-moving Mercury or impulsive Mars. We can work more consciously on recognizing and reappraising events and actively working on letting go when our tendency is to hold on.

Attention has two important dimensions. Can we stay focused even with distractions around us or are we likely to be taken off course by whatever distraction emerges? On the other hand, do we over-focus and lose sight of the environment around us? This manifests in situations large and small, within one's daily life or one's career, and in long-term relationships. As with many functions governed by the Moon, the right amount of flexibility is important in our daily lives. Otherwise, we're apt to lose track of our purpose or what is in the background.

As astrologers we're not in the business of diagnosing the already over-diagnosed ADHD. We can, however, note tendencies toward over-focus or diffused focus and distractibility. Note the interplay between Moon and Mercury in their respective modes, aspects from other planets, and sign rulership.

Self-Awareness, *Social Intuition*, and *Sensitivity to Context* involve ability to read ourselves from our body's signals, to sense the other person, and to involve ourselves properly within situations of daily life. All these involve the Moon's role in adaptation to changing circumstance; all require modulations within extremes of over and under-sensitivity.

The Rhythm (and Adaptation) Section

When we ride a bicycle or play the piano, we are continually fine-tuning small movements, responding to changing conditions that arise by the millisecond. Similar fine-tunings occur when living our daily lives.

Quotidian Realities

How does a US President, with Moon in Capricorn conjunct the Lot of Spirit and square Mars, manage daily life during a Civil War? Abraham Lincoln is American history's most extensively researched person and we have a birds-eye view of his daily routine during this time.

Up and working at 7 AM, sometimes he would forget breakfast; when he did show up, it was routinely eggs, toast and coffee. Then it was off to the East Wing for appointments, speech writing, and correspondence. If he missed lunch, he would snack on apples with nuts, cheese, or crackers. Work continued and sometimes his wife could talk him into taking a walk in the late afternoon.

After dinner – a simple affair but always including apple pie – he might socialize with friends but usually would retire 10-11 in the evening except when awaiting news from the war front. With this kind of schedule and a rather stressful job, Lincoln suffered from insomnia and sometimes needed a late-night solitary walk to recalibrate.

As befitting Moon in Capricorn square Mars in Libra, his was a hard-working, organized but not overly rigid schedule. There were some comforts but not much physical activity. He was indifferent to food indulgences except for apples and apple pie that he consumed regularly.

Even if we are not administering a country during a civil war, much of our lives is about the daily care of bodies and our energy. We're alike in many respects, yet our Moon placements can signal important differences between our management of daily life. If we hold onto specific life rhythms for too long or too fiercely, we become rigid and unable to adapt to circumstances as they change. The ability to change – and to set new

Astrology and the Lives of People

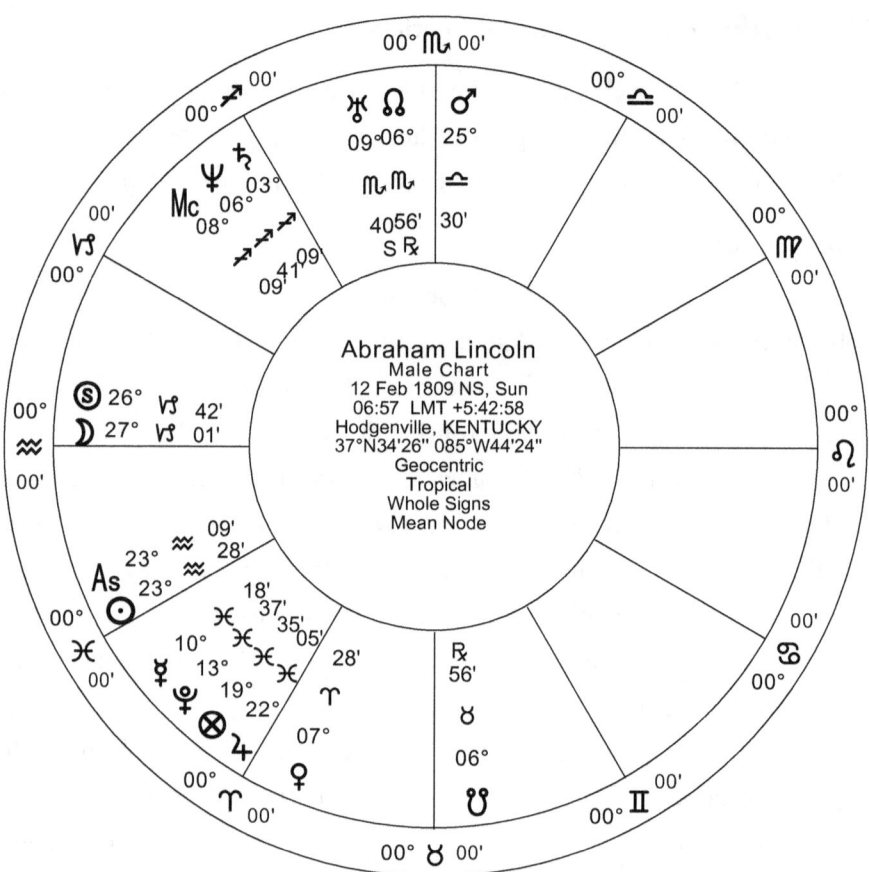

rhythms or respond differently to the larger rhythms of life – is one of the Moon's important functions. Many of us anticipate our activities on a given day but must be at the ready for "Plan B" when the day begins to drive its own agenda.

Anticipation and Improvisation: The Moon as Our Daily Planet
Early in his monumental *Anthology*, second century astrologer Vettius Valens provides quick depictions of the seven planets. The Sun, he tells us, is "the eye of intellect" (*nous*), but the Moon is "foreknowledge" (*pronoia*). *Nous* is an ordinary ancient Greek word for "mind" or "intelligence" and is related to words in many languages for knowing. Although *pronoia* was

later affiliated with Divine Providence, it is an ordinary Greek word that means anticipating the future. It can manifest in very ordinary ways. If we want to buy a new car, for example, we must decide what kind of car is best for us, decide whether we want to keep one for a longer or shorter time, and figure out what we can afford.

Sometimes we also need to "turn on a dime". While in the process of acquiring a new car, our job changes and our income is suddenly insecure, or the brand of car we are looking at has been recalled due to defective parts or has been named in a safety lawsuit. Perhaps an elderly relative wants to give you their car and it's free, but the car is also elderly but our relative would feel hurt if we didn't take it. These situations call on us to respond quickly but sensitively. Skillfulness in negotiating these conditions is an ingredient of *emotional intelligence* that we'll discuss in a future chapter. The job of practical anticipation, however, is strictly lunar.

Moon and Saturn – Other Possibilities

No doubt the reader is familiar with Jane Austen. Her many novels from early in the nineteenth century continue to be popular today, launching movie adaptations, academic research, and more than a few book groups. Austen's works were also successful during her short lifetime (she died at the age of 42), although her popularity today tells us much about ourselves and our culture.

Compare Dorothy Parker's Moon in Capricorn square Saturn in Libra with Jane Austen's Moon in Libra, conjunct exalted Saturn in Libra and with a strong square from Mars that is exalted in Capricorn. [29]

Up close, she was not overly social but was decorous and generous and with an instinct for irony. Austen never married but remained within a close knit-family, with her sister as a close friend and correspondent and a brother as her literary agent. Her unconventional perspectives were covered

---
29 Rating A: from memory

Astrology and the Lives of People

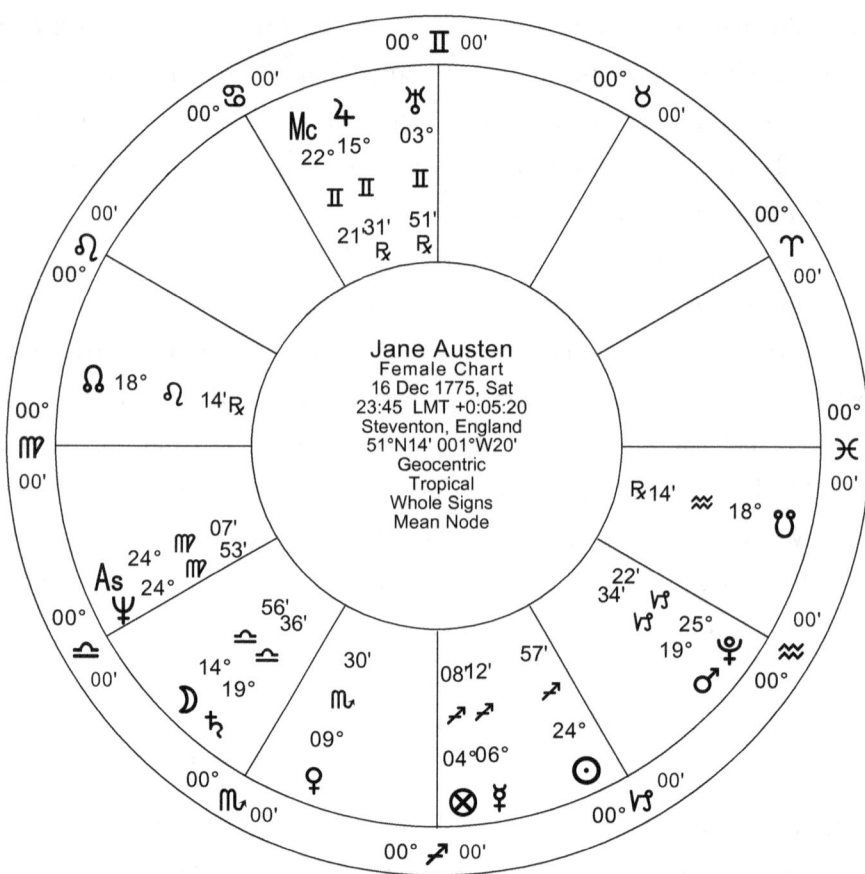

over by politeness; they came out in her novels alongside overarching reasonableness. Moon in Libra conjunct Saturn gave comfort with formality, but Mars gave an edge to her decorum. Austen's Mercury and Venus placements await examination in later chapters.

Envy, Resentment, and the Lunar Side of Bigotry

The Moon is at its best when its responses are empathic, non-ostentatiously generous, and appropriate to the needs of the moment. The Moon is at its worst when it separates, when it posits a zone of protection – around one's body, ego, or ethnicity or national origin – so that what is outside is

The Moon's Many Appearances

met with indifference or hostility. This results from the protective lunar response of anxiety and its effects can be poisonous. Of the traditional seven cardinal sins, the Moon is most often associated with envy.

> *…what light through yonder window breaks?*
> *It is the east, and Juliet is the sun.*
> *Arise, fair sun, and kill the envious moon,*
> *Who is already sick and pale with grief,*
> *That thou, her maid, art far more fair than she.*
> *Be not her maid, since she is envious;*
> *Her vestal livery is but sick and green*
> *And none but fools do wear it; cast it off.*
>
> Romeo and Juliet, Act 2. Scene. 2

Three hundred years before Shakespeare, Dante took us further into the psychology of the Moon's envy. Upon the terraces of the Mountain of Purgatory, those afflicted by envy (*invidia* in Italian and Latin) purge themselves of this affliction. Today we have the commonly used German word, *Schadenfreude*: taking delight in the misfortunes of another. Why do we do this and why is it protective?

When we don't see the possibilities of gaining what we want for ourselves and cannot fix a situation, one lunar remedy is to fantasize and enjoy the downfall of those who we think deserve it. Directly or indirectly, they are often object of our envy. In this way our urge to protect ourselves opts for a narrow but comforting scenario. We lose sight of the fact those we envy or resent breathe and bleed like we do, that their supposed superiority is perhaps more our projection than what is real.

As an antidote for envy, Mahayana Buddhism recommends rejoicing in the good fortune of another. This cuts at the heart of envious relationships. This is a central practice for the aspiring bodhisattva and most find it difficult.

Lunar protectiveness at the heart of *bigotry* serves to isolate and protect ourselves from those who are different in some way. The word itself originated from Old French from those who looked down on the Normans and was later used by the English Normans who looked down on their Anglo-Saxon and Viking co-inhabitants. Bigotry has been around for a long time and shows no sign of decreasing.

Our lunar nature sensitizes us to external threats, and we automatically fear those who could threaten us in some way. By instinct, who and what we don't know can hurt us. From anxiety, hidden or right on the surface, we circle the wagons, creating an outer barrier to protect the vulnerable inner self from some perceived external threat. On the solar and jupiterian side, bigotry also indulges in the intoxication of identifying (Sun) and belonging (Jupiter).

Lunar Values and Heroics

The Moon operates at its best when we affirm and appreciate our commonality with others, and when we rejoice in ordinary goodness that occurs around us all the time. I offer three scenarios from different cultures and times that illustrate some of the Moon's values and virtues.

Get A Life

We first go to the distant past, to a poem that was recovered over a century ago in Nineveh in modern-day Iraq. It tells of the king of Uruk, the self-designated solar hero Gilgamesh.

Gilgamesh was a special kind of person: partly of divine origin, he was both a king and heroic warrior. Things were going swimmingly for him but then his best friend Enkidu died of an illness. Enkidu's death greatly upset our king/hero and, knowing that eventually the same fate will befall him, he set on a journey to find the one deathless mortal. Gilgamesh felt that he, unlike everybody else, was worthy of immortality.

Our warrior's quest, including journeying through the underground path of the Sun before he becomes incinerated, took a heavy toll on him. By Tablet 10 of the epic, he is worn out and emaciated, looks more animal than human; even if still a human being, he seems mentally troubled. Siduri, a woman who runs a tavern "at the edge of the sea [of death]", sees him coming; fearing his appearance, she escapes to the roof of her building for safety. Eventually she descends and they converse. After Gilgamesh tells her how he fears his own death, Siduri replies that immortality is reserved only for the fully divine, not for humans. She tells him,

> "As for you, Gilgamesh, let your stomach be full,
> Always be happy, night and day.
> Make every day a delight,
> Night and day play and dance.
> Your clothes should be clean,
> Your head should be washed,
> You should bathe in water.
> Look proudly on the little one holding your hand,
> Let your mate always be blissful in your loins,
> This, then, is the work of mankind,
> He who is alive [should be happy]." [30]

Many of us have heard such things from our worried parents when, in younger years, we wanted to backpack around the world or join the Peace Corps or live in an ashram or monastery, and so on. "Can't you just find a nice girl/guy, get a decent job, have a house and family and be a normal person?" (Say this in whatever accent you wish.)

When we are young, we tend to ignore risks and long-term consequences: that is the strength of being young. As many of us have gotten older, we appreciate more the perspective of Siduri and our parents

---

[30] *The Epic of Gilgamesh* (Second Norton Critical Edition). Trans and ed. Benjamin Foster (2019) p. 79

– life is fragile, we should appreciate the richness of ordinary life. Much later, at the end of the epic, having failed in his quest, Gilgamesh does settle down into a life that Siduri would have approved of. But would he have regretted not continuing his quest, his "noble folly" as George Orwell would have it?

Astrology's Moon speaks with Siduri's voice, not for rising above but staying grounded, as our opportunities for happiness and contentment are limited in possibility and in time. Note her emphasis on the pleasures and adornment of the physical body and with relating to others physically. Astrology's Moon is this kind of body.

Abstract Lunar Heroism: Developing Connection and Unity

Our journey now moves to sixteenth century China, to the schoolroom of the philosopher Wang Yangming (1472-1529). Wang inherited China's Confucian tradition of learning and self-examination and of loyalty to family and social structures. He also was influenced by the Buddhist and Taoist emphasis on the development of compassion and harmony with the natural world. Wang Yangming discusses our natural sympathetic responses that can extend progressively from a small child in danger toward the plants and the stones around us. His is a lunar style of fulfillment.

> "The great [person] regards Heaven and Earth and the myriad things as one body. [One] regards the world as one family and the country as one person. As to those who make a cleavage between objects and distinguishes between self and others, they are small [people]. That the great [one] can regard Heaven, Earth, and myriad things as one body is not because one deliberately wants to do so, but because it is natural to the human nature of one's mind to do so. Forming one body with Heaven, Earth, and myriad things is not only true of the great

person. Even the mind of the small person is no different. Only [one] makes it small." [31]

This breathtaking vision of unity and compassion cannot exist without a sense of commonality with all that appears and all that exists in our worlds. The development of character is not about *self*-improvement but tuning into the universal, and this from the beginning is what makes personal love possible. The philosopher continues,

> "Manifesting a clear character consists in loving the people, and loving the people is the way to manifest the clear character. Therefore, only when I love my father, the father of others, and the fathers of all [people] can my humanity really form one body with my father, the father of others, and the fathers of all [people]. When it truly forms one body with them, then the clear character of filial piety will be manifested." [32]

Most of us are not where Wang Yangming would have us be, and the philosopher was aware of this. Although this quality of universality is present innately, we easily become numb to our worlds through blocking our genuine feeling and taking on a mistaken view of personal separateness. We remedy this through self-cultivation that engages in the actual worlds in which we live (as opposed to memorizing Confucian maxims), by living in our worlds more closely and attentively. In this way we can recover our true nature over time. Our commonality with the world overcomes our specialness and astrology's Moon overcomes an over-individualized Sun.

Although this is clearly a difficult path to accomplish, a sage is not necessarily the Confucian scholar-gentleman or a recluse in the mountains, but can be an ordinary person living an uneventful life. Centuries afterwards, the English novelist George Eliot would heartily agree.

---

31   6. 659; *A Source Book in Chinese Philosophy*. I have rendered the pronouns gender-neutral.
32   Ibid p. 660

Practical Lunar Heroics: George Eliot's Praise of the Everyday

At the end of her novel *Middlemarch*, in its final two paragraphs, the author concludes the story of a main character who had renounced her inherited fortune to marry the man she loved (it's complicated), and settled down to a life of relative obscurity after having once been a "somebody."

Here, in the final page of *Middlemarch*, George Eliot sings the song of lunar heroism, worthy of committing to memory:

> "Certainly those determining acts of her life were not ideally beautiful. They were the mixed result of young and noble impulse struggling amidst the conditions of an imperfect social state, in which great feelings will often take the aspect of error, and great faith the aspect of illusion. For there is no creature whose inward being is so strong that it is not greatly determined by what lies outside of it...
>
> "Her finely-touched spirit had still its fine issues, though they were not widely visible. Her full nature, like that river of which Cyrus broke the strength, spent itself in channels which had no great name on the earth. But the effects of her being on those around her was incalculably diffusive: for the growing good of the world is partly dependent on unhistoric acts; and that things are not so ill with you and me as they might have been, is half owing to the number who lived faithfully a hidden life, and rest in unvisited tombs."

The heroism of Eliot's character Dorothea, like that of other lunar heroes, does not follow some preordained divine decree but is simply the accumulated responses by ordinary people to ordinary situations of life. And, in these times, I think of many people thrust into extraordinary circumstances who simply have done what comes naturally. They too are our heroes.

Chapter Four

Astrology's Sun, Its Shadows, and the Stories We Tell

In the early 1940s Orwell described Don Quixote and Sancho Panza as a "dualism of body and soul...noble folly and base wisdom, [which] exist side by side in nearly every human being."

> If you look into your own mind, which are you, Don Quixote or Sancho Panza? Almost certainly you are both. There is one part of you that wishes to be a hero or a saint, but another part of you is a little fat man who sees very clearly the advantages of staying alive with a whole skin. He is your unofficial self, the voice of the belly protesting against the soul. [33]

In the previous chapter we encountered our "base wisdom", our "voice of the belly", our Moon. In this chapter we consider the Sun, roots of "noble folly" and sometimes nobility.

The Traditional Sun

Guido Bonatti, who lived about a century after Ibn Ezra, wrote the encyclopedic *Book of Astronomy*, within which is this concise depiction of the great luminary.:

---

33 George Orwell, "The Art of Donald McGill," in *The Collected Essays, Journalism and Letters of George Orwell*, ed. Sonia Orwell and Ian Angus, vol. 2: My Country Right or Left 1940-1943 (Harmondsworth, Middlesex: Penguin Books, 1968), p. 192.

Astrology and the Lives of People

> "[The Sun] signifies light and splendor, and beauty, and intellect and faith. And he even signifies a great kingdom, and all other lay dignities, both of magnates and others. And this, because he is posited in the middle of the others (just like a king), and the others stand next to him – certain ones on one side, certain ones on the other side (namely the superiors to his right, the inferiors to his left) ... Moreover, his motion is practically uniform, and is not varied nor altered, but always keeps the same similar advancement annually. And his motion is most noble above the motions of the other planets, nor does he go retrograde like others go retrograde." [34]

From astrology's geocentric perspective, the Sun is royally placed between the six planetary ministers of the sky. The Sun's appearance and speed remain steady, not slowing down or hastening. In contrast, all five starry non-luminary planets change speed as they move in their direct and retrograde motions, determined by their changing distances from the Sun. Also based on its moving relationship to the Sun, the Moon's appearance changes from night to night.

From the second century C.E., Claudius Ptolemy set the agenda for much of western astrology to come. Toward the end of *Tetrabiblos III* and its discussion of the Quality of the Soul, Ptolemy discusses the Sun when configured by aspect or dignity with another planet that has rulership over the soul. The positive side of Sun has nobility of character and a commanding presence.

> "...when in dignity of disposition, it contributes toward the juster and more successful and honorable and august and more religious. But [when disposed] in the opposite and unfamiliar manner, it contributes toward the more lowly and laborious

---

[34] Bonatti, *Book of Astronomy*, Vol .1 Translated by Ben Dykes p.164.

Astrology's Sun, Its Shadows, and the Stories We Tell

and insignificant and savage and obstinate and austere and the more difficulty in life, and on the whole more difficulty of success." [35]

Other sources say that astrology's Sun brings natives to seek power, to be in charge of their world: hence the association of the Sun with kingship and the head of government. Other people, lower-down, do the real work. The king or queen reigns, standing above it all.

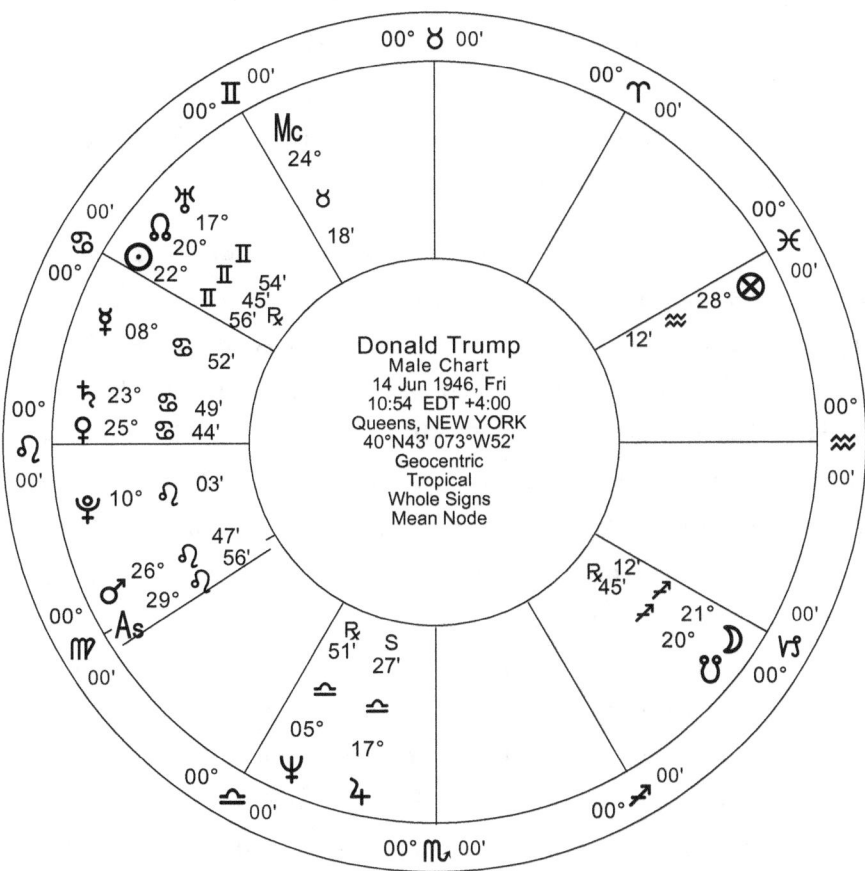

Here is the natal chart of a strongly "solar" person with a strong dash of Mars. I supply this just in case one is tempted to glamorize qualities represented by astrology's Sun.

---

35 *Tetrabiblos III*, trans. Robert Schmidt. P. 64

An ill-disposed Sun inclines one toward low status, bringing much work and meager success. (We will find that an "ill-disposed" Jupiter also tones down that planet's positive features.)

Moving forward about nine hundred years from Ptolemy, the Jewish polymath Ibn Ezra brings together the Sun's qualities of leadership with intellect and the energy of life.

> "The Sun signifies life, for he is the greater luminary and the light for all the bodies, the metals, the plants, and all animals. The Greek philosopher [Aristotle] said that the spirit of man is owed to the Sun, therefore he signifies wisdom and honor, like a king, and benefit, for he signifies the good fortune by aspects, and the grace as well."[36]

And from his *Beginning of Wisdom:* "*In its share is every dignified quality. Of human nature it has knowledge, intelligence, majesty, beauty, courage, seeking high positions, desire for wealth, garrulity, expeditiousness, and excess of desire.*"[37]

These days we do not find many kings and queens but there are all kinds of leaders. Some are Jupiter-like consensus builders, others are authoritarians or authoritarian wannabees. A true leader provides surface stability but is also constantly in motion, is inspiring when inspiration is needed, is more responsive and less in charge than many would admit. Sometimes they are called to act decisively. They often serve best as an example for others, for better or worse.

Astrology's traditions also cite the Sun as the governing center of intentional awareness. This differs from the instinctive responsiveness of the Moon. Together they form a broad picture of who we are.

Marsilio Ficino lived over two hundred years after Bonatti and was one of the guiding lights of the early Renaissance. He was well-versed in the astrology of his time and in classical antiquity, routinely referring

---

36   Ibn Ezra, *Book of Reasons,* translated by Meira Epstein, p. 34
37   *Beginning of Wisdom,* p. 99

to the Sun as Apollo. His applications of astrology look ahead to a more psychologically focused modern era. Many of his letters have been translated into English and appear in *Meditations on the Soul*.[38]

In one letter, co-written to a "fellow philosopher," he writes of the Sun – metaphysically, psychologically, astrologically. Ficino, scholar, sage, and politically avoidant, emphasized the Sun as aware consciousness.

> "According to the Orphic tradition, the whole sphere of the Sun has a life-force far excelling that of all the other spheres. It is this which causes life and movement to course through the entire body of the sphere and then to pour out through everything. But through the actual globe of the Sun, it first brings about understanding and sight: it brings about the understanding through the light of consciousness ruling in the very center of the Sun, as it were in the head; and it brings about sight through visible light that shines everywhere within the full circuit of the Sun, as it were in the eye. It is certainly in the Sun that visible light is created from the light of consciousness, and there is also sight is created from understanding."[39]

In the same letter, Ficino brings together intellect and a unity of self or will:

> "[The Sun] does not see these many [compounded] things through many forms but through one form, that is, the one light, the origin and model of the various colors. Nor does it make use of numerous powers of seeing and choosing, to see and choose multiplicity, but it sees multiplicity through a single power of seeing, and likewise chooses with a single will.

---

38 London: School of Economic Science (1996).
39 *Meditations on the Soul: Selected Letters of Marsilio Ficino*, p. 160-161

> Therefore, it seems that multiplicity is perceived by intelligence alone, that is, by the clear sight that discerns innumerable things and by the will that judges them.[40]

Sun is our ability to depart, if only for a moment, from the ordinary and the habitual, to think and decide, to project personal will and vision. Sometimes our brilliance shines only fleetingly but it persists in our aspirations and in our projections. Not everybody is a leader, but everybody has a discerning and creative intelligence that is solar. Since everybody has a Sun in their astrological chart, everybody is capable of this intelligence. Usually, it needs to be cultivated and practiced.

Astrology's Sun also gives a broader and deeper range for who we are. Falling deeply in love or creating art are matters too important to be left to Venus alone. Rising above obstacles, "beating the odds", are matters that should not be left to Mars alone. The Sun manifests when we reach back and find our genius, vision, or ethical courage, our capacity to endure suffering within the context of something more important. We rejoice when others with whom we identify reach these possibilities for themselves (fiction or nonfiction): we like to tell stories about them, as we tell stories about ourselves.

How to Recognize a Solar Person

From "The Philosopher"
Although our astrology would have been foreign to Aristotle, his *Nicomachean Ethics* depicts many of our qualities that are interpretable from astrology's symbolism, especially that of the Sun. Book Four of this work discusses, among other virtues, greatness of soul (his word is *megalopsychia*), often rendered into English as "pride" or "proper pride." Today we might recognize such a person as having an aristocratic demeanor. We see this

---
40   p. 163

character type in Homer, with characteristic ambiguity, but Nietzsche considered this a worthy alternative to the meeker and milder Christian style. Jane Austin's depiction of Darcy in *Pride and Prejudice* first criticizes this kind of person but eventually the novel uncovers its positive qualities.

Aristotle asserts that honor, i.e., justified esteem by others, is the object of *megalopsychia* – but honor that is neither more nor less than what one deserves. Claiming more than what one deserves is a sign of vanity; not claiming honor sufficiently makes one too humble and small-minded. (Today, as in the past, we have contempt for those who imitate a great-souled person without being one.)

This great-souled person is courteous toward those of moderate station, but not high-handed with those of inferior position, for that would be vulgar. Aristotle asserts that a justly superior person renders aid willingly but is reluctant to ask for help: that would put one in a position of dependency. One does not bear a grudge, nor gossip, and never complains when adversity occurs: these responses are marks of lesser mortals. Additionally, one walks slowly with dignity and speaks with a deep voice. For Aristotle, these characteristics signify one who is confident and self-assured, and these can be praiseworthy qualities. They are also subject to abuse from societies organized by class or status (that would be all of them), often falling into elitism and snobbery.

A Less Aristocratic Alternative
The American essayist Ralph Waldo Emerson was the central figure in the nineteenth century Transcendentalist movement. Instead of the haughtiness of Aristotle's formulation, Emerson taught and wrote of one's dignity, divinity even, that is essential to all of us, a common human nature that has solar characteristics. These qualities may emerge through relying on intellect, a good heart, solitude in nature, or being with worthy friends when needing inspiration. Emerson's writings, especially his first set of essays, are strong remedies when our self-esteem takes a hit.

Astrology and the Lives of People

Emerson's astrological chart finds the Sun and Mercury in Gemini in the ninth house.[41] The ninth is the place of philosophy and religion. In the mutable air sign Gemini, we find variability and rather verbose expressions of spiritual principles. The Sun is in its joy in this house and Mercury is in its own sign here in Gemini.

There are many strong aspects to Emerson's Sun: a sextile from Mars in Leo, a trine from Uranus, and a square from Pluto. To top it off, the Lot of Spirit is in Leo, keeping company by sign with Mars and Moon, all governed by his Gemini Sun. They all attest to the strong, exuberant, but intense individuality that he embodied and proclaimed to all who would listen.

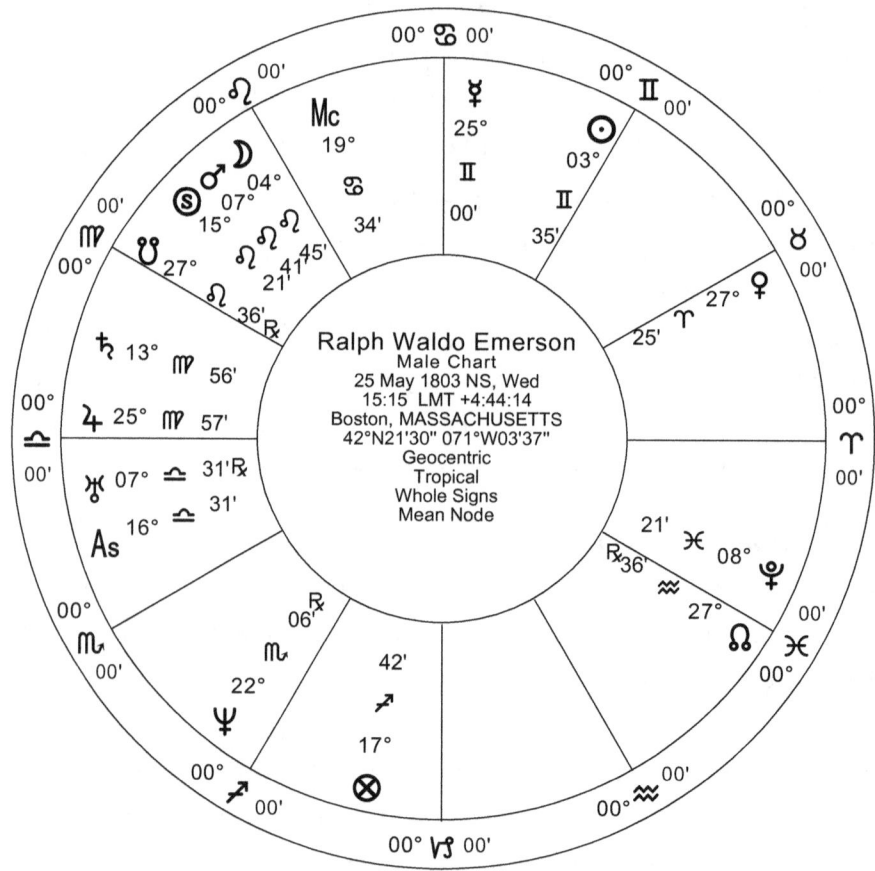

---

41 Rating AA: recorded in a diary

True to his Sun-Uranus trine, Emerson's famous essay "Self-Reliance" shows a distinct preference for greatness that comes from oneself alone. "Whoso would be a man must be a nonconformist. He who would gather immortal palms must not be hindered by the name of goodness but must explore it if it be goodness. Nothing is at last sacred but the integrity of your mind."[42] This includes the courage to tolerate being misunderstood by others: "Pythagoras was misunderstood, and Socrates, and Jesus, and Luther, and Copernicus, and Galileo, and Newton, and every pure and wise spirit that ever took flesh. To be great is to be misunderstood."[43] In line with his times, Emerson held the importance of "great men", but also asserted that *all* should strive to be great, to develop within ourselves the independence and courage that we admire in others.

Aristotle and Emerson promote an active intelligence and discernment that separate one from the rest of the pack. This accords with our own desires (or fantasies) to be self-sufficient, to have mastery over ourselves, to be truly the center of our universe.

You may find Aristotle's *megalopsychia* and Emerson's self-reliance to be one-dimensional, even narcissistic. A distain for the ordinary and the conventional easily covers a veneer of personal insecurity and a fragile sense of identity. Yet their descriptions of greatness indicate something most of us aspire to, and is the nature of astrology's Sun. This manifests in our own ambitions and is projected toward those we admire.

Another "Gemini"

According to the birth time generally given for Alice Bailey, Mars is conjunct the Ascendant in Leo, governed by the Sun in Gemini – just like that of Donald Trump whose chart is above. What a difference between them! Instead of being a businessperson and politician, this woman's sense

---

42 Emerson, p. 261
43 Emerson, p. 265

of purpose and perseverance nurtured the New Age movement in the mid-twentieth century and her influence continues today.⁴⁴

Born into an upper-class English family, Bailey was oriented toward religion and service from the start – and she received a strange visitation from beyond when she was a teenager. She could be of service to the world, this apparition said, if and when she could tame her strong-willed nature.

As a young adult she went to India, married then later divorced another missionary, found her way to California as a single mother, and began attending meetings of the Theosophical Society. She found her calling.

Within a decade Alice Bailey had established her own power base. She again married, this time the secretary of the Theosophical Society. She and her husband then split off from the Theosophical Society. Bailey began her own career of lecturing and publishing.

Most works from her typewriter, she asserted, were inspired by an evolved being. Included in her (or their) works were writings on Initiation and Discipleship, the Seven Rays (including the famous volume *Esoteric Astrology*), and Spiritual Hierarchy. Bailey was one of those promoting a new Aquarian Age where these esoteric teachings would become more available to more people and help turn the tide against this age's materialism.

Bailey's astrological chart gives her a robust personal presence, a reluctance to suffer fools gladly, and a strong drive. We must include the expressive nature of Leo rising, especially when it is governed by the Sun in Gemini that is happily situated in the eleventh house.

A modern astrologer would find that the midpoint of Uranus and Jupiter is the Sun. This combination can give rise to sudden revelations, quick strokes of good luck, and an enterprising nature unfazed by notions of conventionality.

---

44 This birth time has been long given as 7:32, was later corrected by Dane Rudhyar for ten minutes later, although Bailey herself speculated that she has Pisces rising. (I disagree with her.) Given C rating. https://www.astro.com/astro-databank/Bailey,_Alice_A.

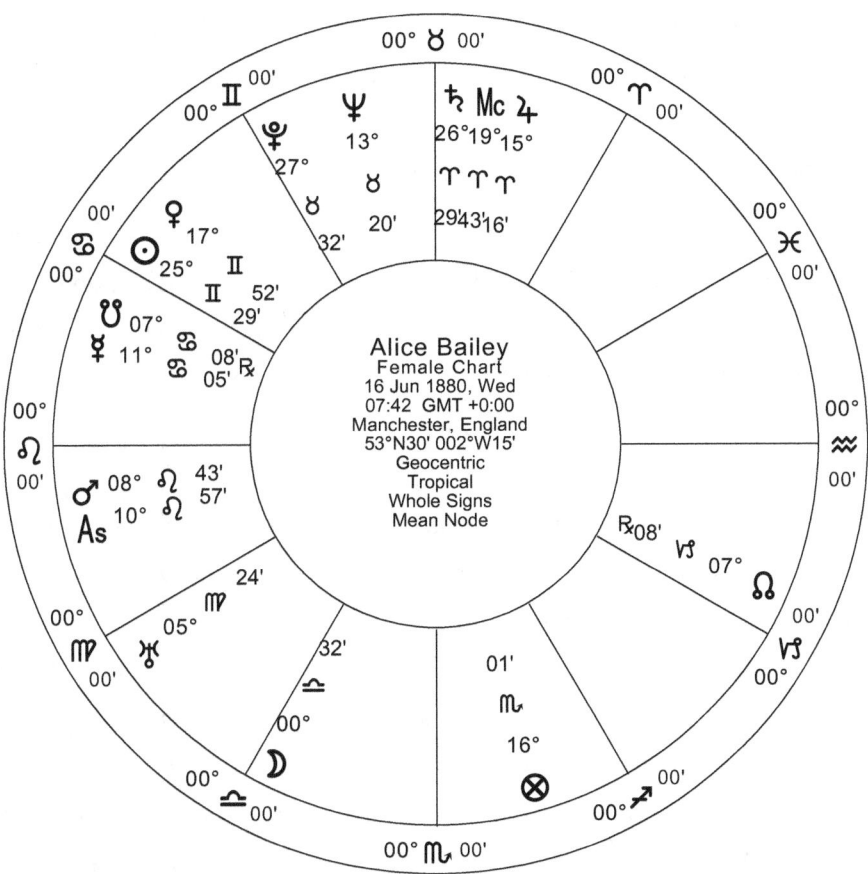

When we look at Bailey's ninth house, we find Jupiter and Saturn and the Midheaven degree governed by Mars, which is on her Ascendant. Saturn is in fall in Aries, which may have brought about an overbearing and dictatorial side of her, but Jupiter is in better condition and perhaps compensated. Both Jupiter and Saturn are in sect in her diurnal chart and are oriental to the Sun. Both planets also contributed to this woman's grandeur – with a Mars-like edge, as that planet was likely on the Ascendant when she was born.

Alice Bailey seems to have taken Ralph Waldo Emerson's teaching to an ultimate manifestation: divinity is not only available to us all, but as we evolve spiritually, we too may become prophets and eventually world redeemers in this lifetime or a distantly future one.

The Solar Luminary Develops Within Us

The early development of Sun, the planet of our centralized self, is more subtle than that of the Moon and grows out of the Moon's developmental arc. The Sun's version of our first years helps us better understand ourselves, especially those for whom psychological developmental failures have led to personality deficits, some of whom we call "narcissists".

Many years ago I was fascinated by the contributions of psychoanalyst Heinz Kohut (1913-1981) who investigated disorders of the self. He provided one developmental schema that, from an astrologer's point of view, depicts a solar self that emerges from our early lunar matrix.

Our innate need for personal structural integrity comes about through our early relationships. In our early years we display our growing capabilities to others, and we are built to respond to their admiration. Over time this develops into an inner sense of self-efficacy and personal ambition. We also form idealized images of others who are close to us, and our growing sense of self merges with qualities we project admiringly onto them. Throughout our lives we strengthen our solar specialness from identifying with those we admire.

From needing to be admired to relating to identifying, we are led into maturity – if all goes well enough. Situational failures, if they occur incrementally and gradually, lead to our becoming less dependent on others for self-integration. Our sense of self becomes coherent and clear to the world around us. This is never seamless: we are all subject to deflation when we encounter adverse circumstances; we all have a measure of personal insecurity. On the other side, most of us are burdened with pride – conscious or unconscious – that can be costly to us personally and interpersonally. Even spiritual aspirations and displays of humility can become fuel for a fixed ego, for myopic self-enhancement.

Pride Before, During, After the Fall

The ancient world gave us the concept of *hybrus* or "overweening pride" that comes from our not recognizing limits. It survives in Dante's depiction of Ulysses in Hell and in our modern stories of politicians and entertainers who thought (or still think) they are immune from consequences that lesser beings suffer from doing bad things.

On the first ledge of Dante's Mountain of Purgatory, the largest ledge for the purification of pride, penitents walk slowly carrying huge boulders on their backs. The poet singles out pride in family heritage, political power, and – most interestingly – in one's own talent or genius, and the poet indicated that he was particularly vulnerable to this last one.

What is the problem with pride in one's talent or genius? For Dante, these gifts are given by God and they have a place on in this world for doing good; one should not be puffed up but humbled at the responsibility this entails. I add that inborn talent must be nurtured by hard work that is supported by the love and generosity of others – it does take a village to produce a genius.

Geoffrey Chaucer, who lived a few generations after Dante, discusses pride and humility in the over-long Parson's Tale that concludes *The Canterbury Tales*. The Parson divides pride into categories that include presumption, insolence, and contempt. The Parson adds ostentation in speech, appearance and especially provocative dress, the latter being vanity about one's attractiveness. Included is also the garish presentation of food and drink to impress one's friends and house guests. True nobility, states Chaucer's Parson, is from keeping in mind all the kindness received from others. Gratitude toward others (or to God) seems to be a universal remedy for pride and arrogance.

Moving toward the present day, we find a different representation of pride and humility (true and false) within the recovery community. Here again is the natal chart of Bill Wilson. In 1935, the arrogance of the vulnerable addict grew into helping lead a healing movement.

His vulnerability to pride and arrogance are accounted for through the trine and mutual reception between the Sun in Sagittarius and Jupiter in Leo. Wilson's Jupiter in its joy in the eleventh house has the ancient meaning of the "good spirit" and the modern meaning of friendship – one could even call it fellowship. The arrogance of fame and celebrity – of being an important person – dogged him throughout his life.

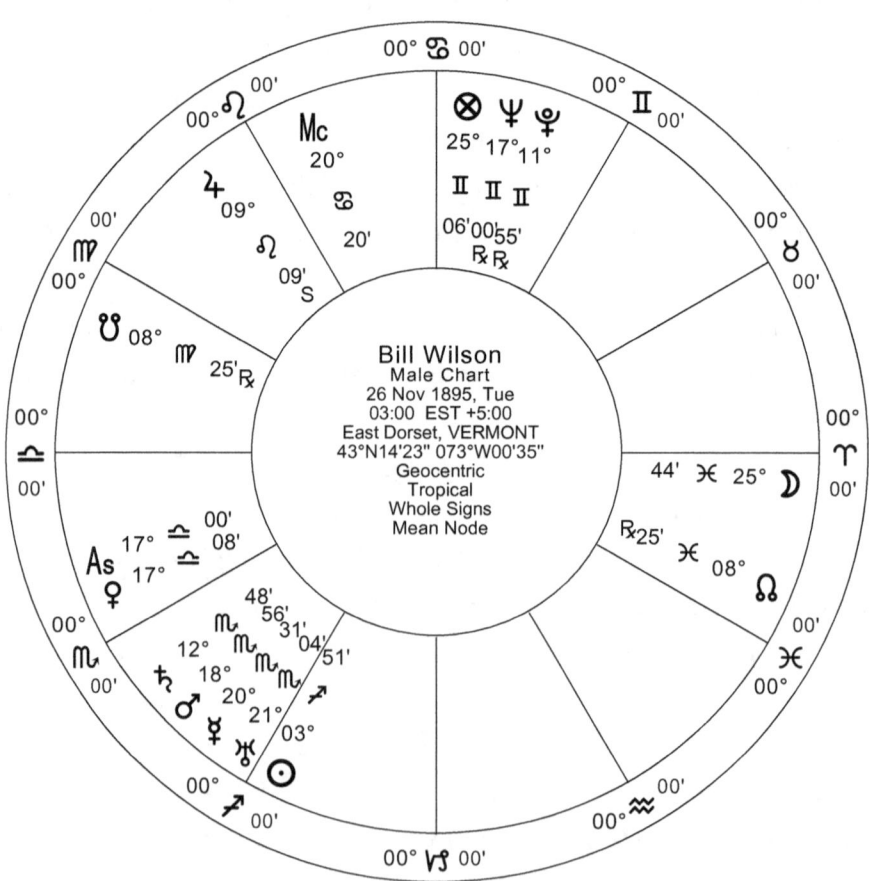

Learning from his experience, Wilson wrote of humility not as affectation or self-disparagement but as a kind of *intelligence*, getting clearer perspective on oneself. Humility seems to include positive pride from being the "right size". This begins by recognizing our deficiencies and attempting to correct them. He discovered, as many of us do, that this is a lifelong, ongoing process.

Solar and Not Proud

One need not be a "solar person" for the luminary to strengthen a sense of our significance. A fine example is Fred Rogers of children's television fame who displayed both intuitively empathic responses and direct skillful action.[45]

Although Rogers is remembered with nostalgia for his empathy and ability to connect, there was an important advocacy side of his nature. As a young man pondering his future career, he noted the gratuitous cruelty and violence on display on television that posed as childhood entertainment. This helped motivate him to enter that industry with the goal of uplifting entertainment for children. Rogers and his mentor Margaret McFarland later devised children's programming focusing on children's emotional development and fostering their understanding, tolerance, and kindness.

With his Sun in Pisces, how was Rogers solar in nature? Certainly not in Aristotle's aristocratic sense: he was closer to Emerson, whereby everybody has a chance to be a unique and irreplaceable person. That this could be part of his solar identity is reinforced by its companions in Pisces: Moon, Mercury, and Venus the ruler of his Taurus Ascendant. You may also notice the Lot of Spirit in Gemini. The "Lot of the Sun" reinforces his unique solar identity and how it could manifest. Additionally, the four Pisces planets stand in the tenth house from the Lot of Spirit, and thus are related strongly to the Lot.

---

45 From a letter by him; rating B

Astrology and the Lives of People

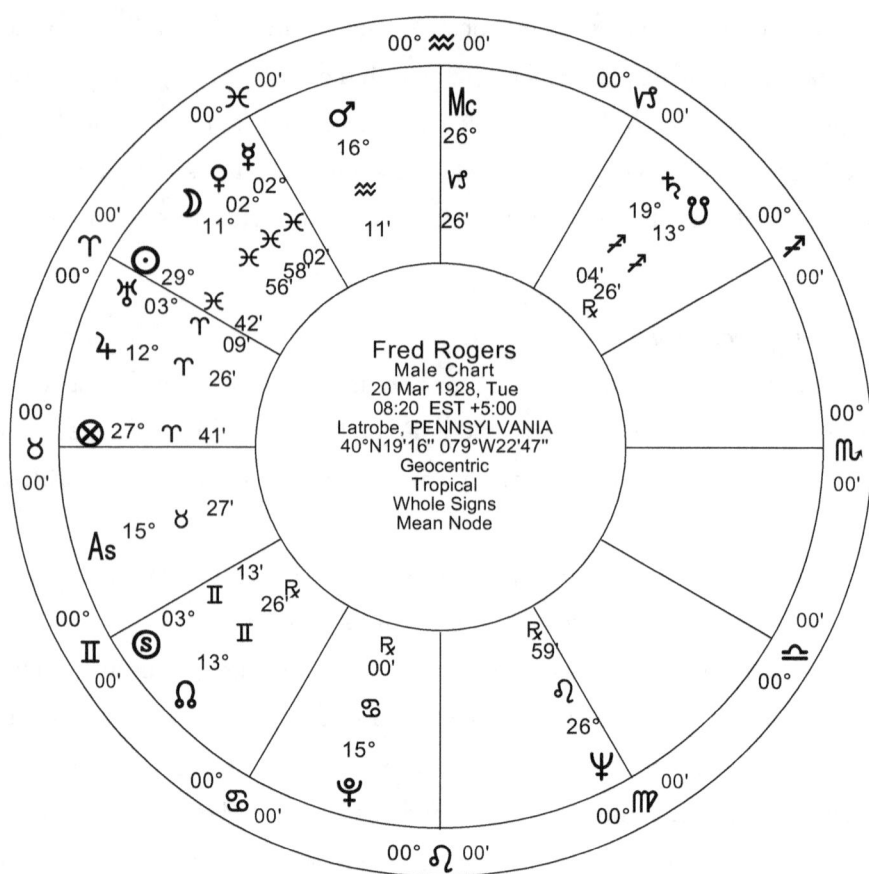

Identity and the Stories We Tell

At the center of our universe, the Sun is our sense of *personal identity* that governs our patterns of *identification and idealization*. The stories we tell reveal our patterns of identification with and inspiration by our gods and heroes: ancestors, saints and historical figures, favorite writers and artists, athletes, rock stars, movie celebrities, even politicians.

Let us not forget the Sun's role in promoting the "isms" of our lives, those principles we consciously value and identify with. (Jupiter's function is how to use our "isms" to make larger connections.) This may range from our identification with humanitarian or social causes to "greed is good", to

Astrology's Sun, Its Shadows, and the Stories We Tell

the superiority of being white or wealthy, to wanting to "own the [liberals]", to valuing authority or democracy, or secular or cultural hegemony by one's religion. When we are loyal to and proud of our country, it is *patriotism*; when it excludes other peoples and cultures it becomes *nationalism*. Why are these "isms" we have so hard to change? Because they constitute a large part our understanding of and projection onto the world.

We display ourselves in the stories we tell of ourselves and others. Sometimes they contain a recognizable trajectory, like battling immaturity in a coming-of-age story, of defeat and coming back, fall and redemption, defying the odds, or the slow steady activation of individual purpose.

Maya Angelou's most significant literary work relates her own story of overcoming personal and cultural obstacles seemingly to live many lives in just one: teenage streetcar conductor, brothel madam, dancer, civil rights activist, poet, and novelist.

She was born two weeks after Fred Rogers and the Sun has moved into Aries. Her Sun is conjunct Jupiter, in the ninth house of the Sun's joy, in its exaltation in Aries and also governing the Ascendant.

Somebody with her strong intensity and drive must not have been easy to live with, or to be married to. Happily, she had a strong family background early in life and a keen intellect from the outset. Accompanying the Sun and Jupiter in Aries is Saturn, in trine from Sagittarius, with a willingness to keep moving no matter what.

Without obstacles and difficulties there would be less to tell of ourselves and of those we admire; there would be no large-scale or small-scale heroism. We are not like the deathless gods in Homer's *Iliad* – shallow and self-absorbed, relying on those mortals below to give them a meaningful existence, nor are we like the bored angels in that fine 1987 film "Wings of Desire".

Our stories of ourselves change as our life circumstances change. They tell us what is important to us right now and they are the stuff psychotherapy and support groups. If our stories stay the same and cover

Astrology and the Lives of People

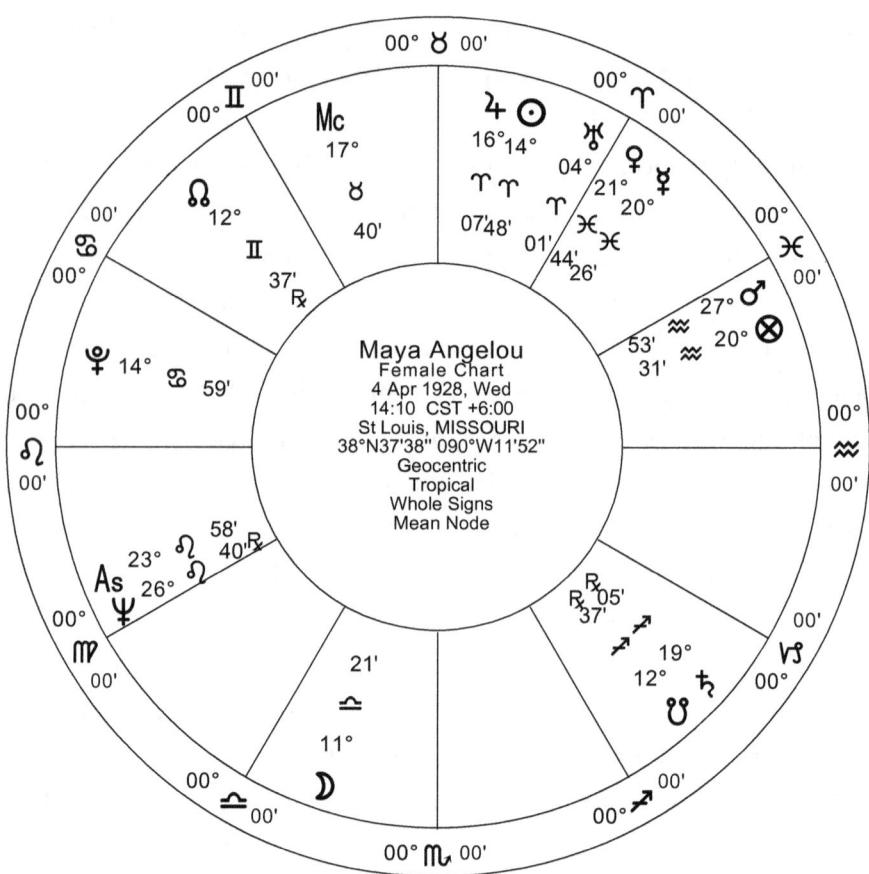

the same ground again and again, current limitations probably have brought us into a chronically defensive position. We have let our identities rest on previous events because we are afraid to move on to the present, to the future.

We are all subject to failure, weakness or cowardice, little hypocrisies and ethical cutting of corners, and all the ways we diminish ourselves and others – sometimes intentionally, sometimes not. They become parts of our solar story. If the stories we tell of ourselves and others are not redemptive in some way, we may have diminished ourselves.

As the Sun's shadows are formed by the intersection of light and solid matter, we encounter many little "deaths" in our lives.

Astrology's Sun, Its Shadows, and the Stories We Tell

The Imprint of History, Personal and Cultural

We Live On Beyond: Solar Options

Ludwig Wittgenstein, esteemed philosopher of the past century, famously wrote that "death is not an event in life". Perhaps this would be so for our *lunar self*. The "self" of the Moon is about maintenance, about the common nature of daily life and our body's rhythms. By contrast, the Sun is willing to sacrifice itself in battle for a noble cause, for the sake of family or country, or God's Providence. Instead, the Moon freezes us on the battlefield, gives us post-traumatic syndrome afterwards, and comes back after our deaths as ghosts trying to finish the unfinished.

The Sun encounters its mortal shadow and strives for meaningfulness and immortality. Our physical deaths do not necessarily interrupt the solar selves that we leave for others. We survive our physical deaths in different ways, even though we are subjectively not "here" anymore. Many of us have our descendants, of course. Parents project hope and fear into the life paths of their offspring, some of which is motivated by seeking immortality of a sort. Searching for personal continuity, some leave behind legacies and have their names placed on buildings and foundations.

We know that not being recognized within one's lifetime does not guarantee eternal anonymity. People who have left behind writings and art sometimes survive their unappreciated lives and become historical figures. Earlier we noted the life of Vincent Van Gogh. We can also think of the work of poets and philosophers, even composers like J. S. Bach or Wolfgang Mozart whose esteem increased only in the years following their deaths.

George Orwell's work had attained some fame before his death: *Animal Farm* and previous works had brought him some recognition. Orwell died a year after the publication of *1984* and, since his death, he has achieved a kind of immortality; his name has morphed into the adjective "Orwellian". Simone Weil, whose chart and life we will consider later in different contexts, was a French intellectual who was not well-known outside a small circle of friends and colleagues during her lifetime. When she died at the age of 34, she left behind a trove of diaries and half-written books and articles that were collected by her parents and others; dissecting and evaluating her life and works continues to this day.

They Are Still Alive For Us: Ancestors and Saints

A large part of our identity is tied up with family bloodlines, and if we were adopted it is just a bit more complicated. When young we identified with the nuclear and close family, when older we think more broadly and further back, we even take pride in our ancestral horse thieves and politicians, corrupt or clean, who show up in our research.

Families in some ancient societies – especially those families who were well-to-do –– constructed shrines to ancestors, and often had statues that preserved the likenesses of them, whether these likenesses were real or made up. When you live on land that was also home to your ancestors, that place becomes a source of pride. Some of this has endured to modern times: much of the splendor of old cemeteries lies in the monuments constructed where generations were interred.

Our family heritage gives us a discrete identity and a mode of identification with those past. Yet in spite of our sense of uniqueness, sober investigation reveals that our lives have come from happenstance piled upon happenstance. If so-and-so had not met so-and-so, and so on, multiplied over and over, who would we be if at all? This has astrological implications: had my mother married the Republican-leaning country-club type instead of the man she did marry, would her first-born with my astrological chart still be "me"? Half of my ancestry would be gone, and half of this part of my identity.

The fourth and tenth places or houses are both important when discussing the Sun. The fourth was called the "Place of Father" in ancient astrology; let us not forget that it was through the father that the family name and property moved through the generations. The fourth house, interpreted more widely than one's biological father, signifies the multi-generational background that has given rise to you and also the source of identity and pride. I have long labelled the fourth house "where you come from" and the tenth "what you make of it", seeing usually not an opposition but a continuity between one's roots and one's place in the larger world. *Both are solar places*; neither are lunar.

Illustrative is the astrology and life of English novelist George Eliot (born Marianne Evans).[46] We consider George Eliot's natal chart. Although she had to make her own way through a male-dominated literary society and gain fame on her own, she never was distant from her family of origin or the place of her upbringing.

Noteworthy is the Moon in Capricorn in close sextile to the Sun in Scorpio in the first house.[47] By sextile and trine respectively both luminaries strongly aspect Saturn and Pluto in Pisces. Here we note stubbornness and intense drive to rise above her background and also maintain loyalty to it.

Jupiter is in her fourth house: many of her best-known characters in her novels are transparent replicas of people in her family, including her hard-nosed father and difficult brother – both of whom she was attached to, and from both of whom she had to endure rejection for a time. Contrasting is Mars in Leo in the tenth house in mutual reception with Sun in Scorpio in the first house. This will manifest itself in her strong drive a name for herself (actually another name) in the world, inner and outer tenacity, and an ability to endure private and public storms.

As a young adult, Marianne Evans was developing her own mind on matters of religion: one day she decided to not go to church with her family anymore. This caused quite the domestic disruption, and an agreement was eventually reached whereby she would keep her own counsel in these matters but attend church with her family. Later she would stay in her

---

46 For a fuller presentation see https://www.astrologyinstitute.com/articleprofile/profiles/2019/mary-ann-evans-a-k-a-george-eliot-and-the-harvest-of-experience
47 Rated AA: quoted birth record

Astrology and the Lives of People

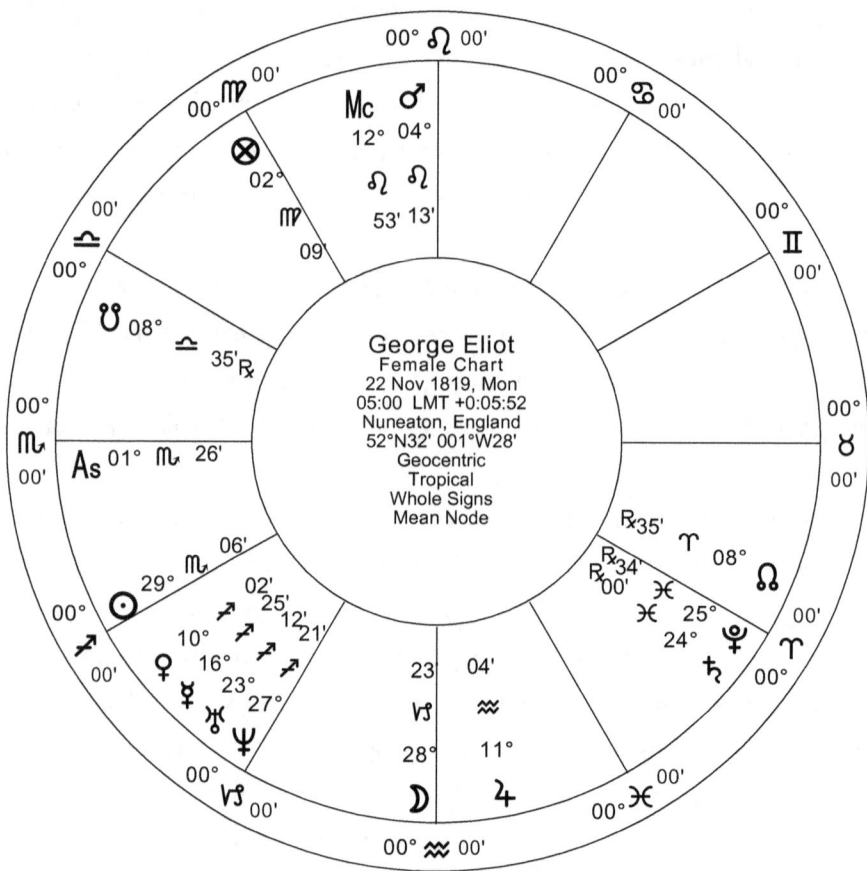

hometown and care for her elderly father – and shortly after his death she left town for wider horizons. After her father's death and her Saturn return, this "plain" woman found herself within the London literati. (We will pick up her story later.)

To Be Continued
Those of us who are artists, writers of literature, philosophers, and astrologers also claim identity from past figures of accomplishment and often partake in informal dialogue with them. Many years ago, literary critic Harold Bloom noted the "anxiety of influence", the need to rely on figures of the past but also set oneself apart from them.

In religious circles there is the practice of venerating and even praying to those who lived in the past and are designated "saints". Christianity has had this tradition of venerating saints for a long time; during the medieval era, their relics were the foundations of many a European cathedral and, memorialized by Chaucer's Pardoner, a source of personal corruption, exploiting the piety if the naive. Reliquaries also exist in Asian Buddhism, as is loyalty to a "lineage", a succession of spiritually accomplished people whose achievement is thought to continue and transmit to the present day. These historical or quasi-historical figures became celestial-historical figures that can also be part of one's solar identity.

Legacies are bestowed by future generations in a process of group identification: consider all the locations in the United States that are named after George Washington. As historical appraisals change, so do some names on our buildings, and city streets – social and cultural patterns of identification have changed. Today some public statues have been removed, replaced by those of other historical figures. All these people, most long deceased, have been transformed into symbols.

Ancestors, saints, historical figures, and others are figures from the past whose lives inspire and instruct long after their lifetimes – paradoxically they reinforce our specialness. Who are they but different kinds of *heroes*, with whom we identify and about whom we tell stories? They perform solar functions by being those whose stories are valued as inspirations and models of how to live well – and living well takes on different characteristics through them.

The concept of "hero" and "heroics" pervades our entertainment industry and world events, but what is it? Are heroes only those we tell stories about, who are held out as inspirational people for one's culture? At the end of the previous chapter I looked at heroics from the viewpoint of the Moon, from empathy, desire to care for others, and the quality of usually being "unsung". Maintaining the need for us to recognize lunar heroism, we need to examine carefully our modern solar concepts of heroism.

Chapter Five

Twelve Ways to Be Heroic

Solar and Lunar Heroes

The previous chapter discussed the ancestors; now is time for our heroes. Traditionally and today, heroes accomplish great deeds and are memorialized in song and story. Often one battles destructive forces and rescues the larger world from harm. Usually fighting men with great physical strength, they flourished within the so-called heroic ages that were characterized by instability and warfare. Although given to violent Mars-like activity and achievement, these individuals also carry many of the features of astrology's Sun.

A Mars-like heroic ideal was questioned by Homer whose depiction of Achilles is complex and his main character morally ambiguous. This warrior's retreat to "sulk in his tent" ended only after the death of his companion Patroclus. When Achilles re-entered battle, he went on a killing spree motivated by rage. Only after the pleading of Priam, King of Troy, for the return of the body of his son Hector did Achilles return to being human.

Ancient heroes were often subject to hybrus, a solar pride that takes one beyond natural limits and leads to unfortunate outcomes. Achilles is often contrasted with Patroclus whose concern for others was his noble trait, yet even Patroclus went too far by attempting to scale the walls of Troy and was killed by Hector. The Trojan Hector, usually cast as a model of family loyalty and civic piety, overestimated his ability to command his destiny; later, with his death immanent, he was reduced to begging Achilles for mercy.

Past and present, from the ancient bard's tales to our modern entertainment industry, just being physically strong or successful in sports, politics, or the performing arts does not qualify one as heroic – having natural ability is not good enough. Instead, the hero encounters obstacles and difficulties, incurs great risk, and may be seen to triumph even in failure. What is Superman without Kryptonite and his ill-fated love for Lois Lane? His efforts to fight the bad guys and uphold justice and rightness would not be much of a story, certainly not heroic, without these accompanying problems. At our best, nature and circumstances, especially problematic circumstances, work together to bring out the best in us. This is the nature of our solar potential and astrology's Sun.

An unlikely person to be heroic, Oskar Schindler was a businessman and Nazi party member who, at great risk to himself, finagled the rescue of over a thousand Jews during in the holocaust. (You may remember him from the 1994 movie *Schindler's List*.) Nobody –certainly not Schindler himself – could have predicted a heroic response.

We do not have a birth time for Schindler.[48] His date of birth reveals Sun in Taurus with a square from Jupiter in Leo. The Moon, Mercury, and Saturn are all in Aries, Saturn forming a trine to Jupiter in Leo. A combination of initiative from planets in Aries and resolve from the Sun-Jupiter square first served him personally and later saved the lives of others. Highly adaptive in a lunar way, Schindler's chart also displays solar characteristics.

Previously we looked at lunar depictions of heroic: the "unsung heroes" of daily life, those who sacrifice much to work with victims of natural disaster, war, and pandemic: their heroics do not gain them glory but meet

---

[48] Born April 28, 1908 in Svitavy of the current Czech Republic. That's all we know.

the urgencies of immediate need. Many inhabit the "unvisited tombs" that George Eliot mentions at the end of *Middlemarch*.

A recent publication by Maria Tatar, *Heroine with 1,000 Faces*, makes the important argument about the role of *narration* to heroism: "...in the gendered division of heroic labor, men acquire glory and are remembered for what they *do*, and women for what they say, tell, or report."[49] She discusses the imposition of silence on women and their courage to speak out, as manifested in traditional myths, fairy tales and recent history.

Tatar updates traditional tales to include, for example, women who have had to speak out about sexual abuse and blackmail. All these people, past to present and from legend to today's news stories, incurred risks to themselves by speaking out, but have indirectly helped others with similar stories but more precarious circumstances. Those who heroically speak up must include those of either gender who have become "whistle-blowers"—not because they wanted to but because they had to. These and many other unsung heroes are no less important than those better-known to us.

Heracles as Solar-Hero and Everybody

Heracles had superhuman abilities that co-existed with complexities and flaws familiar to the rest of us. Although Heracles is sometimes cast one-dimensionally as wondrously strong, his story contains difficulty, suffering, and redemptive consequences for himself and others.

He began life both blessed and cursed, as the son of Alceme and Zeus who had disguised himself as her husband. Another child, Eurystheus, was conceived at the same time through Alceme's real husband. Zeus had designated that her next-born son would be a king and protector for Greece. Jealous Hera delayed Heracles' birth so that Eurystheus would be born first, and indeed he became king instead of Heracles.

---

49 Tatar, M. p. 9

Various stories accrue about the growing muscle man who amazed others with his strength, including his sexual prowess. However, having settled down to a marriage and some children, Heracles was possessed by Hera induced madness and in a fit of possessed rage killed his family. Later, having come back to his senses and repentant, he consulted an oracle on how to purify himself from this evil, and was told to serve king Eurystheus. So began the Twelve Labors of Heracles. These Labors, or *athloi*, more like contests in an athletic competition, are varied and each one seems to have its own variations including side trips and adventures on the way to or back from the assigned task.

This solar hero had the saturnine task of working for somebody inferior to himself. Nor was he always compensated or credited justly, as, for example, when he cleaned out the stables of Augeas by re-routing two nearby rivers, disappointing Augeas who wanted spectacle.

Cleaning the stables also illustrates the varied means used to accomplish a task, especially the use of intellect, not just brute strength. There are other examples, such as leading the captured golden-horned hind back to Eurystheus, all the while persuading Artemis that this endeavor was a good thing to do. All this took patience and delicacy, not automatic for this strongman.

Heracles also made mistakes: by one account, when given the task of acquiring the girdle of Hippolyta, queen of the Amazons, he started a war and killed her and many others, when all he had to do was just to ask her for it. On a famous side trip well-known to many astrologers, Heracles carelessly opened a bottle of wine for the centaurs at a wedding reception; this began a battle which resulted in Chiron receiving his incapacitating wound from one of Heracles' poisoned arrows.

Heracles also had to encounter and conquer death. During his Labors this was signified by his last two tasks, obtaining the golden apples of immortality from the Hesperides, later retrieving Cerberus from the

Underworld. (A trip to the Underworld seems mandatory for the solar hero.)

Heracles finally settled down with Deïanira as his wife. When she was about to be carried off by Nessus the Centaur, Heracles shot him with a poisoned arrow. Dying, Nessus told Deïanira that his blood would help bring her husband to his senses if he loved another woman more than her. True to form, Heracles fell in love with somebody else and, upon hearing about this, Deïanira gave him the blood-dipped robe to make a sacrificial offering. When heated, this robe stuck to Heracles, and he was consumed by excruciating pain. On his request, our hero was taken home to be burned in a funeral pyre and his wife accompanied him onto the flames.

Heracles' end was immortality, as the mortal part of him perished (or went to a gloomy underworld) and the immortal part –from his father Zeus – ascended to the heavens to live among the Gods. The hero's solar symbolism culminates when he transcends mortal and physical limitations.

Finally, heroes are redemptive to the larger world, personal failings and all. Many of the Labors of Heracles rescue the surrounding community from death-dealing monstrous creatures or pestilence. Virgil gives us a clear example in his depiction of Aeneas, who was fated to flee Troy and become the ancestor of the Roman state; he participated in fulfilling his preordained destiny unwittingly and often unwillingly.

Into the medieval era, we see Beowulf saving the Danes from the man-hungry Grendel, gives credit to his lord afterwards, but much later is killed trying to save his realm from a dragon. Parsifal overcomes his youthful innocence and insensitivity to rescue the King and save the kingdom from their ruler's malady. Sir Gawain rescues King Arthur from a dangerous contest with the Green Knight and learns later that he is not so virtuous after all, and in that way becomes a more complete model to his knightly community. In Tolkien's modern rendition of old Germanic mythology, the ever-underestimated hobbit Frodo succumbs to the evil power of the

Ring at the very last minute, and only by accident does he becomes the person who saves his world from encroaching evil.

Zodiacal Identity and Solar Heroism

The attribution of a personality type to each sign is a prominent feature of modern popular astrology. Since astrology's Sun manifests in how we attribute identity to ourselves, and since many people call themselves a Libra or a Capricorn or a Pisces, it seems fitting to depict a solar heroic journey for each zodiacal sign.

How each Sun sign defines us and our environment is recognizable within the standard stereotypes. Perhaps we could call this ego. Reality – such as it is – usually has other plans. In the face of adversity, blind spots emerge, mistakes happen, there are destructive and self-destructive paths for all of us, but new possibilities arise. . All determinations (like the identities given to the twelve zodiacal signs) are ego sand traps – and potential sources of greatness.

(For purposes of clarity and consistency, I'm pretending that we are each of the twelve signs as we go along.)

Aries is cardinal, fiery, the domicile of Mars and the exaltation of Sun, the fall or depression of Saturn. This energizing place for the Sun can provide a strong place in the world. Difficulties stem from outer resistance to our inspirations and impulses – from those around us, from our extended social or cultural environment, or even from our own bodies.

The naivety of Sun in Aries is its greatest strength and greatest weakness. Our ability to size up situations freshly and act spontaneously can lead to insight and decisive action or rashness, poor discipline, and indifferent follow-through. In response to outer or inner resistance, an underachieving Sun in Aries may go for over-caution or sullen resentment. Alternatively, poor impulse control and bad judgment causes us continual difficulties in life.

Adding together the initiative of cardinality, the activity of the fire element, and the assertiveness or aggression of the Mars rulership, we gradually acquire more versatility, understanding, and attunement to the larger environment. We continue to act strongly and decisively but also inventively, perhaps moment by moment. This takes courage, especially since challenges happen continuously: sidetracks and backtracks are simply part of the landscape of our lives.

Taurus is fixed, earthy, the domicile of Venus and the exaltation of the Moon
This is a steadier sign and appreciates the large and small pleasures of life: body, sense perception, physical contact with others, and environmental richness. Yet, with feet placed firmly on the ground, we can be both strong and effective in action. Here we encounter and are irritated by volatility, unpredictability, and the inevitability of discomfort and frustrated desire.

One response is to lower expectations and relax with whatever comes our way, but there is the added danger of digging in our heels, settling for the narrow and the certain, ignoring possibilities within our reach. Instead, we may follow a spiritual path of renunciation and gain a larger perspective from the uncertainty and pain that envelops us all. Another is to provide for others, to find resources to provide greater happiness for them. If stinginess is a sign of Taurus defensiveness, generosity widens its capacity for enjoyment. Taurus' radiance occurs with an appreciation of life's circumstances, even a love for one's immediate circumstances as they are – together with the need to be decisive when that is called for.

Gemini is mutable, airy, a domicile of Mercury, without a planetary exaltation or fall. We know the stereotype of the chatty life-of-the-party person, capable of dispensing their knowledge with great eloquence, but whose knowledge on anything is exhausted after five minutes of conversation. At the core is an open-minded inquisitive nature that can hold multiple perspectives and find ingenious solutions.

Here we need to deepen its range of identity and activity and strengthen our resolve and sense of responsibility, as life rarely gives do-overs when we go astray. Enjoying our many possibilities and connections comes to a screeching halt when we realize that who we are is a result of choices we have already made and not made. We need to deepen our relationships: other people are less interchangeable than we thought, they burden us with their demands, they force us to understand and not run away from those who are sticky.

Like a block of stone to a sculptor, a palette to a painter, or a fixed budget to a movie producer, limitations are where Gemini's solar qualities could manifest itself. What we do, if in harmony with the limitations that accompany all situations, sets the stage for the next possibility, and so on.

Cancer is cardinal, watery, the domicile of the Moon, exaltation of Jupiter, and the fall of Mars. The Moon's rulership provides a heightened sense of the everyday and the close. As this luminary's domicile, our identity is wrapped up in personal and emotional connections. In that way we can access intuitive wisdom that develops from caring for others. We also know this sign's reputation for nostalgia, sentimentality, and overly-fused relationships.

Reality intrudes as the unfamiliar. The task for Sun in Cancer is to include the unfamiliar in an expanding world – and also keep a strong and engaged personal touch. Failing this, we have "xenophobia", a fancy term for bigotry, based on the fear of or hatred of what we consider outside our range of concern. Often this is based on a mistaken fear of loss or personal diminution. Within our own circle there is usually a capacity for generosity and empathy and we can use this to go beyond the familiar. Jupiter, the exaltation ruler of Cancer, may come to the rescue, challenging us to expand our scope of sensitivity and empathy, even to be concerned with others we will never meet.

Leo is fixed, fiery, and the domicile of the Sun, without exaltation. The Sun here may bestow greatness – with some tempering. At its best Sun in Leo makes no excuses for nonengagement, for not taking up the mantle or baton of leadership when it is appropriate to do so. As the most intentionally public of the zodiacal signs, the shadows cast by the Sun are also there for all to see, like the person beaming before a crowd and not noticing the open zipper on the pants or the piece of spinach lodged between the teeth. Over time and with work, this embarrassment at being ourselves, being ordinary after all, becomes a path to our greatness.

For heroically-minded Leo, it is easy to become blind to our pettiness, pomposity, and attitude of superiority that are often disguised as good intentions. If of a more narcissistic orientation, we become dependent on surrounding adoration. Given some charisma and power, this narcissism becomes toxic interdependency between fraudulent leader and gullible crowd. The Sun's proud ego can easily become a comedic stock character.

The ongoing solution is to affirm our nature as a flawed hero, to appreciate that the limitations of others echo our own. Humor, generosity, and character are qualities worthy of being inspirational to others.

Virgo is mutable, earthy, and is the domicile and exaltation of Mercury, the depression or fall of Venus. The Sun in Virgo does not radiate – or does not want to be caught doing so. Yet pride – as a virtue or a defect – persists here as in Leo, just more quietly. Virgo's solar fantasy is not about attracting an audience but about being indispensable, rising above the gross defects and incompetence of others and being unparalleled at what we do. Our skills can benefit or intimidate, sometimes both.

The Sun in Virgo has limitations because it is possessed by a mere human being. Like the rest of us, Virgo too may not rise to the occasion, from laziness or indifference, or an unwillingness to go without proper gratitude. When Virgo's failure looms, we tend toward cynicism and withdrawal, but later, we are haunted by the thought that precious time is being wasted. (Sun in Capricorn shares this affliction.)

The ongoing challenge is, in the well-known directive of American football coach Bill Belichick, to "do your job." This does not mean to outshine everybody with our skills, but to be part of a coordinated endeavor that also allows our teammates to do their jobs better. We might be the highly paid quarterback or the lesser-known player on the line, but both are equally asked to just "do their job". The corollary is "next man up": when we are suddenly called to replace somebody ahead of us, we step up and do as well as the person we replaced. Perhaps our job is to "ride the bench", but then, to quote the great poet John Milton who never played American football, "they also serve who only stand and wait."

Libra is cardinal, airy, and the domicile of Venus and fall or depression of Sun. The Sun's light in Libra is just as strong as elsewhere but its light is *diffused*, not seeming to generate from ourselves but in relationship. Sun in Libra is famous for its kindness and consideration, for an ability to see ourselves in larger contexts.

Libra can have its own kind of egotism: being attached to a pretty version of things and ignoring the plainness or ugliness of reality. Our lives all contain messiness: petty self-dealing, treachery in relationships, betrayal of our own stated principles – that Libra would prefer to do without. The ability to stand up and do something, so easy to the Sun in Libra's opposite sign Aries, is compromised by caution, over-thinking, and the feeling that if we allow ourselves to go out on a limb, others will be sawing away at the branch.

Instead of putting our head in the sand, this Sun placement may face those difficulties head-on as they arise, letting ensuing discord be part of repairing or initiating new things. We can be a spokesperson for higher ideals while keeping our feet on the ground. Finally, we might contribute through being a hidden benefactor, one who quietly benefits others but stays out of the spotlight. All these alternatives leave Sun in Libra with much nobility, even without visibility.

Scorpio is fixed, watery, the domicile of Mars and the depression or fall of Moon. We have the steadiness of being in a fixed sign and with the drive associated with Mars. If well cultivated, the inner honesty and emotional depth of Sun in Scorpio can make these individuals exemplary. Conventional descriptions of Scorpio stress that when frustrated or feeling unfairly treated, outrage can lead to sullen resentment, fantasies of revenge or becoming passive-aggressive. It is entirely too easy for Scorpio to hold onto negativity so rigidly that it becomes toxic. These are admissions of helplessness that undermine our solar possibilities.

The Sun in Scorpio identifies itself with its passion, its drive, and, at its best, is eager to commit to something important. It is equally capable of decisive action and operating behind the scenes, whichever is appropriate. There are fewer qualms about acting ruthlessly if that is what is called for. Then, even after having worked our magic, we must walk into the sunset.

The Sun in Scorpio may also yield the whistleblower who takes risks to expose wrongdoing, or maybe another anonymous benefactor who contributes in hidden ways. Both benefactor and whistleblower forget themselves and their desires for fame or notoriety. If we try to go out in a blaze of glory, or make a show of our devotion or self-sacrifice, the result can be more destructive than helpful. By losing ourselves in a just cause, we find ourselves but finding ourselves turns out not to be very important.

Sagittarius is mutable, fiery, a domicile of Jupiter and no exaltation or fall. This placement inclines toward public activity, an ability to manifest within a broader horizon. The mutability of Sagittarius allows for a flexibility of response that is more difficult for the other two fiery signs, but this can bring about this Sun's well-known attributes of inconsistency if not hypocrisy. Additionally, our desire to have the answers collides with those occasions in which we are found to be wrong but will not admit it.

Like the other fiery Signs Aries and Leo, we must look around first before doing anything rash or embarrassing, but sometimes there arises the need to act quickly at the risk of being wrong or becoming vulnerable. Yet, for all its buoyancy, Sun in Sagittarius often experiences life as an ongoing collection of disappointments. The trials for optimistic Sagittarius are in facing its smallness within the larger world, that we are not as significant as we would like to be but are subject to the same vicissitudes as those ordinary people.

Jupiter's sign then can hold onto its veneer of self-importance – or we can become truly wise and effective. If wisdom and concern for others overcome arrogant defensiveness, we can embody higher principles and inspire others. This would be not so much from charisma but from a wider outlook that contains both one's pride and humility.

Sun in Capricorn is cardinal, earthy, governed by Saturn, the exaltation of Mars and the depression or fall of Jupiter. With this line-up of planetary connections, why would anybody want to be identified with *this*?

The Sun in Capricorn is well-suited to acknowledge painful realities and to carve out new possibilities, not from wishful thinking but applying resources that are already there. This occurs through being the "Mountain Goat", not from a fixed disposition but an ability to stay on course while navigating setbacks and unanticipated difficulties - but also keeping our eyes on the prize. However the prize must be worth the steep climb.

The other side is our perception of limitation and failure. In response we can become cynical, greedy, stuck in a fixed identity, mistrustful of others. We can become a throat-cutting overachiever or go passive and inept, ignoring the richness our life circumstances offer.

The Capricorn life is a lonely journey, but when dedicated to sharing with others, austere self-reliance becomes a way to enlarge ourselves in the world. Drive and defiant stubbornness express themselves through Capricorn's affinity to Mars (exaltation) and Saturn (domicile) respectively.

These days some contemporary psychologists call this "grit", a concept we will consider later.

Aquarius is fixed, airy, and is domicile of Saturn. This Sign, opposite Leo, is the "detriment" of the Sun and a less visibly solar character, like the Sign Libra. Both Libra and Aquarius diffuse the Sun's radiance outward. Aquarius is less Venusian, more concerned with implications of ideas than how they harmonize with one another. Fixed Aquarius is more likely to go toe-to-toe with an adversary.

Sun in Aquarius has a reputation for strong adherence to principle that can cover assigning itself the most positive of motives. With an identity based on asserting honesty and thoughtfulness, Aquarius can rationalize brilliantly, disguising its small-minded actions. We inadvertently fulfill the stereotype that Sun in Aquarius loves humanity but dislikes ninety-five percent of the people in it. Our path of solar heroism is in being honest about our ordinary emotional responses. Our limitations help us to identify with others and be of benefit to them. In that way allegiance to principle becomes a beacon for us and potentially for others.

Pisces is mutable, watery, the domicile of Jupiter, the exaltation of Venus, and the depression or fall of Mercury. One would think that this combination of attributes would be less burdened by ego than the other signs – mutability gives flexibility, wateriness yields empathy and sensitivity, and the dignity of the benefics Jupiter and Venus incline toward the positive. Alas, there are pitfalls for this solar condition as well.

If ideas and values are tentative and based on intuitions and feelings that are subject to change, it is easy to lack conviction, or to substitute emotional responses for seeing things clearly and being skillful in daily life. We may alternate from the melodramatic to the melancholic, courting sympathy either way. One of my first astrology books used Shakespeare's Hamlet as an example of Sun in Pisces, and it is hard to disagree.

How do we climb over perversions of intuition and distortions of empathy? By acknowledging and embracing those negative manifestations in ourselves and others. Even better would be to follow the words of a prayer attributed (probably falsely) to the thirteenth-century Francis of Assisi, who asks that he understand rather than be understood, to love rather than be loved. This might seem rather unworldly, yet an impersonal but emotionally connected outlook can exist within our ordinary lives. Pisces has a radiance that is more atmospheric than driven by personality. We may shine from creating an environment for others rather than from displays of personal charisma. .

In summary, how do we bridge the wide river between our disappointing actualities and our inherent possibilities? It does take a village to raise a hero or, put differently, an exemplary person. We must also consider the many kinds of perceptiveness and intelligence that uncover and act upon better versions of ourselves. Examining these qualities in the following chapter concludes our discussion of the luminaries.

Part Two

Planetary Excellence and Not So Much

Chapter Six

Planetary Character

The word *character* has an interesting history and a double meaning. The word's original meaning was for an instrument for cutting or making something sharp, so it meant something engraved, impressed, or stamped – made distinctive in some way. When we refer to somebody as a *character*, we mean that this person makes a noteworthy impression. To muddle matters we also have the notion of *character development* that I unfairly free-associate with sanctimony or the Victorian era's ideal of a "gentleman."

This second version of the word implies having moral strength. One can have many character flaws even when the same person is a character, a distinctive person.

As an introduction to the five visible planets, this chapter begins with the first meaning which is sometimes used synonymously with "personality" – what kind of character are you? Our discussion of the five planets will demonstrate some people of greater moral character and some with less. We discuss character strengths with the luminaries and the five planets in Part Three.

Many modern astrologers assign character, synonymous with personality, to zodiacal signs. Astrology conference organizers often give attendees name tags for them to write down signs of their Sun, Moon, and Ascendant. This serves mostly as a social icebreaker, a way to introduce yourself to your peers. My Sun in Capricorn means I'm traditional and goal-oriented, my Sagittarius Moon is emotionally changeable and sometimes insensitive, and Libra rising tries to be nice to others.

Long before Sun-sign astrology, the five visible planets Mercury through Saturn represented five different modes of attitude and behavior. Although we have all these visible planets in our astrological charts, one or two of them were considered the most critical to our happiness and activity, or, if poorly handled, to our detriment. We could be *saturnine* or *mercurial*, even *venereal* or *jovial*, or maybe have "too much Mars". Which planet or planets best capture your physical presence, your personality and range of activity?

The Sun and Moon rarely become an overall chart ruler since they each governs only one sign and they both express life issues common to us all. The five planets are better suited for depicting individual differences.

As one can use the twelve signs of the zodiac to put people into little boxes marked with keywords, one might think the same problem occurs using planets, yet it does not. Here some complexity is our friend: even when a particular planet bursts into prominence in a natal chart, one must consider its condition and its relationships with other planets. One needs to consider zodiacal placement, house (as in "ninth house") in which planets reside or govern, aspects and other associations between planets, and temporary conditions linked to transits, progressions, or planetary periods. Additionally, sometimes there are two dominant planets, and sometimes none rise to the occasion. Even if one planet seems to dominate, there are other voices – accompanying or contrasting – we also need to hear.

Planets Dignified and Disposing

This is an opportunity to review the astrological information that will help us determine planetary character. One issue is *dignity*, from the Latin for "worthiness" and depicts nobility or elevation of rank. Often planetary dignity is divided into *essential dignity*, for its sign placement, and *accidental dignity* for house placement as well as aspects from benefics and malefics, speed, and nearness to the Sun. *Disposition* denotes how one or two planets may govern one position like the Ascendant or Mercury or many places in the chart.

Three or Five Categories of Planetary "Essential" Dignity
We begin with domicile. As shown in the chart here, each of the five planets is in its own "house" or domicile in two signs, one in a so-called masculine sign (fire or air element) and the other is in a so-called feminine sign (earth or water element). As we may act differently when in the city of the country, each planet acts differently in its two places.

Differences between the planets' two domiciles also link to planetary sect, diurnal and nocturnal, that correspond to the masculine and feminine

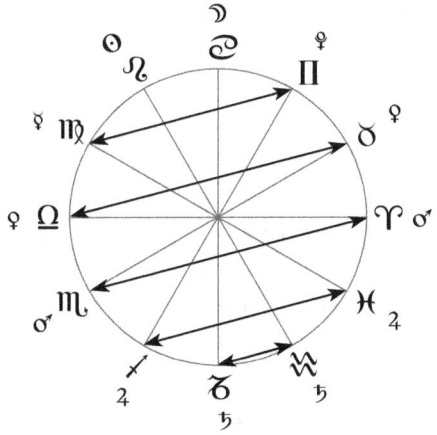

signs respectively. Remember that Saturn and Jupiter are of the diurnal solar sect and Venus and Mars of the nocturnal lunar sect, and Mercury goes either way. (Saturn prefers the lighter qualities of the diurnal sect and Mars the downshifting energy of the nocturnal sect.) A planet in sect has a more comfortable environment in which to operate.

Clearly influenced by these considerations, ancient astrologers often posited that each planet prefers one domicile or sign to the other: nocturnal Venus prefers (feminine) Taurus to (masculine) Libra, nocturnal Mars prefers (feminine) Scorpio to Aries, diurnal Saturn prefers (masculine) Aquarius to Capricorn, diurnal Jupiter prefers (masculine) Sagittarius, and Mercury, as usual, is a toss-up between Gemini and Virgo, giving (feminine) Virgo a slight edge.[50] Ancient astrologers were less interested in detriments (placement in sign that is opposite domicile: for example, Mars

---

50 Hephaistio of Thebes, Bk I Chapter 7; Al-Burini concurs except he asserts that Mars prefers Aries to Scorpio, p. 257

Astrology and the Lives of People

in Libra opposite Aries or the Sun in Aquarius opposite Leo) than their medieval and modern successors.

Another category of dignity is that of exaltations. If a planet in its domicile sign is strong because it is comfortable in its own home, then a planet in the sign of its exaltation is like being an honored guest and behaves at its best. In contrast, a planet opposite its exaltation sign is said to be in "depression" or "fall" (or both, like Mercury in Pisces) gets a ruder welcome. The exaltation of the Sun is Aries; that of the Moon is Taurus. Planets with opposing signs of exaltation give some opposite strengths and characteristics, as with Mercury/Venus and Mars/Jupiter.

Here are the assignments of exaltation and depression/fall:

	Exaltation	Fall
Sun	Aries	Libra
Moon	Taurus	Scorpio
Mercury	Virgo	Pisces
Venus	Pisces	Virgo
Mars	Capricorn	Cancer
Jupiter	Cancer	Capricorn
Saturn	Libra	Aries

Although common understanding is that the system of exaltations and depressions (signs opposite planets' exaltations) arose independently from that of domiciles, considerations of planetary sect seem to bring them together. Behold an amazing pattern: think of trines as more diurnal, the nature of Jupiter, and sextiles are more nocturnal, the nature the nocturnal benefic Venus.

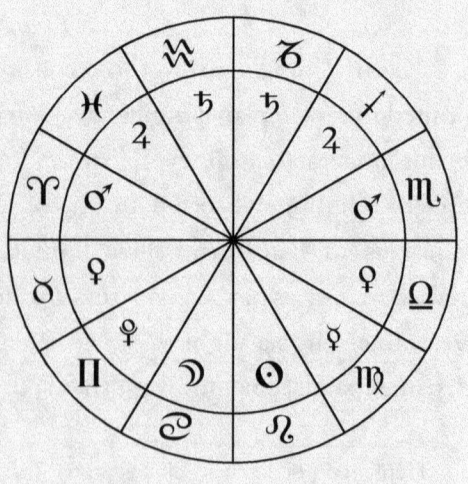

120

Planetary Character

- The Sun, exalted in Aries, is in trine with its domicile Leo.
- Saturn in exaltation in Libra is in trine with its domicile Aquarius
- Jupiter's exaltation sign Cancer is in trine to Pisces.
- The nocturnal sect does similarly with sextiles, as the Moon's exaltation in Taurus is in sextile to its domicile Cancer,
- Venus, exalted in Pisces sextiles Taurus
- Mars exalted in Capricorn sextiles its domicile Scorpio.
- Mercury, of neither planetary sect, has the distinction of Virgo being both domicile and exaltation sign. Mercury is always a bit different from the others.

This system of domiciles and exaltations, including opposite signs for detriment and fall, is a glorious pattern from traditional astrology that helps the information from a natal chart be clearer. It is unfortunate that many modern astrologers, by including outer planets and asteroids and the like as governing signs, have made this elegant system asymmetrical and confusing.

A third category is used for dignity but not for debility. We discussed triplicities in the first chapter, and it may be helpful to supply these distinctions again.

- For planets in the *fire* signs by day, the Sun is the triplicity ruler; by night it is Jupiter.
- For planets in the *earth* signs by day look to Venus and by night look to the Moon.
- For planets in *air* signs, Saturn is the triplicity ruler; by night it is Mercury.
- For planets in the *water* signs, it is more confusing. Everybody agrees on Mars for nocturnal charts; for those who are diurnal, I and most sources look to Venus.

Two other categories of dignity – the "minor dignities" – are sometimes used, although I tend not to use them actively in my client work. *Terms or bounds* divide each sign of the zodiac into five unequal parts. Early degrees of a sign tend to be governed by a planet with some other dignity in that sign, and the final degrees are governed by either Mars or Saturn, whichever has less dignity in that sign. Different lists of terms have accumulated over the centuries. The fifth dignity is the *faces or decans* that go in descending planetary order and fit in nicely with planetary days and hours.

So far we have looked at a planet's status in its own position. The next section takes up another critical factor for determining the planet or planets of character. What planet or planets govern planets in their signs or in other factors like the Ascendant?

Planetary and Chart Dispositors
Although the modern meaning of *dispositor* is closer to "attitude" as in, for example, "I'm not disposed to going to the movies tonight" the word originally meant an arrangement. Think of the English "dispose of..." not in the sense of getting rid of something but as in settling a matter. Beginning simply, my Lot of Fortune in Scorpio is disposed by Mars and my Lot of Spirit in Virgo is disposed by Mercury.

Alas, this becomes more complicated in traditional astrology, as they use different categories of disposition, corresponding to the categories of dignity cited above. For example, if I have Mercury and the Moon in Sagittarius, then Jupiter (both domicile and triplicity lord of Sagittarius in my nocturnal chart) figures strongly as dispositor for both important planets. Then I have to look at the condition of my Jupiter placement.

A planet may be important by disposition but be weakly placed in a natal chart, or an angular planet in essential dignity may not be dispositor for any important positions in a natal chart. Ideally one would find one or two planets with strength of *both* dignity and disposition to determine planetary character, but if you don't, that is also important information about a person.

There are different traditions for finding a dispositor over many positions, the "Ruler of the Nativity" or "Lord of the Geniture" or the chart "Almuten". (This has come down to us in modern astrologers in the simplified form of the domicile ruler of the Ascendant being the "chart ruler.") There are complicated and simpler ways to assessing one's planetary character and I tend to favor the (relatively) simple.

On the more complex side, astrologers often counted points for the dignities, adding more for "accidental dignities", and then note which planet has the greatest number of points.[51] One begins with the standard essential dignity table (available in many astrology software packages) that usually includes number values: domicile is 5, exaltation 4, triplicity 3, term or bound 2, face 1.[52] The result is that the domicile lord for a position is important but does not always prevail.

Over time my focus for dispositors became the domicile, exaltation and triplicity lords only. The advantage of stopping at triplicities is that you can dispense with the standard dignity table and easily memorize domiciles, exaltations, and triplicities, for these pertain to entire signs, not their divisions as do terms and faces. For those who may be interested in trying this out, I will cite point systems here, although I tend not to use them in my practice. Let's try this out where it counts: interpreting the lives of a few famous people.

---

51 See Ibn Ezra, *The Book of Nativities and Revolutions,* (2008) trans. Meira Epstein p. 13-14; Johanne Schoener, *Opusculum Astrologicum,* (1994), trans. R. Hand p. 35,64

52 To calculate a planet's dignity in its sign, many computer programs will deduct five points if a planet is in detriment and four if in depression or fall. If a planet does not appear in any of these five categories, five points are also deducted for being peregrine. Additionally, if two planets are in mutual reception in any of these five categories, the number of points for that category is added. Some currently practicing traditional astrologers follow these procedures closely: I do not.

Astrology and the Lives of People

Governing One or More Positions

We begin with finding the dispositor for one planet only. What planet or planets are in charge of Eleanor Roosevelt's Mercury? The swift planet is in the third degree of Libra in her eleventh house in a diurnal chart.

- Venus gets five points for domicile.
- Saturn gets four for exaltation, and Saturn gets another three points for being triplicity ruler by day.

Saturn beats out Venus in this position, seven to five, although Venus is domicile ruler of Libra.

Now we expand and consider Saturn's position in her chart: in Gemini and placed in the seventh house, Saturn is in its own triplicity in her day

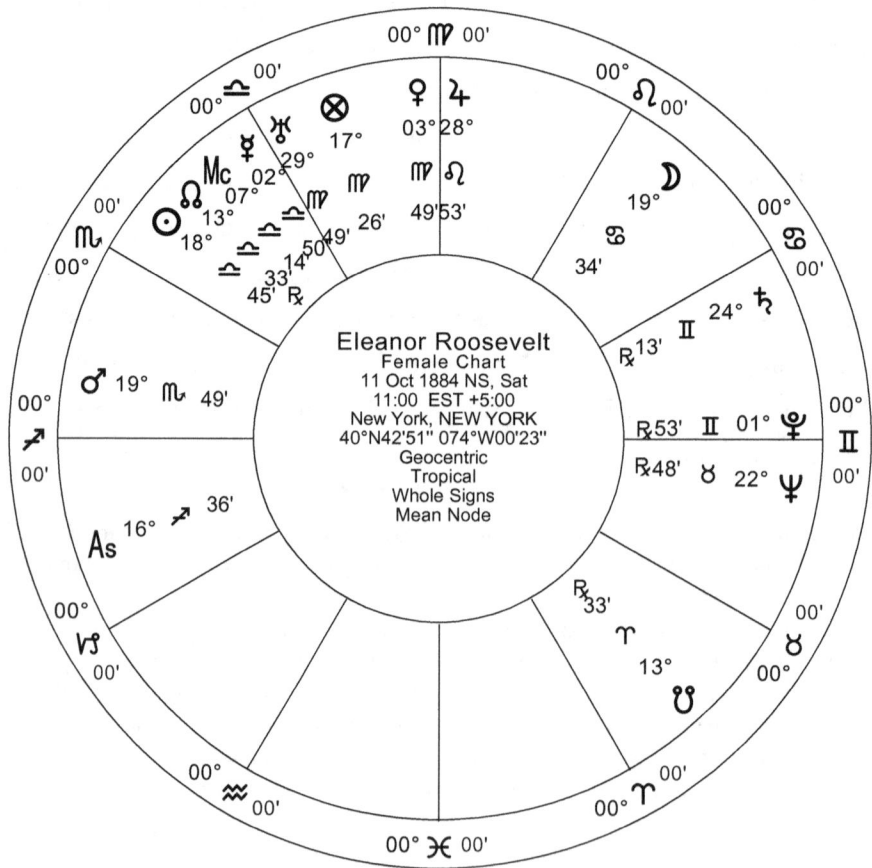

chart: one should not ignore this planet for matters mercurial. Noting also that her Libra Sun also has Saturn as exaltation and triplicity ruler, our slow dark planet has a critical role in the nature and life course of this woman. Yet Saturn will not always dominate.

Eleanor Roosevelt's Ascendant is in Sagittarius, so Jupiter in Leo is the Ascendant's domicile ruler (Sagittarius has no planetary exaltation ruler and the Sun is triplicity ruler). Since Jupiter is also the Moon's exaltation ruler and is conjunct the fixed star Regulus, we might look for an alternation, oscillation, or polyphony between Saturn and Jupiter. Which planet might you see from Eleanor Roosevelt and when? For example, after she learned of her husband Franklin's affair with Lucy Mercer, Franklin confronted more of Eleanor's Saturn; over time the public saw more Jupiter.

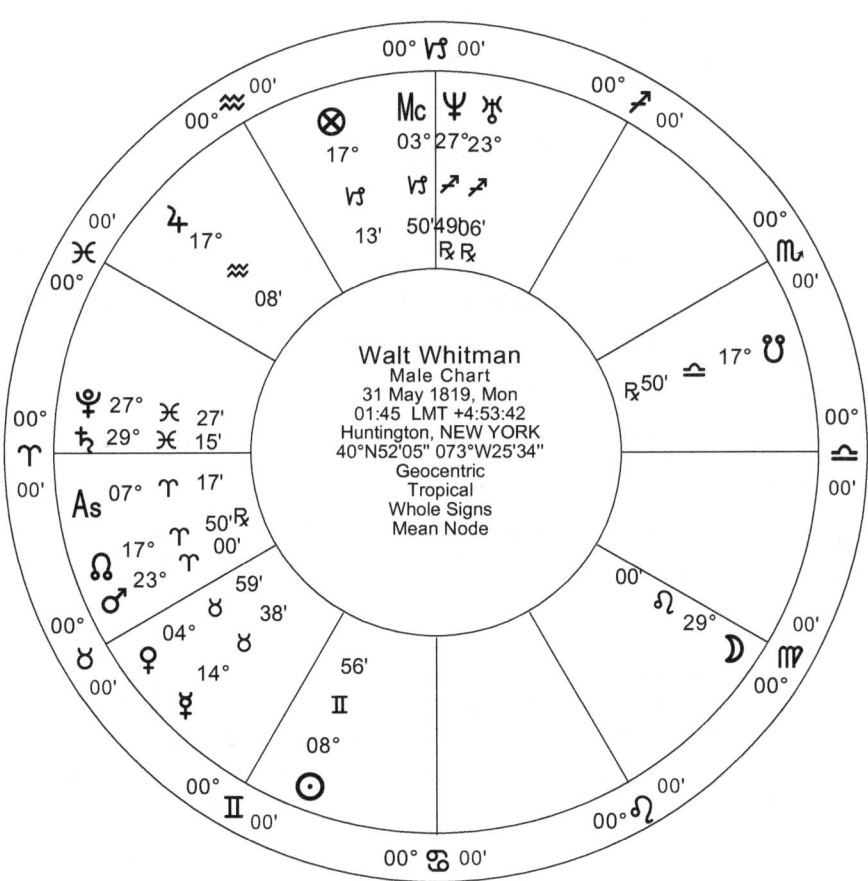

In comparison with Roosevelt's Mercury in Libra, we get a different picture of Mercury with Walt Whitman. Our American poet, with Mercury in Taurus in the second house in a night chart, yields five points for Venus in its domicile, four for the Moon in its exaltation, and an additional three for the Moon as triplicity ruler for nocturnal earth-element charts. The Moon prevails over Venus in this zodiacal position. Previously we discussed the Moon's importance in Whitman's chart; its rulership for Mercury emphasizes this luminary even further.

Looking further at Whitman's chart as a whole, we see the importance of Mercury, domicile and triplicity ruler of both Sun and Jupiter, but also Mars in the first house in Aries. Whitman gives us a varied nature: attuned to both a larger cosmic picture and the immediate, his writings revealed great energy but not in a competitive way, and if you met him you would find him to be quieter and more reflective.

Who is in Charge Around Here?

Ibn Ezra, from the twelfth century, considered the strongest planet as the one with the most points of dignity over the two luminaries, Ascendant, Lot of Fortune, and Moon's position at the New or Full Moon preceding the birth. Johannes Schoener, from the sixteenth century, used the Midheaven degree instead of the prenatal New or Full Moon. Ibn Ezra and Johannes Schoener also included numbers for house position.[53] William Lilly, two centuries after Schoener, stated that it is simply the planet that has strong disposition over important chart positions, with essential and accidental dignity – perhaps Lilly was a busier man.

---

53   In descending order from twelve points to one, both authorities give 10th =12 points, 1st=11 points, and then in descending order 7, 4, 11, 5, 9, 3, 2, 8, 12, 6: e.g., a planet in the first house would receive eleven additional points but another in the second would receive four. One may disagree with some of these number values; my solution is to look specifically at angular houses and those that aspect the Ascendant sign by trine or sextile.

Planetary Character

Here is the astrological chart of the former Italian Prime Minister Silvio Berlusconi, whose birth record says one thing and his word says another. He is a glowing example of a "character" in the first sense as a distinct personality and style, but with apparent deficits of moral character.

As a younger person Silvio Berlusconi was a successful businessman, a media mogul with political ambitions. During his political life and during his three stints as Italy's Prime Minister, he spent much of the time battling charges of corruption and sexual misconduct, providing the Italian media and the public decades of entertainment and intrigue. This came at a cost: nobody could take him or his country seriously while he was in office.

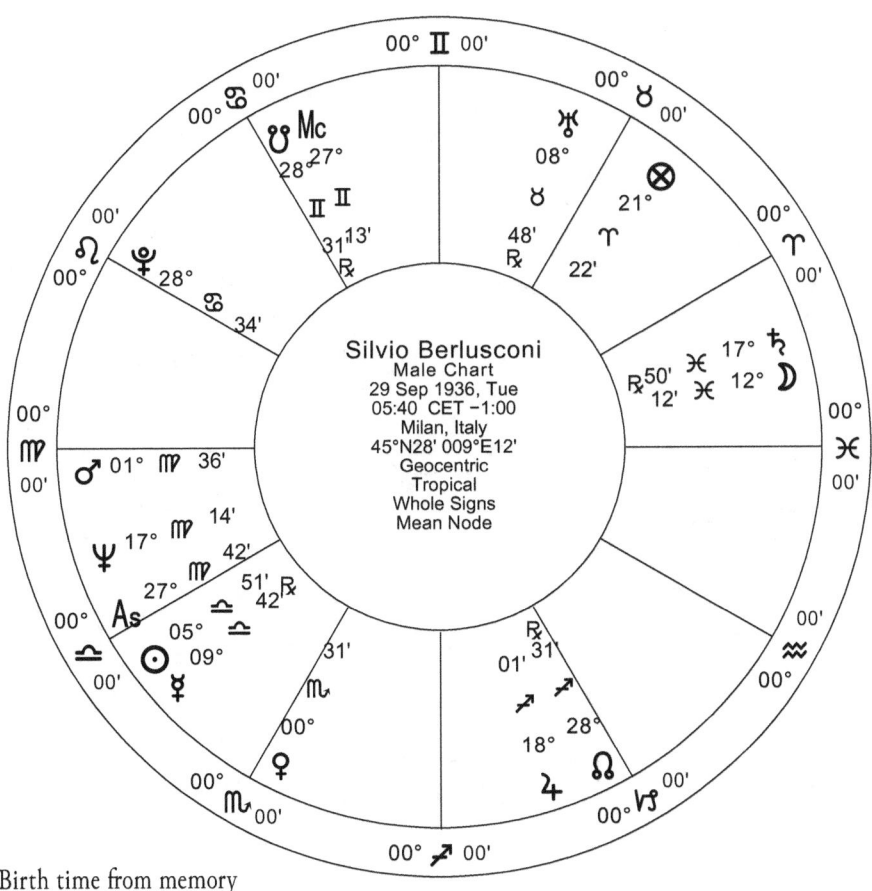

Birth time from memory

Here's his natal chart, if you believe the time he gives. What is his almuten or Lord of the Geniture? If you did the calculations without using the Prenatal New Moon, Jupiter comes out slightly ahead; otherwise, using the Prenatal Moon it is Mercury by a few lengths, especially as Mercury is also ruler of the Ascendant. (Considering his wealth and political involvement and its superior house position, I am tempted not to include the Prenatal Moon and to go with Jupiter.)

Berlusconi's actual birth record indicates that he was born just under an hour later, with Libra rising and a diurnal chart. It's another picture entirely, one that emphasizes Venus as domicile of his Ascendant and Sun and exaltation ruler of the Moon and Lot of Fortune.

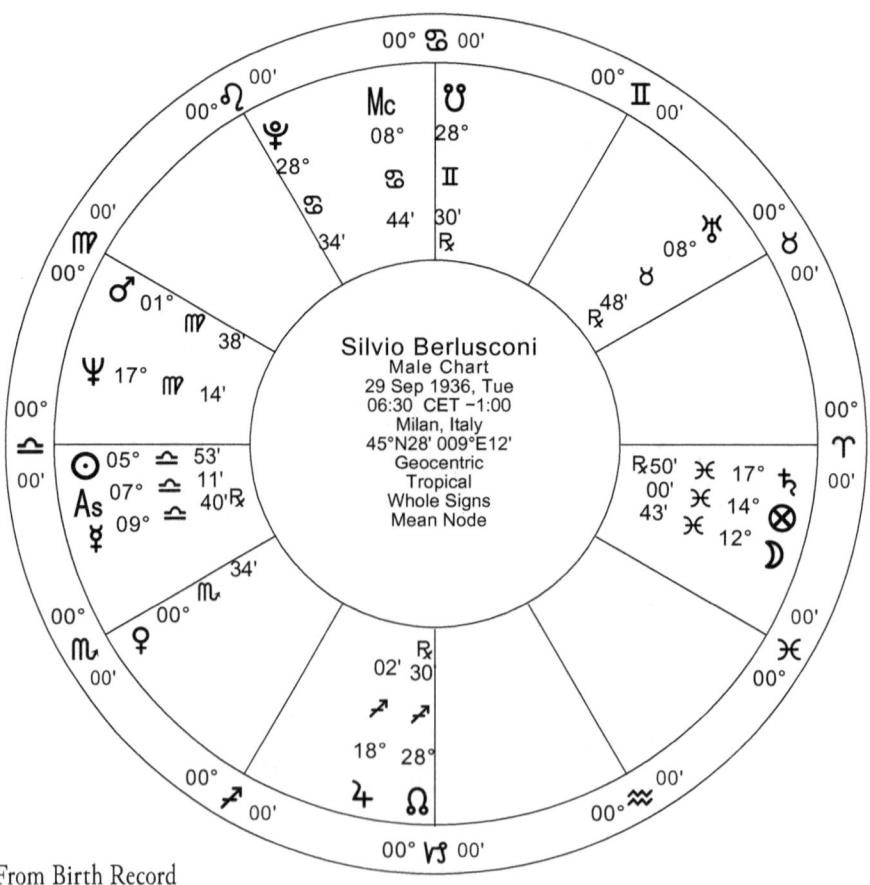

From Birth Record

Planetary Character

Adding the Sun and Mercury so close to his Ascendant (Mercury in also its "joy" in the first house), Venus completes a portrait of a charming but possibly manipulative person. The position of Venus in Scorpio, however, brings in Mars, since the red planet is not only the dispositor for his Venus; the two planets are also in close sextile. All this gives us a mixed message of one who could be appealing and entertaining but also gruff and coarse. Jupiter maintains its important position as the governing planet for Berlusconi's Moon.

When we consider Albert Einstein, all roads appear to lead us to Jupiter, domicile of Sagittarius and Pisces respectively, and exaltation ruler of Ascendant in Cancer. Yet Jupiter in Aquarius is in the mediocre eighth

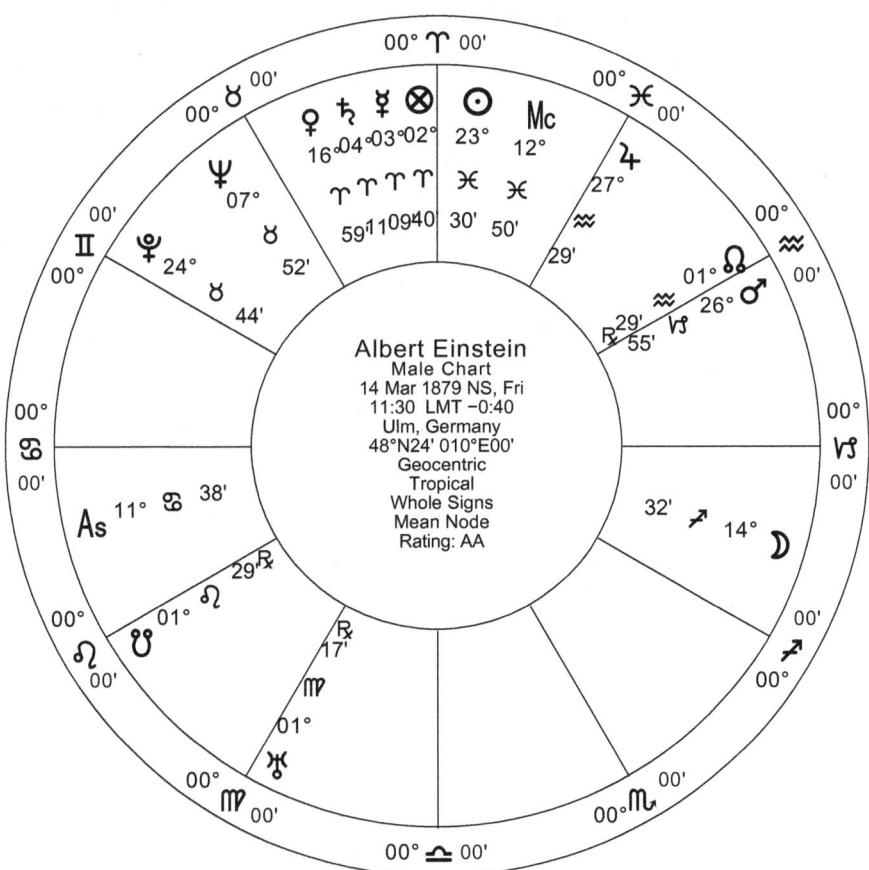

house and has no aspects to personal planets, although the square from Pluto may be a factor.

Einstein's Mars, angular and in exaltation, and with a sextile to the Sun, could be another candidate for dominant planet. The three-planet combination in Aries in the tenth house, all governed by Mars but with the Sun in exaltation and triplicity, may have given rise to his early fame, but his enduring legacy seems to have the nature of Jupiter.

There are different approaches you can use to determine planetary character. You may try out point systems, including points given to the houses, and you may want to include lords of terms/bounds or faces. You may opt for the Hellenistic alternative of each category of dignity having an equal value but each one used differently. You may consider the Lord of the Ascendant to be the planet with which one has the easiest access, but a Lord of the Geniture – if it is different – may represent more of a person's complete nature or potential. In my view, by using planetary sect, three traditional categories of dignity and disposition, and factoring in location of houses and contacts from other planets, it is not difficult to identify one planet or two that are most critical for a person.

As these planets will be differently placed for all of us, and as our life conditions vary, a character governed by the five planets will manifest differently for one person than for another. This creates complexity, but it's a complexity that parallels who we are.

In the following chapters we will consider each planet on its own. What it is like to have a character that is mercurial, jovial, venereal, Mars-like, or saturnine?

Chapter Seven

The Wit and Wisdom of Mercury

Astrological Mercury is perplexing to the modern mind, perhaps related to the fact that most of us don't know if we have ever seen it in the night sky. Mercury appears only briefly, if at all, only shortly before sunrise or after sunset low or the eastern or western horizons. Our astrological ancestors, who observed the night sky more closely than we can, would have noted this planet's quick and fleeting appearances.

Ibn Ezra from the twelfth century gives us a picture of Mercury and of those under its influence. He focuses on Mercury's quickness and changeability.

> "Mercury is mixed and variable since he changes according to the nature of the rest of the stars and the signs, and his nature is somewhat tending toward coldness and dryness. In his share are the soul of man and the power of intelligence."

> "In his share of human nature are speech, intelligence, education, wisdom, science of the stars, divination, all sorts of magic, eloquence, accuracy of language, fast talk, ability to recite and rhyme, knowledge of hidden secrets and prophecy, [also] kindness and compassion and avoiding evil, [as well as] musical talent, love of anything miniature, negotiating, verbal arguments without resorting to blows, all sorts of trickery and deception, and writing forged documents. His hand is trained in all skills, and he is eager to do all [kinds of] activity, and

[he is inclined towards] acquiring wealth and squandering it.

His nature varies according to the individual nativity..."[54]

Mercury is the planet of the mind's movements and the marketplace, the political forum, the advertising campaign, virtual or physical offices of managers and lawyers and astrologers, temples of prophets, and schemes of today's internet scams. Mercury forms the basis of friendships and humor and builds toward a larger social self.

Mercury's language ranges from the profound to the glib to the knowingly deceptive. Mercury is ethically neutral and often enjoys pushing the proverbial envelope: this can be a good thing, for it allows us to examine our assumptions and perhaps appreciate moral complexity as it arises. It also may try to get away with what is bad.

Mercury's Households and a Tall Tale

Like Jupiter, Mercury's domicile signs, Gemini and Virgo, are in square to each other and yield different planetary effects. Gemini's version is more familiar, one that loves different perspectives but is loyal to none, and that dances with situational, informational, and moral boundaries. The ancient Greeks gave us that man of many turns, Odysseus, who will spin a tall tale because that's his nature. The Romans, out of envy and mistrust, maintained a stereotype of the Greeks as too clever and subtle, overly prone to double-talk, and ethically challenged. The Romans considered themselves closer to Mercury in Virgo, practical if not always interesting, trying to make the best of what is immediately at hand.

To make more vivid the contrast between the two Mercuries, here's an old tale that sharply divides a Virgo Mercury from one in Gemini. We go back to late medieval Italy in the years following the Black Death. Giovanni Boccaccio's tales in the *Decameron* often value cleverness and intellect

---

54 *Beginning of Wisdom*, p. 101, 102

The Wit and Wisdom of Mercury

over phony assertions of power or class dominance. On the third day of storytelling among the privileged escapees from the city, this day's theme was "people who by dint of their own efforts have achieved an object they greatly desired or recovered a thing previously lost". Here is the second tale of the day.

In the Kingdom of Lombardy in Northern Italy, in the very distant past, King Agilulf had a wife who was of course beautiful and virtuous. One of the grooms working for the Queen, a low-born but intelligent young man, fell in love with her. This dangerous inclination he kept to himself, but then, having given up all hope of happiness in life, he decided to die in a way that would demonstrate his love for her.

The Groom quietly observed the behavior of Queen and King and decided to impersonate the King at night and take to the Queen's bed. The King often slept by himself but did visit his wife from time to time. Our Groom put on attire like that of the King, imitated his mannerisms, found his way into the Queen's bedroom and onto the Queen. Straining credulity, she did not notice that this man was not her husband. The satisfied Groom then left the Queen's bedroom – but, alas, a short while later the King arrived for some marital pleasure for himself. The Queen was surprised to see him, since she thought he had just left and was now returning for more, and questioned her husband on the wisdom of these nocturnal exertions for his health.

Agilulf, noting his wife's surprise upon seeing him, realized that somebody else had just been there with the Queen, unbeknownst to her. Hiding his anger – what good would it do for his wife to know somebody else had taken advantage of her? – he pretended to heed his wife's concerns and he leaves the bedroom.

The King surmised that the transgressor was one of the male servants and went to the dormitory where they are all asleep: one of them surely had a pounding heart that would give away his crime. Agilulf found one such person pretending to be asleep, and quietly cut a portion of hair on one side of his head for detection the following morning. After the King left, however, the Groom got up, found a pair of scissors, and made a similar cut of hair on the others asleep in the dormitory.

The following morning the King assembled his household, expecting to find the culprit and have him executed, but instead he saw that all the men had a similar cut of hair! The King simply said, "Whoever it was who did it, he better not do it again. And now, off with you all!" This ends the story: the Groom's transgression was never repeated, and the young man kept his head. King and Queen preserved their dignity and nobody but King and the Groom were the wiser.

The Groom is the extreme mercurial trickster of dubious morals, but we are tempted to ignore his transgression and focus instead on his cleverness. (Note that the Groom, his longing now satisfied, had no desire for an honorable death in consequence of his transgression.)

By occupation the King is the nature of the Sun, yet he endured this blow to his masculine pride to preserve the honor of his household and kingdom. The King shows Virgo Mercury's resourcefulness and ability to act quickly and skillfully when this is called for. Mercury gets the job done for him.

Mercury and *Realpolitik*

Previously we've seen individuating and "aristocratic" values for the Sun and physical, interpersonal, and "common" values for the Moon. Mercury has another set of values.

Nicolo Machiavelli is best known for the adjective "machiavellian" that denotes tactics that are cynical and often amoral but effective. Some of us may have once read *The Prince*, that short advice manual that Machiavelli wrote in exile as a job application to the Florentine leadership. His work counseled the Florentine leadership of the time on how to rule successfully and hopefully guide Italy toward union.

Machiavelli didn't get the job he wanted, and *The Prince* was only printed after his death, but his role as an important political thinker has endured to this day. Machiavelli famously asserted, for example, that it is far better to be thought virtuous than to be virtuous, better to be feared than to be loved. He asserted that an effective leader sometimes may need to be strong like a lion and sometimes clever like a fox. Thus began modern political theory.

Nicolo Machiavelli was not only a political and military theorist and advisor but an able diplomat, satirist, and playwright. He may also have been a good farmer but that clearly wasn't his preference when he began *The Prince*. Machiavelli's natal Mercury was capable of all these enterprises.[55]

In Gemini, Mercury is in its own domicile and triplicity (in this nocturnal chart), and is moving toward its retrograde station; all this helps give him a steady intellect alongside a quick mind.

Additionally, his Lot of Spirit is in Virgo, governed by Mercury that is in the tenth house from Lot of Spirit – the intentional choices he made would take on a mercurial quality. Hence his famous job application. (I wonder whether Mercury's placement in his sixth house also inclined him to overwork as a writer.)

Machiavelli's penetrating thinking and persuasiveness may stem from the square from Mars to Mercury. Mars, in its own triplicity, inclined Mercury toward the polemical; he was forceful in the presentation of his ideas. We also have a window on his interests in military structure and strategy.

Pluto, in square to both Mercury and Mars, will not bring out much idealism. Machiavelli bequeathed to us one of the gems of Italian comedy. *La Mandragola* or *The Mandrake* that presents bribery, sexual hijinks, and church corruption. Everybody, no matter how virtuous one seems, has his

---

55 AA rating – we have a birth record for him!

Astrology and the Lives of People

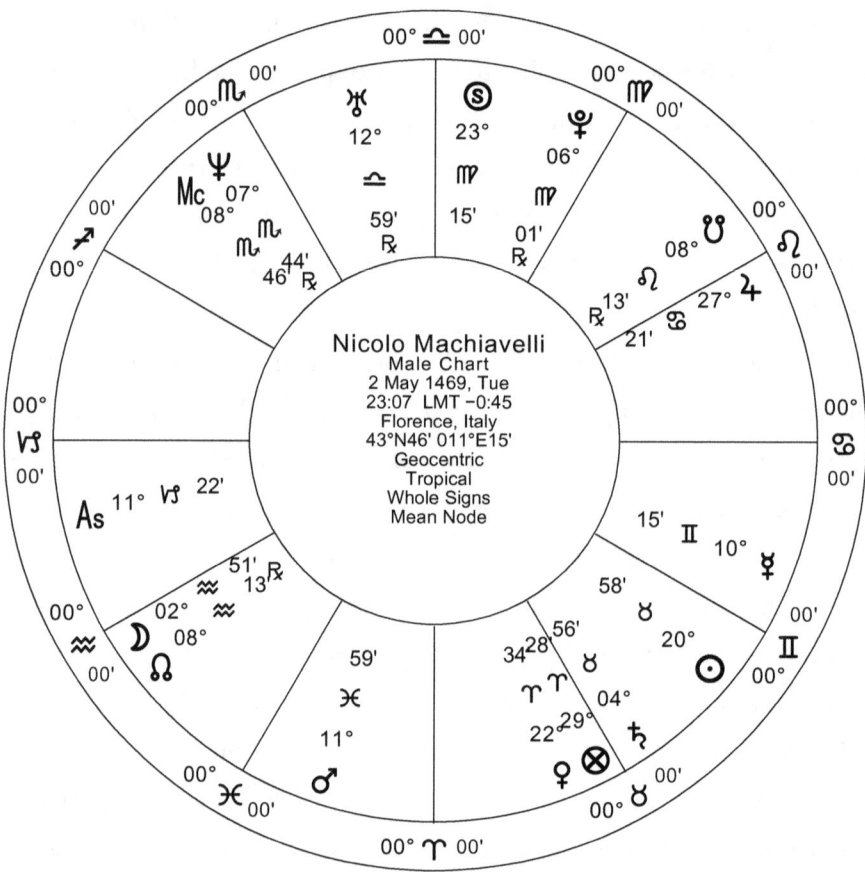

or her price. It's a play consistent with Machiavelli's personal and political views and one the great successes of the Italian Renaissance stage.

Uranus also is in trine to Mercury, giving him a knack for the unconventional and even the disturbing. Unlike his contemporaries who idolized Plato and metaphysical idealism, it's likely that Machiavelli was influenced by Lucretius, the banned epicurean ancient philosopher. Machiavelli's outlook had a roundly pessimistic side: he considered human nature as driven primarily by self-gain.

If Machiavelli's Mercury produced a wide-ranging intellect and a variety of literary and diplomatic enterprises, that of Margaret Sanger was more focused, more disciplined, and more successful in the long run. She

The Wit and Wisdom of Mercury

was a decades-long advocate for the availability of birth control information and methods in the United States.

Early in Sanger's crusade for available birth control, she decided not to align herself with allied causes of workers' rights and women's suffrage, although many of her followers were also passionate about these causes. This turned out to be a wise move that simplified her advocacy: although the cause of women's suffrage was eventually successful, there was a suppression of other causes that were deemed communist or anarchist.

Instead, Sanger used her nursing credentials and affiliation with the medical establishment to promote birth control rights as a health issue. Using whatever means necessary for her purposes, she also used eugenics

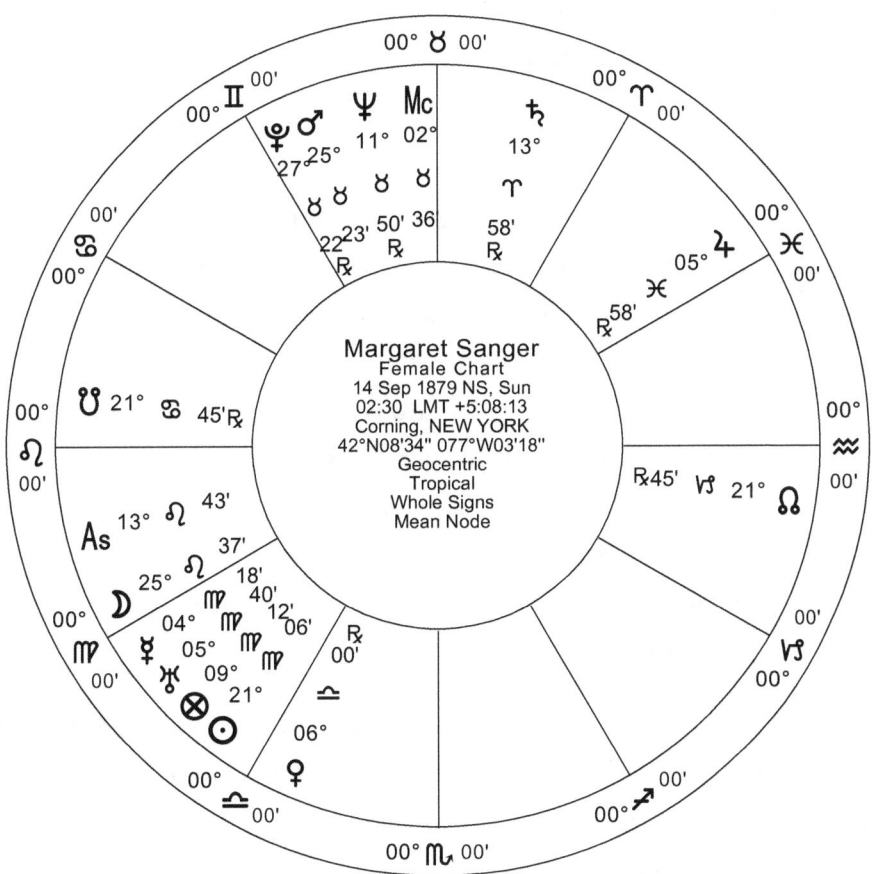

arguments in support of her cause, a line of thinking that was strong at the time. Unfortunately, these and other sets of arguments led to the accusation that she was racist – this was never true.

Sanger's Mercury in Virgo illustrates well the pragmatism and focus of her work. Jupiter and Uranus, configured with Mercury, helped her to keep her "eyes on the prize" and employ creative and at times unconventional strategies. Sanger was neither an ideologue nor was she inflexible – except in her overall purpose.

The Excellences and Corruptions of Mercury

We return to William Lilly and his depiction of the character of those influenced by this quick planet.

> "Being well dignified, [Mercury] represents a man of a subtle and politic brain, intellect, and cogitation; an excellent disputant or logician, arguing with learning and discretion, and using much eloquence in his speech, a searcher into all kinds of mysteries and learning, sharp and witty, learning almost anything without a teacher; ambitious of being exquisite in every science, desirous naturally of travel and seeing foreign parts; a man of an unweared fancy, curious in the search of any occult wonders; given to divination and more secret knowledge; if he turn merchant, no man exceeds him in way of trade or invention of new ways whereby to obtain wealth." [56]

Alas, our next person is a talented and mercurial self-promoter and conman in both business and politics, closer to Lilly's depiction of the poorly placed Mercury.

---
56 Lilly, *Christian Astrology*, p. 77

The Wit and Wisdom of Mercury

Donald Trump has been a master of emotionally tinged and subjective communication, specializing in grievance and resentment. Many have been repulsed by him over the years, but for a vocal minority he has spoken directly to their concerns and aspirations. He also transcended normal standards of truth/falsity: according to the *Washington Post* and other sources, Trump spoke about thirty thousand fabrications during his term as US President, many of them assertions that had been debunked previously by others. Trump has been able to ride popularity and distain for decades – as a great communicator of sorts – at least up to the present.

Donald Trump's Mercury seems unremarkable compared with other features of his natal chart. In Cancer in the twelfth house, and not in any sign of dignity, Mercury also receives a square from Neptune; this aspect is suggestive of fantasy replacing reality but hardly describes the habitually deceptive nature of his thinking and communication, *and its effectiveness.*

Sometimes modern astrologers will talk of the twelfth house as the "collective unconscious" – this seems to be a relic of "Twelve Letter Alphabet" whereby the twelfth house and Pisces (and Neptune) have a common quality. Instead, I am inclined to look traditionally at this house as self-undoing or, like the sixth house, implying gradual improvement with time and effort.

Donald Trump's Mercury needs to be special, reflecting his unique characteristics. Mercury in Cancer is governed by the Moon and could have an emotional, subjective, and a watery intuitive quality, but that's not what is interesting. Instead, it is Mercury's relationship with both luminaries that is special, for there is an important connection between his Mercury in Cancer and his Moon in Sagittarius and his Sun in Gemini.

You may recall the discussion of symmetries to the cardinal axes 0 degrees Cancer/Capricorn and Aries/Libra in the introductory chapter when we looked at the natal chart for Abraham Lincoln. We saw a connection between Jupiter at 22 Pisces and Venus at 7 Aries along the Aries/Libra axis and between Saturn at 3 Sagittarius and Moon at 27

Astrology and the Lives of People

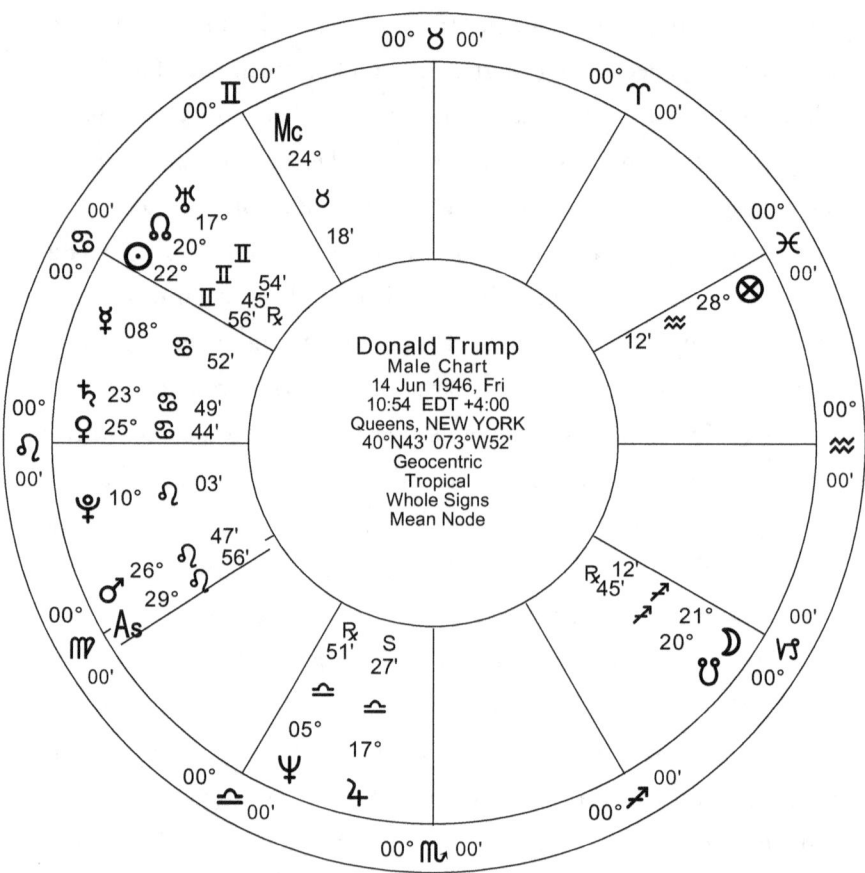

Capricorn along the Cancer/Capricorn axis. Based on these symmetries, signs without major aspect nonetheless relate to each other, corresponding to antiscia and contra-antiscia. We apply this to Trump's natal chart and the result is striking.

- Donald Trump's Mercury is 8 degrees Cancer and 51 minutes.
- Add that to the Moon's position of 21 degrees Sagittarius and 12 minutes, and we get thirty degrees and three minutes! Moon and Mercury are in a close contra-antiscion relationship along the Aries/Libra axis.

- Gemini and Cancer connect along the Cancer/Capricorn axis. If we add Mercury's number of degrees to the Sun at 22 degrees Gemini 55 minutes, the result is thirty-one degrees 46 minutes that is wider than between the Moon and Mercury but also relevant.

Thus Trump's Mercury has a close connection with the Moon, more distantly with the Sun. Adding that Trump was born on the night of a lunar eclipse, we see another dimension to his Sun-Moon opposition —one that includes Mercury.

A Cancer Mercury/Sagittarius Moon connection gives a capacity for both empathy and inspiration, a "common touch" that can relate to all kinds of people and their situations *and* make people feel included within a common vision. This configuration also manifests in Trump's style of communication: direct, subjective, also grandiose. The Moon-Mercury combination may give an ability to read others, but this need not imply kindness nor a caring attitude toward them. Instead, one may take personal advantage of others' aspirations or vulnerabilities. Nor does a common vision imply that this vision is uplifting or transformative in a positive way.

Trump's crafty Sun in Gemini, configured with Mercury in Cancer, helped make him a salesman, showman, relentless self-promoter, and trafficker in personal resentment. His heroic promotion of himself comes in when we add the Sun in Gemini governing his Leo Ascendant with Mars. We cannot blame Donald Trump's negative characteristics on his astrology alone. They could have manifested differently for him, as we will see through Alice Bailey's similar configurations.

In the Sun chapter we discussed the resemblances between the astrological charts of Trump and Alice Bailey. We noted the expressive nature of Leo rising, especially when it is governed by Sun in Gemini happily situated in the eleventh house. Mars in Leo conjunct the Ascendant adds forcefulness and both individuals could be irritable and difficult.

Those with Sun in Gemini may fear new experiences less than the rest of us; indeed, they may even they crave them. Alice Bailey's motivating vision was not about her own wealth and importance but about the spiritual evolution of humanity and the planet. Both Bailey and Trump would consider themselves prophets – but with wholly different agendas.

Alice Bailey also had Mercury in Cancer in the twelfth house, swift of motion and moving away from the Sun. Bailey's Mercury, however, has a square from Jupiter in Aries in the ninth house of religion. Since Mercury is in Jupiter's exaltation, this is an aspect with reception. This could yield grandiosity, and no one could call Alice Bailey humble.

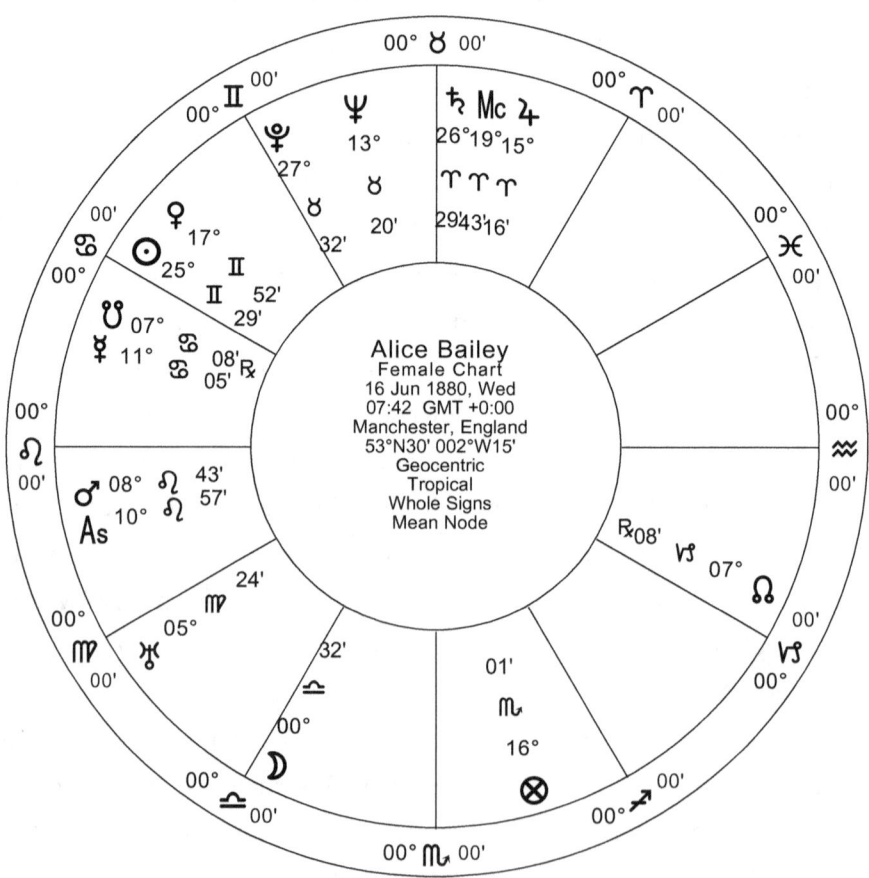

Bailey's Mercury also has a close sextile to Neptune that may correlate to the prophetic and allegedly inspired source of her work. Trump, whose Mercury in Cancer is square to Neptune in Libra, used his configuration differently. (Neptune is also in Bailey's tenth house of career; the Midheaven degree in the ninth house may add a religious sensibility.)

In many spiritual traditions, otherworldly beings, from God to angels to evolved beings, directly inspired or even dictated their most important texts. By removing a living writer from the sacred writing, one better legitimizes the text as sacred. I am not qualified to attest to the truth of Bailey's visitations or the sources of her writings. Alice Bailey's purported otherworldly presences rendered her Mercury placement in Cancer subjective but not personal, giving her writing an ecstatic quality that has appealed to many but sound very strange to others.

We have gone from Trump's self-absorbed grandiosity to Bailey's grand vision for humanity and the planet. Now, we further explore the dimensions of Mercury through some writers whose works were neither ghostwritten (Trump) nor from an otherworldly being (Bailey).

Great Things Come from Debilitated Planets

Mercury is the domicile ruler of Jane Austen's Ascendant and Midheaven degrees; Mercury is also conjunct Lot of Fortune. All this seems perfect for a writer, but what of Mercury's debilitated status in Sagittarius?

When placed in this sign of detriment, Mercury is sometimes stereotyped as inelegant or clumsy, prone to substitute fact with opinion, and prone to verbal puffery. From what we know of Austen, she had none of these attributes (some of her characters did).

Think back to her novels that you've read or the movie and television adaptions you've seen: in the end the right women and the right men marry each other, most financial problems are resolved, and most enmities between people are reconciled. On their own, these happy endings would

Astrology and the Lives of People

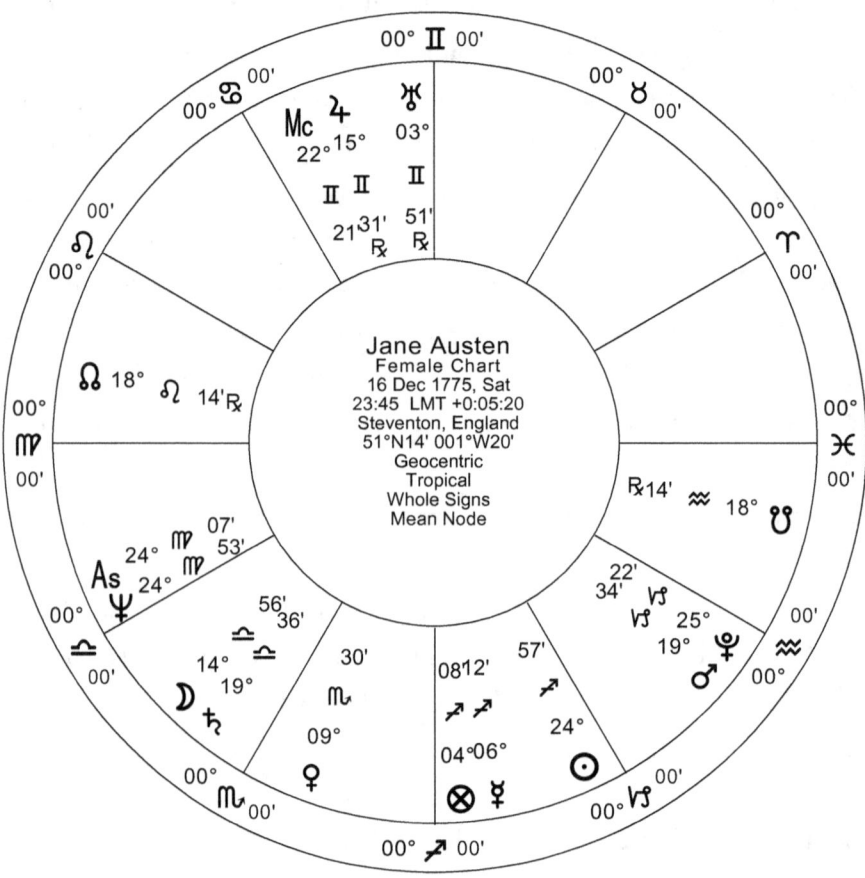

make Austen's work enjoyable but shallow, instead they are classic. Austen's interweaving plots and subplots are a joy to behold; her prose style is clear and often ironic; her depiction of nuanced social nicety shows a clever wit and steady hand.

We could begin in modern fashion with the opposition from Uranus to Mercury. One might think of an unconventional thinker – perhaps one with some weird ideas – or someone with a calling to open the minds of others. This opposition shares the stage with the late nineteenth century philosopher Friedrich Nietzsche, with a similar quality but a more provocative style. Instead of the German philosopher's desire for the "transvaluation of values", Austen questioned her contemporary mores but did not attempt to change human nature.

For Austen, Mercury's dispositor is Jupiter in Gemini and there is a mutual reception by two planets that are in their respective signs of detriment. Or is *mutual deception?* Do these planets in their signs of detriment signify difficulties expressing the range of their potentials? Yes, and they also contain unique possibilities of growth and eventual flourishing – with the requisite hard work.

Mirroring Jupiter's importance in Austen's chart, moral dilemmas are often foundational for her work. But instead of preaching to her readers, her role was to get them to think through the cultural and interpersonal difficulties she presented, and not provide easy answers. Austen harmonized a moral compass with an appreciation for life's complexities. Her "debilitated" planets helped give rise to what made her novels unique.

In person, Jane Austen may have been polite company but also perceptive and given to expressing irony. The fixed star Antares, the alpha star of the constellation Scorpio, often called the "Heart of the Scorpion", is conjunct, co-rising, and co-culminating with Mercury. One would underestimate this woman at their peril.

Jane Austen's novels also display her characters' personal growth, often shown as their impulsiveness becomes reflective, as they begin to understand better their limitations and possibilities, or find out that there is not one way to be happy or be a good human being. A planet in its own sign, its domicile, may reveal ability from the beginning, but a placement in "debility" can expand possibilities over time, facilitated by circumstance and effort. For Jane Austen, her debilitated planets helped make her a great writer.

How does Mercury in Pisces, its other sign of debility, make a great orator, as was Abraham Lincoln? The outer planets have their voices as they aspect Mercury – toward unusual thought and expression (trine Uranus), embodying through speech a depth of intellect (conjunct Pluto).

Astrology and the Lives of People

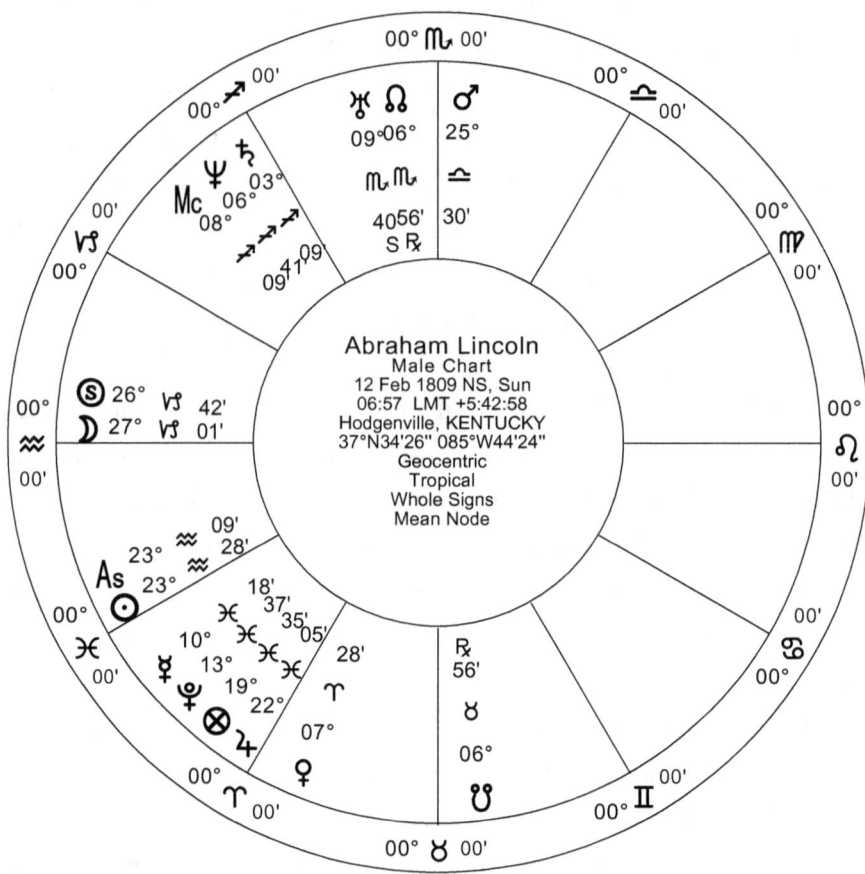

Yet these potentials must be put into action, even when expressed through his reputedly high-pitched voice.

When we look at Lincoln's earlier life, he had many opportunities for practice, practice, and more practice: as a country lawyer, as a politician, and as a wartime President. His early immersion in Shakespeare, the King James Bible, and the rhetorical nature of nineteenth century American language gave Lincoln opportunities – and political situations gave urgencies – to develop his Mercury to sublimity. Remembering that Lincoln was mostly self-taught (as have been many creative thinkers and writers), we must also give credit to his melancholy but determined saturnine influences.

The Wit and Wisdom of Mercury

This brings us to the peculiar Mercury placement of a great modern writer. We encountered James Joyce briefly at the beginning the chapter on astrology's Moon. Recall the first line of his final work: "riverrun, past Eve and Adam's from swerve of shore to bend of bay, brings us by a commodious vicus of recirculation back to Howth Castle and Environs."[57] As frustrating as Joyce can be to read and understand, he is one of the great artificers of the English language.

Bumbling through this author's writings, often what appears to be nonsense instead has multiple layers of meaning. The sentence cited above, and so many others he wrote, attempt to burst the boundaries of language

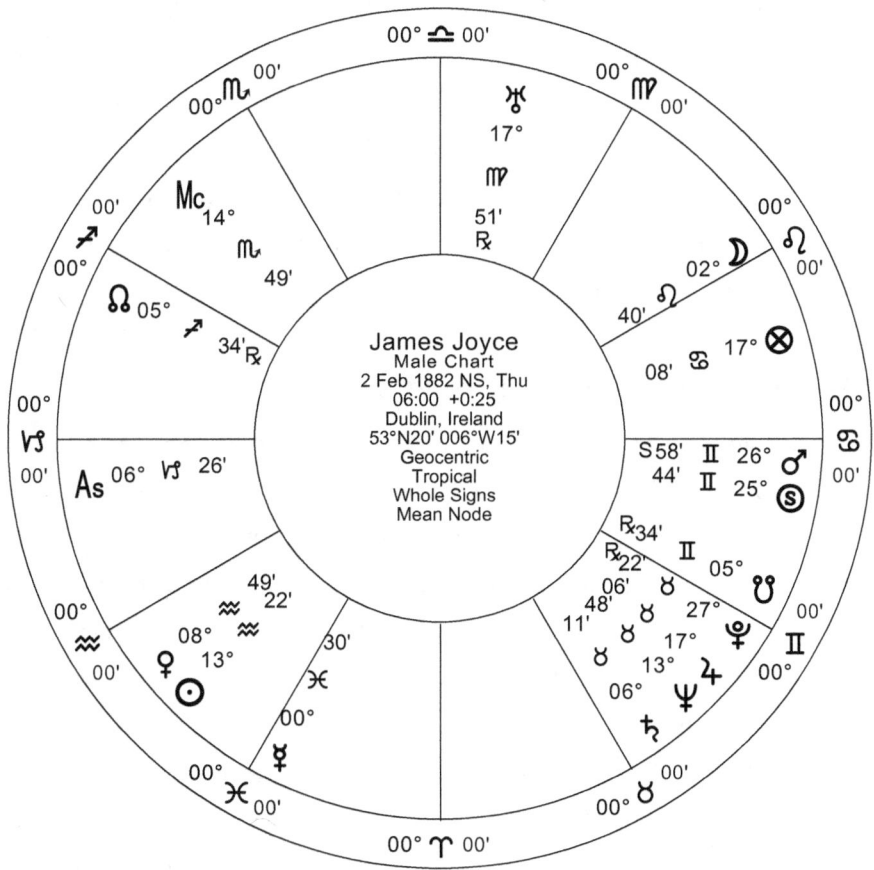

---

57 Joyce, J. *Finnegans Wake* (1939), p. 3

to express multiplicities of mind and thought. Yes, Pisces is a mutable sign but a strange one for Mercury.

Mercury is also the ruler of Joyce's Lot of Spirit in Gemini, and so Mercury in Pisces is in the tenth house from this Lot. (Lot of Spirit is also conjunct Mars in Gemini that is in its joy in the sixth house, adding Mars-like toughness but also Gemini's versatility.) Mercury is an important planet in this man's chart and life, but we must also note the importance of other fixed and saturnine features in his natal chart.

Without the discipline and determination indicated by Mercury's application to Saturn in Taurus, Joyce's Mercury in Pisces may not have gone beyond limericks, word games, puzzles, comic expressions, and word-salads. In fact, he was quite discerning: as a young man, in often-futile attempts to make some money, he wrote many brilliant reviews of literature and theater productions – and he was a difficult critic.

Under direct or indirect influences of a discriminating Saturn, Mercury can become wiser over time. It can also become irritating, like your friend whose eyes roll when you say something grammatically suspect.

Mercury in Decline, Saturn as Remedy

Language follows thought and thought follows language: if you misuse one, the other suffers as well. George Orwell and Hannah Arendt were contemporaries who likely never met but whose understanding of the perversion of language have become an important part of their accounts of totalitarianism. Their respective astrological charts show prominence not only of Mercury but also Saturn. Together, these two planets brought a conservative bent to these two individuals who of the consequences of the abuse of language by the powerful. Unfortunately, their insights continue to be relevant.

Using the chart previously noted with Virgo rising, George Orwell has a Mercury to be envied: in its diurnal domicile Gemini, in the tenth house

The Wit and Wisdom of Mercury

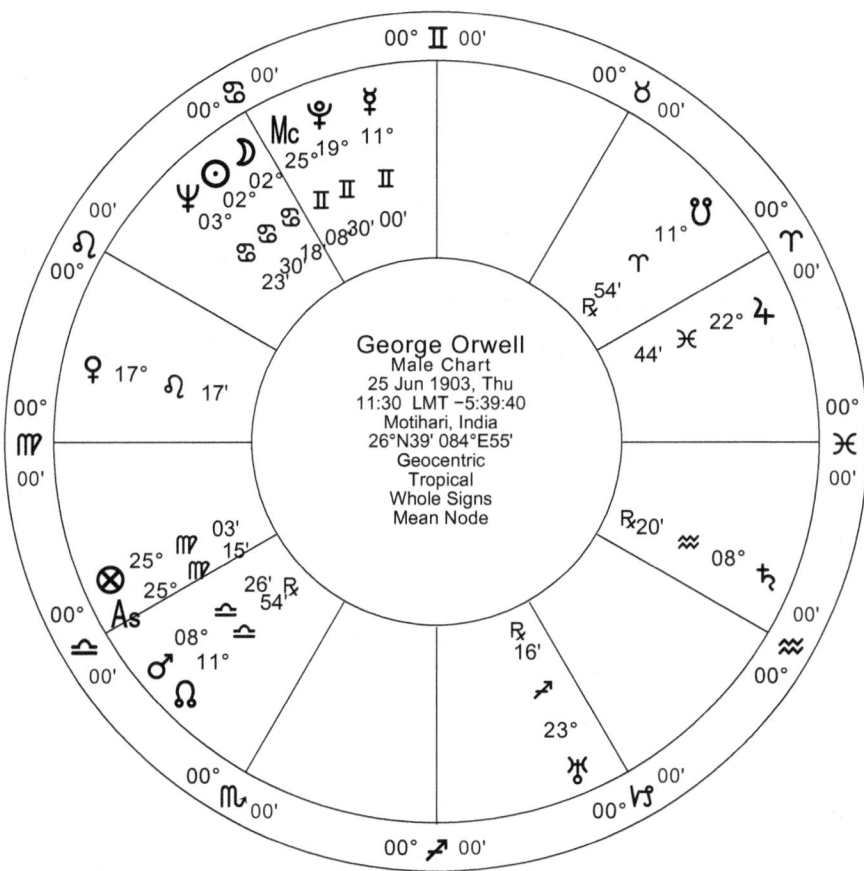

from the Ascendant and the Lots of Fortune and Spirit – and governing all three positions.

Mercury in its diurnal sign Gemini is given to quickness, adaptability, curiosity, playfulness, and verbal expressivity. Additionally, Mercury is oriental (rising at dawn from the Sun) and is in sect in Orwell's diurnal chart.

This planet's placement helps account for the range of his experiences, his ability to place himself in different environments, and to communicate significantly about his experiences. George Orwell (Eric Blair by birth) grew up in the English countryside, spent his early adult years in the military in Burma and grew to hate colonialism; he lived with impoverished people in France and England and wrote about their lives; he participated in the Spanish Civil War in the late 1930s; he spent time in Morocco to strengthen his respiration. Orwell was in London during the Second World War where he wrote *Animal Farm* and lived on a tiny island in Scotland where he wrote his masterpiece *1984*.

Saturn in Aquarius, in its own sign, and Mars in Libra are both in trine to Orwell's Mercury. This three-planet configuration is imbalanced toward Saturn: in a day chart Saturn is the triplicity ruler of all three planets. Saturn is also in its own (diurnal) sign Aquarius and is the exaltation lord of Mars in Libra. Unlike Jane Austen's Mercury-Jupiter novels with their miraculously happy endings, Orwell's Mercury-Saturn great works all end unhappily.

There are similarities between Orwell and Nicolo Machiavelli, as both have prominent Mercury and Saturn placements. Both have their prophetic and pessimistic legacies, yet Orwell's Sun-Moon-Neptune combination in Cancer gives him an empathic nature we do not see in our Italian Renaissance man. More than four centuries apart, both men were the most intelligent persons in most rooms they walked into.

Orwell's essays on language advocate a simplicity and directness of style. With Virgo rising and a strong Mercury configured by Saturn and Mars, Orwell looked at language and its ability to confuse and oppress. We see most clearly Orwell's combination of Mercury and Saturn when we look at his essay "Politics and the English Language" from 1946. Its second paragraph, excerpted here, should be read by politicians, those in the broadcast media, and all those who consume their products.

> "Now, it is clear that the decline of a language must ultimately have political and economic causes: it is not due simply to the bad influence of this or that individual writer. But an effect can become a cause, reinforcing the original cause and producing the same effect in an intensified form, and so on

indefinitely. A man may take to drink because he feels himself to be a failure, and then fail all the more completely because he drinks. It is rather the same thing with our English language. It becomes ugly and inaccurate because our thoughts are foolish, but the slovenliness of our language make it easier for us to have foolish thoughts."[58]

Orwell argues for dispensing with pretentious diction and vocabulary, dying metaphors, and meaningless or foreign-derived jargon when something more straightforward would do. He sensitizes the reader to language that fills space, deadens thinking, and substitutes blather for conveying real information and ideas. He also dismisses words derived from Greek or Latin when those derived from Anglo-Saxon would do: Mercury plus Saturn once again.

Orwell's critique of language shows its ability to enable oppression. In *1984* Orwell suggested that authority could debase language and thought, termed Newspeak and Doublethink respectively, and limit our resources of thought and language. Newspeak, for example, aims to reduce deviant thinking by making its words and concepts, and potentially subversive communication, impossible. From the inquisitor O'Brien to the hero of the novel, Winston Smith:

> "Don't you see that the whole aim of Newspeak is to narrow the range of thought? In the end we shall make thought-crime literally impossible, because there will be no words in which to express it. Every concept that can ever be needed will be expressed by exactly one word, with its meaning rigidly defined and all its subsidiary meanings rubbed out and forgotten. . . The process will still be continuing long after you and I are dead. Every year fewer and fewer words, and the

---
58 Orwell, *The Orwell Reader* (1956) p. 355

range of consciousness always a little smaller. Even now, of course, there's no reason or excuse for committing thought-crime. It's merely a question of self-discipline, reality-control. But in the end there won't be any need even for that. . . Has it ever occurred to you, Winston, that by the year 2050, at the very latest, not a single human being will be alive who could understand such a conversation as we are having now?"

Hannah Arendt, a major political theorist of the previous century, had an agenda similar to those of the final works of George Orwell. Today she is best known for having written *Origins of Totalitarianism* and *Eichmann in Jerusalem*. Both works comment on the deficiencies of thinking and their tragic consequences. During the past several years, as different governments around the world have descended or attempted to descend into authoritarianism, *Origins of Totalitarianism* received renewed attention and has been the starting place for many who have also analyzed this trend.[59]

Looking at Arendt's astrological chart, Mercury's trine to Saturn gives focus and, with the Midheaven degree so close to Saturn, a strongly intellectual lifestyle and set of values. Mercury also has a partile sextile to Uranus that can bring about unconventional thinking and expression.

We find forceful intellect and expressiveness indicated by the mutual reception between Mercury in Scorpio and Mars in Virgo: this is an intellect that was sharp and penetrating.

Mercury also governs Arendt's Moon in Virgo that is opposed to Saturn: this speaks of her determination and willingness to adapt to changing circumstances in her life, like starting over and eventually flourishing as a prized intellectual in a new country and speaking and writing in a non-native language. (Saturn shows up in yet another way: note the symmetry to the Aries/Libra axis by the Sun in Libra and Moon in Virgo – their numbers come close to thirty. Both luminaries form their own symmetry to Saturn!)

---

59 Rating AA: birth chart quoted

The Wit and Wisdom of Mercury

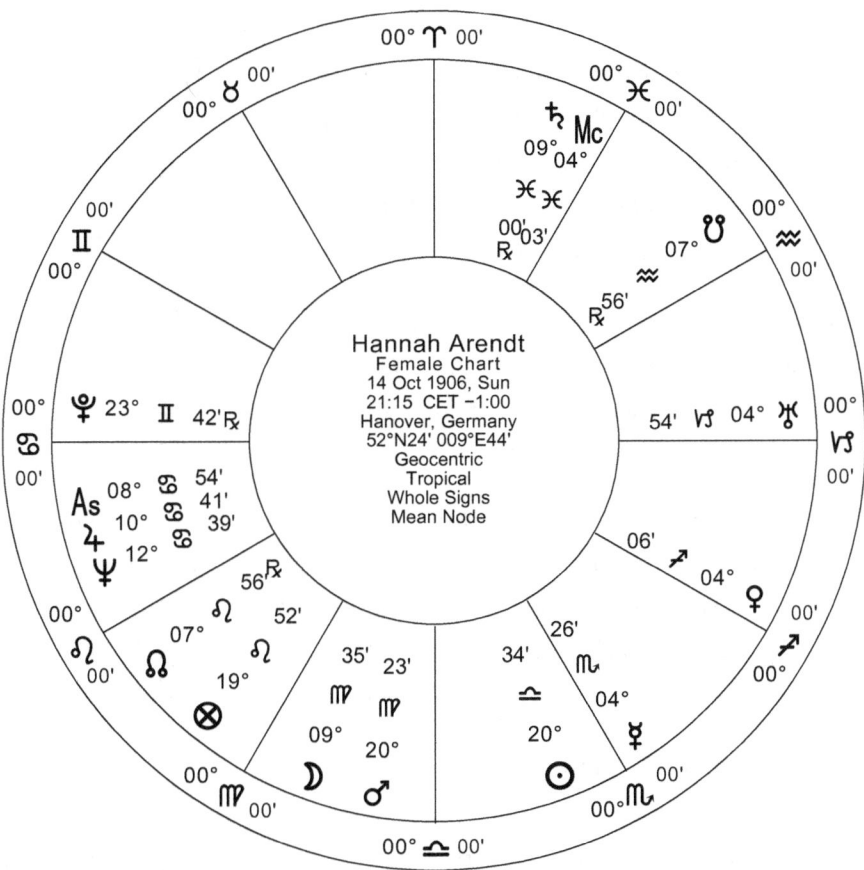

In the early 1960s, the *New Yorker* magazine sent Arendt to Israel as a correspondent to the trial of Adolf Eichmann, who had overseen the logistics of the Holocaust and had been recently captured in Argentina. From this assignment grew *Eichmann in Jerusalem,* a work that was controversial from the outset. This book coined the phrase "banality of evil". Preparing for Eichmann's trial, Arendt studied transcripts of police interviews with Eichmann.

> "Officialese became his language because he was genuinely incapable of uttering a single sentence that was not a cliché... The longer one listened to him, the more obvious it became

> that his inability to speak was closely connected with an inability to think, namely, to think from the standpoint of somebody else. No communication was possible with him, not because he lied but because he was surrounded by the most reliable of all safeguards against the words and the presence of others, and hence against reality as such."[60]

Echoing her previous *Origins of Totalitarianism,* Arendt does not classify Eichmann as an ordinary criminal. Instead, we need to look at the state culture that nourished his lack of thought and language, that placed him into prominence.

> "German society of eighty million people had been shielded against reality and factuality by exactly the same means, the same self-deception, lies, and stupidity that had now become ingrained in Eichmann's mentality. These lies changed from year to year, and they frequently contradicted each other..."[61]

This may seem eerily familiar to the reader.

This chapter has contained only a few dimensions of Mercury's activity. Aside from its roles in prophecy, humor, discernment, eloquence, sublimity, and creativity of spoken and written language, we need to also look at Mercury's role in fraud, seduction, polemic, and of course in sustaining elegance. These we reserve for the next chapter on Venus and for the ones to follow.

---

60 Arendt, *Eichmann in Jerusalem*, p. 48, 49
61 Ibid, p. 52

Chapter Eight

Venus, For a Good Time

A Glittering Example

Nobody today seems to have as many Venus qualities as did Elizabeth Taylor. She was in movies from childhood, was a young movie star and later a glamour queen, managing to be a good actress while her personal life helped fuel the American tabloid media for a generation. She could be breathtakingly beautiful and seductive, garishly materialistic, but also very kind. Her memoir was entitled *My Love Affair with Jewelry*. Later in life she founded a line of perfumes, the first one called "Passion". [62]

But first, there were other dimensions to Elizabeth Taylor beside the Venusian. She was afflicted with health problems throughout her life and had to battle addiction to alcohol and painkillers. Following the death of her friend, actor Rock Hudson, she dived into AIDS activism. She was then known as a champion of people and causes. After a long illness she died in 2011 at the age of 79, surprised she made it that far.

Taylor's astrological chart, like the woman herself, is multifaceted and glittering.

If we begin with her Sagittarius Ascendant, we land on Jupiter in the ninth house in its own triplicity and conjunct the Part of Spirit. Some contemporary astrologers think of this abundance of Jupiter means that anything that can be done can be overdone – and many say Elizabeth Taylor pursued extravagance to the point of bad taste. Jupiter also gave

---

62 Rating AA: birth record available

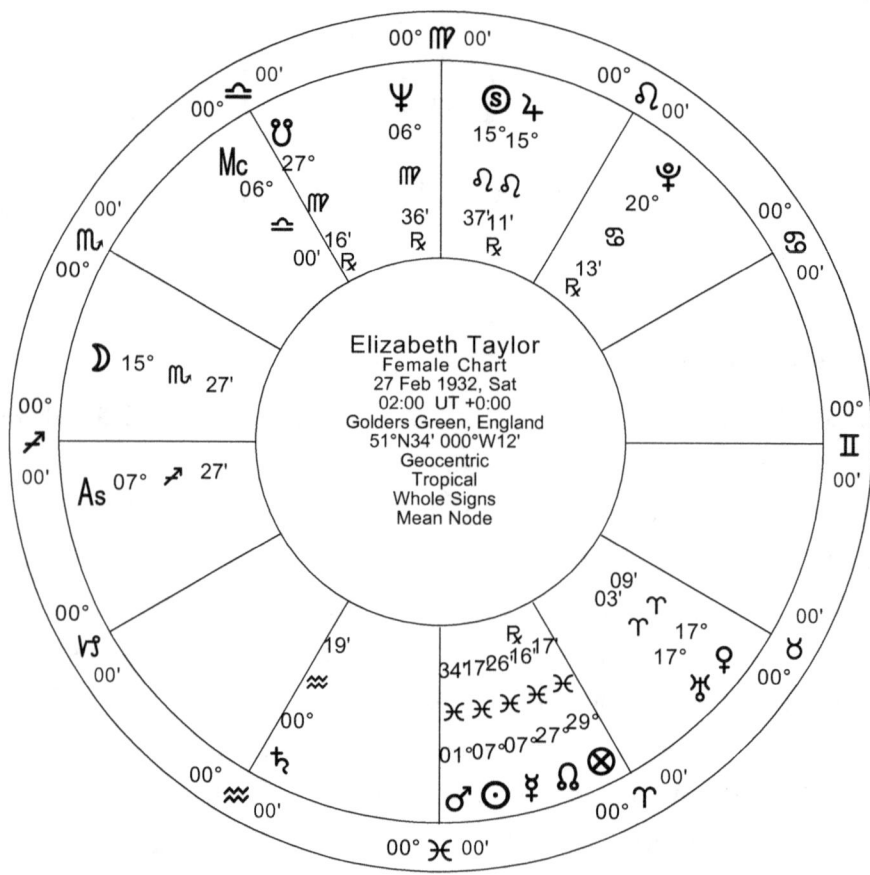

her a presence that was not only grand but magnetic, and later in her life made her social activism more compelling. Although out of sect in her nocturnal chart, Taylor's Jupiter has many enviable qualities that displayed themselves during her lifetime.

Moon in Scorpio in the twelfth house has a partile square to Jupiter in Leo and adds complexity and potential toughness to Jupiter's grandness. The aspect to the Moon aligns well with Taylor's many emotional and relational shadows *and* her sympathy for the vulnerable. This configuration points to her talent as a dramatic actress, especially in roles that called for emotional complexity. We also see Sun and Mercury in close opposition to Neptune. It would be difficult for her to determine her own identity; Neptunian glamour filled in the gap for many years for her.

Venus is in Aries, in its "joy" in the fifth house, and only a few minutes of zodiacal distance from Uranus. At first glance, the Venus-Uranus conjunction speaks directly to her variability and excitability, to her expressions of sexuality and desire for an exciting partner. At least twice Taylor married men who were married to others at the time she became intimate with them. The married-divorced-married-divorced-together again bond with Richard Burton afforded her a lot of time in the public eye and very few dull moments.

The square from Pluto to Venus/Uranus shows the darker sides of Venus. Yet there is no indication that Elizabeth Taylor was sexually promiscuous for its own sake; instead, her instincts were more relational and often maternal and protective. Taylor's first two marriages seemed motivated by her desire to be free from parental oversight. Her third husband Mike Todd seemed to be perfect for her, but he died in a plane crash a few years after they were married, and she needed to move on.

The trine from Jupiter to Venus manifested itself in the superabundance of her romantic relationships, jewelry and adornment, and charm and charisma. Attesting to her identity being wrapped up in the fair planet, Venus and Sun are mutual reception by exaltation. Venus and Mars are in "mixed" reception – Venus is in Mars' domicile and Mars is in Venus's exaltation: it was difficult for most men to say "no" to this woman.

Her many marriages become clearer as we also survey her seventh house and its ruler Mercury that has an opposition from Neptune. This may indicate confused perceptions, enchantment followed by disenchantment, perhaps a heightened ability for different versions of herself to emerge within her relationships. Together with Moon in Scorpio in the twelfth house, I wonder whether Elizabeth Taylor's complex and chaotic personal life was in part an effort to retrieve a fundamental incompleteness she felt about herself. In her case a completely mutual relationship would be difficult to come by and instead she would find alluring substitutes in either torrid sexuality or in tumultuous relationships.

"The Fair Planet that Inclines Us to Love"

In the opening of Dante's *Purgatorio*, pilgrim and guide see Venus in the eastern sky before sunrise. With a sweet bluish color and escorted by the stars in Pisces (this planet's exaltation sign), Venus brings delight after a traumatic journey through Hell. Venus offers the first glimpse of a new day and a more positive journey ahead.

Many people, including many professional astrologers, think only of romantic love and sex when they think of Venus. Venus does encompass a spectrum of romantic behavior, from casual flirtation and "going steady", to varied (and hopefully fully consensual) expressions of physical desire. Yet Venus has a broader range that we also need to explore.

Medieval astrologers were more straight-laced in their depictions of this planet than our contemporaries. In this way they also help us understand this broader range. We begin with the twelfth-century astrologer and sage Ibn Ezra.

> "Of clothing [she denotes] all embroidery and pretty garments; of human nature [she denotes] cleanliness, friendship, laughter, playfulness, merriment, dance, pleasant talk, love, adultery, playing dice, generosity, excessive lust for everything, false testimony, tendency toward drunkenness, natural and unnatural sexual intercourse, love of children, fondness for the marketplace, {and in general love of justice and of places of worship}. Of the trades [she denotes working with] anything that is dyed, and in sewing. She indicates all eating and drinking, the mother, the daughters, and the younger sister."[63]

---

63 *Beginning of Wisdom*, p. 100-101

Venus stands for many of the finer things that we want to have or to behold. Here we find art, beauty and adornment, gaiety and gatherings, elegance, and entertainment. Venus brings us out of ourselves into a world of beauty, pleasure, and fulfillment. Venus operates to bring us into our versions of beauty or sublimity: when we attend a concert, or a movie theater, or when we gaze at a work of art not wanting to move from where we're standing. Unlike Jupiter's reaching out toward broader horizons, Venus experiences life at shorter range but intimately.

We know of paleolithic remains with body decorations and there is no indication of this going away anytime soon. Venus does not decorate oneself to intimidate others (Mars) or show one's status or group affiliation (Jupiter), but for purposes of enhancing one's presence through beauty and to make oneself more attractive by pleasing others. Parallel is the sociability associated with Venus – not for purposes of competitiveness (Mars) except when competition increases the joys of companionship (think beach volleyball or a date at the bowling alley), but instead establishes and maintains ties that are personal and exciting.

Venus in Contrast

Features of comfort and familiarity are associated with the Moon. Lunar love is informal and quotidian, as when partners share comfort food, movies, and television, often clad in sweatpants and sweaters with holes in them. As one client said to me when wanting not to be single anymore, "I want somebody to go food shopping with!" Some of us are with someone whose sentences we can complete, and they can complete ours, and even anticipate our attempts at bad humor. As intriguing and Venusian as they may be at the outset, most romantic relationships increase a lunar component over time and then must strive to maintain the Venusian.

Venus symbolizes our excitement of being with the *other*, fascinated by this person who brings out new experiences and facets of ourselves.

Combining you and somebody different, together but also distinct, can produce a new person, but sometimes that new person, the "child", is the relationship itself. Perhaps this is part of eros, the joy and challenge of going beyond oneself. "Fear of intimacy" is often the fear of sacrificing one's fixed identity to the unfamiliar other.

With miraculous or tragic results, we may throw caution and others' good advice to the wind when Venus strikes, when the erotic excitement of new beginnings and new creations arise. If circumstances make this a distant possibility, we have an entire entertainment industry to provide compensating fantasy.

Venus that governs Taurus of the earth element is about sensuality and physical satisfaction. Our five senses reach out toward our surroundings, into a world it finds pleasing and beautiful. (Our sense faculties have a defensive side, of course, but this is not Venus.) Musically, a Taurus Venus appreciates the quality of *sound*. This side of Venus values texture and color and the richness of environmental display, the warmth of our partner right next to us asleep, or at a higher temperature when aroused. However, the sensuality of Venus need not imply a lower form spirituality or sublimity.

As a sign of the air element, Libran Venus is attracted to the composite, where the parts come together to form a greater whole. This may be from grand architecture or a fulfilling romantic or friendship connection, or a dance performance. This is reflected in some of the West's greatest art, literature, and music, where their strength is from a complex but harmonized structure.

Does Venus have symbolic resonance with the second house? No, this is a relic of the "Twelve Letter Alphabet", whereby the first house is like Aries and so the second house is like Taurus. This violates the centrality of finance for the second house. The possessions of Venus are better classified as "nice stuff" than liquid capitol or property ownership for profit that are second house matters. Instead, I look to the tradition attribution of Venus in its "joy" in the fifth house that is the place of "good fortune" in ancient astrology, and what I call the "party house" to my clients.

The Sensory and the Sublime

Because Venus has an ability to take people outside of themselves, this planet brings us into religious and the spiritual dimensions. Music and eros, with their sensuality and rhythmic natures, easily distract us and bewitch us but also can enhance spiritual experience and insight. We may also become slave to our senses, shallow in the company of others, and selfish in our pursuit of satisfaction. Western tradition and ancient mythology extol the powers of Venus but do not trust this planet.

Guido Bonatti, depicting Venus a century after Ibn Ezra, adds an interesting feature. The first two sentences are similar to what we've just seen but note the final sentence that I've put in italics.

> "And venereal men are of games and laughter and dancing, and gladness and joy, and freely using food and drink in company; and venereal men get drunk more quickly than others, and they trust in others, and often are deceived by them. And Venus signifies esteem, generosity, love, and justice, and the like. *And venereal men spend time in houses of prayer, so that they may appear to be what they are not, and they restrain their faith, and long to hear the sounds of musical instruments, and they are strong in them more so than in other men.*" [64]

Depicting "venereal men" at church, Bonatti alludes to a downside to Venus – a tendency toward superficiality and social pretense. Yet sacred music also uses our physical, sensory, and emotional natures to bring us closer to experiencing divinity. Christian Church "father" Augustine of Hippo, in Book Ten of the *Confessions*, argues both sides of the issue. He weighs

---
64 Bonatti, *Book of Astronomy,* translated B. Dykes, p. 168-169

the emotional power of music to bring us closer to God with music's ability to pull us down into worldly sensuality. (In centuries following, these reservations have been applied to sacred visual arts as iconoclastic campaigns against representing divinity visually.) Augustine's discussion is a small part of a contemplation of the spiritual defect of pleasure derived from all our senses.

Plotinus was a philosopher two centuries before Augustine, whose thinking continued to be influential through the Renaissance to modern times. Following the earlier Plato, Plotinus was concerned with the *object* of love, beauty (*Ennead* 1.6). To Plotinus and his followers, love of the sensory was inferior to that of the formal or immaterial. He spoke of beauty in a Libran intellectual way: harmonies and proportion. Sources of beauty may manifest among our sense experiences but their beauty is more purely rendered from the soul and faculties above the soul. As it reaches into matter, the pursuit of beauty becomes a spiritual quest "When he sees the beauty in bodies he must not run after them; we must know that they are images, traces, shadows, and hurry away to that which they image..."[65] And when the purified soul thinks back on what he once thought beautiful, "he laughs at all the other loves and despises what he thought beautiful before."[66]

To our modern sensibilities, love and beauty are distinct as one need not imply the other. We know from our relationships that when we love somebody, we bestow beauty on that person regardless of any lack of conventional "good looks", and their perceived beauty diminishes as the relationship diminishes.

To Plato and Plotinus, love is closer to an assessment of beauty as it appears outside of ourselves and inside and expresses itself through form. In their defense, consider the heightened experience when one is familiar with gothic architecture, the color wheel, sonata form or the form of a

---
65 Plotinus *Ennead* I.6.8 6-9 Armstrong translation, Loeb Classical Library
66 I.6.7 18-20

sonnet when encountering an exemplary medieval cathedral, painting, symphony or such a poem.

Music and Love

Marsilio Ficino, whose descriptions of planets we've previously quoted, was the sage and polymath of the early Renaissance in Florence, Italy. Son of a medical doctor to Cosimo de Medici, Marsilio Ficino received the best education his culture could offer. He seemed to have been an intellectual prodigy from the beginning. Just before Ficino turned thirty, Cosimo named him head of the "Platonic Academy", gave him a place to work and live outside the city, and put him to work on translation projects from ancient Greek into Latin. Ficino's translations were considered of high quality and were used for centuries before these works were translated into vernacular languages.

Among today's astrologers he is best known for the third part of his *Three Books on Life:* "De Vita Coelitus Comparanda" or "On Obtaining Life from the Heavens", where he combines astrology, Neoplatonism, and sympathetic magic. How to attract favor from the heavens, for purposes of physical health and mental flourishing?

Marsilio Ficino was familiar with his astrological chart, although an early letter gave some planets in incorrect positions. This chart, from a different letter, reflects his later understanding of his natal chart.[67]

A modern astrologer would notice the outer planets in opposition to his luminaries. Uranus opposing his Sun in Scorpio lends itself to an unorthodox sense of purpose. Pluto opposing his Moon in Capricorn in the twelfth house, on the other hand, contributed to an anxious temperament, and there was much for him to be anxious about.

---

67 Rating A: Ficino letter as source. See Kaske and Clarke, *Three Books on Life*, Intro. p. 20-21

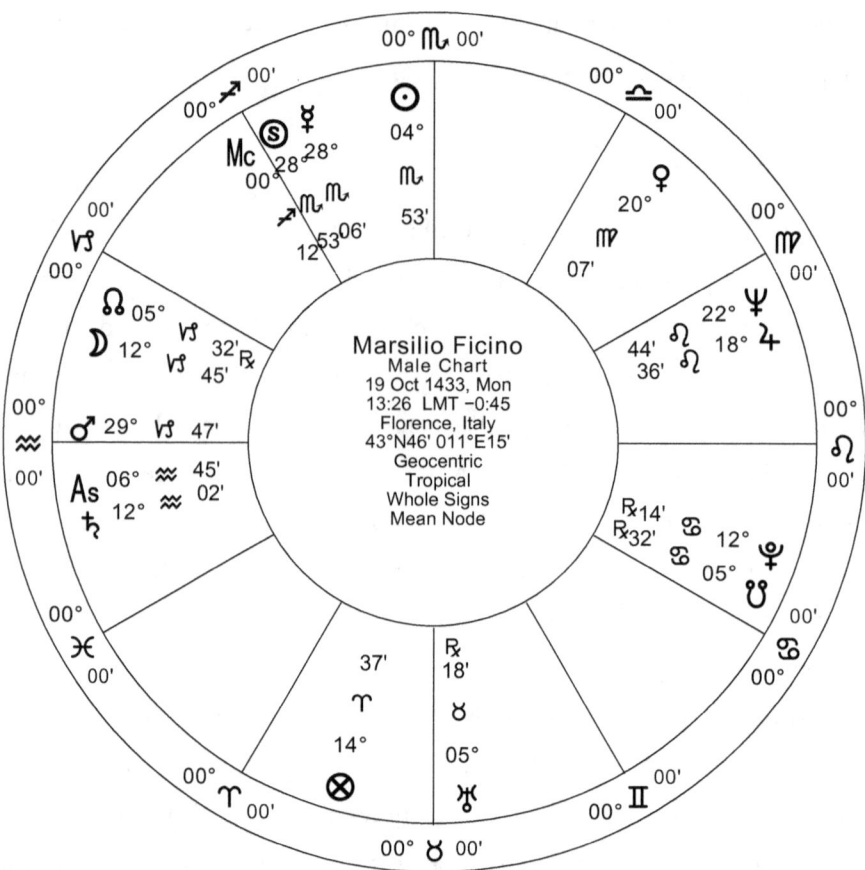

For a polymath like Ficino, Mercury bears a close look. Mercury is in the tenth sign from the Ascendant, is very close to his Midheaven degree, and is also conjunct Lot of Spirit, elevating further its importance. Mercury's partile sextile with Mars, exalted in Capricorn, adds forcefulness and expressiveness, and Jupiter in Leo relieves some of Saturn's gravity.

Venus is more remote, placed in the eighth house, in fall in Virgo but in her own triplicity, with only a distant trine from an already stressed-out Moon in Capricorn. Both Venus and Moon in earth signs give him practicality and assisted him in his self-appraisal as a doctor of the soul. Ficino also strongly promoted music as therapy as we would call it. It is through music but also conviviality that we can approach Venus and partake of her benefits. This is very important for saturnine intellectual temperaments of him and his friends.

> "We come under the influence of Jupiter by civic occupations, by those occupations which strive for honor...of Mars, by anger and contests, of the Sun and of Mercury, by the pursuit of eloquence, *of song*, of truth, and of glory, and by skill; *of Venus, by gaiety and music and festivity*; of the Moon, by a vegetable existence." (Italics mine)[68]

Ficino describes musical voices attributed to different planets – if that of Jupiter is deep and earnest and sweet, then Venus is "voluptuous, with wantonness and softness", i.e., seductive and not always trustworthy. (Saturn's voices are slow, deep, and harsh, and those of Mars are quick, sharp, and fierce, menacing.)

One often-cited letter discusses music as healing of the spirit (a corporeal soul or subtle body), alongside with medicine that heals the body and theology that heals the soul. "Spirit, which is the airy vapor of our blood and the link between body and soul, is tempered and nourished by airy smells, by sounds, *and by song*" (my italics).[69] Ficino practiced this in his life, spending much time consoling and refreshing himself in song, accompanied by his lute.

Venus was also about charm and delicacy. She is the mother of the graces, enhances "with her all-bountiful and joyful rays," adding "wonderful and life-giving charm that always delights and profits."[70]

Marsilio Ficino does not speak of his personal life in a way that hints at sexuality and romance. He never married and possibly was celibate throughout his life – one would not be so surprised for one of the formulators of the concept of "platonic love." The relatively weakly-placed

---

68 *Da Vita*, Chapter 2, p. 253-255
69 *Selected Letters*, p. 63-64
70 p. 109

Venus in Virgo need not bring about a life of chastity but may be inclined toward a mental version of love.

Ficino had many close friendships with artists and intellectuals – all male, as far as I can tell – and we can look at Jupiter in Leo in the seventh house for his interpersonal good fortune. Unfortunately, later in life his adversaries accused him of homosexuality, an accusation likely without foundation but damaging to his reputation.

Following Plato and Plotinus, Ficino made a strict distinction between worldly and divine love. In one of his letters, ordinary human love is "full of anxious fear," noting many ways in which desire arouses "fiery choler" or melancholy and then "groundless fears". (These extremes correspond well to Mars and Saturn respectively.) "Divine love, however, kindled by the flames of the virtues and growing strong from celestial rays, seeks to return to the sublime heights of heaven that no fear of earthly ills can ever trouble".[71]

Transcendent and Practical: Music and Marriage

We continue our discussion of Venus with the life and astrological chart for Martin Luther, younger than Ficino and with a greater influence on later European religion and culture. He chose a different path for our planet that inclines us to love.

Luther was, by his own lights, a failed spiritual man. As a young man within a severe monastic setting, he tried to earn future redemption through living as perfectly as he could – not successfully. He came to believe that salvation was achieved solely through the grace of God, not solely by exertions toward spiritual perfection. Most important, therefore, was a personal relationship with the Deity, unmediated by a priestly class or church hierarchy. As the primary Christian reformer of his time, Luther sought to enhance a personal connection of ordinary people to God.

---

71 (Letter 82, p. 175)

Venus, For a Good Time

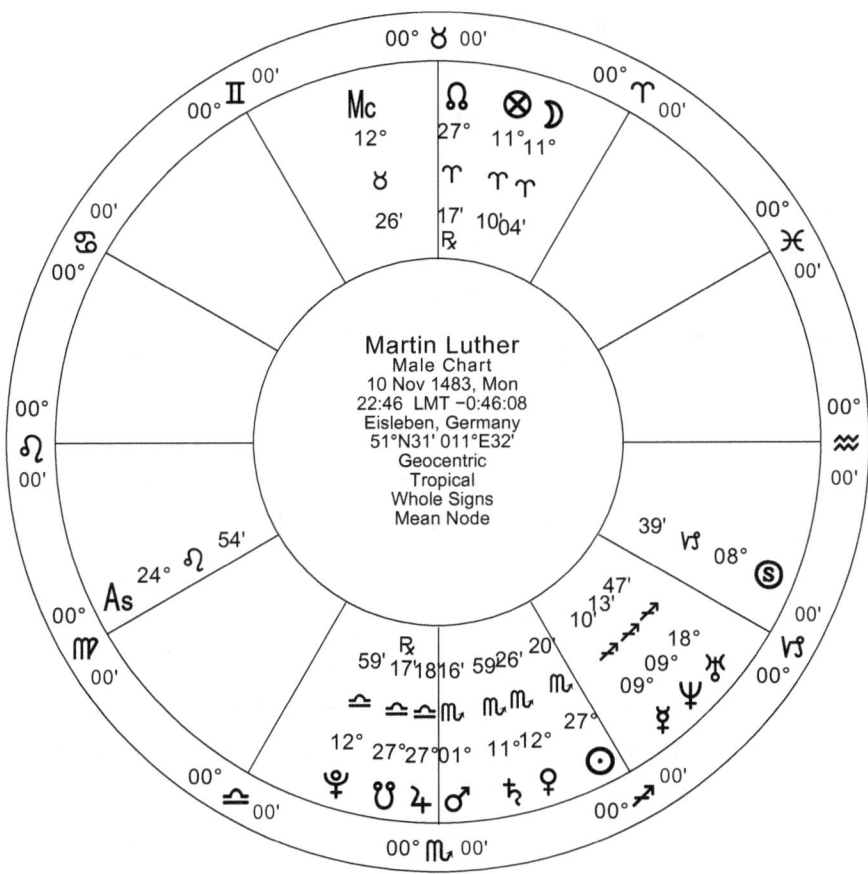

Martin Luther's Venus is placed in Scorpio with a close conjunction to Saturn, the dispositor of both planets being Mars also in Scorpio.[72] This is not a Venus prone to idealize beauty or engage in pleasing and charming social discourse. Martin Luther was intense, passionate, and practical – and manifestations of his Venus placement were no different.

To support the religious life of his followers, building grandiose cathedrals and subsidizing famous artists was out of the question, for theological and practical reasons. Luther instead focused on music that was portable, accessible to ordinary people, and could communicate

---

72 AA rating – birth record

directly. His lasting contribution was the introduction of the "chorale" – vocal music that was tuneful and easy to remember, using biblical passages in the vernacular, and sung by a congregation together.

Venus in Scorpio helped Luther use music here not as entertainment or diversion but to penetrate one's psychological and spiritual make-up. His astrological conjunction of Venus and Saturn gave practical application priority over what is merely pretty, what is meaningful and lasting over what is trivial but shallow. When we consider Luther's cultural influence on the German baroque era and especially on Johann Sebastian Bach, we sense his impact on the western music of the future.

Likely unable to master his own sexuality as a young man and later desiring to end the dominance of a celibate priestly caste on spiritual life, Lutheran priests were allowed to marry and became "ministers". No longer would a celibate life put a finger on the scale of redemptive possibilities: an ordinary person with an ordinary love life was as equally qualified to be saved as somebody who lived more austerely. Luther himself married probably not as much from romantic yearning but to make a statement. His was a saturnine Venus governed by Mars.

From a similar Venus placement, but with a different result, we return to Jane Austen. She wrote extensively about marriage and romance but appears to have experienced little of it herself. We have little reliable information: one possible flirtation, one marriage offer that was first accepted then declined the next day, and speculation or fiction. Noting Neptune closely conjunct her Ascendant and closely in square to her Sun, we are left with an enigmatic character, her Scorpio Venus adding to the mystery.

Austen's Venus has no major aspect to any other planet and stands in contrast to those in the more upbeat Libra and Sagittarius. Mars, exalted in Capricorn and in a favorable house, is the dispositor for Venus. It has been said that Austen's novels are, at bottom, all about "female sexual selection" and its complexities. The novelist was tuned into the currents

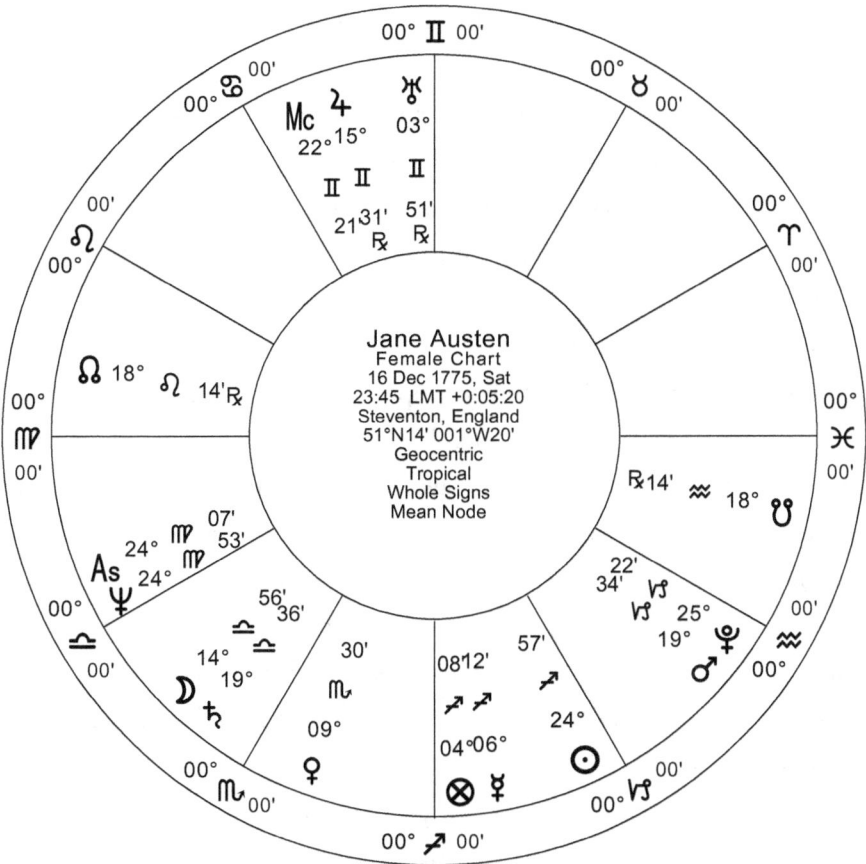

and undercurrents of how people form couples with fulfilling or disastrous results, how they marry happily or unhappily.

Most of us realize the importance of context – timing, opportunity, resources – and Jane Austen's work contains much that is relevant today, regardless of the polite affectation and social rigidity of the era in which she wrote. There is nothing naïve about her Venus or her depictions of romantic love. We need look no further than *Pride and Prejudice* that is popular in book form, movie versions, sequels, and fan fiction. Venus in Scorpio stands out clearly in one incident, when we focus on our heroine's friend Charlotte who is married to the romantically lacking Mr. Collins.

We first see Mr. Collins first as an ironic character: buffoon-like and full of pretension, he has the gall to ask for Elizabeth's hand in marriage. However, as Collins is decreed to inherit her family's property after father's death, Elizabeth marrying him would have provided financial security to her family. Being fiercely independent, however, she vigorously refuses his offer. Reflecting the opposing priorities of her parents, Elizabeth's mother is furious at this rejection, her father is relieved.

Fast-forward a few years and Mr. Collins has a bride and it's Elizabeth's best friend Charlotte. Elizabeth is disappointed that her friend would marry him, but Charlotte takes a more somber approach: "Happiness in marriage is entirely a matter of chance", she says. Reflecting her fragile social status, Charlotte also states that marriage is "the only provision for well-educated women of small fortune." Charlotte has reconciled herself to being with somebody she does love but who provides financial security for her and her family. Charlotte's first statement reflects Austen's Venus in Scorpio; the second one soberly reflects the social and economic conditions for women of that time.

For Venus in detriment in Scorpio, governed by Mars in Capricorn that is square Saturn, there is no getting carried away by sentiment or the temporary flutters of affection – marriage is a business institution where most women have few options and romantic love must be just one factor among others. Yet in her stories true love (mostly) prevails in the end.

Power and Sociability

We now arrive at the interpersonal side of Venus: communication and behavior with others. Venusian behavior is often very effective in meeting our needs, particularly in romantic/sexual situations where we can take advantage of our charm and good looks.

Baldesar Castiglione's fifteenth-century *Book of the Courtier*, unfamiliar to most modern astrologers, is interesting for describing many of the interpersonal dynamics that apply to Venus. Castiglione's work considers the qualities of the "perfect courtier" and was popular for several centuries afterwards, often serving as a handbook for upper-class gentlemen. His work was roughly contemporary to Machiavelli's *Prince* and is a worthy complement to that better-known work. (You may recognize Castiglione's image from a famous portrait by Raphael.)

A "courtier" is one who is in service to a prince: his or her duties are unspecified and may consist in taking up arms, playing music, serving the prince's court, or just keeping the prince entertained. Of course, it's helpful to be well-spoken and talented at activities like music and the martial arts. One can be fierce or harsh with opponents, "and in every other place, humane, modest, reserved, avoiding ostentation above all things as well as that imprudent praise of himself by which a man always arouses hatred and disgust in all who hear him."[73] In contrast to Mars-like boorishness we have Venusian grace.

Defining "Cool"

Is personal gracefulness from "noble birth" or from "the nature of the heavens"? For some this quality flows naturally, for others, if well-trained and attentive, grace can become second nature. For the rest of us it does not happen.

Castiglione coins a word for behavior that comes off as graceful – *sprezzatura* – that could be there by nature or can be acquired by imitating those who are good models. Interestingly sprezzatura derives from the Italian word for distain or scorn and indicates a kind of studied detachment. This word is usually translated as *nonchalance*: "make whatever is done or said appear to be without effort and almost without any thought about it. ...we may call that art the true art which does not seem to be art."[74] It is coupled with *disinvoltura* that means ease or effortlessness.

---

73 Castiglione, B. *Book of the Courtier.* Norton Critical Edition. (Bk 1:17, p. 25).
74 Bk 1.26: p. 32

This is neither flattery – always looked down upon by Castiglione's speakers – nor appearing to put so much effort that it brings unwanted attention to oneself. One presents oneself in a pleasing way, performing well, seemingly naturally, and without making demands on others. Sprezzatura is correlated with a sanguine temperament that has a lightness and sociability that enhances one's surroundings and quietly attracts others to oneself. Upon reflection, it articulates the difference between most of us and the "cool" people, those without the social desperation that characterized our younger years.

Is *sprezzatura* inauthentic or phony? It depends on the situation, for often what is called for is not blunt honesty but needing to gain some advantage or remain in the good graces of somebody one depends upon, like a boss, client, or patron. When there are divergent roles and inequalities of station, when oppositional Mars or advice-prone Jupiter would back-fire, a gentler planet must take over.

Flexibility

Book Two of *Book of the Courtier* discusses fashion in clothing, advising one to be attired in appropriate styles, but not dressing garishly to make oneself look like a fool. Otherwise, one is seen as without taste and is easily duped by what is "in fashion."

The courtier also needs to accommodate their conversation and language to the occasion and the expectations of others, especially one's prince. In general, they must have a gentle and pleasing way: "Our Courtier will not indulge in foolish presumption; he will not be the bearer of unpleasant news; he will not be careless in speaking words which can offend, instead of trying to please; he will not be obstinate and contentious..."[75] The courtier must mirror the needs of the moment: "...he must become another person and lay aside grave matters for another time and place and

---

75 Bk 2: 18, p. 81

engage in conversation that will be amusing and pleasant to his lord, so as not to prevent him from gaining such relaxation."[76]

Biographies of the author give his date of birth as December 6, 1478, time unknown. Regardless of time of birth, he has Venus in Scorpio, close to an exact (to the minute) Uranus-Neptune conjunction. Our author was neither a rebel nor an idealist but a creative gentleman with a grim outlook.

Castiglione's Venus is also configured with Jupiter in Taurus and it's likely he had also Moon in Taurus: a believer in beauty and elegance, he was also in touch with the real world with its complexities and dilemmas. (His writing style that leans toward the pompous may be attributed to the fashion of his times or Sun and Mercury in Sagittarius.)

Sex and Being Funny

Dorothy Parker, whose Moon-Saturn configuration we noted previously, possesses an astrological chart as multi-layered as the woman herself. Natal Mercury in Leo is in play when considering her wit and intellectual incisiveness. The only visible planet that is angular in her chart, Mercury has aspects from all three outer planets: sextiles from Pluto and Neptune in Gemini and a square from Uranus. (Modern astrologers may also note an exact quintile – seventy-two degrees – from Jupiter to Mercury.) Here was intellectual restlessness plus a desire and ability to shock others. We also note the sextile from Saturn in its exaltation but in the sixth house. This helped give her language a discipline and brevity that contributed to her talents as a writer and as a very witty conversationalist.

Parker's Venus brings us to her exuberant sexuality, at least in her pronouncements. Sometimes her best quotes were just plain fun, as in "Wasn't the Yale Prom wonderful? If all the girls in attendance were laid end to end, I wouldn't be at all surprised." There are a surprising number of lines like this, often rendered less delicately.

---

76   Bk 2: 19. p. 82

Between and during her three marriages (one a re-marriage), Parker had numerous affairs, a few times fell in love disastrously, often had a casual sex life, and at one time had an abortion followed by a suicide attempt. She was equally famous for her alcohol consumption. For all her seeming success in life, Parker had a streak of self-deprecating and self-destructive behavior.

Parker's Venus is in Libra, in its ruling sign with an emphasis on relating. Jupiter in Gemini, in exact trine to Venus, brings abundance if not steadiness in love. Parker's difficulties were not about romantic appeal or sexual expression: sexuality was easy, and relationships were difficult. Parker gives us a jaded bitter look at the powerful world of sexual love, with a tone of melancholy that pervaded much of her life and literary work.

> "By the time you swear you're his,
> Shivering and sighing,
> And he vows his passion is
> Infinite, undying –
> Lady, make a note of this:
> One of you is lying."

Venus is also the ruler of Parker's Taurus Ascendant, in its own sign but in the difficult sixth house that is more about struggle than Venusian pleasures. Parker could easily have been a stereotypical psychoanalysis client with "hysteria", physical symptoms pointing to repressed sexual desire. Instead, she yielded to her sexuality with both creative (literary) and destructive (personal) consequences. Sigmund Freud, had he known Parker, would have been impressed by her high intelligence, raw talent, and the pitched battles within her soul.

The Life of The Rose

Antoine Saint-Exupéry, best known today as the author of *The Little Prince*, was well known as both aviator and writer. Less well-known at the time was his difficult marriage. When younger and as he was becoming a rising literary star, Saint-Exupéry married the wealthy and magnetic Consuelo Suncin, herself a writer and artist. He had not expected this exciting woman to be so emotionally demanding and difficult to please. Saint-Exupéry was no easy person either, consumed with his careers and with a tendency toward extramarital affairs when abroad, which was often. Additionally, he moved to America after the French defeat by the Germans at the beginning of the Second World War, leaving his wife at home.

The Little Prince was published during the War, shortly before his plane was shot down when he had re-entered the war. The book contains reflections on culture, life purpose, and love and has been translated into almost as many written languages as there are on this planet.

Antoine Saint-Exupéry's natal chart is wonderfully transparent, displaying an eagerness for excitement and a mind full of curiosity and expressiveness. We find a pilot – maybe a reckless one – when we consider Mars in Gemini conjunct the Midheaven degree and with Jupiter opposing from Sagittarius. The sextiles from Moon and Mercury in Leo to Mars, also with trines to Jupiter, might additionally argue for a writing or theatrical career. His life was probably sufficiently theatrical.

Venus, on the other hand, seems sedately placed in Cancer and is retrograde, although further instability is marked by a contra-antiscion from Uranus (the midpoint between Venus and Uranus is the Aries-Libra axis). Uranus is also prominent as the Moon's application by trine. He would find Consuelo Suncin exciting – I have no doubt that she was – but when she created too many problems for him, there were other exciting women to be with, at least temporarily, at a lower emotional cost.

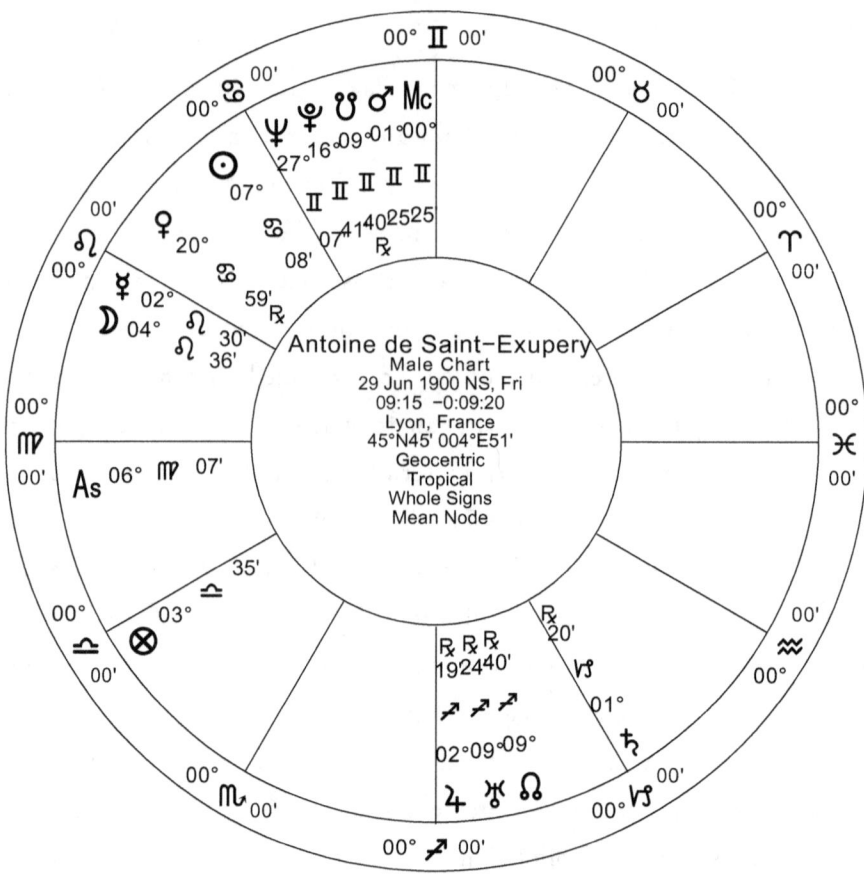

The Little Prince begins when an aviator is trapped in the desert with a disabled plane and must repair his plane before his water supply runs out. Unexpectedly there is a strange child-like character – The Prince – from his home on Asteroid B-612 that is about as large as a house.

The Prince tells the narrator that there are various plants that grow on this small asteroid. One day, a new one appeared: a rose. The rose took her time emerging because she wanted to look her best for the occasion. She had a "rather touchy vanity" and a complex and exhaustingly vulnerable emotional nature. Eventually the Prince tired of her and wanted to get away, in a touching farewell, the rose told the Prince to "try to be happy" and that she would fend for herself.

After visiting nearby asteroids whose sole inhabitants were engaged in useless abstract or egotistic activities, Earth was recommended, and the Prince landed here. He surprisingly finds a rose garden with five thousand roses, all of which looked like the rose he had left behind – she has deceived him, she was not unique after all! The Prince became thoroughly depressed.

He encounters a snake (a death principle) but also a fox. The Prince asks the fox to play with him but the fox will not. The fox has not been "tamed" by the Prince, meaning they have not created ties that would make the fox unique: "I'm a fox like a hundred thousand other foxes. But if you tame me, we'll need each other. You'll be the only boy in the world for me. I'll be the only fox in the world for you." (p. 59). In reply, the Prince states that perhaps his flower back on the asteroid had tamed him. "Taming" or creating ties happens through physical proximity over time and sharing time and daily activity. Sounds lunar.

The Prince revisits the rose garden with its multitudes and tells them that, because no one has tamed them, that they insignificant. "But my rose, all on her own, is more important than all of you together since she's the one I've watered. Since she's the only one I sheltered behind a screen…Since she's the one I listened to when she complained, or when she boasted, or even sometimes when she said nothing at all. Since she's *my* rose." (p. 63)

The fox asks the Prince to remember one thing: "One sees only with the heart. Anything essential is invisible to the eye." Later, as the Prince is going to die and disappear or return to his home planet and his rose, he states to the narrator that the stars above are beautiful because of a flower that you do not see. What is essential but not visible? Is it the relationship of love that builds quietly as one cares for another being?

We return to our author's Venus in Cancer. He establishes love as an indicator of meaning, brought about by caring not for the beautiful but by what is particular but seemingly ordinary. There may be thousands or millions that look the same as one's "rose", only this one is *his*. It seems that all the problems and emotional tumult with his wife had the effect of "taming" him; because she forced him to care for her, he began to care for her in a new and meaningful way.

Saint-Exupery's Sun in Cancer, along with Venus, tells us that the daring adventure-seeking qualities of his chart only gave one dimension – the public dimension – of this man. There was much more, invisible to the eye during his lifetime, that he was able to appreciate only in exile and when writing his book. It's unfortunate he didn't live long enough to accomplish what *The Little Prince* realizes, although we as readers can benefit from his wisdom.

Concluding our discussion of Venus, we arrive at a very different piece of modern literature. Hold onto your hats.

Venus and "Obscenity"

> ...theyre all mad to get in there where they come our of youd think they could never go far enough up and then theyre done with you in a way till the next time yes because theres a wonderful feeling there so tender all the time how did we finish it off yes O yes I pulled him off into my handkerchief pretending not to be excited but I opened my legs I wouldn't let him touch me inside my petticoat because I had a skirt opening up the side I tormented the life out of him first tickling him I loved rousing that dog in the hotel...[77]

We return to James Joyce. Many will recognize the style, if not the exact content, from the final "Penelope" chapter of *Ulysses*. This passage, in which Molly Bloom recalls an early sexual experience, is from what Joyce's contemporary writer D. H. Lawrence called "the dirtiest, most indecent, obscene thing ever written."[78] Lawrence was not alone in his estimation.

---

77 Joyce, James *Ulysses* (Gabler edition, 1984) Chapter 18, lines 805-814, p. 626
78 From Chabon, Michael, "Ulysses on Trial", *New York Review of Books*, Vol. LXVI, Number 14, September 26, 2019

Venus, For a Good Time

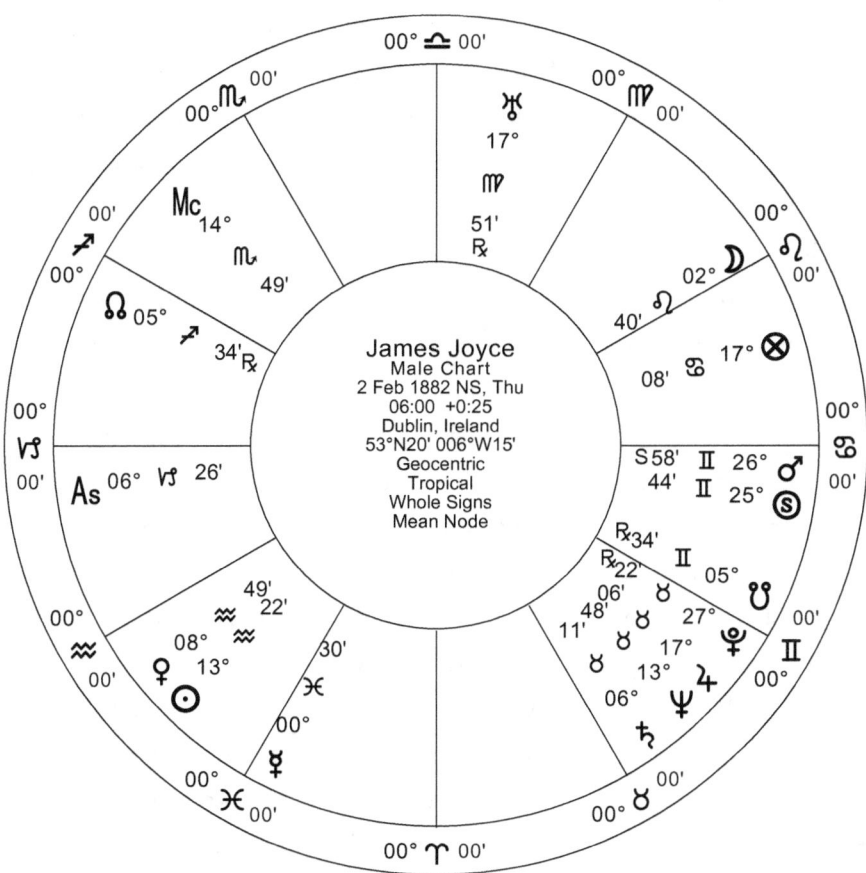

Now considered a literary classic, this work was first published in France a hundred years ago, but its distribution was delayed for years in many countries on account of its "obscenity."

Sexuality in this novel appears in many forms, from its main character Leopold Bloom admiring his penis in the bathhouse to masturbating at the sight of a comely young woman, to a hallucinatory visit to a brothel, to separate accounts by Molly and her husband Leopold of their first sexual rendezvous, to graphic accounts of Molly's tryst with a dapper gentleman felicitously named Blazes Boylan. In many ways and often in Molly's bedtime monologue that concludes the book, Joyce captures sexuality on its own terms as pleasure, self-expression, and merging with another.

Jesuit-trained and from what he considered an oppressive priest-ridden national culture, James Joyce attempted to make our human bodily functions into art, including emotional and mechanical aspects of sexuality. In *Ulysses*, Joyce brings Venus's loving attention to sexuality and how sexuality reaches out to others.

Joyce's astrological chart gives us a heady dose of Venus but with Saturn in strong aspect. We see a strong mutual reception by sign between Venus in Aquarius and its ruler Saturn in Taurus with both planets in close square aspect. There is tension between Venus and Saturn, between Aquarius and Taurus, but also possibilities of creative accommodation.

Capricorn rises, governed by Saturn; Sun and Venus are in Aquarius, also governed by Saturn. Joyce's adult life was characterized by singleness of purpose and a (reluctant) willingness to endure poverty, ill-health, a torrent of controversy and rejection to reach his literary goals.

The universality and detachment of Aquarius blends with or can be at odds with the immediacy and earthiness of Taurus. Inspired by his education in Aristotle and Aquinas, James Joyce renounced the abstraction and otherworldliness of the platonic perspective for a greater emphasis on sense perceptions and embodied existence. Advantage Taurus.

Joyce's adolescent sexual desires were satisfied temporarily and not inexpensively from his visits to a "red light district" of Dublin and, combined with a traditional homelife and strict Jesuit training, he felt rather guilty. Yet Joyce emerged from this confusion to develop a strong (if at times unstable) marriage and an appreciation of our sensual and sexual lives.

Joyce could not have accomplished this by himself; a strong romantic partnership was invaluable. *Ulysses* acknowledges this by placing the "action" on the day that the author and his lifelong companion Nora Barnacle went out "walking together" for the first time. That was June 16, 1904.

As a teenager Nora had gone to Dublin to escape from a physically abusive family situation and was working in a hotel when she and James

Venus, For a Good Time

happened to converse on the street. Only a few months afterwards, she and Joyce left Ireland for Europe where they would remain together the rest of their lives.

Unlike many other women of her time, place, and social status, Nora Barnacle's marriage to James Joyce gave her a chance to live an interesting life of consequence. She also had to endure her partner's self-centeredness, inconsistency, his drinking, and their many early years of poverty.

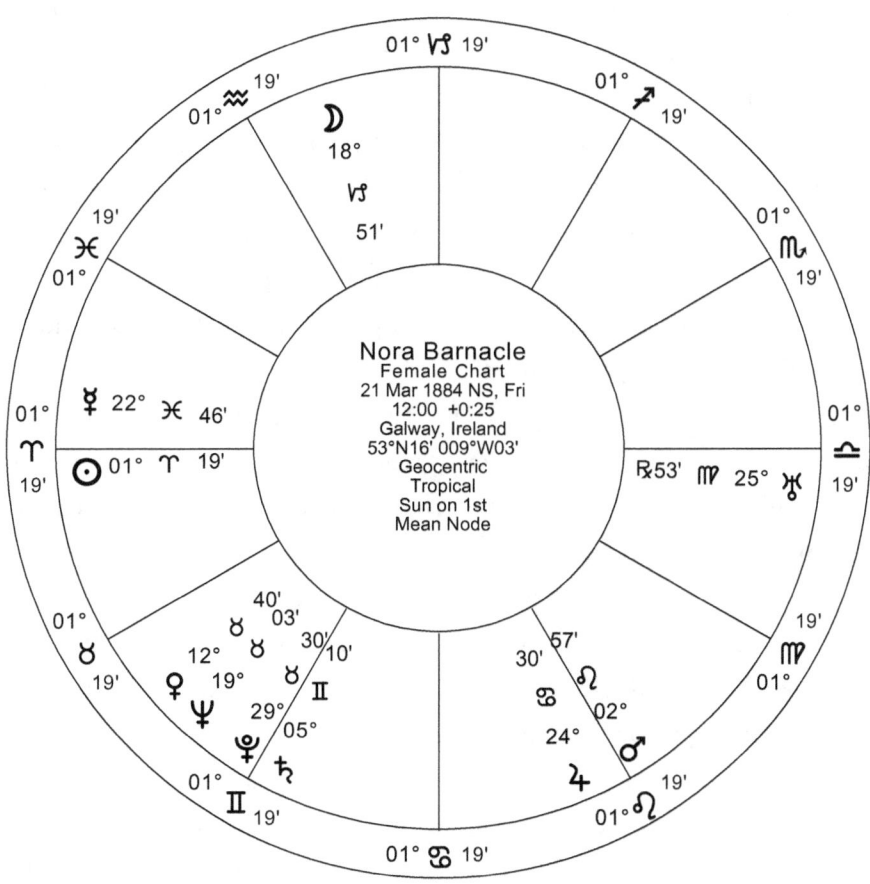

She was born either this day or the day after, so what may appear as house positions are irrelevant.

Unlike her genius renegade husband, Nora was not well educated, was rather conventional in her interests and attitudes, but, with her man, was emotionally and sexually expressive.

Nora Barnacle was born on March 21, 1884, or the next day, so our astrological information is sadly incomplete. For either date, Nora was born with Sun in early Aries in close trine to Mars in Leo. With this combination we could call her headstrong. James Joyce's Moon is two degrees of Leo, conjunct Nora's Mars, and trine her Sun. At mid-day on March 21 of that year, Moon was in the middle of Capricorn; if Nora was born on the following day, her Moon would have been in Aquarius, a "match made in heaven" perhaps.

We see the sexualized nature of their relationship in her Venus placement at twelve or thirteen degrees of Taurus that is conjunct James's Neptune. Nora's Venus is also square to James's Sun and Venus, helping to tip his scales from intellectualizing Aquarius toward earthy Taurus.

Western culture has too often cast sexuality as a worldly distraction at best and evil at worst, to being tolerated for the purposes of procreation or for the purposes of expressing love, not part of our nature without any need to be justified. James Joyce was not a Freudian nor an exponent of what we might call "free love" (too much Saturn in his chart); instead, he attempted to bring into literature more of the richness of our human experience.

From an astrological point of view human sexuality is a multi-planetary phenomenon, ranging from supporting lunar homeostasis to solar self-expression, from jupiterian cultural membership to a field for saturnine self-mastery, repression, or oppression. The role of Venus seems twofold and relates to its two domiciles – we have the joy of physical pleasure for oneself (Taurus) and the joy of reaching out to and merging with somebody who is other (Libra). As we all know too well, sexuality and self-expression have some dark sides: dimensions of competition, intimidation, blackmail, and abuse that are the realm of Mars, the next stop on our journey.

Chapter Nine

Mars: Good-Doer and No-Good Doer

The two "malefics" or "no-good-doers" are Mars, the lesser malefic and Saturn, the greater one. Both embody unfriendly realities of life, and both provide the resources to confront them. Saturn digs in or circles the wagons and Mars fights back. Both planets strengthen divisions within oneself or between oneself and the world. Both planets have tendencies toward extremes: Saturn can turn self-containment into oppressing others, Mars can turn pushing back and competitiveness into hatred or violence.

Medieval Literary Elemental Mars

Dante's *Inferno* is not an American burger chain but a classic of western literature, a depiction of a tour through the medieval Christian Hell in pursuit of salvation. Its middle cantos, where the "violent" are confined, contain many Mars-like environments. (Dante's version of violence is more extensive than ours.) The poet's use of Mars symbolism especially in Hell is abundant. Note the red planet's parched lifeless bloody qualities and how Dante uses them to evoke an atmospheric Hell.

> "Phlegethon begins as a *boiling river of blood* that awaits the violent ones; *centaurs* shoot them with *arrows* if they ascend above their allotted levels in the river. It flows onward, cutting through a *lifeless landscape within gnarled trees* and are preyed upon by *harpies*: these trees are the remnants of those who killed themselves. Further down is a *dry desert of flaming rain* for the "sodomites", prodigals, and usurers...The usurers sit in

> the *hot sand* ... Mars is affiliated with excess heat that brings sterility and diminishes life. Mars is not just its psychological attribute of anger; it has an entire range of qualities that Dante uses to depict Hell's Seventh Circle."[79]

Geoffrey Chaucer, seventy-five years after Dante, depicted Mars in *The Knight's Tale*, the first story of the *Canterbury Tales*. In addition to one of the protagonists being of the nature of Mars and dying from a Mars-like affliction, Chaucer depicts a temple and shrine to Mars, god and planet. Chaucer emphasizes qualities of toughness, steeliness, darkness and sounds that are harsh and grating. From a modern translation:

> Wrought of burnished steel, and the entryway
> Was long and narrow -- ghastly, by my faith!
> And from this passage, rushing with frenzied roars,
> Came blasts that shook and rattled the massive door.
> There were no windows; the only light was across
> The entryway, shining down from the north.
> There was no other way to see.
> The door was made of eternal adamant, attached
> From side to side, its entire length, with clamps
> Of tough and hammered iron..."[80]

Quality, Sect and Dignity

Hellenistic and medieval astrology casts Mars as dry like its fellow malefic Saturn but hotter than astrology's Sun. When conditions are too wet or too cool, or when we are too soft or inert or depressed, Mars toughens and arouses. Left untethered, however, Mars can "lose it."

---
79 Crane, J. *Between Fortune and Providence* (2011), p. 7-8
80 Burton Raffel Translation, Modern Library, lines 1120-1128

This tendency toward immoderation led ancient astrologers to place Mars as part of the Moon's nocturnal sect. The relative coolness and wetness of the nocturnal sect helps temper and sensitize the fiery planet. In an earth or water sign, Mars has a measure of containment and is less likely to go off the rails and become counterproductive.

Accordingly, Mars prefers its evening domicile Scorpio more than the diurnal Aries (Al-Biruni disagrees). Scorpio Mars seems better able to methodically pursue its goals, being patient when required. It can operate in a hidden way until the time is right. Contrasted is Mars in Aries, strong-willed but prone to ignite or accelerate too early or too late. A pure form of Mars in Aries is like people we know who have a short fuse, but what has upset them is forgotten five minutes later. We also see containment and positive purpose for Mars when we consider its exaltation in Capricorn that is governed by Saturn. Mars is also in its joy in the sixth house, a place of covert or unrecognized activity.

We all know the keywords – Mars energizes, stimulates, aggresses, and lashes out. Mars also seethes, plots revenge, can turn on itself when helpless or disempowered. Mars makes a good comrade in arms and a useful servant or employee but can be ill-tempered or impulsive as a boss.

In the chapter on Venus, we considered Castiglione's concept of *sprezzatura* or "nonchalance", an ability to make what is effortful seem effortless. The action of Mars is the opposite, the visible application of effort. Note those television commercials for athletic gear and sports beverages – we see young men and women sweating and grunting and putting in herculean efforts that always leads to future accomplishment. Venus is built to charm, to enchant, to seduce; Mars inspires, arouses, breaks a sweat, suffers greatly, and may emerge triumphant even if not always victorious.

Astrology and the Lives of People

Mars as People

Medieval astrologers often depicted people with a prominent and favorable Mars as violent and abusive, but even worse when Mars was prominent but unfavorable. Ptolemy from the Second Century CE gives the customary negative attributes but also some positive ones. From Robert Schmidt's translation, we see some of the red planet's more positive attributes:

> "When the star of Ares alone assumes the rulership over the soul in dignified dispositions, it makes the natives noble, commanding, passionate, fond of weapons, versatile, powerful, venturesome, foolhardy, insubordinate, indifferent, obstinate, keen, willful, contemptuous, tyrannical, active, irascible, fit for leadership.
>
> But for the opposite disposition, it makes them savage, insolent, bloodthirsty, fond of uproar, extravagant, bawlers, precipitous, drunken, rapacious, malefactors, merciless, those who are unsettled, mad, haters of family, impious."[81]

Here we are not concerned with those who are violent or pathologically aggressive but with those closer in temperament to you, me, and our clients. Somebody of a Mars-like nature need not be a Worldwide Wrestling contestant or be in prison. Of course, there's much room for ordinary people to be impulsive, ill-tempered, and abusive. All of us have these potentials, for we always have Mars somewhere, yet Mars often operates more benignly in our daily lives.

At its best a Mars-like personality can be decisive. They can be physically, emotionally, or intellectually vigorous or tough, somebody you'd like to have looking out for you in a rough neighborhood or in your high school where the bullies run amok. Despite many possibilities for excess, the energy expressed by Mars can assert leadership, be protective,

---
81 Trans. R. Schmidt, Claudius Ptolemy, *Tetrabiblos Book III*. P. 62

Mars: Good-Doer and No-Good Doer

and drive toward accomplishment. We will encounter Ptolemy's range of Mars' character throughout this chapter.

My Favorite "Martian"

No, we're not concerned with that mediocre sitcom of American television in the 1960s, instead we go to the Sorbonne of the 1920s. "The Martian" was an affectionate moniker given by an eminent professor and philosopher to his favorite student Simone Weil (pronounced like "vay"), who we mentioned in a previous chapter. Weil's writings on history, philosophy, politics, and religion, mostly collected and published after her death, are ingenious, and as we will see below, relevant to the times in which we live.[82]

Of those who knew her personally, many considered Weil challenging, some found her sanctimonious and insufferable, others adored her despite her eccentricities. Although most of us may never meet somebody of her dominant intellect, we've all encountered Mars-like personalities like hers. Weil shows that a Mars-like personal style can abide alongside a compassionate nature.

Weil's contemporary, the future writer Simone de Beauvoir, had wanted to meet Weil when they were both young and at the Sorbonne and she gives this memorable account.

> "[Weil] intrigued me because of her great reputation for intelligence and her bizarre outfits...I managed to get near her one day. I don't know how the conversation got started. She said in piercing tones that only one thing mattered these days: the revolution that would feed all the starving people on earth. I retorted, no less adamantly, that the problem was not to make men happy, but to help them find a meaning in their

---

82 For full profile see https://www.astrologyinstitute.com/articleprofile/profiles/2019/simone-weil-a-radically-extra-ordinary-person

existence. She glared at me and said, 'It's clear you've never gone hungry.' Our relations ended right there. I realized that she had classified me as a high-minded little bourgeoise, and I was angry."[83]

Weil's astrological chart is wonderfully multifaced, just like the woman it belonged to. We see Mars in the first house, in sect in her nocturnal chart and in close sextile to the Sun. Aided by Mercury in Aquarius in partile sextile to her Ascendant degree, she would rather be right than well-liked.

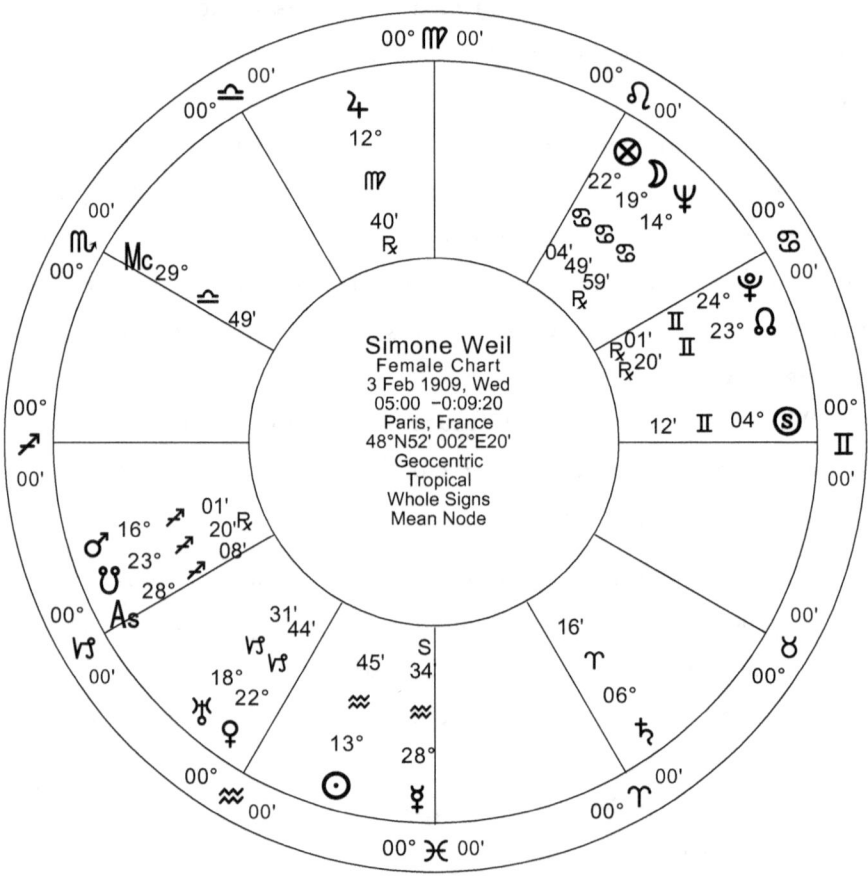

---

83 Quoted in Gray, Francine du Plessix, *Simone Weil* (2001)

Weil's Ascendant and Mars in Sagittarius are disposed by Jupiter in Virgo. Although in the powerful tenth house, Jupiter is wholly out of sect and will have more difficulty. Jupiter's placement in Virgo, in its detriment, gave her insightful and broad brushstrokes of judgmentalism. Simone Weil's short life, marked with increasing intensity during her last years, was strongly aided by her Mars placement and its relationship to Jupiter, both in strong places.

Mars with Other Purposes

Sometimes, when an astrology client asks me about how they can become involved in the larger world, I'll ask, "What out there makes you most angry?" This is often a clue where one's passion and purpose can be found.

Fred Rogers, of children's television's *Mr. Roger's Neighborhood* fame and beyond, was known for sagacity and articulateness but especially for kindness.[84] Mars was also the planet that helped motivate him toward a fulfilled life and benefit to others.

Rogers' four planets in Pisces, including the luminaries and an exalted Venus that governs his Taurus Ascendant, conforms to his reputation for kindness. Complementing this was a Mars-like zeal.

The fiery planet is in Aquarius, out of sect – possibly unruly – but in the tenth Sign of career and prominence, in sextile (and midpoint) to both Jupiter and Mars' dispositor that is Saturn. Rogers was no sentimentalist, even with the Pisces planets, but also had toughness and endurance.

As a young man studying music, with an interest in children's education and maybe the ministry, Rogers' first exposure to television was at his parents' home on college break. He was immediately convinced of

---

84 In the United States a few years ago Fred Rogers, deceased for more than a decade, became the subject of much laudatory press and a movie starring Tom Hanks playing the television personality. I rode that wave with an astrological profile https://www.astrologyinstitute.com/articleprofile/profiles/2018/fred-rogers-2018s-favorite-person

Astrology and the Lives of People

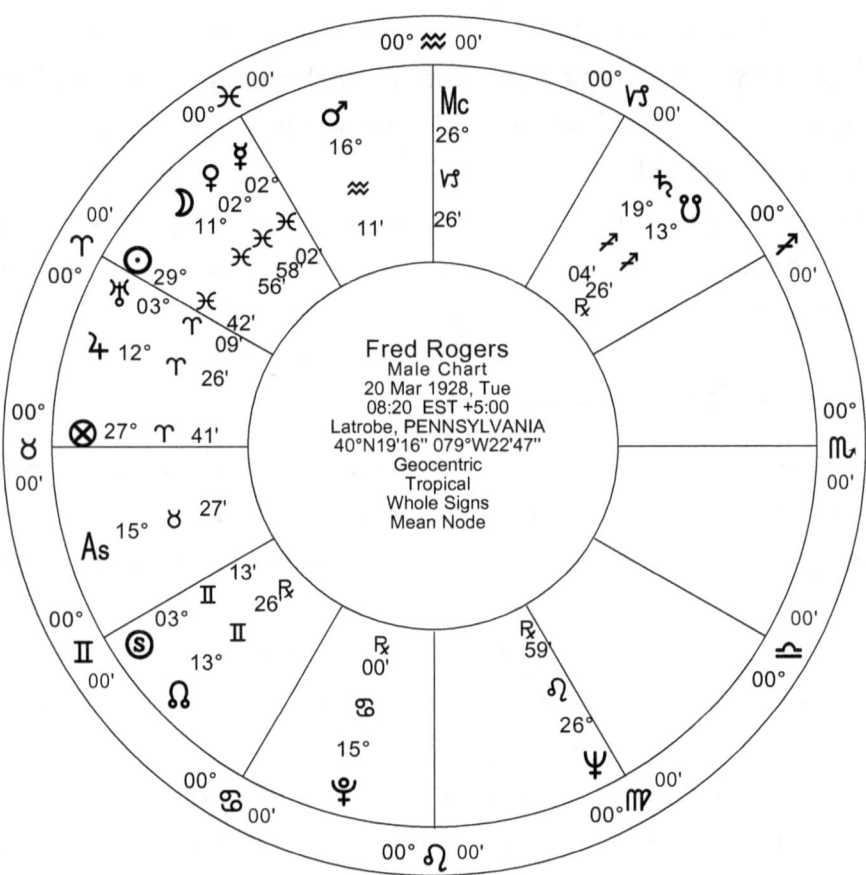

television's potential but was appalled by what he saw. "I saw people dressed in some kinds of costumes, literally throwing pies in each other's faces. I was astounded at that." His distaste for "the crass, low-grade humor of the television he saw" helped bring his talents together on a mission.[85] Throughout his career Rogers was upset by attempts to exploit or deceive children through television and other popular entertainment. His television career aimed to counteract those tendencies in our culture, tendencies that have since expanded to include video games and much online media.

Rogers was also known for tackling difficult subjects with children. He was not afraid to take controversial subjects to television. To fight

---

85 King, Maxwell, *The Good Neighbor* (2018) p. 67

against racial discrimination in public swimming pools, for example, Rogers devised a character, "Office Clemmons" an African American, and they shared a wading pool and towel.

Malcolm Little, better known as Malcolm X, was a few years older than Rogers, was more controversial, and died too early. Malcolm X, a name he adopted in renunciation of his "slave name", also had a mission that was influenced by Mars but in the light of personal and cultural oppression. (In discussing his life and his astrology, I will refer to him as "Malcolm", not from disrespect but grammatical convenience.)

Malcolm's Mars is in fall in Cancer, but in sect and its own triplicity in his nocturnal chart. Bringing these factors together, one can encounter

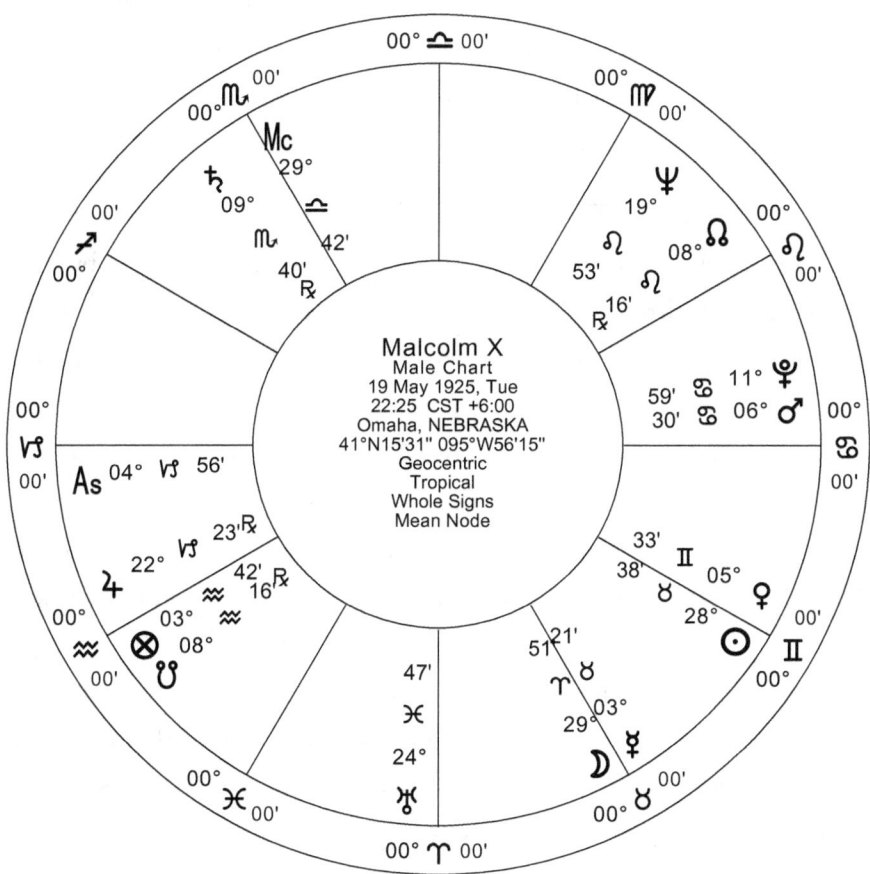

situations intuitively and with sensitivity and respond accordingly. This is not the impulsiveness of Mars in Aries but one that can make connections.

Mars in Cancer is also in mutual reception with Moon, in the last degree of Aries, in the fourth house of parents, family, ancestry. For this important planetary relationship, we have an origin story – unfortunately not so unusual for his time and skin color.

> "In 1925, Klan members on horseback attacked the Omaha [Nebraska] home of Reverend Earl Little, an organizer for Marcus Garvey's "Back to Africa" movement. Little wasn't home, but his pregnant wife and three children were. The Klansmen galloped around the house with flaming torches and shattered all the windows. In Michigan, where the family moved after the baby was born, vigilantes burned their house to the ground. The baby grew up to become Malcolm X." [86]

Two years afterwards, Earl Little was found dead in what was judged to be a streetcar accident; his family asserted that he was murdered by white racists and then thrown under the streetcar. Malcolm's mother then had to support her family and fend for herself; a few years later she was committed to an asylum where she would remain for decades. Although Malcolm and his siblings were scattered into various foster arrangements, their network remained strong throughout his life.

As a teenager in New England, Malcolm became a street hustler. He was part of a house-breaking gang but was arrested and sentenced to prison. In jail everything changed: Malcolm converted to Islam, began a rigorous self-education program, and upon his release he joined the Nation of Islam and quickly became an intellectual and rhetorical star. (Mars closely sextiles Mercury in Taurus and is in trine to Saturn in

---

[86] *New York Review of Books* (Dec. 7, 2017), "Ku Klux Klan Klambakes" by Adam Hochschild.

Scorpio, governed by Mars, and can bestow strong communication and discipline.)

The strong relationship between Moon and Mars can indicate emotional or defensive responses, a difficulty with anger or impulse control, or a tendency to put oneself in danger. None of these were the case with Malcolm X. During his lifetime the white liberal press loved to interview him, as he was outspoken and was very quotable, but he was never hostile. He was a deliberative provocateur.

Although not adversarial in his personal relationships, Malcolm's Mars, closely opposing the Ascendant, engaged most strongly when there were clear opponents for him. His life and times gave him plenty of them. During his final years he had been expanding his horizon and developing more inclusive viewpoints. If his life had not been cut short by assassination, would he have continued to be effective if greater wisdom tempered his Mars-like competitive nature?

We now move to somebody very different. Pablo Casals was a renowned cellist, conductor, and composer. He is famous for unearthing, performing, and recording the Unaccompanied Cello Suites by Johann Sebastian Bach. Casals also came from a tumultuous place and lived during a tumultuous time. He was a Catalan patriot and Spanish Republican who opposed the military campaign and government of dictator Francisco Franco.

Mars is in its own sign Scorpio and additionally is in sect in his nocturnal chart. This Mars is intense, persistent, and can be single-minded when roused. Mars has a sextile to Mercury in Capricorn, helping focus to the latter planet. Mars is in the fourth house that includes family tradition and heritage, ancestry and ethnicity, "motherland" as well as "fatherland". Casals was raised in a family that prided itself on being Catalan and he supported greater autonomy for this region throughout his life.

Astrology and the Lives of People

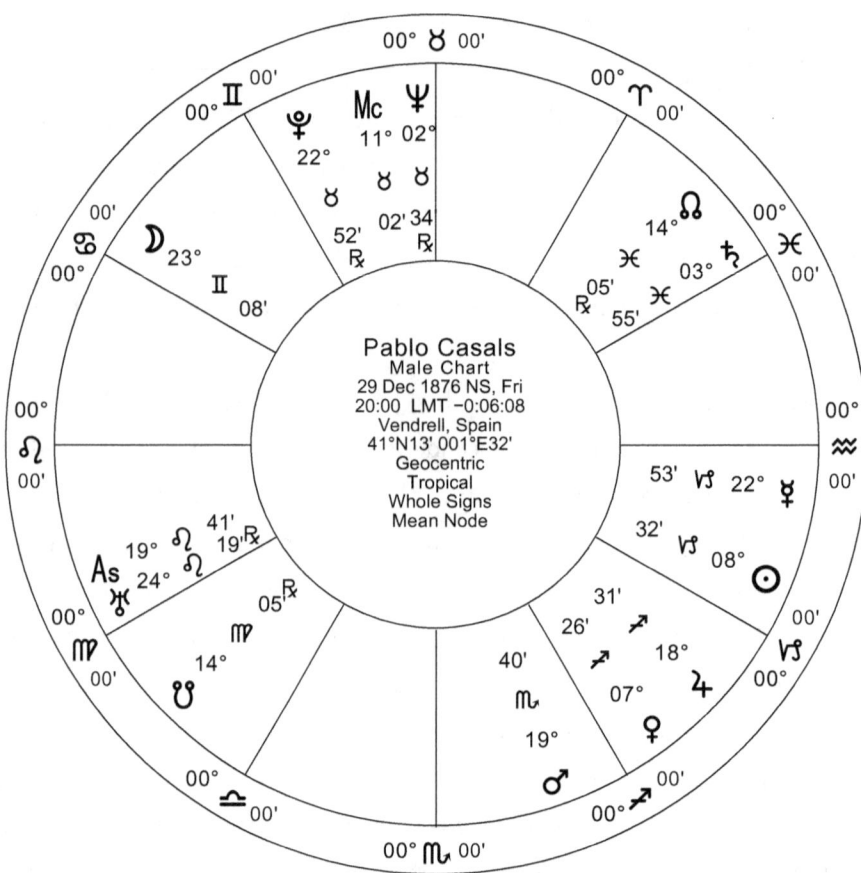

Pluto opposes Mars from the tenth house of career or calling. The tenth house is not only career but the larger world of which one is a part. After the Second World War, when western democracies began to establish diplomatic ties with Franco's regime in Spain, Casals responded by declaring that he would not perform publicly in any country that recognized Franco. As an older man Casals moved to Puerto Rico, remained active in his music into his nineties, and died two years before the end of the Franco regime. Upon Franco's death, Casals was given honors by the Spanish state and in 1979 his body was taken back to be reburied in Catalonia where he was born.

Adversarial Mars

Our ability to polarize, to split reality into "for me" and "against me", is crucial to survival in dangerous situations and energizes us into decisive action. In tennis, chess, or debating, a superior opponent improves our performance.

An illustrative life – and a revealing astrological chart – is that of the chess champion and subsequent recluse Bobby Fischer.[87] When I was young and aspired to be a good chess player, Bobby Fischer was somewhere between hero and deity. A childhood chess prodigy, Fischer burst onto the national chess scene very young, won "the game of the century" at the age of thirteen, and at the age of fourteen became the youngest person to become a grandmaster. He then became the American answer to the Soviet-dominated world of chess. Fischer's quest for a world championship culminated in 1972 when he was victorious over Boris Spassky in a match that drew worldwide attention and subsequent fame for Fischer.

Like much of his chess playing, Fischer's astrological chart is a thing of beauty. Although there are are no specific astrological indicators for "genius", Mercury can give us some clues.

Placed in the seventh house in Aquarius, we must also note Mercury's contra-antiscion relationship to an exalted Moon in Taurus. Additionally, Mercury is in a mutual reception with Saturn, strongly placed in Gemini in the eleventh house and not far from Lot of Spirit. This linkage of Moon and Mercury can give a highly intuitive mental approach but also point to mental or emotional inflexibility. Saturn's influence on Mercury was also seen in his strong preparation and research that often uncovered past techniques that had become neglected. As with Wolfgang Mozart, another prodigy in a different field, hard work accompanied natural gifts to create great accomplishment.

Mars in Aquarius is in square to the Moon, adding even greater fixity and aggressive involvement. Mars also has trines from Saturn, Uranus,

---

87 Rated B: quoted in biography

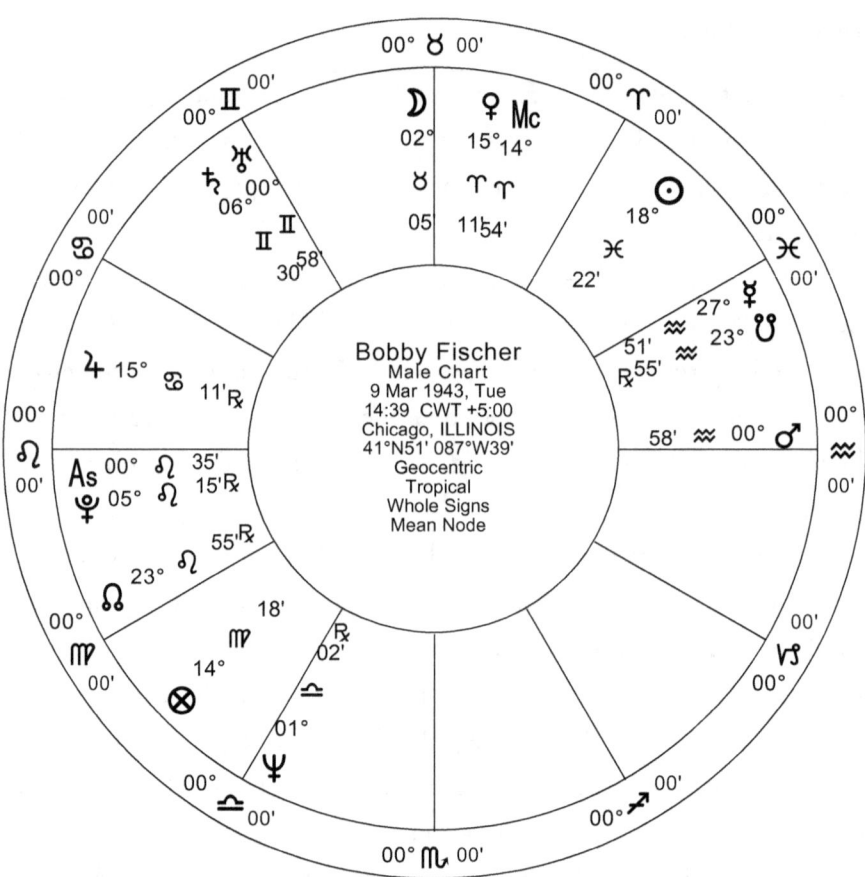

and Neptune, configurations that would play itself out in different ways throughout his lifetime.

Mars at the first degree of Aquarius is in exact opposition to his Ascendant. Pluto is not far from the Ascendant degree and is opposing Mars. Chess was a perfect game for Fischer, a game that involves being close to and directly across from one's opponent. Fischer would note their surprise when he made an unexpected move; he especially enjoyed watching them squirm at their first surmise of inevitable defeat.

According to a *New Yorker* article written when Fischer was still a teenager, "When he started playing in tournaments, he burst into tears each time he lost a game, but now he merely bites his fingernails and glowers."[88] As a chess master in his prime, Fischer could be difficult and demanding, assuming that adversaries were cheating by trying to distract him. Here's a description of him in his championship match.

> "Mr. Fischer's characteristic petulance, loutishness and sense of outrage were the stuff of front page headlines all over the globe. Incensed by the conditions under which the match was to be played — he was particularly offended by the whirr of television cameras in the hall — he lost the first game, then forfeited the second and insisted the remaining games be played in an isolated room the size of a janitor's closet."[89]

At the heights of his celebrity in the summer of 1972, Mars was in Leo, transiting his first house. Transiting Uranus was in mid-Libra, opposing his Venus-Midheaven conjunction and squaring Jupiter in Cancer. This was a brilliant but tumultuous time for him.

In the days and years following his victory over Spassky, Fischer was over his head in his new role of international celebrity. He refused public appearances, went into seclusion, and later refused to defend his world championship title. Paranoia and conspiracy theories seemed to have replaced his love for personal competition.

The remainder of his years were dismal: after emerging briefly for an illegal rematch against Spassky in 1992 in embargoed Yugoslavia, he spent his last years wandering the globe as an émigré. He gave radio interviews about worldwide Jewish conspiracies, hailed the terrorist attack on the World Trade Center in 2001, was jailed in Japan for a time for using an illegal passport and finally found refuge in Iceland where he died at the age of 64.

---

88 Bernard Taper," Prodigy" *New Yorker* August 30, 1957
89 Obituary, *New York Times,* January 18, 2008

Mars in Action

We return to Margaret Sanger and her decades-long fight for the legalization and availability of birth control in the United State.[90] Mars in Taurus, configured with tenth house Pluto and square Moon in the first house, tells us much about her drive and tenacity over decades.

After she and her sister opened the first birth control clinic in October 1916, Margaret Sanger catapulted to national visibility. Authorities quickly

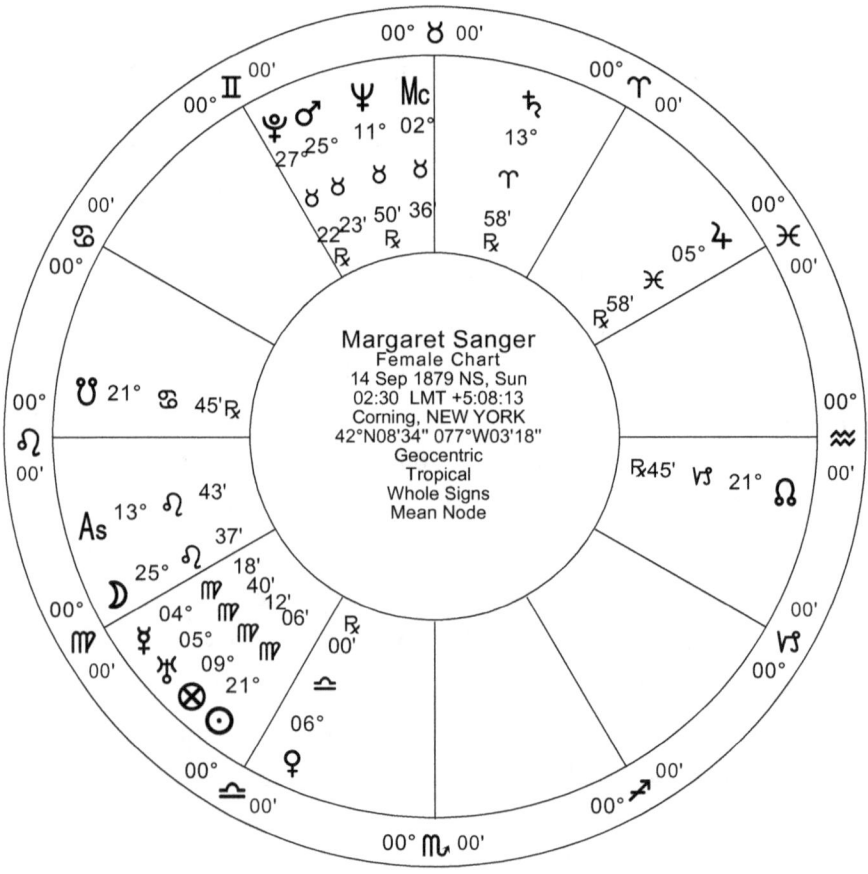

---

90 For my fuller profile of Margaret Sanger, see https://www.astrologyinstitute.com/articleprofile/profiles/2018/margaret-sanger-social-progress-and-the-very-long-road

closed the clinic, and the siblings were briefly incarcerated but a national movement had begun.

Decennials, my favorite ancient predictive technique, show what indicators led up to this occasion. Three years previously, upon her return to the United States after being arrested and then leaving the country, planetary lords changed from Venus-*Saturn* to Venus-*Mars*, and, just before the clinic opened, they changed to Venus-*Moon*, the same Moon in the first house that squares Mars natally.

On the same day that the clinic opened, secondary progressed Mercury formed an exact sextile to progressed Uranus – a fine combination for civil disobedience. Signifying that her act of rebellion would give her public visibility, transiting Jupiter was in conjunction to her Midheaven degree at that time. And where was transiting Mars? It was at 26 degrees of Scorpio, in square to her natal Moon and opposing natal Mars and Pluto.

Mars-Mercury: Lifetimes of Fabrications

Bringing together neutral Mercury and lesser malefic Mars gives us a spectrum of positive manifestations: penetrating intellect, strong speech and an ability to act intelligently in the face of difficulties. A darker side of this combination intimidates and manipulates for selfish ends, also routinely lies and defrauds.

Mars and Mercury need not be in contact by aspect or dispositor to cause mischief; they can freely cooperate in the same person. We previously considered the astrological chart of Donald Trump, noting the antiscion/contra-antiscion contacts between Mercury and the two luminaries opposing each other. Mars in Leo on Trump's Ascendant is not directly involved with Mercury, but indisputably adds to the many ways the swifter planet goes down the wrong path.

Another person, less well-known outside of the United States than Trump, set a different standard for fraudulent behavior: financier Bernard

Madoff. He died in prison in April 2021, having served twelve years of a 150-year prison sentence and leaving behind great personal and financial destruction.[91] For about twenty years before his arrest and conviction, Madoff had operated the largest known Ponzi scheme in history, with losses to investors totaling over sixty billion dollars.

Madoff made his money by using current investments (including from philanthropies) to pay off previous withdrawals, the money given never being invested in anything but quietly taken to support a lavish lifestyle for him and his family. This ruse was undetected until the financial downturn

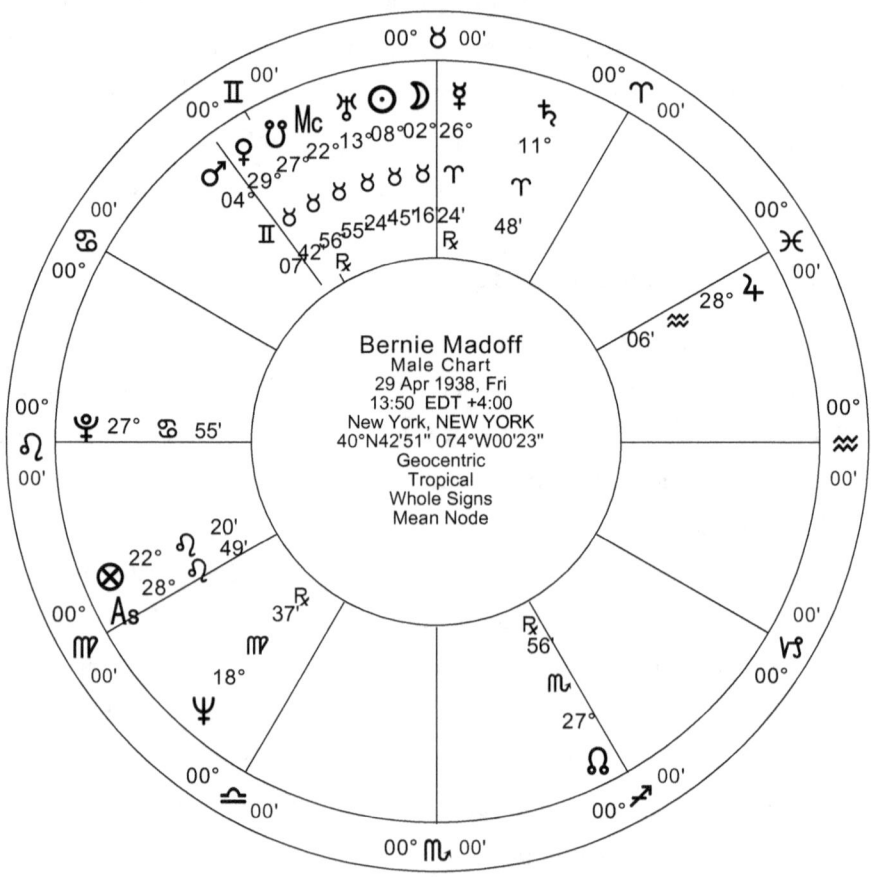

---

91 Rated AA: birth record available

of the late 2000's, which left Madoff without the resources to pay back investors. At this point everything fell apart.

Madoff's astrological chart does not show a Mercury-Mars contact by major aspect. Mercury is in Aries, retrograde (complicated but not terrible) with a square from Pluto. But Mars in Gemini brings the two planets together in mutual reception.

Both planets on their own have added advantages: Mercury has a trine to his Ascendant degree and Mars is in the fortunate eleventh house. More positively manifesting, this combination could have made for a savvy investor or investigator.

Our eyes also turn toward many planets in the tenth house in Taurus, including both luminaries.[92] How did they manifest for Madoff? He presented himself as cautious and self-contained like his Taurus planets. His public face was steady and reliable, unlike the flamboyant Charles Ponzi of the early twentieth century. Madoff promised moderate but steady growth to his investors.

Madoff's Jupiter is in the seventh house, opposing the Ascendant by degree: Madoff lived off the wealth and good reputation of those who trusted him. To be an investor in his enterprises was to join a group of special and important people.

Most of us could not emotionally tolerate attempting to perpetuate such an operation. It's likely we'd be having nightly visions of getting caught and our lives ruined. Perhaps Madoff's exalted Moon in Taurus was not his friend here, for he certainly knew how to make himself comfortable and emotionally steady while taking enormous risks.

Madoff's Mercury-Mars mutual reception helped ignite and sustain his brazen enterprise; Mars perverted Mercury's cleverness into fraud. His Taurus planets certainly had a role in the self-perpetuating nature

---

[92] A traditional horary astrologer may notice the Moon being within the Sun's rays, indicating hidden activity – in the tenth house, hidden in plain sight.

of his operation. Its twenty-year success stems from his Mercury-Mars connection – along with naïve investors and poor governmental oversight.

Sexualized or Sexually Abusive Mars

Mars can be a useful ally upon entering the field of battle to accomplish one's (solar) purposes. Allied to the Moon, Mars can help one prevail over difficult circumstances. But when Mars is on its own and in charge things can go astray.

Venus is the planet of connection and affiliation; Mars is the planet of pursuit and victory, including in the field of romance. When Venus is in charge we have passion, eros, excitement, perseverance, our enduring quest for love. But when a need expressed sexually is for power and prevailing over opposition, the results are messy at best, cruel and traumatizing at worst.

Although medieval astrologers tended to be more squeamish about sexual misbehavior, those from antiquity were usually more direct. Vettius Valens, a practicing astrologer from the second century C.E., gives us many aphorisms about sexual behavior. "If Ares [Mars] and Aphrodite [Venus] should have set under the beams [of the Sun], the natives will engage in clandestine adulteries and secret sins. And if they should also happen to be oriental and upon pivot points [angles], it will be more apparent."[93] From the same passage and reflecting the conditions of many in the ancient world: "On account of Hermes [Mercury] witnessing them [in aspect], the native pursues innovative sins, and furthermore are involved with servile personages and children."

Claudius Ptolemy, a generation after Valens and whose work was revived by medieval and early modern astrologers, thought of sexual activity for men governed by Mars and for women governed by Venus. For men, if Mars is with Venus, or if Jupiter is there and Saturn is not, "it produces men who

---

93 Trans. R. Schmidt, *Vettius Valens* Anthology *Book II and Book III, p. 4*

are lascivious and frivolous and who procure pleasures for themselves from all sides." And for women, Mars makes for women who are "lascivious and debased and rather frivolous." If Mars is under the beams of the Sun, these women "have intercourse with slaves and with those of lower rank or with foreigners."[94]

From a lunar side: people with sexual addictions, those who pursue gratification at great risk to themselves and harm to others, are often incapable of real intimacy. More prevalent is an exercise of power expressed sexually. Yet when we look at sexual exploitation and abuse astrologically, we must tread carefully, for one may pathologize or criminalize planetary placements and interactions that are shared by those who do not have these tendencies.

For our purposes, the Marquis de Sade stands for sexual perpetrators of all kinds. He endured thirty-two years in prison, during which time he wrote many of the works that have ensured his reputation. His long life coincided with the emergence of real or fictional people (e.g., main characters of two sublime Mozart operas) who were upper class but "libertines", prone to sexual adventurism. Here we must add de Sade's fascination with sexual violence.

One author discusses de Sade psychologically as narcissistic but her description of him also has the flavor of Mars, or this planet run amuck.

> "Sade had an early sense, candidly admitted to in his writings, that 'the entire universe had to flatter [his] whims, and that [he] had the right to satisfy them at will.' Be it his yearning to whip women with cat-o'- nine tails, or his urge to create a sodomitic daisy chain with several prostitutes and his valet, or his craving to stage orgies at his castle with a company of nubile youngsters, no threats or public censures could

---
94 Trans. R. Schmidt, *Ptolemy* Tetrabiblos Book IV, p. 25

persuade him to curb his most offensive demands. Each of Sade's sexual infractions also reinforced what some psychiatrists call 'narcissistic' cement, offering him an illusory but exhilarating sense of control over others."[95]

Behold a striking astrological chart.[96] We can see de Sade as an unconventional person and a very good writer: Mercury has trine aspects from both Uranus in the first and Moon in Virgo in the ninth house. If de Sade had solar narcissistic issues, we may look closely at his Sun, conjunct

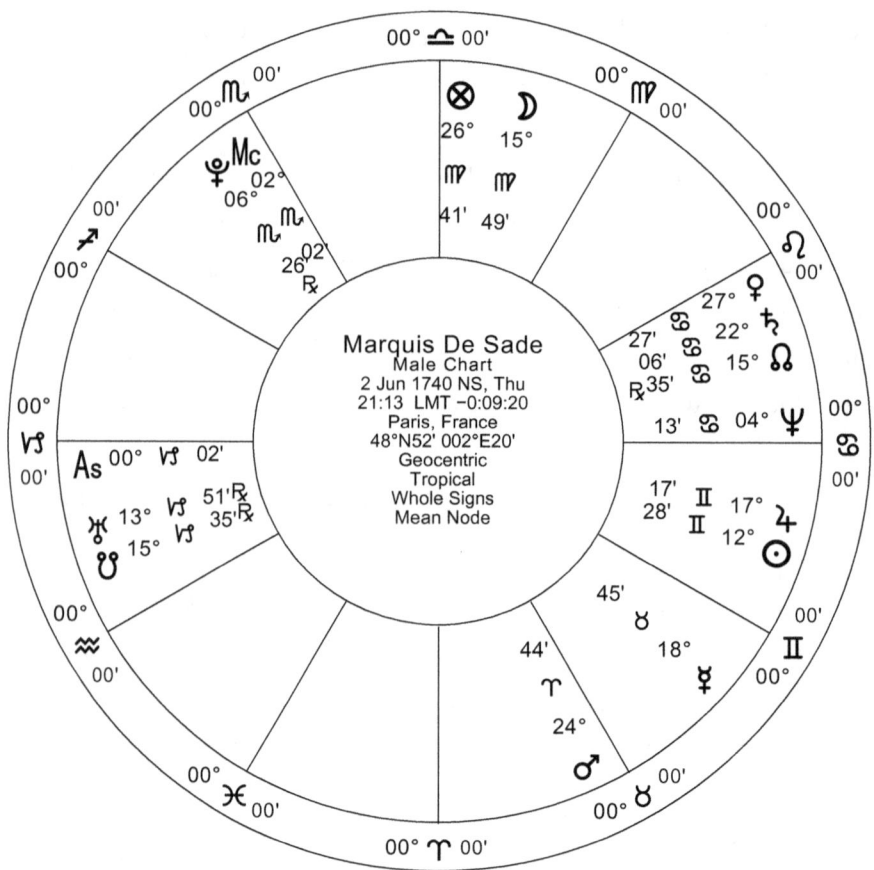

---

95 Du Plessix Gray, Francine: *At Home with the Marquis de Sade.* (1998) Simon & Schuster, p. 157
96 AA rating: birth record quoted

Jupiter in the more difficult sixth house. (For William Blake, discussed in a previous chapter, they were together in Sagittarius; for de Sade they're in the sunnier but the less moralizing sign Gemini.)

Mars is in its strong angular position in its domicile Aries and dominating squares to Saturn (in detriment) and Venus. Mars in the fourth house, manifesting differently than for Casals, may indicate problems in his family of origin and in early childhood; its square to Venus suggests sexual expression of a Mars-like aggressiveness. Perhaps Saturn's placement testifies further about his oppressive brand of sexual excitement. De Sade's Venus in Cancer can't escape from two malefics quickly enough and seems not to have succeeded in doing so.

De Sade's writings on politics and culture were original and sometimes outrageous. His advocacy against a death penalty is commendable and prescient but further reveals his character influenced by Mars. He could understand murder by passion or an extreme state of mind, he wrote, but state-sanctioned deliberate murder is wrong: "To have him killed by someone else after calm and serious meditation and on the pretext of duty honorably discharged is incomprehensible."[97]

Moving from men to women will give us a different picture. We return to Chaucer and consider the Wife of Bath, an unforgettable character from the *Canterbury Tales*. She describes enough of her astrological chart for me to be daring and posit a speculative chart for her.[98] Most of her "tale" is a monologue, at times charming and funny and at other times full of anger. She has been a successful businesswoman in the textile industry. She has also attracted five different men to marry her and she's on the lookout for number six.

---

97 Camus, *The Rebel*, p. 40
98 For a fuller depiction of this unique character and her astrology, see https://www.astrologyinstitute.com/articleprofile/articles/2017/chaucers-wife-of-bath-needs-a-new-astrological-chart

Astrology and the Lives of People

She was born of Venus in her feelings, she states, but her heart belongs to Mars. She shows how a strongly placed Mars and a dignified Venus can produce a creative character or can work at cross purposes and be destructive.

> Venus gave me desire [my lust, my likerousnesse], and all the parts
> I needed, but it was Mars that made me daring [hardynesse].
> My astral ascendant was Taurus, with Mars sharing
> The sky. Alas, alas! that love should be sinful.
> I followed the path my stars placed me in,
> I had no choice but to be what I have been.
> I never was good at holding back: my chamber
> Of Venus was open to any man who was able.
> And yet, remember, I wear Mars on my face
> And also in another private place.[99]

Here is a chart that conforms to her description and would correspond to a time and place of her birth.

Mars rises in Taurus and sextiles Mercury in Pisces: Chaucer presents her style of speaking as intense but rambling. Later commentators note her frequent errors when she cites historical and biblical precedent. Dignified Saturn in trine gives Mars directness and consistency, even if what she says sometimes seems contradictory. Mars and the Ascendant are both governed, however, by Venus in Pisces in the eleventh house.

Her dignified Venus would be fond of love and sex, music, adornment, and parties and luxury – the good things in earthly life. These all seem true for her, but they are sullied by the strong influence of Mars on her personal style. She dresses strikingly but garishly. At times she comes off as rough, coarse, and aggressive.

---

99 Raffel translation, from *Wife of Bath's Tale*, lines 609-620

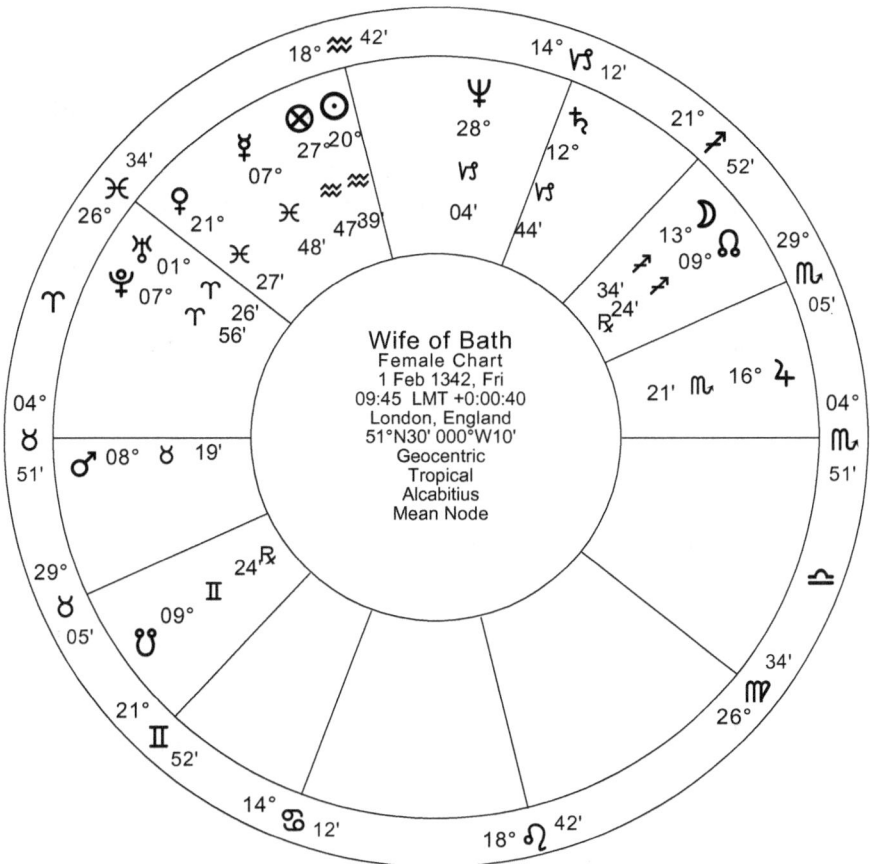

She boasts of her use of power games in the bedroom, sometimes refusing sexual contact but at other times demanding that her men fulfill their "marriage debt" by "working" all night. As with some other characters in Chaucer's poem, sex is not an expression of love or an impersonal instinct but a weapon to dominate others – or, in her male-dominated marital culture, to get even.

Her lesson for men, in her monologue and her story that follows, is that women want authority in their marriages. But at just the point where we are softened by her and the positive conclusion of her tale, Mars-like anger comes out. She ends with a prayer that Jesus send to women those men who are young, meek, and "fresh abedde", and that Jesus shortens the lives of those who will not be governed by their wives, and to the worst of them, send a pestilence.

One can see a Mars tendency to fly off with its own energy. For all this, the Wife of Bath has personal appeal and would be an entertaining dinner and drinks companion – but I'd be sure to leave the tavern by myself.

Chaucer's depiction of the Wife of Bath is neither from a misogynist's playbook nor is she an early feminist. Although she found a place within the restrictions on women of her time, she was also excessive and ultimately self-destructive.

Affliction: Another Dark Side of the Red Planet

We briefly return to Simone Weil to consider her essay "The *Iliad* or the Poem of Force". She uses Homer's work to discuss the effects of force to "make a thing of whoever submits to it" with soul-deadening effects she called "affliction." We can think of affliction as being on the receiving side of oppressive circumstances.

Many of us are familiar with the *Iliad's* depictions of death in combat, often told with grisly realism, of the cruelty and claustrophobic savagery of warfare, and the ambiguous glorification of some of its heroes. We may also recount the poem's brief moments of grace and its sublime conclusion. Writing as the Nazis had taken northern France and as the Second World War was gathering steam, Weil argues that the true hero of the poem is not a person but *force itself*.

From one memorable passage we see the intoxication, destructiveness, and self-destructiveness of Mars when brought to extremes.

> "The human soul seems ever conditioned by its ties with force, swept away, blinded by the force it believes it can control, bowed under the constraint of the force it submits to. Those who have supposed that force, thanks to progress, now belongs to the past, have seen a record of that in Homer's

poem; those wise enough to discern force at the center of all human history, today as in the past, find in the Iliad the most beautiful and flawless of mirrors."[100]

Although violence (personal or national) embodies the most blatant and literal application of force, it is simply an extreme degree of oppression and affliction. Weil cites the submissive posture of the suppliant and the condition of the slave whose body is an object of use and whose soul withers. Previously in her life, when Weil was working in a factory, she noted how the assembly line made people into machines so that workers eventually became weak and submissive and petty. Additionally, when one country makes a colony of another, one country subdues the other with the same consequences. We see both malefics at work.

Although the *Iliad* is a poem of extremes of human condition and behavior, there are subtler versions of force, ones closer to our normal lives. When we look at the role of Mars with Mercury and then with Venus, we note fraud and deceit (even if the receiving party seems willing) and sexual exploitation and abuse. Both excesses carry with them an indifference to those who are the objects of fraud, systematic deceit, and sexual exploitation and abuse. Weil's essay reminds us that Mars easily enhances divisions between one's will and the object of one's will, and how easy it is for us to fall for an intoxication of dominance.

Later in her essay, Weil notes redemptive qualities in Homer's epic and in our lives. She cites the "fleeting and sublime moments when men possess a soul. The soul thus roused for an instant, soon to be lost in the empire of force, wakes innocent and unmarred; no ambiguous, complex, or anxious feeling appears in it; courage and love alone have a place there."[101]

---

100 Holoka, James P. (translator and editor) *Simone Weil's The Iliad or the Poem of Force: A Critical Edition* (2008) New York: Peter Lang Publishing. p. 45
101 Ibid, p. 62

Astrology and the Lives of People

Moments of true friendship, camaraderie, and understanding, even between enemies, bring illumination that punctuates the dominance of soul-crushing force, of the ever-present realities of oppression and affliction.

Transcendent Mars

Having explored some of its darker possibilities we should close with more admirable manifestations of the red planet. At its best, Mars is found in some people who have been able to blend vigor with vision, and sometimes in ordinary people who must act quickly.

Dorothy Day (1897-1980) never led an easy life, went through profound changes of direction in pursuit of her life purposes. She became a prominent leftist activist who may be declared a saint by the Catholic Church.[102] In stark contrast with today's "abundance spirituality" and evangelical authoritarianism, Day endeavored to blend political causes and a personal touch with her adopted Catholic community.[103] This was not an easy combination for her.

Day was co-founder and main spokesperson for the "Catholic Worker" movement that began in depression-era United States. Along with co-founder Peter Maurin, she helped set up nonsectarian Hospitality Houses -- not to preach or convert anybody but help assist those in need.

Mars is in its own sign, is in sect in her nocturnal chart, and is in its house joy in the sixth house (especially helpful with the adversity she frequently encountered). Mars holds its own and adds its strength to Mercury and Sun that are also in Scorpio.

The strong connection between Mercury and Mars tells us about her personal intensity, unyielding attitudes, and early penchant for advocacy journalism. These two planets, together with a more contemplative Sun in Scorpio, also point to her continual spiritual self-examination.

---

102 Rated AA: birth record quoted
103 For a fuller astrological profile of Day, see https://www.astrologyinstitute.com/articleprofile/profiles/2018/dorothy-day-untimely-prophet

Mars: Good-Doer and No-Good Doer

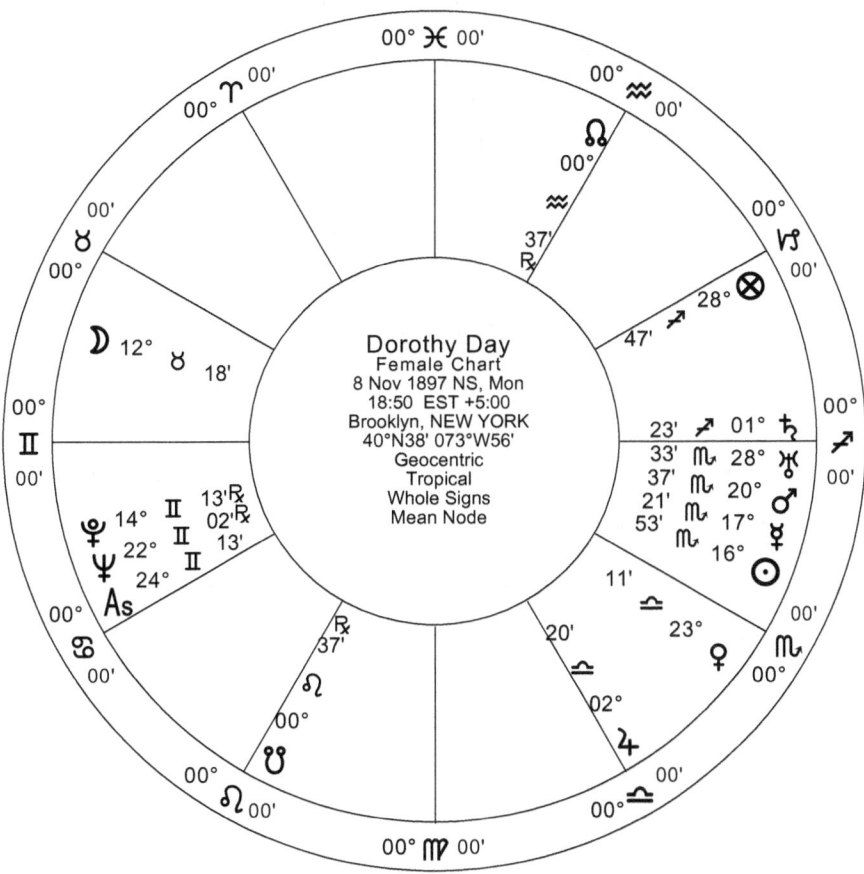

Conversations with psychiatrist-author Robert Coles, later published as *A Radical Devotion* (1987), picture her as somebody who was honest with herself, aware of her self-righteous do-gooder arrogance, and the attitude of self-importance that often goes with being a public person. Without lapsing into false humility or self-deprecation (additional manifestations of pride, of course), Day approached her activist life in a contemplative manner as best she could.

Had she been a lesser mortal, her combination of planets could have rendered her intensity unbearable to others. If on the side of faith and virtue, she would have come across not as saintly but as a sanctimonious nuisance. Venus and Jupiter in Libra do come to the rescue, giving her personal charm and a comforting presence.

In an article from 1994, Garry Wills writes about what separates a good person from a great person, a charitable person from a saintly one. One must step beyond our usual self-protectiveness into something creative – and often outrageous – regardless of personal consequences. Evoking Dorothy Day, Wills states:

> Such people are "outsize," for better or worse, escaping the boundaries that hold the rest of us constrained by self-regard, convention, or fear. The protection against their challenge is to dismiss them as outstandingly crazy. Most saints met that response at some point. [104]

If Mars has a transcendent side, how Dorothy Day manifested this planet may show us how to do it.

---

[104] https://www.nybooks.com/articles/1994/04/21/the-saint-of-mott-street/

Chapter Ten

Big and Vast Jupiter

What We See and Who We Are

Jupiter is a wonderful planet to watch in the sky. On a clear night, especially when Jupiter and the Sun are directly across from each other from our viewpoint, Jupiter shines brightly. Year after year, Jupiter's journey through the heavens is stately and dignified, taking twelve years to travel the zodiac. Jupiter is our first step above the immediate realities of our lives, encompassing a broader horizon.

Jupiter is the "great benefic" or doer of good, signifying the world as friendly, accommodating, and full of possibility. In our ordinary lives, Jupiter is the planet of inclusion into communities and larger enterprises – cultural, social, political, and planetary. These communities provide opportunities for meaningful connections with those we have not met, and manifest in our lives from the playpen to the local senior center. We all know how important is our sense of belonging to us and how frightened or resentful we can be when feeling excluded – isolation is Saturn's domain, togetherness belongs to Jupiter.

Many of us have experienced the thrill of being part of a concert performance or watching our favorite sports team. Perhaps you've been with fifty thousand like-minded political demonstrators when you think collective chanting and clever placards will change the world. These experiences are some of our more joyful experiences in life. If unchecked, however, the intoxication of togetherness can become thoughtless, impulsive, and cruel to others.

Today, we also form virtual communities. Mass mailings and social media include us algorithmically, placing us into groups outside our control. We have become sets of interests, preferences, and marketing potentials. Virtual communities, closer to statistic-weaving social psychology and marketing principles, miss our real nature. Citing Walt Whitman again, we too are "untranslatable." Yet we belong with others; we are also statistical units.

Jupiter also travels across time, bringing with it our common heritage and history, our intellectual, artistic, or spiritual lineages, from a past we were born into, to a future that we may yet contribute to. When astrologers consider their field only from the viewpoint of the last century and ignore the richness of its more distant past, their astrology loses some of its depth and richness.

Jupiter yields principles that are abstract and have universal application that can motivate greatness or rationalize evil. This planet's tendency to generalize may ignore unpleasant realities closer to home or within oneself, resulting in sometimes comical inconsistencies. In the United States it's fashionable these days to condemn rising gas prices and excessive oil corporate profits and ignore the high gas-consumption of the fashionable vehicle one is driving. Longer-range results of hypocrisy, small and large, often become an eventual descent into saturnine cynicism.

What They Said

We begin again with astrology's representation in literature. Dante's *Paradiso*, structured by the heaven of the medieval Christian imagination, gives us a striking image of this large planet. Ascending beyond the crusaders and martyrs of Mars, the pilgrim and his guide arrive on the Sphere of Jupiter. They encounter a dazzling assembled light show, part of which transforms into an Eagle that speaks with many voices. Together they represent both worldly and divine justice. Although some individuals comprising this assembly are identified, the focus is on collective righteousness and advancement of God's providence.

A few centuries earlier, Al-Biruni's *Book of Instructions* cast Jupiter as a creature of society, its culture and its principles.

> For Disposition and Manners: "Good disposition, inspiring, intelligent, patient, high-minded, devout, chaste, administering justice, truth-telling, learned, generous, noble, cautious in friendship, egoistic, friend of good government, eager for education, an honourable, trusty and responsible custodian, religious."
>
> For Activities, Instincts, and Morals: "Friendliness, a peacemaker, charitable, devoted to religion and good works, responsible, uxorious, laughing, eloquent, eager for wealth, in addition to affability some levity and recklessness." [105]

Five hundred years later Johannes Schoener's pithy handbook on astrology looks at different roles for a person of the nature of Jupiter.

> *Conditions and Peoples:* Those skilled in law, bishops, prelates, nobles, upright persons, judges, honorable, true, benevolent, freeborn, faithful, gentle, pious, truthful, magnanimous, and religious persons.
>
> *Endowments and Magistracies:* Dignities and offices in spiritual matters, jurisprudence and judgement, preferment, royal power, principality. [106]

Astrology's traditional Jupiter is not the king but the minister, maybe the prime minister, but also the foot soldier, even the righteous commoner. Jupiter has virtues that are necessary to help run and participate in a bake-

---
105 R. Ramsay Wright translation (1934), p. 250, 251
106 Schoener, Johannes. *Opusculum Astrologicum* (1994). Trans. R. Hand, Golden Hind Press

sale, book group or a government: loyalty to its mission, consideration for others, and a sense of personal responsibility to perform well.

Traditional Jupiter is also the planet of wealth. (This is different from Venus, the planet of "nice stuff".) Wealth allows for greater standing and influence. Wealth's influence may fund arts or charities, hire lobbyists to further increase business opportunities while reducing one's tax burden, or be used for prominent but useless activities like sending other rich people into space. From the distant past to the present moment and surely into the future, wealth gives one greater pull in society.

What if an "ill-disposed" Jupiter governs one's soul? According to Ptolemy,

> "When the opposite disposition occurs [i.e., Jupiter is unfortunate], it maintains similar appearances for the souls, yet more toward the debased and insignificant and undistinguished; for example, prodigality instead of magnanimity, superstition instead of religion, cowardice instead of modesty, conceit instead of dignity, foolishness instead of kindness, love of pleasure instead of love of beauty, stupidity instead of high-mindedness, indifference instead of liberality..." [107]

Modern astrologers talk of debilitated Jupiter implying grandiosity and overdoing, or perhaps erring to the other extreme and lacking self-confidence. In my view, an inability to establish genuine friendships and relationships can lead to retreating into oneself and constructing an artifice by which one participates in the larger world. Perhaps a debilitated Jupiter is socially anxious.

---

[107] Ptolemy, *Tetrabiblos III,* Chapter 15. Trans. R. Schmidt

Jupiter: Solar and Lunar

Depictions of the Sun and Jupiter sometimes use the word "religious." The Sun, whose joy is the ninth house of the "Sun God", is (potentially) a more direct channel to divinity. Jupiter's religiosity is closer to what is practiced by a community and aims to establish or maintain one's participation within that community.

Astrology's Sun, the planet of identity and identification, may intersect with Jupiter but is not the same as the large planet. You may take pride in your Polish ancestry, but this is not the same as exploring your family's emigration from Poland to the United States, joining the Polish American club, learning to speak Polish, visiting the country, and learning its history. If the Sun is what bestows meaning in our lives, Jupiter puts it into action. When there's a mission at hand Jupiter is the Sun's "wingman".

If Sun includes the stories that we tell of ourselves (and those others tell of us), Jupiter is who we tell our stories to. Whether in the elementary school classroom, a group therapy meeting, among our spiritual companions, or in a time capsule for our descendants or beyond the solar system, Jupiter proclaims who we are to those we do not know. An unholy alliance between Sun's pride and Jupiter's scope often leads to a bloated estimation of oneself.

The *lunar* qualities of Jupiter have a more empathic nature but may descend into sentimentality. Jupiter's larger horizons may include the inner life of others, what it is like to be them when they seem so very different from us. Jupiter fits in well with travel and learning different languages, cultures, and human possibilities. Jupiter allows lunar qualities to take flight from personal caring to broader ranges of compassion.

Astrology and the Lives of People

Joviality

We all know how important humor is to us. We tend not to trust those who seem humorless. When we hear laughter in the next room, we want to find out what we are missing. Now it is time to lighten up and survey a strong but too-often neglected feature of Jupiter: its ability share laughter with others.

Many planets are involved in humor, but Jupiter has a special role. Mercury provides much of the overt content. Venus uses humor to comfort and charm and attract people to us: if there is easy laughter on a first date, the evening is going well. Jupiter's role is not as much the content but the *purpose* of humor, as a vehicle of group bonding and shared pleasure – and to poke fun at those who are not like us.

A First Humorous Cynic

Mark Twain, the beloved American writer and performer from the nineteenth century, had all the planetary dimensions to be a successful humorist, giving him an ability to be appealingly and devastatingly comedic at the same time. Here is a too-brief sampling of his written wit.[108]

> "It could be shown by facts and figures that there is no distinctly native American criminal class except Congress."
>
> "I believe that our Heavenly Father invented man because he was disappointed in the monkey."
>
> "Let us be thankful for fools. But for them the rest of us could not succeed."
>
> "Always do right. This will gratify some people and astonish the rest."

---

[108] On the Internet one finds many famous quotes given to Mark Twain without giving references for them. To prevent attributing something to this famous author that he never wrote, I consulted the well-known *Familiar Quotations* (1980) This work that has had multiple publications and is usually known as "Bartlett's Quotations".

> "Everything human is pathetic. The secret source of humor itself is not joy but sorrow. There is no humor in heaven."

Do Twain's barbs, and similar humor by others, soften or sharpen? The first quote is sharp, accusing prominent politicians of being criminal; others paint a dire portrait of the rest of us. Twain's humor brings people together in laughter, even if its implications are unsettling.

Many planets attest to Mark Twain's incisive mind, appeal, and a melancholic disposition.[109] Mercury, in its joy in the first house would indicate his talent and his piercing humorous style. Mercury in Scorpio gives cleverness and calculating shrewdness to the personality. We also see the sharpness and inventiveness of his wit that is delivered in a way we find pleasing despite a pessimistic underlying message.

Twain's Aries Moon, separating from Jupiter, connects next to Venus that keeps company with a Sun-Mars conjunction; together with a charming presence, this combination adds drive and desire to make an impact on others. Venus in Sagittarius gives us Twain as a robust public performer, somebody who recouped financial losses by going on a world tour and returning home as a celebrity.

Saturn in Scorpio occupying the first house makes for an ability to put oneself forward in a very deliberate way. Saturn makes him disciplined and hard-working but personally defensive. Saturn also speaks of the pessimistic side to Twain's version of the world.

Mercury's witty and playful presence is given context by the trine from Jupiter that is exalted in Cancer. Jupiter adds a humanitarian and caring streak to his otherwise calculating and ambitious nature.

This planet also gave him an ethical sensibility that buttresses much of his work and its impact. This combination between planets in the first and ninth houses brings together personal style and a sense of common

---
[109] This birth time has been handed down from astrological literature and is rated "C". No reliable source has been found, nor have any alternatives.

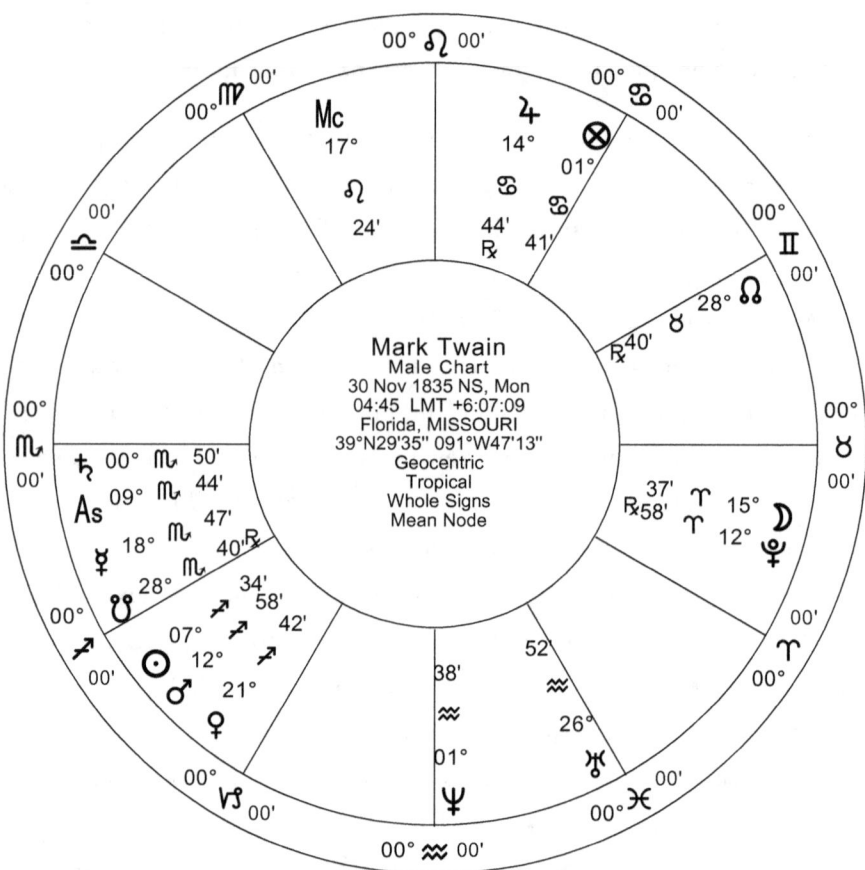

humanity, through which he included himself as morally frail like the rest of us.

Another Humorous Cynic

Recalling Dorothy Parker's chart, we previously discussed her presentation of exuberant sexuality. She was also very funny.

I remember the line "You can lead a horticulture, but you can't make her think" before I was old enough to understand the reference. From *Mad Magazine* I recall that "Beauty is only skin deep, but ugliness is to the bone". *Mad Magazine* changed a few words, but the quote's basic meaning is the same as Parker's original line. Later, in my days of waywardness and excessive alcohol consumption, I would quote "I'd rather have a bottle in front of me than a frontal lobotomy." These days her inquiry "What fresh hell is this?" upon hearing the telephone ring seems appropriate for our times.[110]

As Mark Twain found the entire human race (including himself but especially the US Congress) not living up to its moral potential, Parker found that romance promises much and delivers far less. Parker's sexual humor appealed to our common but usually restrained prurient sensibility, together with a skeptical attitude about romantic longings and their

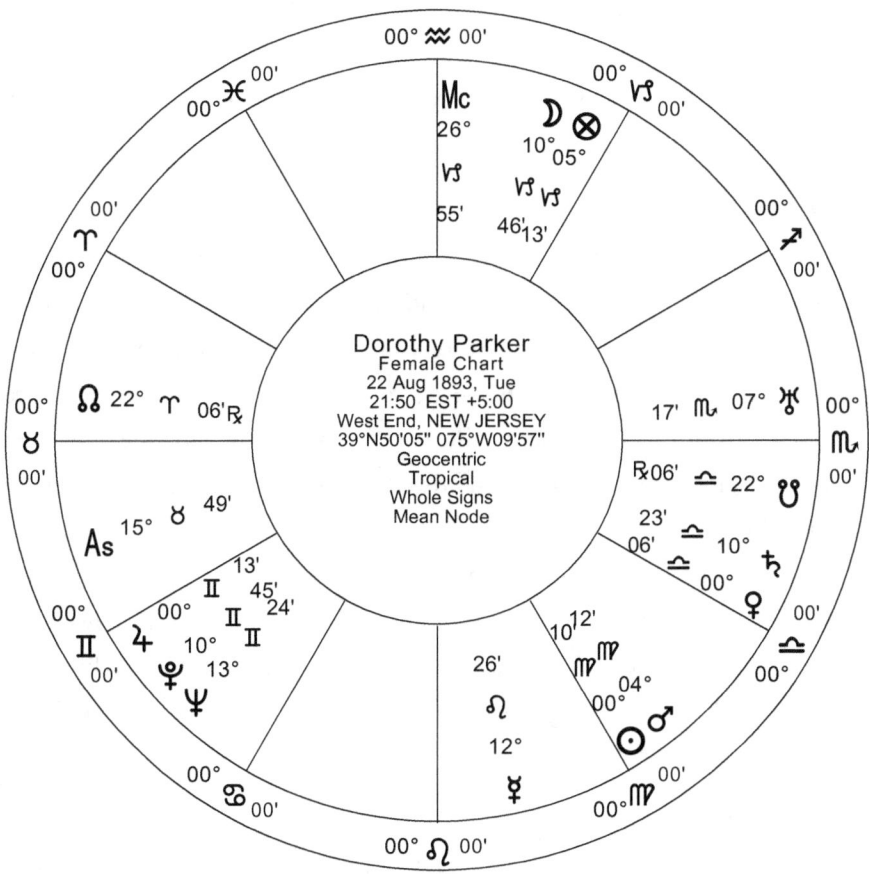

---

110 See her biography *What Fresh Hell is This* (1987) by Marion Meade; this and standard poetry anthologies are sources for these lines attributed to her.

possibilities for fulfillment. From an astrological point of view, part of this tendency can be traced to her dominant Saturn in its relationship with Moon that we discussed previously.

Parker's Jupiter contributes much as her humor was an effective way to bring common experiences to the forefront and to lighten their capacity for disappointment. Jupiter in Gemini is in trine to Venus in Libra. Her writing and her company often displayed a sparkle even when she writes of heartbreak and self-destructiveness.

Parker's Jupiter has a strong square to the Sun, both planets governed by her sharp Mercury. We should note Parker's political and cultural leanings, including her advocacy and activity for liberal causes, from protesting the Sacco and Vanzetti executions in the 1920s, to promoting civil rights in the decades afterwards.

Jovial Failures

We are familiar with the cruelty of humor at the expense of those who are disadvantaged or handicapped, and the joy we take in humor poked at the privileged. Note the nature of ethnic humor to reinforce negative stereotypes. Political humor can border on cruelty to those on the "other side" but reinforces ties within the community of which one is a part. Political humor provides comfort and reduces anger and anxiety by having fun at the expense of others but reinforces personal divisiveness.

Being made fun of, being the victim of humor, often produces a first blush of shame followed by a wave of anger. Being the butt of jokes is the next worst thing to social ostracism, as we are exposed as unworthy of the company of those who laugh at us. The experience of the "in group" may be Jupiter but its effect on us is saturnine.

Jupiter, the Planet of the City

We tend to think poorly of politics but espouse the virtues of being a citizen and having civic responsibility. Both words "politics" and "citizen" derive from the word for "city", in ancient Greek and Latin respectively.

These days we use the word "politics" for situations when people divide into leaders and followers for purposes of organization and making decisions. This pervades our lives from elementary school to retirement home.

Over the past hundred years, few have articulated the political dimensions of Jupiter as well as Hannah Arendt.[111] You may recall her from our discussion of Mercury.

A Jewish refugee from Nazi Germany who eventually settled in the United States and fell in love with its democratic ideals, Arendt was a voluminous writer and a political theorist.

Arendt's Jupiter is exalted in Cancer, conjunct the Ascendant on one side and Neptune on the other. Jupiter is also configured with the Moon as the Moon's next aspect.

The house of the Ascendant is governed by the Moon in Virgo that has an opposition from Saturn; combined with Neptune, this is not an extraverted but a contemplative Jupiter. Although Arendt asserted the need for community involvement, she was personally reserved and loath to be celebrated or made notorious (eventually she would become both). Arendt was sociable with friends, students, and other writers, but rarely sat for television interviews: she disliked being recognized on the street by strangers. Although an "honored guest" as exalted in the sign Cancer, Jupiter is out of sect in her nocturnal chart. True to the nature of an introverted Jupiter, her place was in the public field of ideas, and she loved being a teacher, but strongly guarded her personal privacy.

Saturn in Pisces, with Jupiter as dispositor, forms a trine to Jupiter. Saturn's impact on Jupiter brought her to investigate and analyze oppressive antisemitism, genocide, and totalitarianism. She sought to learn our tendencies toward evil, human possibility and our self-destructiveness. With Saturn in the ninth house of philosophy and academia that is governed by Jupiter in her first house, Arendt worked with these questions

---
111 From birth certificate (AA)

Astrology and the Lives of People

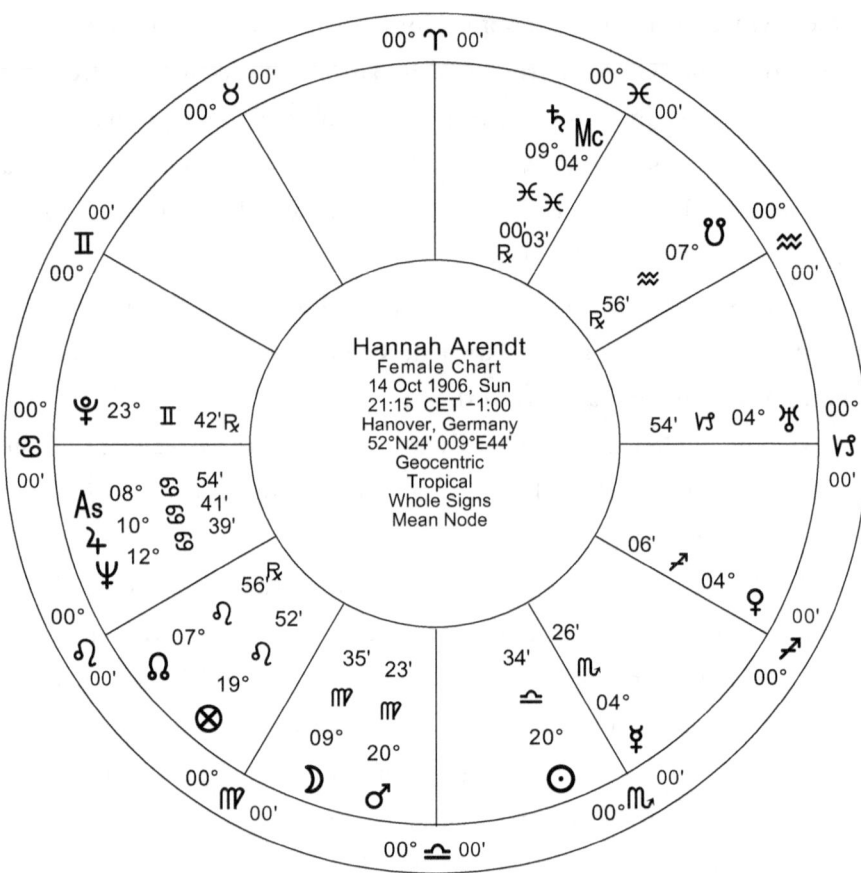

through the lens of history and philosophy. Hers were the musings of a jupiterian – but not jovial – person.

In accord with Jupiter's prominence, Arendt valued the sphere of public life. *The Human Condition* (1958) asserted that western thought has tended to promote the contemplative life over the active life, the individual (and its extension the "social") over the public. Her sense of the political life valued rhetoric, persuasion, and opinion that bring us into a public realm. We are capable of enormous creativity or great harm when, in exchanges with others, we respond to complex situations. These situations have uncertain outcomes which we are accountable for. We also detect a Jupiter-Neptune idealization of political process and the uncertainty it entails.

Jupiter's conjunction with Neptune also relates to her lifelong quest to find a place of belonging, a permanent mooring within the larger world. Before Hitler came to power in Germany, Arendt was involved with pro-Zionist causes, particularly gathering information about heightened Nazi anti-semitic inclinations. After one subsequent interrogation she had the good sense to flee the country and eventually found her way to the United States.

Eichmann in Jerusalem, discussed in the chapter on Mercury, soberly implies that none of us are very far from being conformist and thoughtless like Eichmann, and suggests that with the right circumstances in play, any of us could endeavor to make the Holocaust trains run efficiently. *Eichmann in Jerusalem* also shed a harsh light on German Jewish leaders for working too closely with the Nazis in the 1930s. This book instantly cost the author many friendships, especially among the American Jewish community of which she was a part. It took time for the uproar to die down.[112]

To what community did Hannah Arendt belong? I have this image of her in her New York apartment loudly taking on Aristotle, Kant, and many others, agreeing sometimes and arguing at other times. Her dialogue with past thinkers parallels her depiction of the active political life – ongoing, without predetermined destination, and timeless.

Politician in a Democracy

If Hannah Arendt as a political theorist embodied many features of Jupiter, Thomas "Tip" O'Neill embodied them as a politician.[113] During current divisive times in the United States, O'Neill has been the subject of

---

[112] Subsequent research has indicated that Eichmann was more psychologically abnormal than Arendt had supposed, yet her depiction of the complicity of many (including the Jewish leadership in Germany) with Hitler has been reaffirmed. Arendt's insights into evil's banality, and its challenging implications for all of us, seems more relevant today than they did sixty years ago.

[113] He has had his nickname "Tip" since childhood – it refers to the baseball strategy of a batter tipping pitched balls foul until the pitcher misses four times and the batter gets a "walk" – first base. Birth time "from memory", Rodden A

nostalgia for the political life as it used to be. As Speaker of the US House of Representatives in the late 1970s and 1980s, during a time in which conservativism was ascending, O'Neill fought hard to preserve liberal values but always with personal warmth and institutional decorum.

A biographer commented on his character as he depicted the first day of O'Neill becoming Speaker:

> "A matchless personality was the new Speaker's most profound political strength. His hat still fit him, as they said in his native North Cambridge. He remained an old shoe. Affable. Funny. Gregarious. Approachable. Genuine. A doer of favors. A spinner of tales. His personality was augmented by his physique. In his seventh decade, he was still a robust, big man, who at six feet three towered over most of his colleagues." [114]

O'Neill was born into a political family and at the age of fifteen was going door-to-door promoting the candidacy of Al Smith, an Irish Catholic like himself. After college and one failed political campaign, he was elected to the Massachusetts House of Representatives and eventually became its majority leader. In 1952 O'Neill ran for the US House of Representatives, fifteen years later he broke with Lyndon Johnson over the Vietnam War, and later helped engineer Nixon's resignation. By 1981 he was the most prominent Democratic leader left standing after Ronald Reagan's presidential victory the previous year. O'Neill continued as Speaker until his retirement in 1987.

O'Neill respected the outcome of elections and worked in good faith with those he disagreed with. He was a favorite at banquets and fund-raisers: warm, entertaining, and possessing a thousand personal and humorous anecdotes – or ten that he repeated one hundred times each. We all know this kind of character.

---

114 Farrell, John A.: Tip O'Neill and the Democratic Century (2001)

Tip O'Neill was able to connect with regular people easily and on their terms. His deft use of the common touch was accompanied by his well-known phrase that "all politics is local". He also understood, better than his conservative adversaries, that government decisions strongly impact the daily lives of people.

Astrologers who first see this man's natal chart are tempted to say, "What a lot of Sagittarius!" Planetary interactions help us sort through this crowded chart meaningfully.

The strong Jupiter-Moon conjunction helps us understand his strong personal touch that was inseparable from his political views and practice. He had adversaries and opponents but no enemies. (He admitted to disliking the young Georgia Representative Newt Gingrich who espoused a "take no

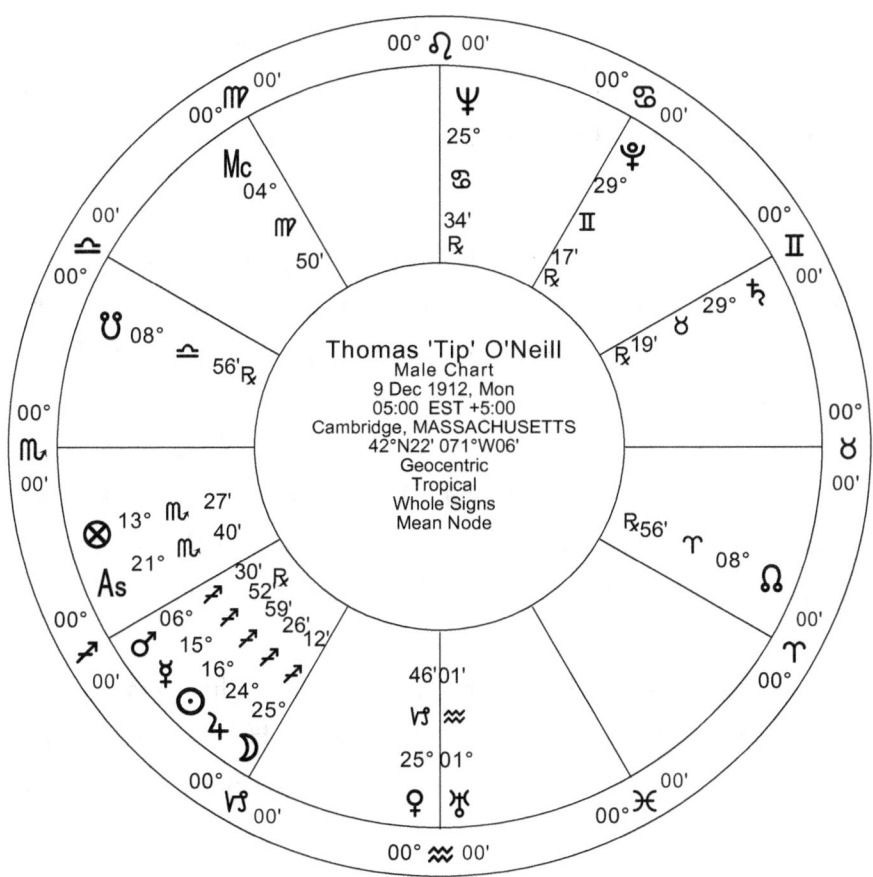

prisoners" approach that O'Neill detested.) Although fiery Sagittarius is well-known for its energy and inspiration, Moon-Jupiter together added a personal and sympathetic attitude.

O'Neill's Jupiter, in its own sign, is also dispositor for Sagittarian Mars, Mercury, and the Sun. It attests to his buoyant sense of belonging. He strongly identified with being Irish and Catholic and had an almost religious reverence for the American political system and valued his role within it. Mars, as ruler of his Scorpio Ascendant and his Lots of Fortune and Spirit, added drive and ambition to the mix.

His successful marriage is indicated by the mutual reception of Venus in Capricorn and Saturn in Taurus in the seventh house of marriage. He was married for 53 years to a woman who could be a political wife when necessary but was his equal in temperament, intelligence, and wit. This configuration, set apart from his Sagittarian cluster, divided his public from his private life and both lives were well served.

Authoritarian Alternatives

Benito Mussolini, the originator of the political approach called "fascism", set the mold for authoritarian leaders to follow. He was also a failed dictator who was killed by his own people toward the end of the Second World War. He was the sole ruler of his country for over twenty years.

Before making a disastrous alliance with Adolf Hitler, Mussolini strove to create a new Roman Empire through autocratic internal policies and military adventures abroad. Aided by paramilitary "black shirts", he came to power in the years following World War One, succeeding a weak liberal government.

Mussolini's astrological chart certainly shows his aggressive and ruthless side, yet Jupiter adds another dimension. He gives us a shadowy side of Jupiter, one that would use personal charisma and a patriotic image for political gain.

Big and Vast Jupiter

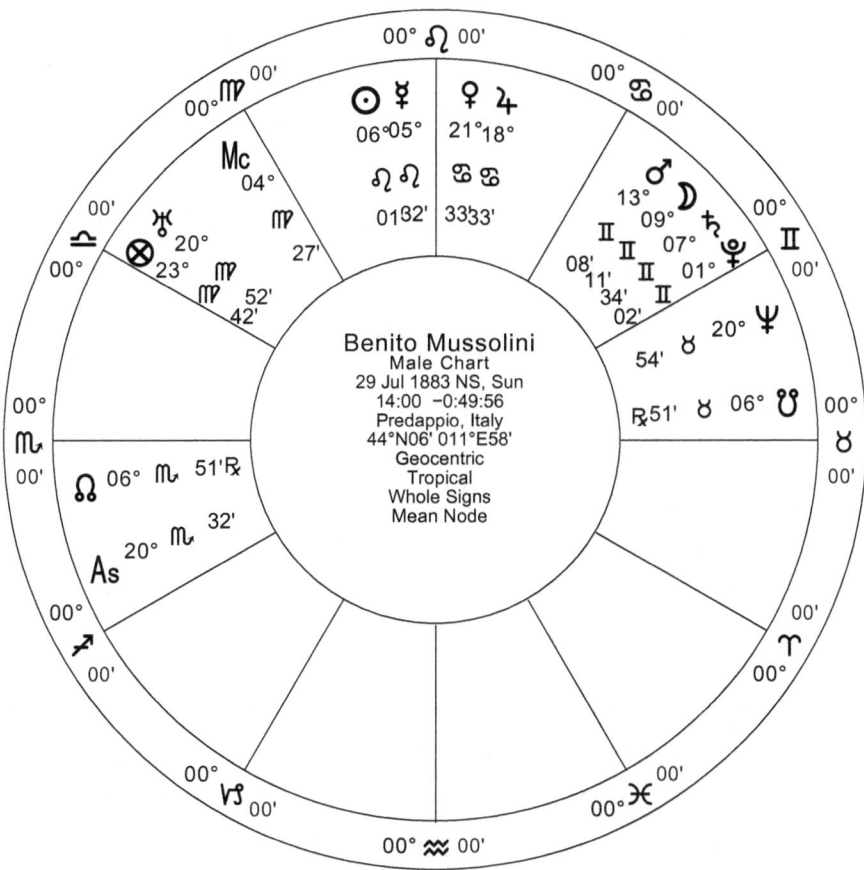

Jupiter in Cancer is in its sign of exaltation, conjunct Venus in its own triplicity, and in antiscion with the Moon that added a common touch. Mussolini had an ability to get others to feel that he was on their side even when he was only on his own side.[115]

Mussolini's Sun-Mercury combination in the sign Leo and in the tenth house could fill a room with personality and energy. He clearly enjoyed the cult of personality that he used along with authoritarian rule.

---

115 To bring another Jupiter placement closer to contemporary life: Donald Trump's Jupiter is in Libra, in trine to the Sun in Gemini and sextile to the Moon in Sagittarius. Jupiter is not strong by sign but its relationship to the luminaries help bring it into action to create a loyal following who also feel he is on their side.

Astrology and the Lives of People

Displaying his knowledge of Machiavelli's classic *The Prince*, Mussolini insisted that a dictator could be loved as long as he was also feared: "The crowd loves strong men. The crowd is like a woman." One author writes:

> "Mussolini lacked all nobility of character, but he knew the Italians and knew how to make them serve his ambition. He was always able to inspire confidence and make people think him sincere, whatever his beliefs or lack of them. Skill consciously employed was allied with a fascination he exerted almost unconsciously...With his bulbous and unsmiling face he created a legend of the strong man who was victorious and always right, the wise man who knew the innermost thoughts of people, the industrious servant of the public photographed toiling in the harvest field stripped to the waist...His most important quality was that of being a stupendous poseur." [116]

The Scorpio Ascendant has its ruler, Mars, in Gemini that is also the Moon's application. In the eighth house, Mars is disconnected from the Ascendant, and can operate differently or more extremely than one is able to manage. Nocturnal Mars is out of sect in Mussolini's diurnal chart, in a masculine sign and on the same side of the horizon as the Sun. Horary astrologers would also see Mussolini's Moon "besieged" between Mars and Saturn – this does not make for sweetness of disposition. Mars also relates to Mussolini's idealization of military leaders and his desire to be one – with disastrous consequences for his country and those he attempted to conquer.

An interesting comparison is with another authoritarian, Francisco Franco of Spain who was born a year earlier.[117] Franco was not a popular leader like his Italian peer but rose through the ranks of the military. With help from Italy and Germany, his army toppled Spain's republican

---

116 Smith, Denis. *Modern Italy: a Political History* (1997), p. 343, 344
117 Rated AA; quoted birth record

government in the late 1930s, and he governed his country for the next forty years. Franco had the common sense not to join with Hitler during the Second World War and managed a diplomatic and economic revival of his country afterwards. None of this redeems him from his role in the humanitarian crisis and bloodshed that followed his taking power.

A quick look at Franco's chart shows a fine collaboration between Jupiter and Mars that served him well: the two planets are in mutual reception by domicile and are closely symmetrical to the Aries/Libra axis. Jupiter is in its own triplicity, in Aries in a nocturnal chart. Additionally, Jupiter and the Sun are in another mutual reception: the Sun is in Jupiter's

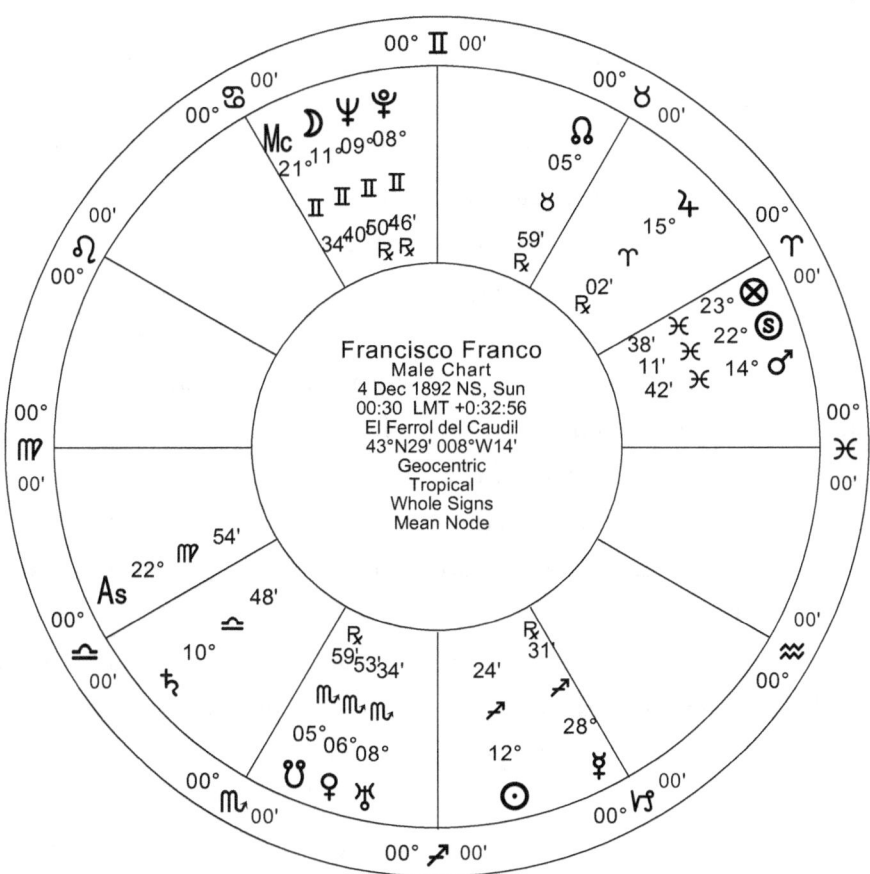

domicile and Jupiter is in the Sun's exaltation. Clearly, Franco was born to be a soldier and fit in well with a military establishment.

When we include Mars being in conjunction with Lots of Fortune and Spirit and in the seventh house: Franco loved a good fight. His chart displays a combination of Mars-like military acumen (he became a general at age 33), and Jupiter's grasp of a larger picture. This allowed him to seize power and stay in power for decades, leaving behind at best a mixed legacy. Upon Franco's death, Spain returned to democratic government and has stayed that way to this day.

Interlude: Jupiter and Hierarchy

We may think of hierarchy as saturnine, but it is important to acknowledge its jupiterian qualities. In our society, top-down command structures are not uncommon: they are in the military and among first responders such as police and firefighters, and often in the ranks of government and industry. We know about the camaraderie that often exists within those professions and the bonds that continue long past active service.

Let us turn back the clock a few thousand years, to ancient China. Confucius lived at a time of pervasive warfare and cultural disintegration and, as a corrective, emphasized hierarchical structures within a family, among those in government, and under Heaven. His emphasis was on the cultivation of personal virtues that would make for interpersonal harmony and for structures that accomplish good for the entire society, not just for those at the top. The *Analects,* compiled by his students after his death, is unsystematic in construction and consists of many interlocking concepts and their applications. It includes principles that make for a good citizen and a good ruler or leader, principles that are of the nature of Jupiter.

Analects 4.15 reduces the Sage's teachings to a "single thread" -- *dutifulness* tempered by *understanding.* The former term *zhong* is sometimes translated as "loyalty" or "giving effort". This concept seems akin to the Roman "pietas" through which one embraces responsibilities within a family or an outside structure. This could also manifest as the obligation of *remonstrance*: this delicate and often dangerous move to call one's superior to account for decisions or behaviors that are perceived as wrong in some way.

Dutifulness is accompanied by *shu* or "understanding" that is closer to our sense of lunar empathy: one adapts to specific situations and does not apply rules without considering their effect on real people. *Shu* is also described as not imposing on others what one would not want for oneself.

These two concepts together make for a good leader and a good citizen. A leader has duties and obligations to those above (including "Heaven") and those below. And, considering life's complexities, a leader must also apply the right amount of flexibility.

The Chinese *junzi* has been badly translated as "superior man" or "gentleman". Its original meaning referred to a member of a warrior aristocracy, but this was later rendered as any person who could lead others by example. The distinction was made between one who acts righteously, as opposed to the small-minded person who is interested mostly in personal gain.

Analects 12.20 makes a distinction between being "accomplished" and being "renowned". The accomplished person is fond of rightness, observes others' words and behavior, and considers the interests of those under him. The renowned person, however, only gives this appearance but violates it in actual conduct. This parallels traditional astrology's distinction between fortunate and unfortunate Jupiter placements.

Virtue is understood interpersonally and manifests as a kind of charisma, a gift from Heaven. In *Analects* 12.19, Confucius states that "If you desire goodness, then the common people will be good. The Virtue of a gentleman is like the wind, and the Virtue of a petty person is like the grass – when the wind moves over the grass, the grass is sure to bend." [118]

To the modern eye, the idea of a virtuous ruler bringing forth goodness in others is a "trickle-down" idea that works about as well as its counterpart in economic policy. More likely is a leader who appears virtuous, letting faults occur behind the scenes, while getting the best of all worlds. Machiavelli, who we will return to in the next chapter, equates the virtuous ruler with the ineffective one who will be taken advantage of by those who are less restrained.

Hierarchies are notoriously subject to ossification and abuse that render them cynically saturnine and oppressive to those lower down. Confucian doctrines were later used to maintain conformity and obedience to those in power and maintain an increasingly frozen meritocracy. Yet, like Arendt's idea of democracy and the active life of the citizen in the polis, hierarchical arrangements that are jupiterian can be both just and effective – if one's eyes stay wide open.

Nonpolitical Jupiter

A Different Kind of Crowd

Born Farrokh Bulsara, Freddie Mercury's musical talent came out early and unexpectedly. As the front man and chief songwriter for the British rock band Queen, his talent and charisma helped bring the group achieve worldwide fame. From the beginning, Mercury was interested in how the band appeared to audiences and how to add theatricality to its performances. Most jupiterian, however, was the band's role in promoting audience participation, fusing band and audience together rhythmically and in singalongs. "My voice", Mercury once said, "comes from the energy of the audience. The better they are, the better I get." [119]

---

118 Trans. Edward Slingerland, *Confucius Analytics* (2003), p. 134
119 Glimore, Mikal, "Queen's Tragic Rhapsody" *Rolling Stone Magazine,* July 2014

Big and Vast Jupiter

There is much to say about Freddie Mercury and his striking astrological chart; our interest here, however, is in his Venus-Jupiter combination. We see Venus's strong position here, not only the dispositor for both planets but also allied with the planet Mercury and the Ascendant in their symmetry with the Aries/Libra axis. [120]

Jupiter brought Freddie Mercury's musical gifts onto a larger stage, and a synchrony with crowds unrivaled so far in his profession. Examples

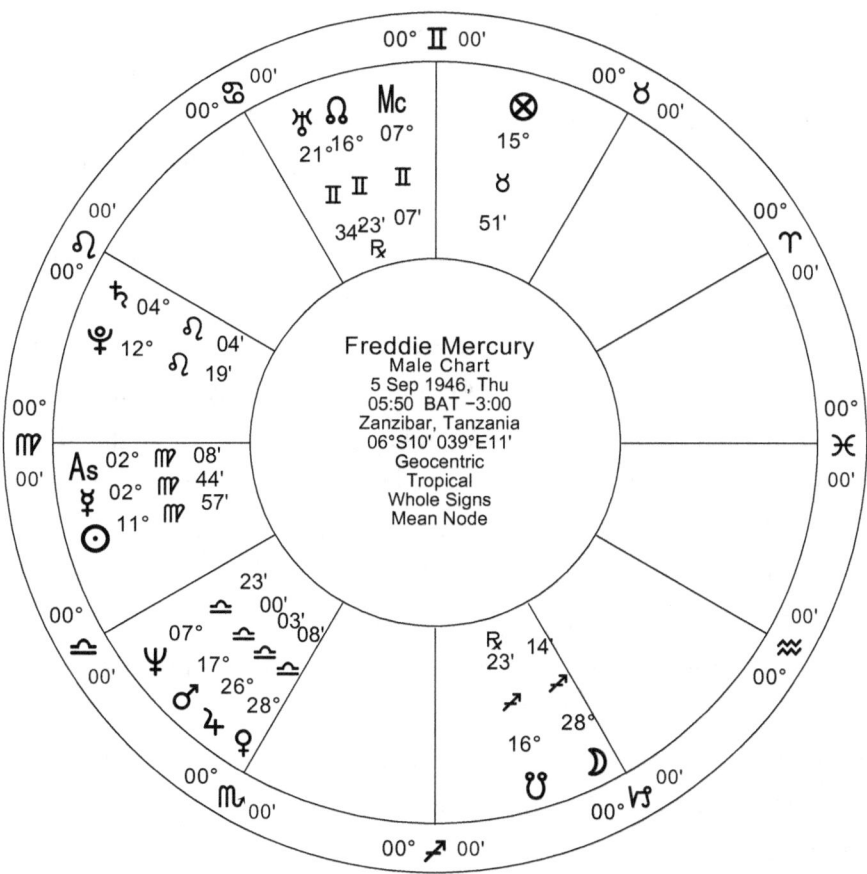

---

[120] There is dispute about Mercury's birthtime, as his birth certificate contains no time of birth. The astrodatabank site mentions the possibility that "Mercury" was chosen as his last name because of the planet rising in his natal chart. Other times given are 4:43 AM and a rectification for 4:46 AM.

are abundant, especially from his Live Aid performance in 1985 and his final performance in front of 200,000 people a year later. Benito Mussolini and Donald Trump would be envious.

Radically Inclusive Jupiter

Walt Whitman proclaimed fusion not with a particular audience but humanity and the cosmos itself. The poet's celebration of physical life and his overall sense of reality was all-inclusive, embracing suffering, ordinary heroism, and our tendencies toward both generosity and evil. Whitman was a poet, not a mystic or philosopher, yet Jupiter tells us much about what made his work distinctive.[121]

We can start with Mercury and Venus in Taurus that brought immediacy and concreteness to his verse. The vast ranges of scenes and people in "Song of Myself" are conveyed with immediacy and without comment.

Jupiter in Aquarius in the eleventh house, the house joy of Jupiter, is Mercury's next application. Without abandoning the immediacy of the Taurus influence, Jupiter in Aquarius gave Whitman a prophetic and visionary voice. Whitman's Jupiter is a conceptual and unifying factor as his Taurus planets revel in what is particular and immediate.

Whitman claimed full participation in his world. He left his peaceful life in New York to care for wounded soldiers during the American Civil War and engaged himself completely in this work. Later, his elegy to Abraham Lincoln "When Lilacs Last in the Dooryard Bloom'd" traces the train that carried the dead President's body across the country to a final resting place. Much of the power of Whitman's verse stems from this creative blending of concrete Mercury and inclusive Jupiter.

In contrast, James Joyce's chart and life show Jupiter's expression differently. Unlike Whitman, Joyce deliberately stood apart from the warfare and political chaos in the background of his life and times. Joyce

---

121 Birth data provided by native

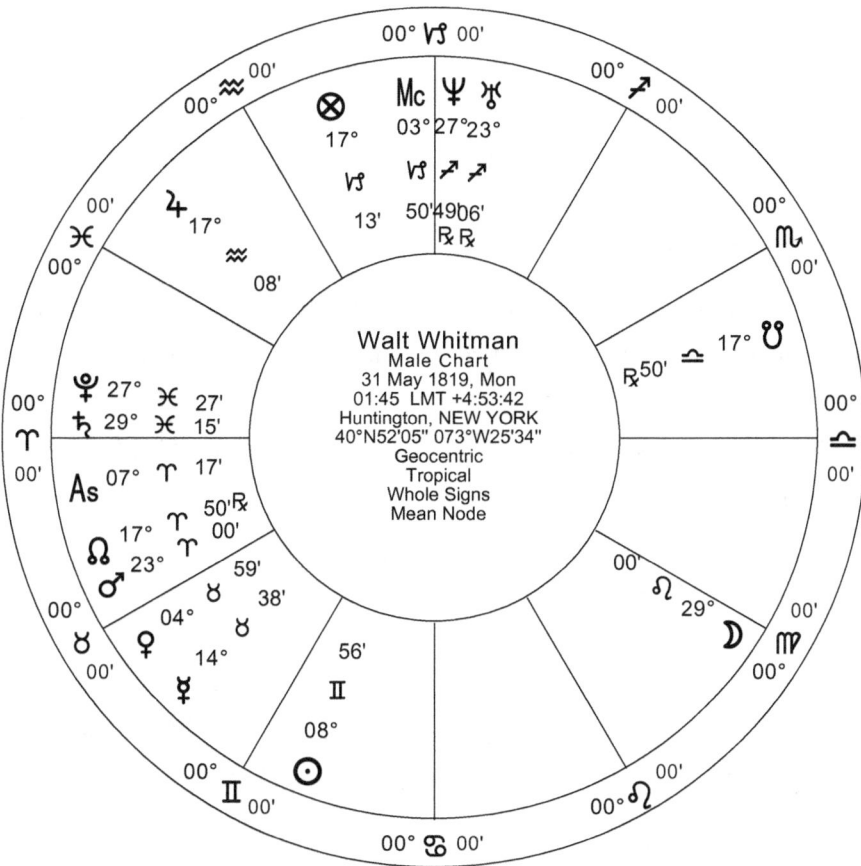

left Ireland in his early twenties and lived in Italy and Switzerland before settling in Paris. He was out of Ireland during its turbulent times preceding home rule and the partition of his country. He played no part in the cultural Celtic Revival and disliked Irish nationalism and cultural chauvinism.

Joyce's Jupiter is in Taurus, which might give Jupiter a narrow range, but it is in a close square to the Sun in broad-minded Aquarius. Both planets are closely symmetrical to the Aries/Libra axis and can find novel ways to express themselves.

Joyce's sense of inclusiveness was more defined than that of Whitman, limiting itself to western history and culture with added emphasis on his literary inheritance. While Joyce's novels are set in Dublin and they demand familiarity with some Irish history, his Irish roots are depicted within larger movements of history and humanity. Jupiter in Taurus gives Joyce's work a level of particularity that only strengthens the conceptual resonance of the Sun in Aquarius.

Limiting Jupiter

In the previous chapter we looked at Simone Weil's Ascendant with Mars and their dispositor Jupiter in Virgo in the tenth house. Jupiter, strong in its house position but weaker in Virgo, expressed itself in many ways. Weil's Jupiter drew its lines deliberately and, thanks to Mars, proclaimed them strongly.

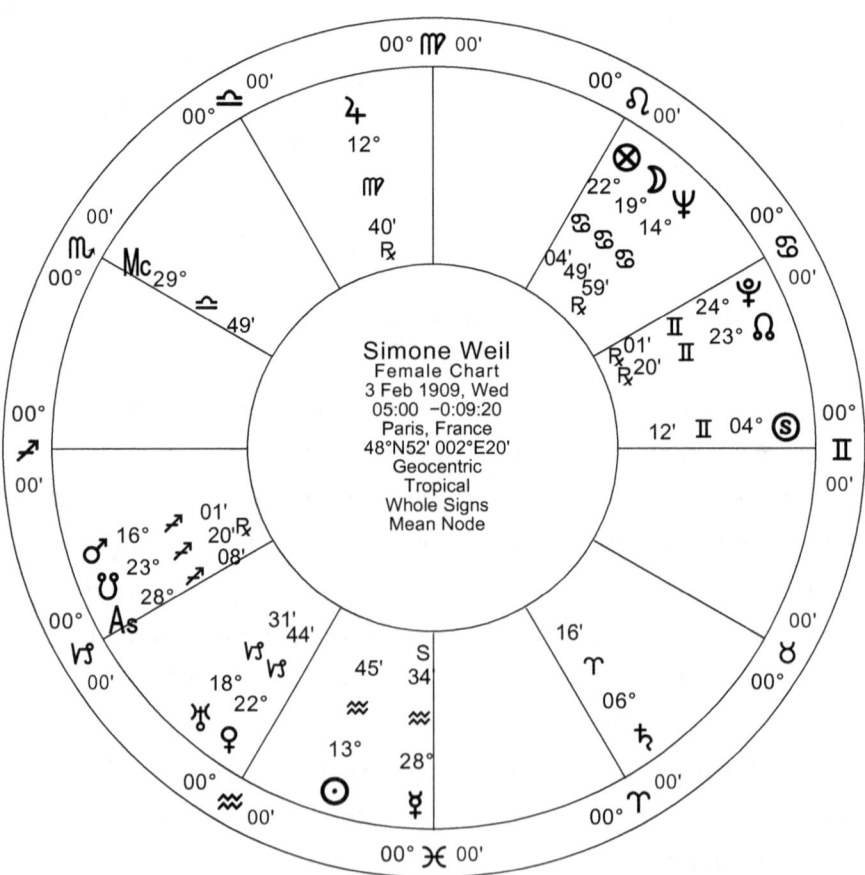

Jupiter led her to study patterns of history and culture in the light of her contemporary world, and its square to Mars brought both insight and a warrior's zeal. She likened the Roman Republic/Empire to the "Great Beast", the medieval Catholic Church as corrupted by Romanism, and Hitlerism as an extension of Roman and Catholic totalitarianism. She contrasted the "true" renaissance of medieval southern France (before the suppression of the Albigensian religion) to the "false" renaissance that began in fifteenth-century Italy. Most startling of all, considering her Jewish family background, was her dismissal of "Hebraism" as a form of religious nationalism.

Weil's historical assessments strike many as outrageous and unfair. However, everybody gains from a perspective that invites a good argument that breaks down stereotypes and leads to greater understanding. Perhaps this is how a strident Mars allied with a sharply defined Jupiter can work together.

"On the Abolition of All Political Parties"
Weil was attuned to and repelled by our ability to lose ourselves in our affiliations. Toward the end of her life and as the tide was turning against the Nazis, plans for post-war France were being made. Her country's pre-war political lines were beginning to emerge from the ashes of catastrophic defeat. A few passages from her article on political parties should suffice to demonstrate Jupiter square Mars:

> "Political parties are a marvelous mechanism which, on the national scale, ensures that not a single mind can attend to the effort of perceiving, in public affairs, what is good, what is just, what is true. As a result – except for a small number of fortuitous coincidences, nothing is decided, nothing is executed, but measures that run contrary to the public interest, to justice and to truth. If one were to entrust the

> organization of public life to the devil, he could not invent a more clever device."[122]

Political parties are notorious for suppressing contrary attitudes and the subordinating vision to a quest for power. Imagine, she writes, of any politician today saying this: "Whenever I shall have to examine any political or social issue, I swear I will absolutely forget that I am the member of a certain political group; my sole concern will be to ascertain what should be done in order to best serve the public interest and justice." It's more likely that somebody will say, "As a socialist..." or "As a conservative...." and short-circuit activity that could come from an independent mind. She likens this to previous efforts by the Catholic Church against heresies; indeed, a political party is "a small secular church that wields its own menace of excommunication."[123]

> "Nearly everywhere – often even when dealing with purely technical problems – instead of thinking, one merely takes sides: for or against. Such a choice replaces the activity of the mind. This is an intellectual leprosy; it originated in the political world and then spread through the land, contaminating all forms of thinking."[124]

Weil's proposed solutions to this problem are impractical yet her message is strong and clear. Her message is not only relevant to our own times but points to problems with Jupiter's tribalism. One-sided political parties, along with corrupt or malignant leadership, are here to stay: how does one respond without becoming complicit and losing one's moral compass?

Alongside her jupiterian tendencies, reinforced by Mars, it's hard not to detect a tough-minded saturnian quality. At first glance Saturn seems

---

[122] Translated Leys, Simon (2013) p. 24
[123] p. 26
[124] p. 34

rather handicapped in its sign of fall or depression and disconnected from other planets.

My Hellenistic astrology friends, using Lots derived from the Lots of Spirit and Fortune and from Jupiter and Saturn, will notice a remarkable symmetry in Weil's chart. For her nocturnal chart, the jupiterian *Lot of Victory* takes the distance between Jupiter in Virgo and the Lot of Spirit at four Gemini; casting that number from the Ascendant degree, the Lot of Victory falls exactly on Weil's Saturn placement! The saturnine Lot of Nemesis takes the distance from her Lot of Fortune in Cancer and Saturn in Aries, cast that number from the Ascendant degree, and the Lot of Nemesis falls exactly on her Jupiter placement! Here is somebody with original and profound perspectives who lived during a difficult with very limited personal success within her lifetime. This also manifested in the uncompromising candor that pervades her writings.

Facing down Jupiter's tendencies toward naivety and hypocrisy, Saturn offers hard paths that have been well-traveled over the centuries, that have saved many a soul from complicit thoughtlessness, corruption, and malignancy. Because it is Saturn, however, it demands a high price. We now depart for those darker regions to conclude our examination of the seven visible planetary bodies.

Chapter Eleven

Saturn's Solitary Realm

Jove's Executioner

Saturn's visibility and path in the night sky contrast strongly with that of Jupiter. If Jupiter's glow is bright, that of Saturn is pale. If Jupiter moves through a sign of the zodiac in one year and twelve years to go around the zodiac, Saturn takes about two and a half years to go through a sign and twenty-nine years to go around the entire zodiac. This slower and more sluggish planet is cast as the Greater Malefic, representing features of our lives that are less inspiring and more confining than those of Jupiter. Saturn and Jupiter, the Greater Malefic and the Greater Benefic, may feel like contradictory principles, but when they work together, outcomes can be very positive.

Jupiter speaks the language of inclusion and has the power of common purpose, a perspective that is broad and hopeful. Saturn deals with exclusions and boundaries, its language is "tough love". This planet reminds us that not only does reality rarely conform to our confident expectations, but usually endeavors to thwart them. If Jupiter responds in the affirmative to the question of whether the universe is friendly, Saturn assumes no such thing.

If Jupiter displays possibilities, Saturn takes us into forced choices where no alternative is wholly satisfactory. For example, most of us have worked with a boss who is less intelligent, resourceful, or sensitive than we are. What happens when we do our jobs better than they do theirs, but they're in charge and they get the larger paycheck and can even fire us?

When this comes up with a client, I sometimes respond that working gracefully with this kind of situation is a sign of maturity. Sometimes, however, the situation is more dire. What if the higher-up or the organization itself is malevolent or conflicts with our moral values, our sense of what is right? This is more difficult, and glib responses or comforting words of wisdom are not helpful. There are no good alternatives.

Castiglione's *Book of the Courtier*, previously discussed in the chapter on Venus, states that this situation may have life or death consequences for the subordinate courtier. In Book Two, the conversation turns to one who falls into service of the wicked. Should the courtier continue working for someone "vicioso e maligno" or should he leave?

Leaving service is one option, and many of us have done this, but this option was less available and more dangerous in Castiglione's time. Today, if we decide to leave a position of prominence, our careers may be in tatters, but our tell-all books sell well.

Castiglione suggests some ways to stay in service and also comply with seemingly difficult situations. For example, a courtier may not understand the complexity of what appears to be an unethical command, and one should have greater trust in one's superior. Alternatively, one may alter commands on the sly, but this can have dire consequences for the subordinate courtier.

In Book Four (Chapter 46), Castiglione offers a jupiterian solution:

> "Since, as we have already said, our habits are formed according to our actions, and virtue consists in action, it is neither impossible nor surprising that the Courtier should lead the prince to many virtues, such as justice, generosity, magnanimity, the practice of which the prince can easily recognize and so acquire the habit of them; which the Courtier cannot do, because he does not have the means of practicing them;

and thus the prince, let to virtue by the Courtier, can become more virtuous than the Courtier." [125]

Being a model of virtue to one's superiors is indeed noble. It is possible to stimulate change around us by setting a good example for others. A saturnian point of view, however, asks how often this really happens and whether the notion is hopelessly naïve.

Today we have examples of whistleblowers, those who have exposed malfeasance and corruption of their bosses and organization often at great personal cost. We have the press or watchdog agencies to report to anonymously. We laud whistleblowers as heroes but most of us would be reluctant to follow the same path as they. These individuals are not uranian, as some astrologers might claim, but saturnine in a virtuous way: they have chosen to go it alone over compliance with what was wrong.

The *Analects* of Confucius mentions the action of remonstrance that we discussed in the previous chapter. Yet according to the Sage, if this fails, one is to go along with the superior's final judgement. But what happens when the authority has lost the Way? Book 8.13 considers alternatives. Extreme situations may leave self-imposed exile as the only option.

> The Master said, "Be sincerely trustworthy and love learning, and hold fast to the good Way until death. Do not enter a state that is endangered, and do not reside in a state that is disordered. If the Way is being realized in the world then show yourself; if it is not, then go into reclusion. In a state that has the Way, to be poor and of low status is a cause for shame; in a state that is without the Way, to be wealthy and honored is equally a cause for shame." [126]

---

125 *Book of the Courtier*, trans. Charles S. Singleton, from Norton Critical Edition, ed. Daniel Javitch. (2002) Book II, Chapter 22
126 Slingerland translation, p. 82

Voluntary or involuntary, the life of exile is the antithesis of Jupiter's hopeful inclusiveness but may serve a greater purpose in the long run. Even without physical withdrawal one may need to flee toxic connections by establishing inner isolation. Otherwise, by remaining and being silent, one may survive but at the cost of one's soul.

Finding Some Balance

Astrology clients sometimes come to me after hearing about the Saturn placement in their charts or fearful about some upcoming Saturn transits. This places me in the awkward role of being a Saturn whisperer. A nuanced approach to this planet will acknowledge and validate its difficult realities but also suggest positive outcomes – if one is undeterred by temporary disappointment and is unafraid of hard work.

Marsilio Ficino, whose chart we noted previously and whose chart we'll consider below, contrasts sequestered Saturn with the more cheerful and communal Sun and Jupiter. Ficino cast Saturn as the planet of "scholars", those who do not lead an ordinary life but one of contemplation. Such a life is often accompanied by setting oneself apart from others.

> "For just as the Sun is hostile to nocturnal animals, but friendly to the diurnal, so Saturn is hostile to those people who are either leading an ordinary life or even to those fleeing the company of the crowd but not laying aside ordinary emotions. For Saturn has relinquished the ordinary life to Jupiter; but he claims for himself a life sequestered and divine. To the minds of those who are truly sequestered as much as possible, he is in a friendly way, as to his kinfolk." [127]

---

127 *Three Books on Life,* Kaske and Clarke translation, "On Obtaining Life from the Heaven", Chapter 22, p. 365

Astrology and the Lives of People

What Tradition Also Says

Saturn is cold and dry, the planet of earth, associated with graves and digging, depth in the graveyard and depth of intellect. Saturn is the planet of anything old, from the venerated and wise to the jaded and decayed. Traditional sources give to Saturn qualities of corruption and fraud, apartness from others, but also an inward life.

Abu Ma'shar's *Abbreviated* and *Great Introductions* were important for later medieval astrology. Saturn is not a nice fellow but does have some positive features.

> "... when he shows provisions, he shows much; and when he takes away, he takes away much; greedy; a pilgrim in faraway and cold places; having one thing in his mouth [but] another in his heart; occupied in evil; a traitor; solitary; a forcer, plunderer, torturer, jailer; but truth-telling, understanding, making things old." [128]

After discussing anger, fettering, and prison, Abu Ma'Ashar continues:

> "... also truth in words, and esteem, and prudence and understanding, and experience, and offense, and obstinacy, and a multitude of thoughts and a depth of counsel, and stubbornness in [his] method. He does not easily get angry, and if he were angry he would not be able to rule his own mind. He wishes good to no one."

A few centuries later, Al-Biruni describes the Greater Malefic:

> Disposition and Manners: "Fearful, timid, anxious, suspicious, miserly, a malevolent plotter, sullen and proud, melancholy, truth-telling, grave, trusty, unwilling to believe good of anyone, engrossed in his own affair and consequently

---
[128] See Ben Dykes trans. *Introduction to Traditional Astrology* (2010) p. 235

indicates discord, and either ignorance or intelligence, but the ignorance is concealed."

Activities, Instincts, and Morals: "Exile and poverty, or wealth acquired by his own trickery or that of others, failure in business, vehemence, confusion, seeking solitariness, enslaving people by violence or treachery, fraud, weeping and wailing and lamentation." [129]

On the slightly more positive side, Guido Bonatti of the thirteenth century notes Saturn's fixity of mind but a kind of integrity.

"And if a Saturnian man undertook to esteem someone (which rarely happens), he will esteem him with true esteem. And if he undertook to hate someone (which often happens), he will hate him with extreme hatred, and will hardly or never desist from hatred...And Albuaz said that if he were of good condition, it signifies profoundness of knowledge, and good and deep counsel, such as another hardly or never know how to improve on it." [130]

During times of difficulty, Saturn can be helpful. Not expecting luck to bail us out can be a gift: one accesses seriousness, frugality, conscientiousness, humility, being careful with one's time and energy, and curtailing overdependence on others. Saturnine people can be untrusting, never naïve, and rarely fooled by anybody's honeyed tongue, purported bank account and connections, or pretty face and figure. Saturn is the jaded planet.

---

[129] Ramsay Wright translation p. 250, 251
[130] Benjamin Dyes translation, p. 150-1

Saturn and Grit

Saturn, influenced in the wrong way by Mars, can become oppressive or dominating. Mars, influenced in the wrong way by Saturn, can become suppressive, driving one's energy inward toward self-destructiveness. However, these two malefics, when acting well together, can produce good outcomes.

They add up to what some psychologists call "grit" which has been correlated with career achievement and prominence. Although innate talent cannot be excluded as an ingredient of adult accomplishment, one must add direction or intention and excitement (the Sun and Mars) and perseverance and self-control (Saturn) while making appropriate adaptations along the way (the Moon and Mercury).

In her book *Grit*, Angela Duckworth gives a snapshot of these qualities. Duckworth's emphasis is on an achievement that is unafraid of confronting one's limitations.

> "Why were the highly accomplished so dogged in their pursuits? For most, there was no realistic expectation of ever catching up to their ambitions. In their own eyes, they were never good enough. They were the opposite of complacent. And yet, in a very real sense, they were satisfied being unsatisfied...
>
> "In sum, no matter what the domain, the highly successful had a kind of ferocious determination that played out in two ways. First, these exemplars were unusually resilient and hardworking. Second, they knew in a very, very deep way what it was they wanted. They not only had determination, they had direction."[131]

---

131 Duckworth, Angela. *Grit* (2016), p. 8

Saturn's Solitary Realm

What follows are some examples of positive saturnine "gritty" qualities exemplified by some historical figures who have important Saturn placements.

Many-Splendored Saturn

Sarah Bernhardt, born in 1844, was the most famous actress of her time. Her astrological chart shows much theatricality – the Moon in Aries, ruler of the Ascendant, is with unpredictable and willful Uranus, opposing Mars.[132] On and off stage, Bernhardt displayed energy and drive – under her command.

Bernhardt was the "illegitimate" child of a Paris courtesan and had unclear paternity. At convent school she learned impeccable diction (see Mercury-Venus mutual reception and symmetry to the Aries-Libra axis). As she was entering adulthood with few prospects for success in polite society, she was set up for an audition at an acting school. Bernhardt's voice alone was enough to secure her a position there.

Unusual in appearance and not conventionally pretty, her career began slowly but then accelerated. She moved from one acting company to the next more prestigious one, breaking contracts frequently and courting wealthy men when it was to her advantage. By the time celebrity arrived for her, she was given sole authority over all productions in which she appeared. She answered the problem of incompetent or unethical bosses through breathtaking ambition and maintaining tight-fisted personal control.

Saturn appears prominently in her chart, gloomily out of sect but in its own sign Aquarius, in partile square to the Sun in Scorpio and a trine to Mars in Libra. As with her acting, Bernhardt displayed aggressiveness or charm or seductiveness as needed, and she was always in charge.

---

132 Born 23 October 1844 at 8:00 PM, according to biographical information. B on Rodden scale. Information about Bernhardt's life taken from Robert Gottlieb, "The Drama of Sarah Bernhardt", *New York Review of Books* May 17 2007.

Astrology and the Lives of People

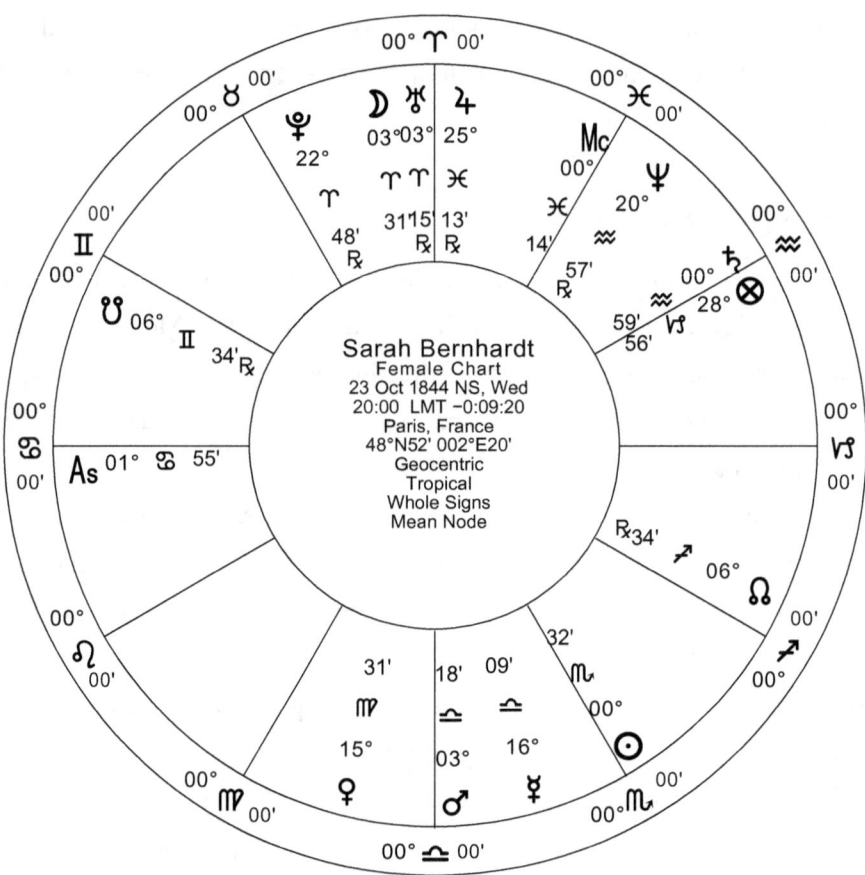

Bernhardt's chart also shows Jupiter in contrast to Saturn. Jupiter is in its own sign in Pisces and is the ruler of her Lot of Spirit in Sagittarius. As a world-wide celebrity, engaging many tours around the world, Bernhard was famous for a string of lovers and many associations with the internationally famous and powerful. She was ambitious but not cynical, using her celebrity to promote causes important to her, including weighing in on the French political controversy known as the Dreyfus Affair.

Mirroring Saturn's tendency to endure, at the age of seventy and with one leg recently amputated, Bernhardt performed her last concert tour. She seemed to relish her work to the very end, and people lined the streets for her funeral in 1923.

More Titans of Saturn

Ficino vs. Savonarola

You may recall how many influences there were on Marsilio Ficino's writings: conventional Catholicism, Neoplatonism, astrology, magic, music, medicine, and today what we call psychology.

Saturn makes a strong appearance in his chart, in its own sign Aquarius and conjunct the Ascendant. In an exchange of letters in which he describes the influence of Saturn, after disclosing (incorrectly) planetary positions in his astrological chart, he writes about himself:

> "I have very little desire for mortal goods, since I am in truth
> too fearful of the surrounding evils, which you reprove in me

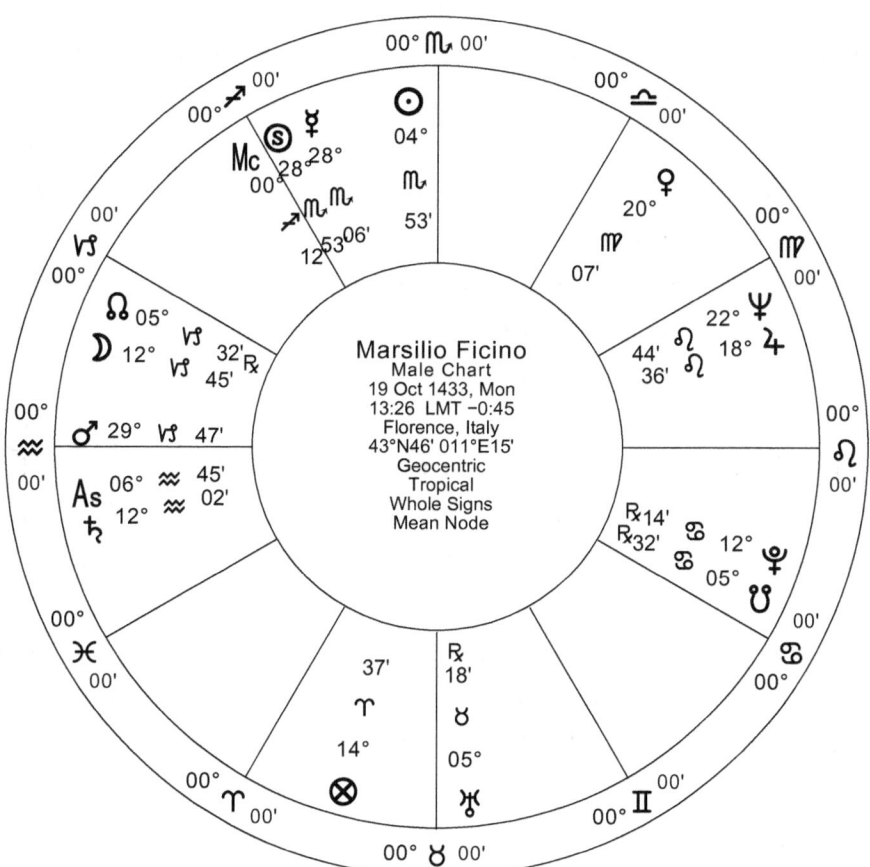

> from time to time. I accuse a certain melancholy disposition, a thing which seems to me to be very bitter unless, having been softened, it may in a measure to be made sweet for us by frequent use of the lyre." [133]

We may add to Ficino's melancholic disposition the Moon in the twelfth house in Capricorn, governed by Saturn, and opposite Pluto: this brings tenacity but coldness, some hidden emotional difficulties, and personal austerity. Saturn is also one his four planets in fixed signs and angular houses. Extraordinary focus helped him weave together many intellectual threads and not become scattered and incoherent, although consistency was not always his strong suit.

During his most productive times, Ficino had an unsteady but successful relationship with city leader Lorenzo de Medici ("the Great") whose fortunes were declining – as was the city's economy. After Lorenzo's death in 1492, Ficino's situation became complicated, as his love of classical learning and intellectual refinement increasingly clashed with new political and cultural trends in Florence.

A strong catalyst for division in the city was the Dominican preacher, Gerolamo Savonarola. His sermons against godlessness, materialism, and the oligarchic rule of the Medici, found many followers – including some closest to Ficino. Savonarola's public identity was of a holy man, a divine seer with prophetic powers and a strident delivery, utter certainty in his message, and an austere personal lifestyle. Part of the preacher's message was apocalyptic: the second coming was near, and Florence could be the new Jerusalem if purified of its sinfulness.

Ficino, who instead wanted Florence to be the new Athens, was finding himself marginalized. He responded first by finding areas of agreement with Savonarola when he could and quietly continuing his own work.

---

[133] *Meditations on the Soul: Selected Letters of Marsilio Ficino*, p. 160

Saturn's Solitary Realm

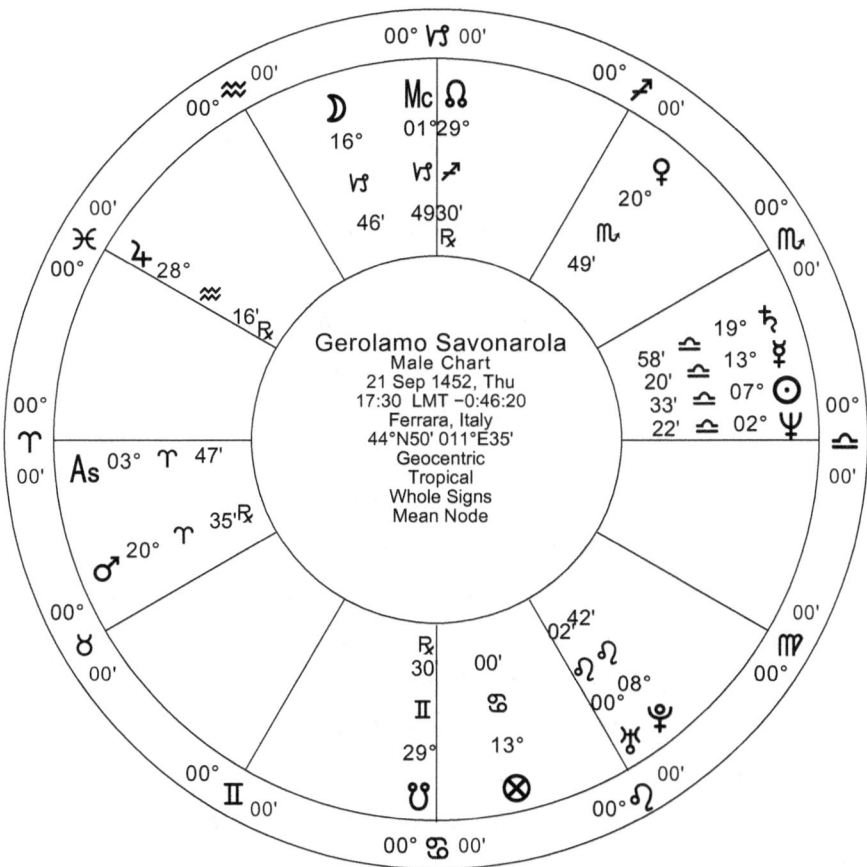

Savonarola's chart also shows a strong Saturn.[134] The Moon in Capricorn (close in degree to that of Ficino's Moon in the same sign) squares Saturn in its sign of exaltation in Libra that is also conjunct Mercury. If one expects a conciliatory and pleasing "Libran" here, they would wrong.

Equally important is Mars in Aries, in the first house and also in aspect with the Moon and Saturn, adding a strong will and stormy self-display. After a lackluster beginning to his preaching career, Savonarola

---

134 Sources differ on his birthtime, with some giving a time slightly earlier that would have a Pisces ascendant. 5:30 PM, a time favored by most sources, speaks more clearly about the man and his character.

took on Mars in full, becoming increasingly fierce and, in its aspect from Saturn, unyielding.

In 1494, when Savonarola became the guiding light of a new republican government, his increasing stridency supported "moral legislation" that was enforced by bands of youthful believers and included the infamous "bonfire of the vanities." Florence had become a combination of a republic and a theocracy: a contradictory and unstable mixture.

Savonarola's rise and subsequent fall mirrors Florence's political instability, the city's economic difficulties, and tensions with the French king and with the Pope. Savonarola's diatribes against the "Antichrist" Pope Alexander VI resulted in excommunication in the spring of 1497, one that the preacher publicly defied. At that time Saturn was at 18 degrees of Aries and Mars was in square from Capricorn: transiting Saturn and Mars were both transiting his Mars-Saturn opposition! Problematic transits would continue as Mars and Saturn both had retrograde periods in the following months. Malefics were piling upon malefics: if only the preacher had not rejected astrology as ungodly, perhaps knowledge of these transits could have convinced him to downshift a bit and weather the storm.

By this time Savonarola had aroused so much animosity, however, that his influence began to wane, in spite of some fervent remaining support. In a sequence of events involving an abortive trial by fire, he was executed in May 1498 in the center of the city. Transiting Saturn had finally moved off his natal Mars-Saturn opposition. At his execution, however, transiting Jupiter in Capricorn had gone retrograde and was no longer protecting his Moon, but Mars in Aries was square natal Moon: a death of the body (Moon) by fire (Mars).

Back to melancholic and careful Marsilio Ficino: with natal Saturn conjunct the Ascendant and the Moon in Capricorn opposing Pluto, he was not going to involve himself recklessly in public affairs. During the years of Savonarola's dominance, Ficino had become a shell of his former self. He was neither comfortable in his villa outside the city nor in the city itself, due to threats of plague outside the city and threats of violence inside the city. Slowly, as Savonarola's influence waned, Ficino became increasingly oppositional in public toward the monk and his followers.

Ficino published a diatribe against the preacher, but not until after Savonarola's execution. He unleashed a barrage of enmity against Savonarola, the "Antichrist Girolamo of Ferrara, greatest of all hypocrites". Since controversies about Savonarola did not end with his death, Ficino releasing his essay was somewhat daring. Yet our saturnine scholar could have acted sooner. Marsilio Ficino died in the year following Savonarola's death, in 1499.

One of History's Great Job Applications
After the deaths of the scholar and the preacher, Florence continued as a republic. This was to the advantage of one brilliant young man who got a job as counselor and ambassador, and who later made an enduring contribution to Western political theory. We met Nicolo Machiavelli previously on Mercury and now we call him to Saturn.

Machiavelli's saturnine nature is easy to see. The Moon in Aquarius is governed by Saturn by domicile (and by Mercury by exaltation and triplicity) and is in a strong applying square to Saturn in Taurus.

Saturn is his Ascendant ruler and is in a favorable position by house and rises from the Sun. Saturn also has a trine from Pluto that also casts its dark shadow on Mercury in Gemini by square. His had an intense and impersonal style, a distrust of sentimentality, and a dispassionate nature. However, he had no idea how to play the political game for his own benefit.

Machiavelli had abundant experience with what he called the malignancy of fortune. His political ascent occurred around the time of his Saturn return, with both Uranus and Pluto transiting his Sun. At that time, Jupiter in Capricorn was conjunct his natal Ascendant and square Uranus – this gives sudden abundance, but also suggests that he should watch his back.

Astrology and the Lives of People

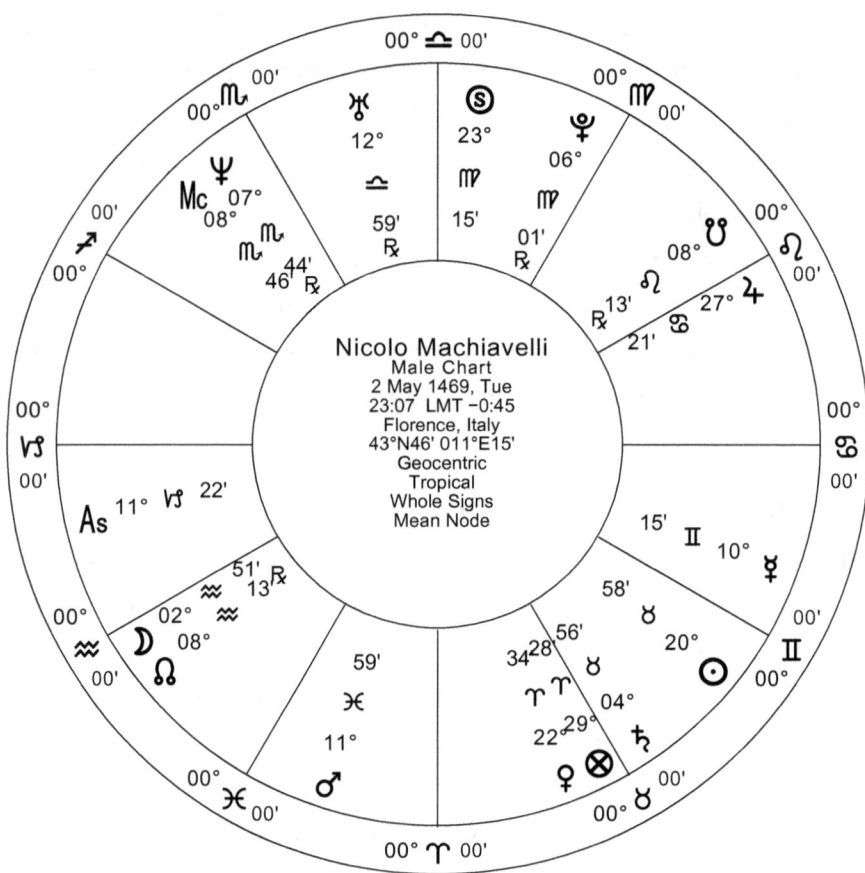

Fast-forward about fifteen years to the autumn of 1512: Machiavelli's previous development of a city militia had backfired, the Spanish army was on its way to Florence, the city leader had fled, and the Medici family was returning. Machiavelli was fired, later arrested and briefly tortured, and by spring 1513 he was on his family farm outside the city attempting to make his living off the land. In these months transiting Saturn in Scorpio was in square to Moon in Aquarius and opposing natal Saturn in Taurus. This time Jupiter was nowhere in sight.

A famous letter from him tells of his evenings. After he finished the day's labor and removed his soiled working clothes, he put on his better clothes and retired to his study to ponder and converse with the ancients and their writings. He began working on *The Prince*.

Machiavelli dedicated *The Prince* to the Medici leader of Florence of the time, in the hope of winning favor. When yet another Medici took over, he reworked *The Prince* and composed an (obsequious or ironic) dedicatory letter to the new leader. Our out-of-favor counselor proposed to help Lorenzo (not the Great) Medici achieve the goal of uniting Italy against the outside "barbarian" nations looking to carve it up.

The Prince remained untouched, the author never received an audience with the city ruler, and only years later, after other projects were undertaken, did Machiavelli return to government service but in a relatively low position. After the author died in 1527, others recognized the book's importance and the rest is history.

Hoover Held the Same Government Job for Forty-Eight Years

Would our Florentine political theorist have envied J. Edgar Hoover who became his own power center and could easily have had *The Prince* by his bedside? Although Machiavelli admired Cesare Borgia's brass-knuckle tactics if his goal was to unite Italy, I suspect he would not have cared for this modern man and his motivations. Hoover ran America's Federal Bureau of Investigation from 1924 until his death in 1972.

Throughout Hoover's decades-long directorship of the FBI, he carefully promoted his reputation as a heroic crime-fighter and protector of "truth, justice, and the American way," to quote a television program whose reruns were popular when I was young. Hoover was protector of an America that was white, protestant, and endowed with "traditional" values that were oppressively saturnine, emphasizing obedience to authority and institutions of traditional culture and government.

Hoover's career began in 1919 when he became head of the agency carrying out the Palmer Raids; its mission was to intimidate and disrupt the work of domestic radicals (like Emma Goldman and Dorothy Day). Hoover maintained his aversion to radicals from the left from that time onward.

Only during the final years of Hoover's life and after his death has the public discovered the extent of his abuses of power. He was found to have authorized illegal wiretaps, used the FBI to intimidate and disrupt leftist groups and and their supporters, monitored the activities of civil rights advocates, and did everything he could to limit the influence of Martin Luther King. Many Presidents toyed with the idea of dismissing Hoover but did not do so because of his vast power.

J. Edgar Hoover's chart is a delight to any interested astrologer.[135] The Sun in Capricorn is on the Ascendant with Mercury and Venus nearby, all governed by Saturn in Scorpio, close to both the Midheaven degree and the Lot of Fortune. His personal demeanor and public image are clearly that of toughness, a no-nonsense approach to himself and his work.

Mercury sextile Saturn shows his embrace of the technology of his time to make the FBI a modern and sophisticated crime-fighting organization. Adding the influence of Mars in Taurus, in trine to Mercury and opposing Saturn and the Midheaven degree, we get a professional style of slow-acting ferocity.

Although Hoover presented himself one-dimensionally his astrology reveals otherwise. The Moon in Pisces is governed by a relatively weak Jupiter in Gemini in the sixth house. The Moon is also conjunct Lot of Spirit and would represent Hoover from a more inward perspective. No, I'm not saying he was a sensitive guy, but that he was anxiously committed to his own institutional survival and maintenance. Squares from Pluto and Neptune can only add to inner fearfulness. The Moon applies to his Capricorn Sun in sextile: the Sun can survive through toughness and a

---

[135] Original account of Hoover's birth data was originally from a diary Hoover kept, although a biography lists his birth time as 7:00 AM and his Capricorn Ascendant would remain. However, there is mystery and confusion, since no birth certificate has been found and there is discrepant documentation. See https://www.astro.com/astro-databank/Hoover,_J._Edgar for the details. For our purposes I stay with the birth data originally given for him.

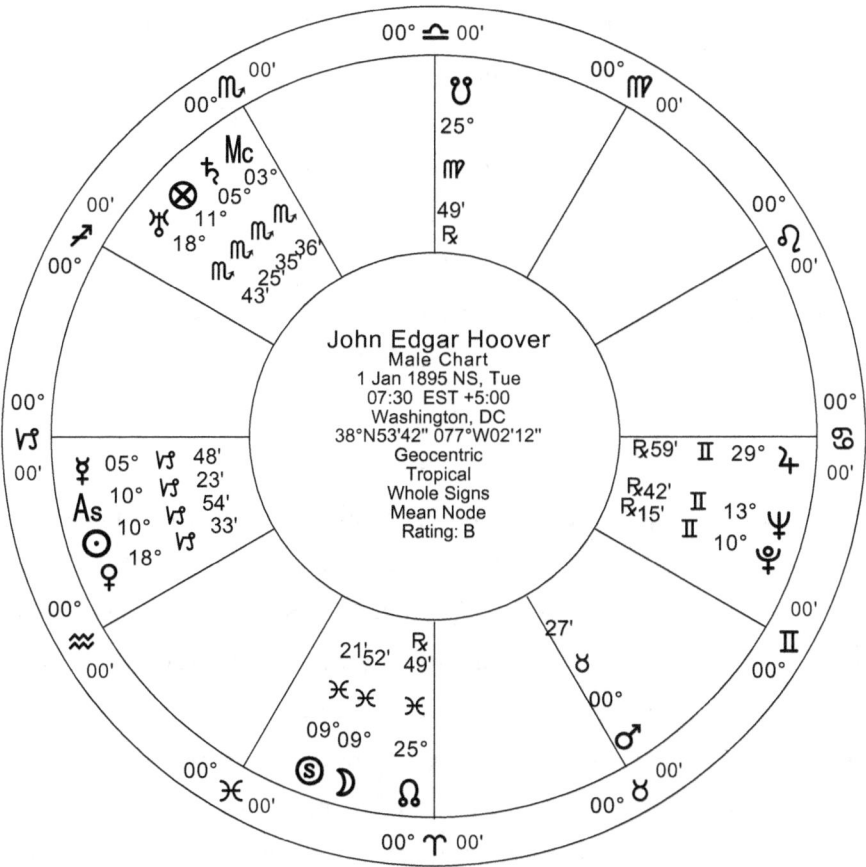

defensive posture. Reviewing a biography of Hoover published in 1987, Alan Brinkley presents our crimefighter's more vulnerable side.

> He was a cautious man almost morbidly averse to personal risk; a man shameless in his sycophancy toward those above him; a man essentially timid in all things except fighting to preserve his own authority. Throughout his life, he was a fervent defender of "traditional" social values; but he was even more fervently committed to his own bureaucratic survival.[136]

---

[136] New York Review of Books, April 23, 1987. Review of Powers, Richard. *Secrecy and Power: The Life of J. Edgar Hoover.* https://www.nybooks.com/articles/1987/04/23/dreams-of-a-g-man/

Hoover's other vulnerability was his sexual orientation and there are differences of opinion about this. There were rumors about his being homosexual and there are indications that point to Hoover as a closeted gay person – perhaps bisexual. Anybody outing Hoover during his lifetime, however, would soon fear for his reputation or his life.

Now that we have swum in the waters of Saturn's upheavals and abuses, it's time for something more inspirational. Can astrology's Saturn be inspirational? Within limits, of course.

Roman Nonholiday

Here's the bottom line: we are all providentially placed in a world not of our making and surrounded by all kinds of conditions outside of our control, and we all end up dead. We are subject to being deceived by our impressions and emotional responses. We habitually chase around what is impossible to catch and bring needless suffering to ourselves and others, but we can rise above this. Our confusion and emotional reactivity is treatable.

To promote the goal of living comfortably in an uncertain world, Saturn must have planetary neighbors. Stoical Saturn requires the company of a Sun's focus on intentionality and using one's critical intelligence to navigate life. It also requires Jupiter's inclusiveness: without focus on responsibility to others and the cosmos, we might be left with passive quietism or a nervous circling the wagons that sidestep our necessary involvements in the world. A stoical attitude tries to temper the Moon's instinctive and impulsive qualities but also applies lunar sensibilities to the conduct of life's details.

Astrology owes an ongoing debt to the ancient Stoics. Their depictions of human bondage and freedom, their quest for serenity in spite of it all, and their emphasis on nobility of character, all continue to influence astrology's underlying assumptions about our lives. Ptolemy, reflecting the stoic attitudes of his time, throws cold water on today's mentality of abundance, that the universe will somehow provide.

> If [the usefulness of astrology] is in relation to the goods of the soul, what would be more conducive to its welfare, joy, and satisfaction generally than such foreknowledge, according to which we come to see human and divine matters together?...

> "First of all it is necessary to consider that even for events that will necessarily result, the unexpected is apt to cause delirious confusion and made joy, while foreknowing habituates and trains the soul to attend to distant events as though they were present, and prepares to accept each of the arriving events with peace and tranquility." [137]

We have previously considered the modern notion of "grit" as vitality + perseverance + self-control. Ancient stoics promoted these same values but under the rubric a philosophical way of life that included self-examination, dialectic, and spiritual contemplation.

From the ancient world three stoics are best known to us – Seneca, Epictetus, and Marcus Aurelius. Their writings are available in many translations and are approachable for the busy modern reader.

Seneca was a brilliant writer. His philosophical writings, particularly his Letters, present a wise older man giving advice to somebody younger. He was conventionally successful and wealthy but pursued the life of a stoic. Seneca is also known to history (and literature and opera) as young Emperor Nero's tutor who was eventually sidelined by his imperial student. To make matters far worse, Nero later ordered him to commit suicide in 65 C.E.

Epictetus was of a later generation and was a slave when young, was physically handicapped, led an austere lifestyle and carried himself with

---
137 Ptolemy Tetribiblos I, 3 (Schmidt translation)

severity. Epictetus's extant writings are noted for their stridency and wealth of detail on how to approach all kinds of situations. Epictetus's writings strongly influenced our next person who is better known to us.

Marcus Aurelius was Roman Emperor from 161 CE to his death in 180 CE. He wrote a series of notes that we call his *Meditations*. They were once thought to be a simple bedside diary but are now understood to have been written systematically. This short work is a guidebook on living a stoic life while also being an important public figure. Reading his writings and pondering his life, we see that Marcus Aurelius was subject to the same personal limitations as the rest of us, plus a few other burdens – like managing a plague and fighting hostile invaders from across the Danube.

What is *solar* about the stoics? Their *hegemonikon* – like our word "hegemony", a dominant force, resides in the heart and is strikingly like astrology's Sun. Applying determined (solar) will is the key to self-mastery, effectiveness in the world, and the soul's freedom. Simplicity – even frugality and chastity – can be used in service to solar purpose, for they train the will to counter distractions and temptations.

The concept of freedom comes up often in stoic writings, being applied mostly to our inner lives. Astrology's Lot of Fortune (Lot of the Moon) corresponds to life conditions over which we have little or no control; Lot of Spirit (Lot of the Sun) appears to correspond more to our freedom, our ability to make choices. Famously, Epictetus' *Enchiridion* or *Handbook* begins in this way:

> Some things are under our control, while others are not under our control. Under our control are conception, choice, desire, aversion, and, in a word, everything that is our own doing; not under our control are our body, our property, reputation, office, and, in a word, everything that is not our own doing. Furthermore, the things under our control are by nature free, unhindered, and unimpeded; while the things not under our

control are weak, servile, subject to hindrance, and not our own....[138]

Epictetus and others suggest that we practice outthinking our habitual emotional patterns, adopting a more detached approach while also acknowledging their power over us. This is an important first step in changing one's behavior. An astrologer, by de-pathologizing but accurately describing some of the emotional traps one can fall into, can help a person be more reflective and reclaim some freedom.

Epictetus, with Jupiter-like cosmic piety, also asserts that our situational limitations are not karmic but providential, part of a larger horizon we cannot see. Note the strength of the simple imagery he uses and his emphasis on aligning oneself with the world as it is.

> Remember that you ought to behave in life as you would at a banquet. As something is being passed around it comes to you; stretch out your hand and take a portion of it politely. It passes on; do not detain it. Or it has not come to you yet; do not project your desire to meet it, but wait until it comes in front of you. So act toward children, so toward a wife, so toward office, so toward wealth; and then some day you will be worthy of the banquets of the gods.[139]

When we are anxious and small-minded, we are lacking the larger horizon that Jupiter provides. In an age governed by large empires, the ancient Stoics valued being *cosmopolitan*, a citizen not just of one city or territory but the whole world. Taking this kind of citizenship seriously requires that we consider all our obligations: as a family member, as part of a community, and as a person on this planet. We must cast petty localisms away.

---

138 Translation W.A. Oldfather, *Epictetus Discourses*, Loeb Classical Library
139 Trans. Oldfather, *Encheiridion*, 15

> If what is said by philosophers regarding the kinship of God and men be true, what other course remains for men but that which Socrates took when asked to what country he belonged, never to say "I am an Athenian" or "I am a Corinthian", but "I am a citizen of the universe (kosmos)?" For why do you say that you are an Athenian, instead of mentioning merely the corner into which your paltry body was cast at birth?[140]

As involuntary burdens, our obligations are saturnine; as parts of who we are they are solar; as they bring us into larger horizons of experience, they are of the nature of Jupiter.

Marcus Aurelius brings the possibilities of living well to an everyday – or an every-morning – level. He depicts an experience we've all had, perhaps this morning.

> Whenever in the morning you rise unwillingly, let this thought be with you: "I am rising to the work of a human being. Why then am I dissatisfied if I am about to do the things for which I was brought into the world? Or was I made to lie under the bedclothes and keep myself warm?"[141]

Saturn in us forsakes the warm bed and warm baths to take our places with others and fulfill our responsibilities toward them. The eventual payoff for self-mastery and discrimination, for taking what is offered at the banquet of our lives and for not wanting more, is that we will someday dine with the gods.

What, then, is the proper place for the lunar rhythms of our lives? They also align with providence if we manage them well. Seneca counsels less travel and less restlessness, greater simplicity of possessions, using plain and unadorned language, attending to one's physical needs for the

---
140 Epictetus Discourses I.9
141 Meditations, Book V Chapter 1

sake of good health (even advocating vegetarianism, then considered a poor person's plight), and living according to seasonal and daily rhythms of nature. Seneca also recommends connecting in friendship to those who are intelligent, virtuous, and trustworthy.

Finally, we should review our thoughts and behavior each day: what ruins our characters, he asserts, is from not reflecting and evaluating regularly.

All three authors espouse philosophy not as study or theorizing but as a style of living, engaging in consistent reflection, questioning, and considering what is required of us in this world and beyond this world. Their vision has qualities of Jupiter, but its bedrock is saturnine, immersed in the cold realities of our lives and the death that we will all experience someday.

Oppression: Internal and External

Does the stoic point of view make excuses for oppression, or does it optimize our responses to oppression? For now, let's consider oppression as an aspect of Simone Weil's view of affliction that we discussed previously: reducing a human being to a thing. This oppression is something we can also do to ourselves.

From the Inside and *the Outside*

Previously we considered Sigmund Freud's natal Mercury and the character strength of curiosity, an ability to follow an inquiry to resolution. We noted the sextile from his Mercury in Taurus to a strongly placed Jupiter at the last degree of Pisces.

Freud considered himself a scientist of the human mind and its ailments. He was concerned with realities of intrapsychic oppression, what we call "repression" when unconscious. Although there is much to criticize in Freud's ideas, nobody can doubt his desire to help reduce self-inflicted human misery. His approach to human nature and its possibilities was more pessimistic than our three stoics above.

Freud posited three demands on our ego (or "I"): (1) from the external world, (2) from the "id" – or "it" – wherein dwells our primitive desires and fantasies beneath conscious awareness, and (3) from the "superego" or set of unconscious unrealistic demands that we have internalized from early childhood. From an astrologer's viewpoint, Freud posits a besieged and diminished solar principle. Psychoanalysis and a supportive environment come to the rescue.

> "[The intention of [psychoanalysis] is to strengthen the ego, to make it more independent of the super-ego, to widen its field of perception and enlarge its organization, so that is can appropriate fresh portions of the id. Where id was, there ego shall be. It is a work of culture – not unlike the draining of the Zuider Zee." [142]

If we first go to Freud's Sun position, in Taurus in the seventh house moving toward Uranus, we see a stubborn style and a reluctant unconventionality. Even at the height of his fame and influence, he was always an outsider, reflecting the influence of Uranus.

A greater difficulty is the placement of Venus: in detriment in Aries, in the difficult sixth house, governed by Mars in detriment and in the twelfth house, another difficult place. It is another example of two planets in mutual reception but placed in signs of detriment, making for a complex push-pull relationship between them. Freud's focus on eros and, in his later writings, destructiveness, casts both urges bringing us through repression to neurosis or to creativity, sometimes both.

Freud's Saturn in Gemini, in its own triplicity in his diurnal chart, has many important roles. "Strengthening the ego" requires that one expand a

---

[142] From "Dissection of the Psychical Personality", *New Introductory Lectures on Psychoanalysis.*

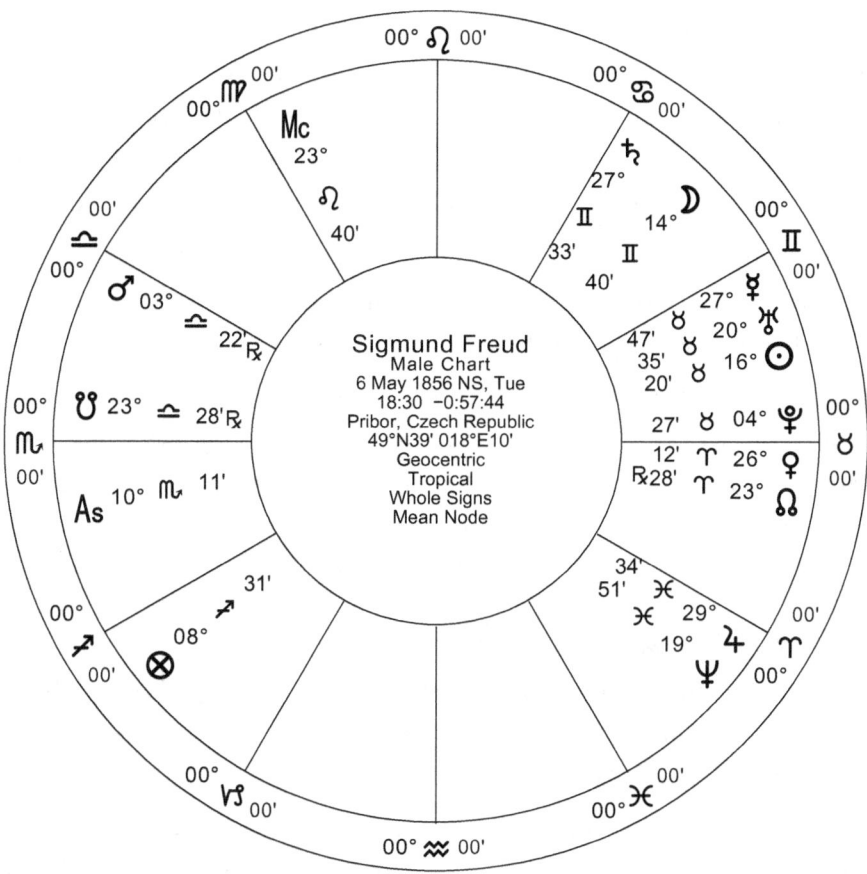

sense of identity to include many features one would prefer not to include. This occurs only through a saturnine descent into the grim realities of one's inner life. One is liberated by dropping impossible expectations, a process that is humbling but loosens our mental afflictions.

Saturn is in sextile to Venus which is the ruler of his seventh house of relationship, also inhabited by the Sun and Mercury. During his long career, Freud's healing methods evolved from cocaine to abreaction to an interpersonal process. Resolution of a patient's issues could be achieved by working through them within the dynamics of the therapeutic relationship. By the end of his career, Freud found a fine use for his strong seventh house.

Freud's Saturn has a square to Jupiter. Freud had no faith that reading the self-help books of our ancient stoics and others, coupled with solitary contemplation, could be effective for disturbances of the psyche. Nor did he believe in the Jove-like "power of positive thinking." One had to dig deeper, and this could not be accomplished by oneself. The sextile between Mercury and Jupiter helped yield a dialectical approach that we now call "psychotherapy," although its content is saturnian.

This square between Jupiter and Saturn also relates to Freud's affiliation with medical and psychological tradition, and with his inherited culture of rabbinical Judaism. Freud's saturnine mind also noted the political situations around him, especially as antisemitism and fascism had grown throughout Europe and war was brewing. His final writings were broad in scope but pessimistic and his final years in England were difficult.

A Reluctant Hero of the People
Another odd mixture of Saturn and Jupiter is the strange case of Dmitri Shostakovich (1905-1975), one of the great composers of twentieth century music.[143] In today's classical repertoire you can find many of his large-orchestra symphonies, concerti, and chamber works. Rather transparently, his natal chart contains Venus in Scorpio in the vocational tenth house, keeping close company with Lot of Spirit.

However, Shostakovich had the ill-fortune of living and working under the totalitarian regime of Joseph Stalin and the authoritarian rule of the dictator's successors.[144]

Saturn is part of a large planetary assembly in this chart. Saturn governs and is in sextile to the Moon in Capricorn. This configuration might be dour and conventional but is accompanied by Uranus which is also in sextile to Saturn. Saturn is also in trine to Jupiter-Neptune and, in

---
143 Birth data B from biography.
144 For much more about him and the astrology of his life, see https://www.astrologyinstitute.com/articleprofile/profiles/2017/dmitri-shostakovich-music-for-interesting-times

Saturn's Solitary Realm

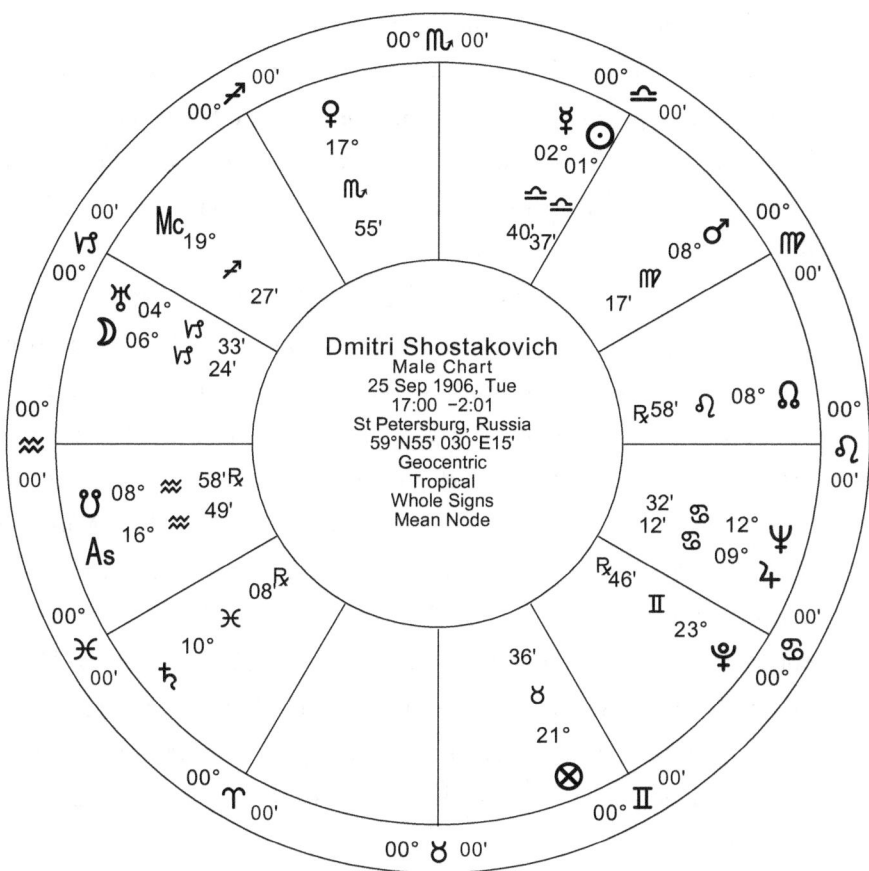

If his natal chart looks a little familiar, it is because he was
born ten days before Hannah Arendt.

Pisces, Saturn's dispositor is Jupiter.[145] Jupiter and Saturn are strongly tied together in his chart.

Jupiter is exalted in Cancer. Unlike Hannah Arendt whose Jupiter was close to her Ascendant, this Jupiter is in the less felicitous sixth house. Instead of becoming an expert on understanding totalitarianism like Arendt, Shostakovich became an expert in surviving totalitarianism.

---

145 Modern astrologers will sometimes lump this configuration together as a "mystic rectangle" with sextiles, trines, and oppositions, yet there seems to be greater clarify just to look at the planets involved in their interrelationships.

At times this meant being a promoter of political and cultural attitudes that he privately loathed. Perhaps we can credit this to a Moon-Uranus conjunction that kept company with Mars, Jupiter, and Saturn: despite the complexities of his public position, Shostakovich endeavored to be faithful to his integrity. With the Sun in fall in Libra, this could not have been second nature.

A few months after Shostakovich's thirtieth birthday and having already gained fame as a prominent young composer, his full-scale opera was finally being performed in Moscow. This was a major public event and Stalin and other government officials were in the audience. Then catastrophe hit – Stalin walked out of the performance! A few days afterwards, an article in the national newspaper *Pravda* appeared with the title "Music or Muddle?", taking the composer to task for many features that conflicted with national interests.

Appropriately and not happily for our composer, Shostakovich's transits for this time included transiting Saturn and Mars in Virgo, both opposing his natal Saturn and in conjunction with natal Mars. (His transits are eerily like those of Savonarola when the latter was excommunicated by Pope Alexander.)

Shostakovich's career immediately dried up, many presumed friends left him fearing for their own lives, and he was left in constant fear for his own. Afterwards his son shared that, during this time, his father always left the house with a bar of soap and a toothbrush: on what day would he be picked up by Stalin's police? Later he would credit his family, his remaining friends, and exercise of will for keeping him going and not committing suicide.

After having to withdraw a melancholy Fourth Symphony, Shostakovich wrote another that he labeled "a Soviet artist's creative response to just criticism." This ambiguous Fifth Symphony, depicting either the triumph of the new soviet man or a pointedly defiant response to Stalin's reign of terror, premiered in 1937 and was received enthusiastically.

The composer thanked the people and their authorities for their patience with him. Shostakovich learned that he could flatter his minders and make necessary public statements that parroted the party and could live and compose another day.

Seven years later, the authorities who spared Shostakovich got their reward. During the brutal Nazi siege of Leningrad, Shostakovich was spirited away to write a Seventh Symphony to boost national morale. Upon its completion, fragments of an orchestra in Leningrad were assembled to perform the piece within earshot of the Nazi soldiers surrounding the city. This provided the positive press and morale boost that was needed. Astrologically, transiting Saturn was now in Gemini and in aspect, once again, to his Saturn-Mars opposition. Mars was returning to its natal position but so was Jupiter, helping this reluctant composer become a national and international hero.

Dmitri Shostakovich's personal suffering and professional triumph would become a mirror for the dark times in which he lived. His saturnian stoic outlook enabled him to be a voice of his culture. Over the thirty years following his Leningrad Symphony, he bounced in and out of favor with the authorities but continued to compose. For someone with no desire to involve himself in the larger situations around him, his music became a lasting testament to the difficult times in which he lived.

A Civil Rights Moment
In 1947, Jackie Robinson broke the "color barrier" in American major league baseball, becoming the first black major-league player since the previous century. During that year Robinson fulfilled a promise he had made to Dodgers' owner/president Branch Rickey: to not retaliate or respond angrily to the catcalls, dirty play, and the thousand insults he would inevitably endure during his debut. Robinson's perseverance resulted in professional success for himself, a route for many black players to follow him into the

Astrology and the Lives of People

major leagues, and an early success in the Civil Rights movement in the United States.

Here is a positive chart for the ages. Leo is rising but Saturn is on the Ascendant, both governed by the Sun in Saturn's sign Aquarius. The Moon, Venus, and Uranus are also in Aquarius. During Robinson's three years of "turning the other cheek", he focused on his game and contributed to his team with quiet dignity – and played aggressively. Once his three years were up, Robinson became more outspoken about his treatment and that of other black players.

Like many successful athletes, Robinson developed his native talent through consistent hard work. As the planet of prudence and discipline,

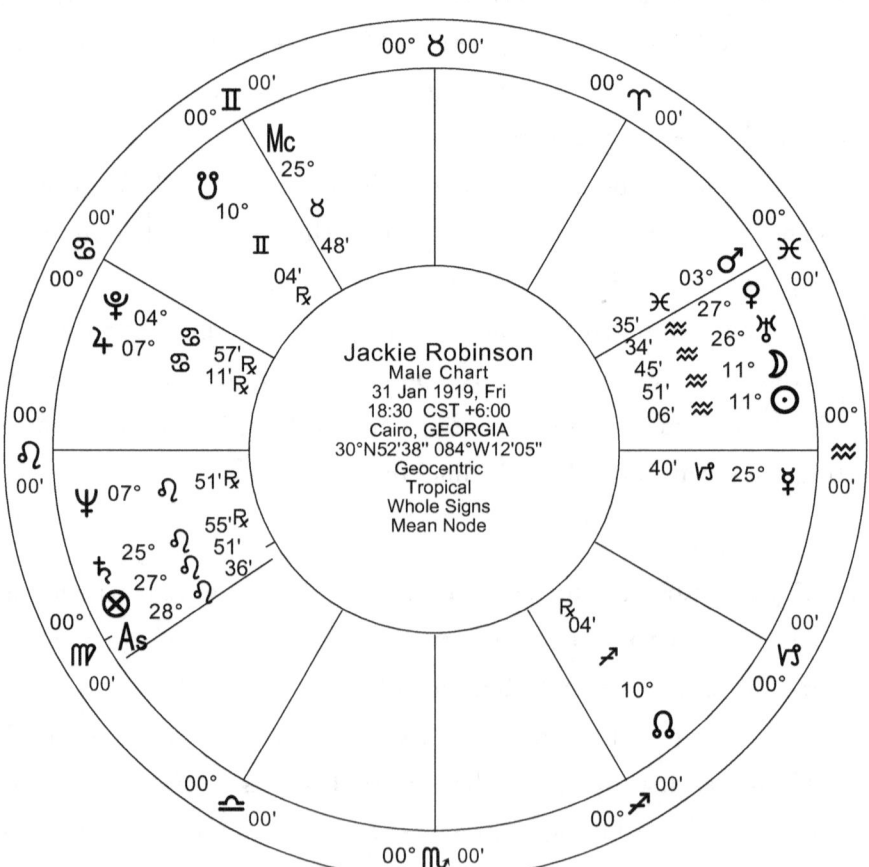

Saturn is not terribly happy in Leo (in detriment) and is out of sect in Robinson's nocturnal chart. As with Jane Austen and Freud discussed above, planets in mutual reception but in detriment contain creative possibilities and an urgency to work out differences.

I wonder about Robinson's physical vulnerabilities that were just under the surface during his athletic career. They manifested in poor health after his baseball career and an early death at sixty-three. Although a self-motivated person with a strong sense of religion and a drive to make the world a better place, psychological stress took a toll on him over the years.

Mars in Pisces is in an applying trine to Jupiter and Pluto in Cancer. Since Jupiter is the domicile ruler for Pisces, we're looking at a strong reception that favors Jupiter in its sign of exaltation.

Pluto's presence with Jupiter only strengthens and deepens the Mars-Jupiter combination. Mars and Jupiter together can bring the warrior who can fight the good fight and suffer defeat gracefully if the cause is good enough. The presence of these two planets in the difficult eighth and twelfth houses may point to a toll this kind of warriorship took on this man. Strongly placed and influential Saturn -- with his wife Rachel, perhaps represented by Venus with Uranus in the seventh house – gave him the strength and support required to perform the role history gave to him.

There was nothing passive or quietist about Jackie Robinson. During World War II, he was drafted into a segregated army unit in Texas. Along with his new friend boxer Joe Louis, Robinson lobbied to be admitted to officer training and, after noticeable procrastination on the part of the military bureaucracy, both were admitted. One day, as his company was boarding a bus, Robinson was asked to go to the back of the bus that was set aside for the black soldiers. He refused to move and found himself in an altercation with the military police that eventually resulted in his being court-martialed for insubordination. He was officially acquitted of these charges but was prevented from going to Europe along with his company.

Saturn also emerges in a famous incident of a black person refusing to go to the back of a bus: Rosa Parks in 1955, in Montgomery, Alabama. This ignited a boycott that kindled the Civil Rights movement. Parks' time of birth is uncertain, yet Saturn clearly dominated her chart: Jupiter, Mars, and Moon are in Capricorn, Mercury and Sun are in Aquarius. Saturn is in late Taurus in trine with her Moon, yielding a traditional mutual reception: Moon is in Saturn's domicile sign, Saturn is in Moon's exaltation sign. Both Jackie Robinson and Rosa Parks embodied a quiet and contained defiance that would make them historically impactful figures.

Standing Apart, Saturn Style

Many of us are inspired by the possibility of going beyond ordinary worldly concerns, although the realities and difficulties of such a path may be more than we bargained for. However, this inspiration is powerful and must be respected. Saturn gives us a revulsion for life's many encumbrances that are roadblocks to a transcendent life. This revulsion can foster renunciation which in turn supports a contemplative and more spirit-directed life.

Two renunciants who have the Sun in Aquarius had different responses to this longing. We first return to Simone Weil: alongside her works of genius that we previously sampled, her personal life was consistent with her views but also problematic. Previously we looked at her Mars-Jupiter square and the interesting connection between Jupiter and Saturn in her chart. Since Saturn is the dispositor for the Sun and Mercury in Aquarius, the dark planet must be considered on its own.

Saturn seems handicapped in Aries, its sign of fall or depression, and has no aspect to her other planets. Mars in fiery Sagittarius in the first house is Saturn's dispositor. Can Saturn, the planet of restriction, also be combustible? A few pages from her life show her depth of self-renunciation but also self-destructiveness.

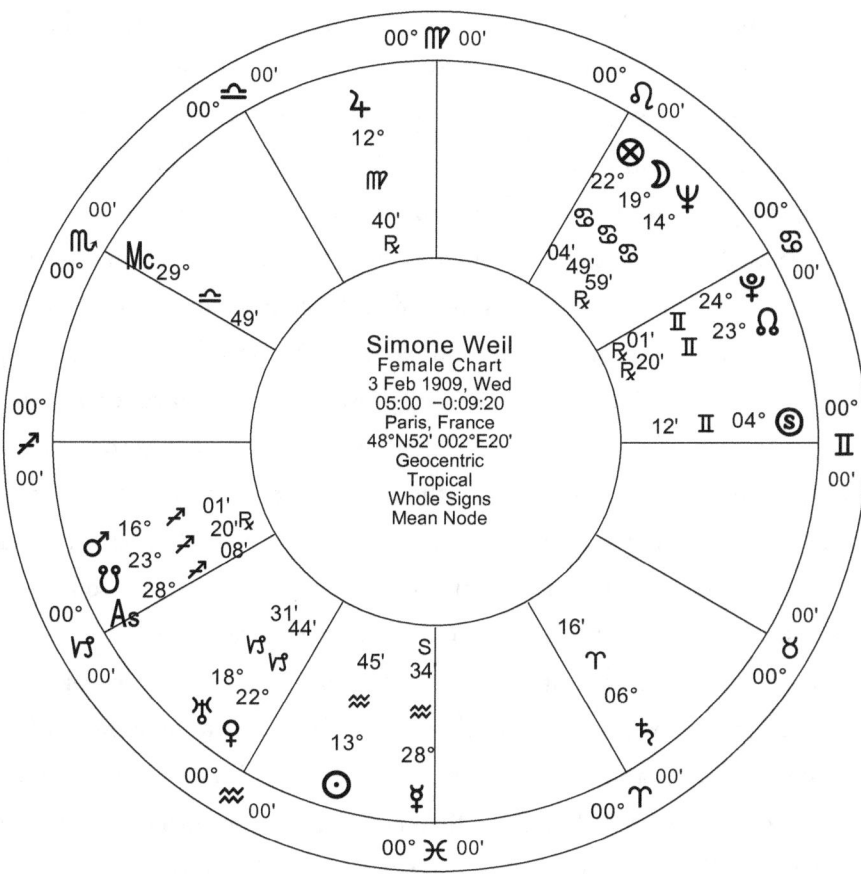

Throughout her life, Weil presented herself as asexual and seemed averse to physical intimacy. Weil loathed dressing for attractiveness, as many photos of her will attest, and wore make-up only once, for a job interview. On a friendship level, however, she was comfortable with both genders.

Weil habitually ignored the cautionary messages the body routinely provides. As a young academic, she left her position for a year to work in a factory, to better understand the lives and conditions of those who worked there. This is laudable, but her frail constitution made this extremely difficult for her. She went to Spain to fight in the Civil War and was undeterred by the fact that she was physically ill-suited for this. Her parents had to rescue their daughter after an injury incapacitated her. During the

Second World War, Weil proposed that a nurses' corps be established to care for wounded soldiers on the front line and that she would be one of the nurses: this was quickly rejected by the authorities.

Food consumption was a major problem throughout her short life. Her astrological chart gives us some indications of this: together with an enthusiastic Saturn was the Moon conjunct Neptune, and her Jupiter was placed in Virgo. Higher callings superseded the commands of physical need for nourishment. Even as a child, Simone went through a phase of refusing to eat chocolate, citing the suffering of those who lived on rations during the First World War. She deprived herself of food during the Second World War from her sympathy for those without food. Her death certificate listed her death as caused by pulmonary tuberculosis exacerbated by self-induced starvation. Much of her self-denial – especially her refusal of food – was linked to concern about others who were deprived elsewhere.

Our second renunciant is Thomas Merton, a monk and well-known writer who was ten years younger than Weil. His books were popular while he was alive, as was the example of his way of living. Today Merton remains a voice for a quieter and simpler life. He had a more benevolent Saturn than did Weil, one that provided structure and limits that enabled his contemplative nature to emerge, transform him, and influence others.

After a chaotic and transcontinental childhood capped off his emergence as a dissolute young adult, Merton landed in New York in 1935 to study literature. He wanted to become a writer but he also had a religious longing. Merton was at first inclined toward eastern systems, but an early teacher, a Hindu monk, instead advised him to dive deeper into Christian traditions.

This advice worked marvelously. By the end of that year Merton had converted to Catholicism; three years afterwards, he became a Trappist novitiate; by the end of the 1940s his *Seven-Storey Mountain* and *New Seeds of Contemplation* were published to immediate acclaim. With critical and popular successes, new challenges were at hand. Merton had to reconcile his recent monastic vocation, his achievement and fame as a writer, and his ecumenical and left-leaning spirit.

We see a restless thinking nature in an Aries Ascendant in close sextile to Mars in Aquarius. If we look at the distribution of the elements between the seven visible planetary bodies, they are all in the so-called masculine signs fire and air. Merton's independent spirit is indicated by his Sun-Uranus conjunction, opposed by a cheerful Moon in Leo in the fifth house. None of this appears suited to a monastic vocation.

Merton's natal chart shows a dominant and positive Saturn.[146] Hellenistic astrology designated the third house as the "Moon Goddess",

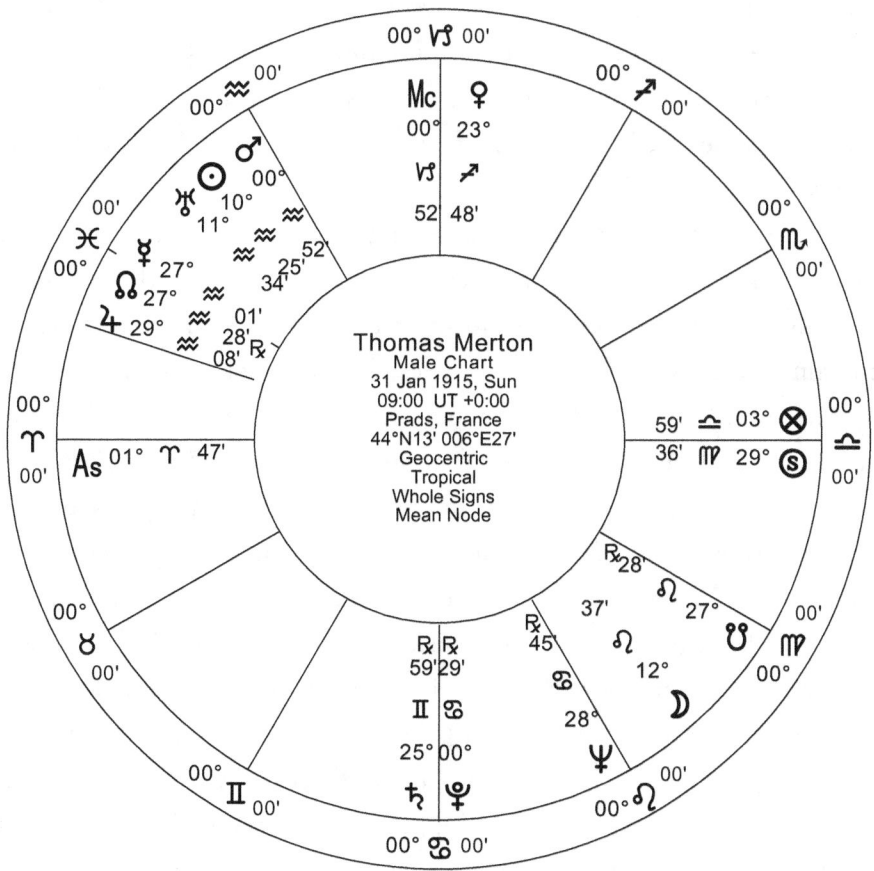

---

146 AA: time from birth record

related to religious observance and practice on a daily or domestic level. Saturn is also in triplicity and in sect in Merton's day chart.

Mercury is in mutual reception by domicile with Saturn: Mercury is in Aquarius governed by Saturn in Gemini which in turn is the domicile of Mercury. They are also in a trine aspect, further allowing this to be a strong and beneficial combination. Merton's Mercury-Saturn combination helped him to find clarity and creative expression within the disciplined life of a monastic.

Four of seven visible planets are in Aquarius in the ancient place of the "Good Spirit", all disposed by Saturn in Gemini. Merton's contemplative life cultivated clarity and self-honesty through silence and simplicity. At its best, developing a strongly inward life limits self-deception and allows one to participate more sanely in the larger world. Merton's message seems prophetic to our modern age of noise, information overload, and culturally induced attention deficit disorder.

Merton maintained a personal discipline that included chastity – not easy for him at all – and obedience to monastic authority that was also difficult for him. Yet, adhering to these disciplines provided a saturnine container for the contemplative life that was also the source of his strength.

Merton's Full Moon displays a split between being special (Moon in Leo) and an impersonal spiritual seeker (Sun in Aquarius). His Lot of Fortune – the Lot of the Moon – is in Libra, governed by Venus in Sagittarius, but his Lot of Spirit is in Virgo and governed by Mercury that is strongly configured with Saturn. Happily, Venus and Mercury are in a favorable sextile to one another. Although one would not consider his life a contentedly happy one, Merton was comfortable with being himself with all his contradictions.

Having discussed these seven planetary bodies individually, we now switch emphasis. Turning our attention toward issues of virtue or excellence, character, intelligence, and friendship, how do the seven planetary bodies provide further insights these important concerns? Part Three also brings together ancient wisdom and modern applications to people and their lives.

Part Three

The Connected and Well-Tempered Life

Astrology and the Lives of People

Astrology's Surroundings

My first astrology teacher, strongly influenced by Dane Rudhyar and gestalt therapy, taught and practiced a *humanistic* astrology that came out of the human potential movement of the 1970s and ego psychology from previous decades. Applied to astrology's symbol systems, this perspective promotes a person's healthier and better-defined self. One difficulty is that as we change along with our lives, we adapt and express ourselves in different ways, and a clear unity of self becomes elusive.

Astrology has also been influenced by a *Jungian* perspective. Overlapping in many ways with humanistic astrology, this approach adds our unconscious tendencies, notes intrapsychic tensions and conflicts, and aims toward a more individuated and integrated self. I have found some difficulties with a Jungian approach: if the goal is integration and someone's astrological chart contains no significant placements in earth or water signs, should the astrologer encourage this person to be more determined and practical? In pursuing a pre-established goal of psychic balance, one could lose sight of the concrete realities of a client's life and their need for practical remedies for immediate situations, i.e., the prospects of moving to Denver to begin a new romance may be far more important to the client than their unconscious motivations for doing so.

Much current astrology also expresses itself within a New Age culture that comes from *theosophy's descendants* that looks for spiritual relevance. This approach has been appealing to many who cannot find a place among other available spiritual and religious options, especially as many mainstream religious traditions have condemned astrology. One drawback, of course, is that only a small number of astrology's clients are strongly focused on spiritual development, although many have some interest. (The final chapter will take up this topic.) Too often the astrologer, not desiring to misjudge the "spiritual level" of a client, misses what is actually in the client's immediate interest.

The Connected and Well-Tempered Life

Over the last several decades, many astrologers have promoted the lunar nodes as depicting psychological dynamics in our lives, the South Node being more about past patterns or comfort zones, and North Node about a path of growth. Some contemporary astrologers address a personal spiritual journey using the image of past and future lifetimes, sometimes employing trauma theory to depict previous lifetimes astrologically. Many employ the lunar nodes to depict past incarnations or present habitual patterns (South Node), and paths of spiritual evolution over lifetimes or personal growth in this lifetime (North Node).

Early in my astrology practice, I dropped using the lunar nodes in this way. Based on how the lunar nodes are determined, I could find no theoretical justification for this practice. More importantly, I found that I was sometimes advising people to adopt attitudes and behavior that were not otherwise accounted for in their astrological charts or in their lives.

The revival of *traditional or "classical" astrology* has given new perspectives on astrological delineation and interpretation. The astrology of the past was less concerned with inner psychic processes and more concerned with the practicalities and difficulties of daily life. In its mission to recover previous astrological approaches and techniques that had later fallen away, there has been less emphasis on how astrology operated within surrounding cultural values and norms.[147] This book has tried to remedy this. Previous chapters, especially those on Jupiter and Saturn, have emphasized the importance of older value systems to astrology, especially its emphasis on life within a community.

Today, in fields other than astrology, there has been a greater serious interest in the wisdom traditions of antiquity and afterwards. Over the past few decades, ethical theory has moved from pondering moral maxims and

---

147 Nicholas Campion has extensively researched the culture that surrounded Hellenistic and medieval astrology. See *The Dawn of Astrology* (2008) and *A History of Western Astrology: the Medieval and Modern Worlds* (2009). These are valuable works for seeing the interplay between astrology and past cultures.

their logic and posing ethical dilemmas to reconsidering the virtue ethics of ancient societies (that were also shared by their astrologers).

Concurrently, and probably not coincidentally, psychological theory and psychotherapeutic practice has developed a branch they call "positive psychology" that looks to the ingredients of a well-lived life, attempting to build from a client's strengths to help them solve problems. To its benefit and relevance to astrologers, positive psychology has relational and contextual dimensions that are emphasized less by offshoots of the human potential movement.

Both modern value ethics and positive psychology overlap with traditional applications of astrology and are relevant to people right now. Both can make strong contributions to astrology's surroundings that form a background to working effectively with clients. These, I feel, are new horizons for today's astrologers.

From an astrologer's point of view and with continued focus on the luminaries and five visible planets, we turn our attention toward traditional and modern depictions of virtues or excellences, character strengths, intelligences, and friendships. How do these issues enrich the symbolism of the Moon and the Sun and the five planets? I conclude with a discussion of spirituality, our seven planets and beyond, and the different applications of traditional virtues to this important part of our lives.

Chapter Twelve

Virtues and Intelligences: The Luminaries

How we act and how we think – *virtue* and *intelligence* – are central in our discussions of astrology's Moon and Sun and their practical applications to people. Today the words virtue and intelligence both carry baggage. It is easy to dislike the word virtue, too often a harbor for the hypocritical or sanctimonious. Fortunately, the modern sense of intelligence has been partly liberated from its former IQ affiliation and now intelligence is better seen as multi-dimensional. Together virtue and intelligence help comprise a life well-lived and well-connected with others. Pondering both enriches our understanding of the luminaries and planets.

Virtue and Excellence

"Virtue" is from the Latin word for "man," as one definition of our modern word "virility", simply means "strength" or "power". The Greek word for "virtue" is "arete" (αρετη) that also has "manhood" as one of its meanings. An attribution of strength helps us understand the expression "by virtue of", an enabling factor of some kind, like our expression "by reason of".

If somebody does something very well, he or she *excels* at it. One can be an excellent violinist, car repair person, pole vaulter, or pole dancer. To become excellent at something usually takes some innate capacity, a supportive environment, sustained effort, and some luck. Accounting for contemporary assumptions, "excellence" is probably a better rendering of "virtue", although for clarity and consistency with tradition, I will continue to use the word virtue in this chapter.

Twenty-three centuries ago, Aristotle looked at moral virtues or excellences – in behavior and states of mind -- as maintaining a mean between two extremes, between too much or too little of some quality. Generosity can veer into careless showboating or stinginess, relative to how much giving is called for and how much one can give. At other times we need to be courageous, by modulating our fears and doing what is necessary even if it is difficult: if we're overconfident when threatened, we become rash or foolish and overwhelming fear may transform caution into cowardice.

Often virtue implies good judgment, based on accurately assessing a situation. Picture yourself at a social gathering full of people you already know. Is it better to help loosen things up with humorous one-liners, claim the center of attention with a good story, be a good listener, or stay in the kitchen and help with the dishes? Some of us are better than others at recognizing what is called for it and acting accordingly. We should not stay within our habitual "comfort zone" when some other response is better.

Aristotle's notion of the "mean" may help us reframe our interpretations of the astrological planets in their signs of dignity or debility. A debilitated planet, in detriment or fall or aspected by a difficult planet or in a house remote from the Ascendant, may be inclined to behave in excess or deficiency. (We can extend this to Mars and Saturn, both notorious for their extremes even when in their signs of dignity, especially when in their domiciles and out of sect, such as Mars in Aries in a diurnal chart or Saturn in Capricorn in a nocturnal chart.)

Our planetary symbolism connects well with traditional depictions of the virtues. This is relevant when we work with planets in their traditional signs of dignity of debility.

Astrologers may look to a debilitated Jupiter, especially when in detriment in Virgo or in fall or depression in Capricorn, as vulnerable to stinginess. Jupiter in detriment in Gemini may be inclined to make a show of one's generosity but forget to send the check. However, intention and practice may result in Jupiter in Virgo manifesting as intelligent or inventive generosity. At a social gathering, sensitive Mercury in Pisces – aided by some discernment – can help redeem awkward moments.

A difficult planetary placement does not disable someone for life, but often, in the words attached to my penmanship grades in elementary school, this planet "needs more work". Time and experience can improve a debilitated planet's functioning. Because these placements contain unusual possibilities, sometimes extra-ordinary things happen.

A dignified planet may display innate capacity but, like a debilitated planet, must be developed over time to be at its best, and its "best" can be superb. Here it may be too easy to coast along and allow one's capacities to stagnate through overconfidence. These planets may also manifest one-dimensionally: without some emotional sensitivity, Mercury in Virgo can miss important information; without humility Jupiter in Sagittarius can be full of noble intention but be weak in getting things done.

Whether your Jupiter or Mercury, or any other planet, is dignified or debilitated, they all need some work. Some of us, as with Mercury in Sagittarius or Venus in Scorpio, start farther behind and need to go further to catch up. As Aristotle wrote and as the story goes about premier pianist Vladimir Horowitz, upon being asked how to get to Carnegie Hall in New York City, he replied "practice, practice."[148] Here I suggest "practice", not in the sense of preparatory work but ongoing activity, like a law practice or an astrology practice. This implies paying attention over time to what seems called for, doing one's best, and learning from successes and mistakes along the way.

Ancient Moral Virtues or Excellences

You may recall Plato's delineation of virtues from *The Republic* or from elsewhere in the ancient world. Plato divided the soul – and the citizenry of the *polis* - into three parts with a fourth to proportion them.

---

[148] There are some variations of this story, but they all contain the same punchline.

The appetitive soul or faculty is oriented toward pleasure and gratification, having nice things and avoiding unpleasantries. This feature does not incline easily to the dictates of our more reasonable nature. When reasonableness comes naturally, the tamed appetitive soul has the virtue of *temperance*. We also have a rational soul that likes to think things through, talk things through, and the associated virtue is *wisdom*. Between the appetitive and rational is the spirited soul that brings energy, proceeds from physical and emotional arousal, and its virtue is *courage*. This uses our energy to support either faculty, to what is immediately gratifying or serves our self-interest, or to the longer-term or to the pursuit and application of wisdom.

Justice harmonizes wisdom, temperance, and courage in the city or the individual. This version of justice is holistic, assuring the coordination of the different parts of our being. Plato's depiction of justice in the individual soul prefigures the modern concept of personality integration.

Temperance, wisdom or knowledge, courage, and justice were known later as the four cardinal virtues. They appear and re-appear throughout the history of Western thought.

Plato's *Republic* discusses courage in ways that are Mars-like and solar, wisdom also with solar features, leaving the Moon and Venus to the lower-down appetitive functions. Jupiter comprises justice, in our usual sense of social contract or proportionality – and as the planet of moderation, as Jupiter was considered up to modern times. Saturn in this context seems like a heavy-handed enforcer of temperance. Of course, Mercury can be anywhere.

In the medieval period, the theological virtues of *faith*, *hope*, and *love* or *charity* were added to the four cardinal virtues to make seven. The four cardinal virtues also added a dimension of being infused by God for the spiritual life. These later developments brought a more affective element into the mix, deepening human excellence and linking worldly virtue with spiritual possibility.

Modern Virtues and Character Strengths

The modern era has different depictions of virtues, including, for example, Ben Franklin's entrepreneurial leanings. The twentieth century de-emphasized listing virtues when our interests turned toward exploring pathology and intrapsychic dimensions. Now only a few decades old, a movement called "positive psychology" has attempted to return traditional notions of virtue to modern clinical psychology. In their view, positive qualities that manifest in our daily lives can be built upon for greater overall fulfillment and to solve psychological problems.

Character Strengths and Virtues (2004) is a hefty tome by Christopher Peterson and Martin Seligman that I have found helpful for examining positive features of our seven visible planetary bodies. This self-depicted "Manual of the Sanities" presents seven virtues, within which are twenty-seven character strengths. Character strengths are selected because they contribute to a good life for oneself and others, are valued culturally, manifest in different attitudes and behaviors, and can be found in some exemplary individuals.

Here is their list of virtues and character strengths. Both categories fit in unevenly with our seven planets, but they are still useful to us. It's a good list for astrologers to ransack.

- *Knowledge or Wisdom* includes curiosity, love of learning, open-mindedness, creativity, and perspective.
- *Courage* is comprised of bravery, persistence, integrity, and vitality.
- *Justice* includes citizenship, fairness, and leadership.
- *Temperance* has strengths of self-regulation or self-control, prudence, humility, but also forgiveness or mercy.
- *Humanity* divides into kindness, love, and social intelligence.

- *Transcendence* consists of appreciation of beauty and excellence, gratitude, hope or optimism, spirituality, and humor.[149]

Transcendence does include an odd collection of character strengths. When we look at them more closely, however, we see that without them we would be angry at the world, depressed, or would be living lives of quiet desperation. These "transcendent" character strengths are also therapeutic interventions that can increase a person's overall well-being. Astrologically most may be included with Venus and Jupiter, the two benefics or doers of good. They may be useful remedies for us and for our clients.

Peterson and Seligman's list of seven virtues contain the ancient cardinal virtues and include two more – humanity and transcendence. Wisdom or knowledge has mostly solar but some mercurial attributes; courage contains both solar and Mars-like possibilities; justice is mostly jupiterian; temperance is somewhat saturnine. Humanity is mostly lunar with a touch of Venus, and transcendence is mixed but seems to lean toward the benefics. We begin our reflection with correspondences of character strengths to the luminaries and will take them up again in the next chapter as they relate to the five starry planets.

Luminaries and Character Strengths

How do Peterson's and Seligman's character strengths align with our understanding of the luminaries? There are many intersections between the ancient and medieval planets and modern application of virtue and character.

---

[149] The later work *Flourish* by Seligman (2011) contains the same list of character strengths with a few changes of category. Under Knowledge or Wisdom is "Social/Intellectual/Practical Intelligence" that instead of Humanity. Two strengths have been moved into Transcendence: "Forgiveness and Mercy" from Temperance and "Vitality" from Courage.

Character Strengths and the Moon

Lunar character strengths of *love* and *kindness* come from their virtue of humanity; from their temperance we have *humility* or *modesty;* from transcendence we get *gratitude* and *forgiveness/mercy.*

Although most of us consider love at least half of what our lives are about, and some of us consider love a cosmic or metaphysical principle, *Character Strengths and Virtues* lists it only as one "strength" under the virtue of humanity. We all know people whose capacity for love seems greater than average, an attribute we generally admire in them. We also may know some for whom the capacity for love seems less, leading to unhappy and unfulfilled lives for them. We know the dire outcomes of our tendencies toward jealousy, possessiveness, and blindness that are love's problematic relations, yet we all aspire to love well or at least better than we currently do.

From love's lunar side grow other character strengths: kindness, gratitude, forgiveness or mercy, and humility or modesty. Kindness steps out from oneself to be helpful for the sake of another. Kindness (or altruism or generosity) includes consideration toward loved ones but also extends toward others, including those we may never meet. As inspiring and lauded as kindness may be, it is often mixed with other motives and often does not show itself in pure form. Since this quality is highly regarded, we are tempted to make a show of it to others. We might also admit that we are more inclined to extend ourselves to those who are more like us, or who we find attractive in some way, or to engage in acts of kindness when they do not exact too high a price on our convenience.

Most of us aspire to increase our kindness toward others, since empathic responses usually make us feel good. Some of us try to practice kindness daily and note how frequently we fall short. All this is astrologically rooted in the instinctual consciousness of commonality symbolized by astrology's Moon. (Indirect contributors to kindness/altruism are more solar or Jupiterian: we may use moral reasoning to focus on others rather than ourselves; we may have a heightened sense of social responsibility. Kindness can be developed in these ways as we go through life.)

Gratitude is recognizing and acknowledging the contributions others have made to us, often accompanied by a desire to pay back their generosity. On an ordinary psychological level, acts of gratitude can lead to one's improved mental health and sense of well-being. Because gratitude acknowledges our connections with others and the unreality of our isolated selves, it is clearly the nature of astrology's Moon.

Forgiveness or mercy seems to be in the same tribe as altruism and gratitude, for it extends to those who have previously harmed us in some way. Instead, this rare but prized response is based on acknowledging our shared vulnerability to cause harm to others. This most saintly of character strengths is based on the reality that we are not saints.

Previously we discussed humility as an antidote to the arrogance or entitlement that solar accomplishment frequently brings. Being realistic about ourselves clips our wings, acknowledges that we frequently fall short of our aspirations, and recognizes our dependence on others. We may be unique, irreplaceable, untranslatable – but so is everybody else we meet! This coordination of solar sense of personal specialness with lunar humbleness is a ground-level Sun/Moon dialectic.

Character Strengths and the Sun

From the virtue of courage, we get *integrity* and *open-mindedness* from wisdom or knowledge, and *appreciation of beauty and excellence* from transcendence. These seem to have solar characteristics.

Integrity is a slippery concept. It allies with concepts of authenticity and wholeness and refers to being true to our internal states, intentions, and commitments. Yet we all think, feel, speak, and behave in different ways and our patterns also change as we move through life. We are situational beings but also possess an enduring sense of identity that is solar in form.

When we are inauthentic or lack integrity, what are we like? We feel like we are putting on an act and we have diminished ourselves. Sometimes this seems required by circumstance. When we are courteous to a boss, client, or customer who we think is incompetent or not too bright, we are not being inauthentic but realistic and maybe a little humble. Many situations require that we appear differently from how we feel. If pushed to extremes, this mismatch between how we present ourselves and who we are leads to resentment and possibly self-destructive consequences. If we attend to this tendency of ours and not ignore it, there is much to learn.

The concept of integrity or authenticity implies an ability to accommodate, even to delight, in facets of oneself that seem contradictory to others. We contain many facets that are not reconciled by some abstract higher principle. Our astrological chart, as it reveals itself over time, can point out these facets.

Appreciation of beauty and excellence is a solar component of transcendence. Since the Sun's activity is often that of identification, beautiful objects or performances or other examples of excellence inspire us and indirectly stimulate our own sense of possibly. We don't have to be a gymnast or piano virtuoso or great scientist or talented artist to be uplifted and even empowered by their examples.

The character strengths that belong to wisdom or intelligence deserve their own section. The Moon and the Sun both have important roles to play.

Ways of Knowing: Intelligence and The Luminaries

The virtue of Wisdom or Knowledge includes *curiosity, love of learning, open-mindedness, creativity,* and *wisdom/perspective* as character strengths. The first two, discussed in the next chapter, may be functions of Mercury and can be used for good or ill. The last three have solar or lunar components and we discuss them here.

Is open-mindedness a lunar potential? Yes, if we call open heartedness, akin to kindness, moving toward wider horizons of awareness based on a deeper sense of commonality. Is open-mindedness a solar potential? Open-mindedness and the other character strength creativity both place us apart from the "groupthink" that surrounds us and that we often unwittingly buy into. As social beings we are pressured to stay in line with our family, network, or group.

Our solar desires to identify ourselves with a particular outlook and pattern of thinking become obstacles to our ability to think for ourselves. For most of us, this takes learning from others and courage to go there ourselves. Open-mindedness as character strength reserves our right to change our minds when considering new information or a differing viewpoint, although it can also hide indecisiveness.

Intelligence is multiform and multidimensional, applied differently to our lives as a whole and to situations we encounter. Loosely following Aristotle, we can categorize these dimensions as wisdom, practical intelligence, and social/emotional intelligence. These categories of intelligence move from the solar, to the lunar and solar together, to the lunar. We begin at the level of the most solar and seemingly abstract to the lunar and most seemingly ordinary.

Wisdom as Contemplation or Reflection

The sage or wise person is one to be listened to, whose actions we can emulate, and most cultures value these individuals. Today we are more likely to focus on the clay feet of those who are thought wise, or on the self-serving ambitions of those who promote themselves as such. In our isolating but interconnected world, a host of hypocrites, moral demagogues, commercial gurus, and quasi-visionaries are readily available. Yet most of us aspire to be wiser than we are, and we admire those who seem genuinely wise.

Virtues and Intelligences: The Luminaries

Wisdom's solar qualities include independence of mind that comes from our life experiences and learning from mistakes – those of ourselves and others. As unwelcome as they are, failures provide the feedback necessary for greater understanding and wisdom.

It can be difficult to find young wise people although they are certainly around. On the average, younger people have a greater need to fit in to a cultural norm and social groups, and their assumptions and prejudices are largely untested by experience. It takes time to learn the limitations of our concepts and the dangerous power of our unexamined perspectives, hopes and fears.

Because wisdom depends on the accumulation of life experiences along with a persistently inquiring, critical mind, there are no straightforward astrological indicators. Given that, however, we may describe some processes and outcomes astrologically.

We begin with a universally acknowledged scientific pioneer who later brought his values and discernment onto a larger stage and whose positive reputation has stood the test of time. [150]

Propelled to fame as a younger person because of his scientific discoveries, Albert Einstein was charming and unassuming for a celebrity. Later in his life he put his heart into causes like nuclear disarmament, civil rights, and inequality. As he grew older, he was increasingly considered a wise elder and today is frequently cited for both intellect and a good heart.

We learn much from examining his Sun placement. Einstein's Sun is in Pisces, in its joy in the ninth house, governed by Jupiter in Aquarius. Because Pisces and Aquarius are disconnected by sign, wisdom would take longer and would not happen easily. The sextiles from Mars in Capricorn and Pluto in Taurus to the Sun help to enhance motivation and a sense of urgency in difficult times. Balancing his intensity and giving him an appealing personal style is the Moon, governing his Cancer Ascendant,

---
150 AA. Birth record available

Astrology and the Lives of People

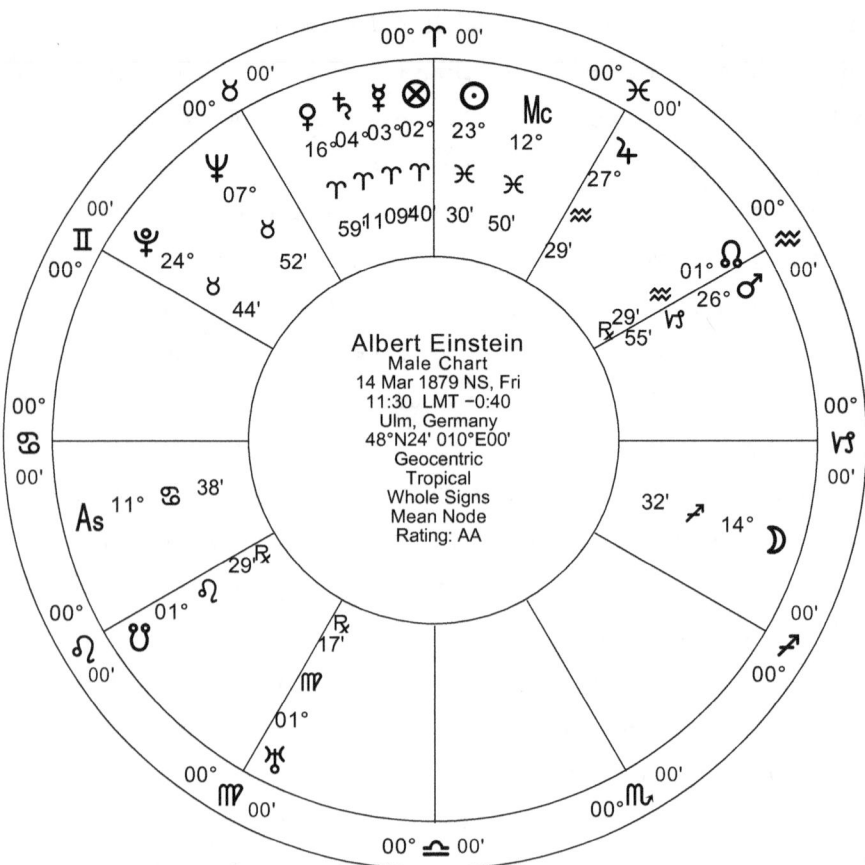

in Sagittarius with a trine to Venus in Aries. Jupiter therefore governs Einstein's Midheaven as well as the Sun and the Moon: Einstein could not divorce his life and his work from the larger world.

A pacifist during World War I and its aftermath, Einstein shut himself off from the world and worked inconspicuously in Berlin. Later, as a celebrity who was Jewish, Einstein was an easy target for the Nazis; he and his family fled Germany and eventually came to the United States. Seeing the possibility that Germany could develop atomic weapons using his scientific advances, Einstein dropped his pacifism and alerted American authorities to this possibility. Thus began the Manhattan Project and eventually the nuclear attack on Japan.

Virtues and Intelligences: The Luminaries

Einstein felt guilty about his role in advancing nuclear arms and redoubled his efforts on behalf of disarmament and putting an end to warfare for good. His advocacy for civil rights and patronage of black colleges were connected to his experiences of being Jewish and German during the Nazis era.

Like Sigmund Freud and Carl Jung's successes at their respective vocations, Albert Einstein's scientific accomplishments alone did not make him a wise person. All three established a base from which they could inquire further and expand their horizons of concern.

In the United States, two successful military men – George Washington and Dwight Eisenhower – became President because of previously gained experience and reputation. We saw the same in the nineteenth century England with the Duke of Wellington and twentieth-century France with Charles De Gaulle. All four individuals built a reservoir of trust and were thought of as both national leaders and wise elders, even when they were not very wise. Others, like Eleanor Roosevelt (and Jimmy Carter who at this writing is still with us), have been political figures in the public eye for so long that they outlasted their detractors and became national role models.

Eleanor Roosevelt's astrological chart shows her many dimensions that came together to give her a singular national role during some of the most difficult days of the twentieth century for the United States.

Eleanor Roosevelt's Sun placement in Libra seems to be without much distinction.[151] There is some strength with this luminary being in the eleventh house and with a strong trine from Saturn in the seventh house. The Sun, however, is the dispositor for Jupiter in the ninth house in Leo – conjunct the fixed star Regulus – that is also in charge of her Ascendant. Jupiter gave broader perspective and Saturn gave discipline to one raised in a privileged environment.

---
151 AA rating: birth record available

Astrology and the Lives of People

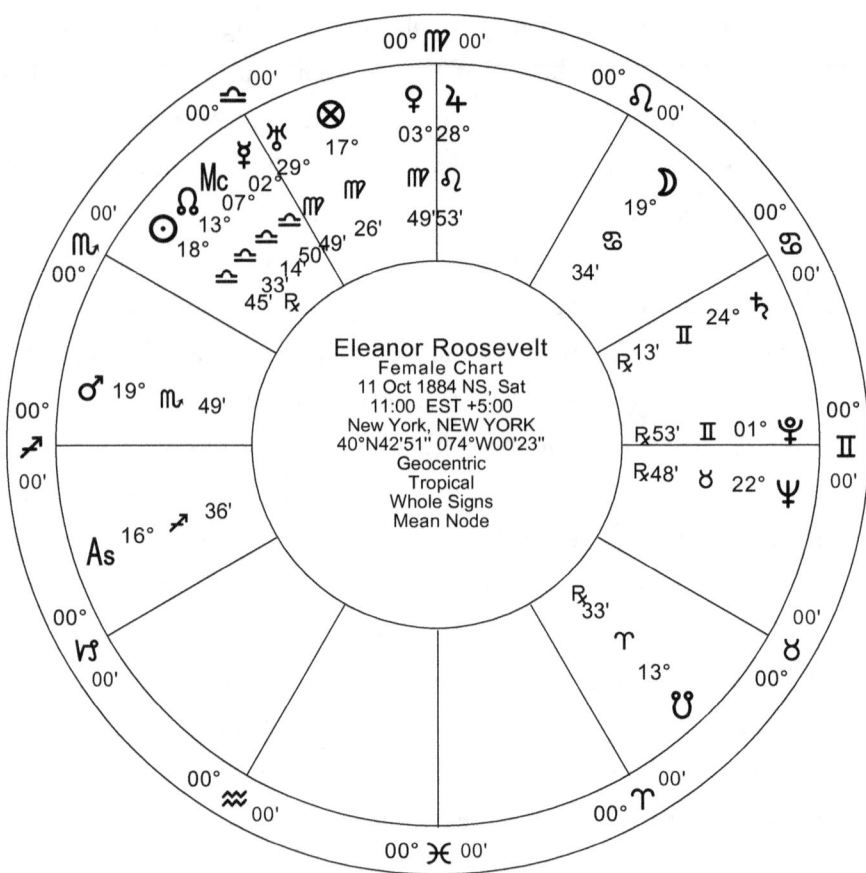

Eleanor Roosevelt's life conditions also relate to her Moon in its own sign Cancer, with a separating square from the Sun in Libra but an important applying trine to Mars in Scorpio in the twelfth house. Her unhappy childhood became a means by which she could access a degree of empathy and commitment unusual for somebody of her privileged situation. She was famous for taking on causes of those on the fringes of society or with a lower status.

Drawing attention again to Sun trine Saturn in the seventh house: her unhappy marriage to a public figure who became U.S. President gave her a public voice, one that resulted in a frequently hostile press and many setbacks. She famously advocated for expanded civil rights and sought help (unsuccessfully) for Jewish refugees desiring entry into the United States. She was a whirlwind of activity during the twelve years she was First Lady.

By the time Franklin Roosevelt died toward the end of the Second World War, Eleanor Roosevelt was an internationally recognized public figure. President Harry Truman appointed her the US delegate to the newly formed United Nations. She responded in part by heading the UN Commission on Human Rights and was a guiding hand in the writing of the Declaration of Human Rights published in 1948. When a new Republican President was elected in 1952, she stepped down from her UN role although she served in other capacities later. Eleanor Roosevelt continued to play a role in American political life until her death in 1962.

When we examine the lives of less famous people like you or me, it is much the same as with famous people like Albert Einstein and Eleanor Roosevelt. We have had our youthful successes or failures, sometimes followed by stagnation or depression in middle age, and through it all we may gain some wisdom to earn the respect of others.

Without getting old first, all of us can develop more of our inner sage. Our experiences and inclinations so far, and our astrological chart, can give us some guidelines.

We can give ourselves more opportunities to practice reflection and self-examination, making this a regular part of our lives. We can look up at the night sky on a clear night, spend time at a seashore, or climb a mountain and look around from the summit. These experiences can bring our minds beyond daily particularities to something vaster. The joy in the reflective life is not in the arrival of certainty but by talking and listening to ourselves, noting how we think, seeing what inspires us and what agitates us. For most of us, self-examination must be punctuated by an inner silence from which new insights can emerge.

From the viewpoint of the luminaries, the Moon discloses intuitions that are already there but unrecognized by us. The Sun brings our multidimensional intelligence into the light of day and brings it into coherence and vision.

Developing and maintaining the right kinds of friendships offer another possibility for developing greater wisdom. We all need others to encourage us, challenge us when we have veered off track, to ask those uncomfortable questions that give us pause. This may also happen when we are with a group of like-minded people *if* there is an atmosphere of open exploration and honest appraisal. The ancient Confucian tradition added study as an ingredient of self-improvement, but also having a mentor or teacher. We have inherited a tremendous amount from the wisdom of the past and there is much to learn from many traditions.

Wisdom is the most obvious form of an "intellectual virtue", as Aristotle would phrase it. Others are far closer to those situations that arise in our daily lives.

Solar Intelligence or "Practical Intelligence": Assessment of Means and Possibilities

The next category of intelligence we sometimes trivialize as "common sense". Sometimes we call this ability "good judgment" The Sun can shed a bright light of objectivity that can be developed as we navigate circumstances and challenges. We are less concerned with abstract principles than with practical applications, and the Moon has an important supporting role.

Here we attempt to balance competing interests of ourselves and those around us, discover how and when to act decisively and when to let things happen on their own. One prerequisite is that we understand our own limitations: – do we hide behind rationalizations and excuses, by our favorite self-deceptions?

In the *Nicomachean Ethics*, Aristotle wrote of "*phronesis*" or practical intelligence that is sometimes badly translated into English as "prudence". He depicted *phronesis* as "characterized by deliberating well about what is good and advantageous for himself, not in a particular respect, e.g., what conduces to health or to strength, but in what sorts of thing conduces to the good life in general."[152]

Yet in the heat of the moment there is usually no time for deliberation, and we must respond quickly. Practical intelligence requires stepping back and looking at different possibilities, to whatever extent that is possible, like a competent chess player weighing different possibilities before making their next move, and the clock is ticking. We need to coordinate solar intention with immediate lunar responsiveness.

The Moon's Contribution: "Emotional Intelligence"

The last category of intelligence is more a modern concept and has a strong lunar quality. The Moon anticipates consequences and can respond quickly. In a game of poker or in a job interview, what is the best move *right now*?

The Moon's situational intelligence is captured with seemingly trivial examples: should I take a "mental health day" from work today or buy that piece of cheesecake or that fountain pen that's staring at me from the storefront window, or should I start a conversation with that quiet person across from me?

Those who think highly of us might not notice our abiding lunar habits and temptations. When we think we should know better, we find ourselves fighting with ourselves. When we're weak-kneed for more vulnerable, we look for a convenient rationale to take the day off, to get the cheesecake or the fountain pen or chat with the easier conversationalist instead of the shy person over there. Our previous responses to similar situations play strongly and can mold bad or good habits over time.

The Moon's intelligence, at its best, notes physical and emotional responses in ourselves and others, neither subservient to them nor tyrannical over them. Our anxieties, rationalizations, and fantasies do not

---

152 From *Basic Works of Aristotle*, trans. W.D. Ross Bk VI, Chapter 4, 1140a; or from Loeb Classical Library, trans. H. Rackham, VI, 4, v.1

solely decide things but are weighed with other factors like obligation, commitments, and our longer-range goals.

Emotional Intelligence, a concept pioneered a generation ago, asserts that success in life (whatever that means) is more closely correlated with Emotional Intelligence than the Intelligence Quotient that was a fixation of prior generations. Not surprisingly, the components of Emotional Intelligence line up nicely with astrology's traditional Moon.

A few years ago, I was in an airport bookstore, a fine place to find self-improvement books for business travelers. I purchased *Emotional Intelligence 2.0* by Travis Bradberry and Jean Greaves (2009), because this work seemed to speak the language of many of my students and clients. According to the authors, there are four components to Emotional Intelligence.

Self-Awareness is the ability to "accurately perceive your own emotions in the moment and understand your tendencies across situations." (p. 24) What "strategies" enhance this attribute? The authors counsel a neutral attitude toward emotions and feelings as they arise and a willingness to feel them physically, and to ponder patterns and causes. They suggest watching our patterns from above "like a hawk", and notice how we react to stress, how these subjective states manifest in our posture, demeanor, and general appearance.

Self-Awareness then morphs into *Self-Management*, which is "your ability to use your awareness of your emotions to stay flexible and direct your behavior positively." (p. 32). Importantly, many of the strategies are physical, focusing on breathing, learning to pause ("count to ten"), take time off to recharge, smiling and laughing more, synchronizing body language with emotion, and improving quality of sleep. Accompanying these are strategies like identifying negative self-talk and finding a friend who can give you objective guidance.

This leads outwards to *Social Awareness,* which is "your ability to pick up on emotions in other people and understand what is really going on with them." (p. 38) Strategies consist of increasing opportunities to watch and listen to others closely, attending to their body language, informal interactions, and being mindful of their social and cultural surroundings. This appears to build on the previous components and enhances our understanding of others.

Emotional Intelligence culminates in *Relationship Management* that the authors deem as "your ability to use your awareness of your own emotions and those of others to manage interactions successfully." (p. 44) Strategies include improving communication style and not giving mixed signals, more skillful exchanges of information with others, and attending to the details of building relationships over time.

The reader may blanch at the words "relationship management", although this goal may be appropriate to the young supervisor who has picked up this book at an airport bookstore. One must ask "To what end does one seek to manage relationships?". From social worker to sociopath, it is important to be skilled at understanding people, assessing their motives, and targeting their needs. Many a con-artist is expert at identifying the feelings and emotional patterns of others – to manipulate or exploit them. The rest of us can develop greater emotional Intelligence in pursuit of self-awareness and positive interactions with others.

Luminaries Together

There are no easy remedies for all our problems, yet astrology can depict potential difficulties and suggest strategies. Much is gained by comparing the luminaries in their respective signs, houses, and their aspects from visible and modern planets. We should consider the luminaries for their strengths and weaknesses and how, in personal application, we can make the best of both. This has been our intention.

Abstracting and moralizing, being prejudiced and self-centered, are downfalls related to the Sun's intentionality and identification of self. One remedy is to develop the virtues and character strengths that make it possible to suspend our inclinations and do what is best in a given situation. This is limited by our blind spots and the creative ways in which we rationalize what we wanted to do anyway. Best is to develop the virtues of the other luminary, the Moon, along with those of the Sun.

Astrology's Moon, with its focus on the body's wisdom, the immediacy of sensory and emotional experience, and connecting through empathy and compassion, is well-suited to compensate for the Sun's self-preoccupation. We may take a sympathetic attitude because someone else's pain makes us uncomfortable, so our sympathy is about us, not the other. Empathy can also degenerate into a kind of posturing, so that this response becomes a front to impress others and us. Here we need Sun's discriminating intelligence and Mercury can also make a strong contribution.

How can the five visible starry planets, Mercury through Saturn, contribute to our solar and lunar aspirations and applications? How can they get in the way and what are some possible remedies? In the next chapter, we will again look at both traditional depictions and modern versions of virtues and character strengths, now applied to these five planets.

Chapter Thirteen

Virtue's Components and Its Neighbors

Returning to Peterson and Seligman's *Character Strengths and Virtues*, we continue our discussion of virtues and their component character strengths and shifting from the luminaries to the five planets. Our discussion of virtues and character strengths will culminate with three kinds of *friendship* in the context of astrology's luminaries and planets.

I am reminded of a famous line from Confucius's *Analects* (4.15) that "Virtue is never solitary; it always has neighbors." Although their depiction of virtue (*de*) includes personal charisma, it is also true in our traditions. The cultivation of virtue and character is not with the intention to circle the wagons around our self-proclaimed goodness but to involve ourselves more skillfully and compassionately our world.

Virtues and Character Strengths

Below is the list of virtues and character strengths from the previous chapter. We see the four cardinal virtues (wisdom, temperance, courage, justice) plus two more that they call humanity and transcendence. Except for transcendence, there are clear correlations to our planets. Knowledge or wisdom includes the Sun and Mercury, courage is partly solar but also of the nature of Mars; justice is jovial, and temperance is saturnine.

- *Knowledge or Wisdom* includes curiosity, love of learning, open-mindedness, creativity, and perspective.
- *Courage* is comprised of bravery, persistence, integrity, and vitality.

- *Justice* includes citizenship, fairness, and leadership.
- *Temperance* has strengths of self-regulation or self-control, prudence, humility, but also forgiveness or mercy.
- *Humanity* divides into kindness, love, and social intelligence.
- *Transcendence* consists of appreciation of beauty and excellence, gratitude, hope or optimism, spirituality, and humor.[153]

Mercury

Character strengths from the virtue of wisdom or knowledge, *curiosity* and *love of learning*, belongs to Mercury. We can think of curiosity in two ways. One is an attitude of "what would happen if I do this?" that can open up new horizons but also backfire. The second curiosity asks questions – of people, procedures, principles, and assumptions that may take us beyond our comfort zone. The opposite to curiosity is closed-mindedness, an inability to see beyond what we already think we know or have experienced. Close-mindedness is often based on anxiety and a defensive attitude toward life.

Sigmund Freud had a positive quality of curiosity that he put to good use. Although vulnerable to over-estimating the value of his discoveries, many of them came from honest and rigorous attempts to solve some of the mysteries of our human nature.[154]

Much of Freud's writing begins with a question and moves systematically toward some answers. He showed an uncommon ability to re-examine and revise in the light of new understanding or the inadequacy of previous solutions.

---

153 The later work *Flourish* by Seligman (2011) contains the same list of character strengths with a few changes of category. Under Knowledge or Wisdom is "Social/Intellectual/Practical Intelligence" that instead of Humanity. Two strengths have been moved into Transcendence: "Forgiveness and Mercy" from Temperance and "Vitality" from Courage.

154 Rating AA: birth record available

Virtue's Components and Its Neighbors

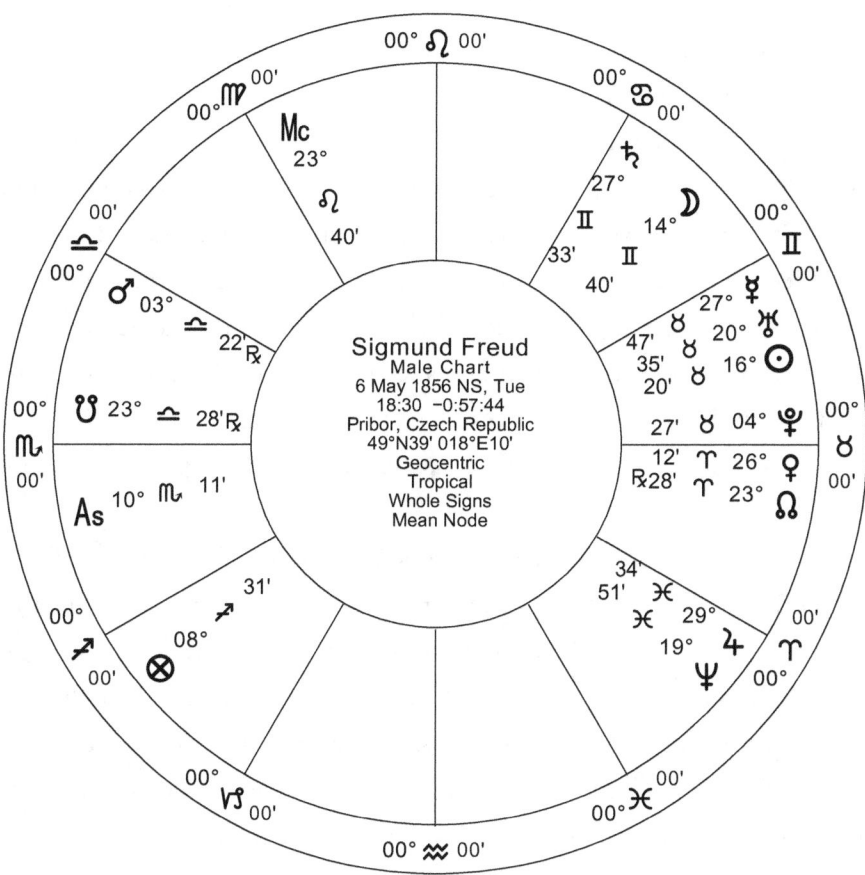

Freud's first major work, *The Interpretation of Dreams* (1900), begins with the simple question "what are dreams for?" In the light of centuries of no significant progress on this matter, he examined previous literature on dreams, rejected some ideas and supported others, contemplated some of his own dreams and those of patients – and came up with notions that are still with us.

Mercury is significant as the domicile of Freud's Moon in Gemini, with an approaching sextile to a dignified Jupiter in Pisces – hence his drive to bring his inquiries into a conceptual framework. (We may credit Mercury's placement in Taurus for the clarity of his writing style.)

Love of learning, a delight in learning new ideas, skills, and activities, is another character strength that belongs to Mercury. For many of us, love of learning must be strong enough to confront our ignorance or lack of ability, to tolerate frustration and self-doubt when learning is slow and effortful. The payoff is, of course, joy in our increasing knowledge, ability, or activity, and a renewed thirst for larger horizons of understanding.

Mercury also partakes of the virtue of humanity through *social intelligence* as "street smarts" or knowing how to get things done in a gang, neighborhood, or governmental bureaucracy. The Gemini side of Mercury can take on different perspectives and find clever ways out of difficulties. The Virgo side is the planet of the *factotum*, the "go-to" person, for good or not-so-good.

We can also look at Mercury's character strength of *humor or playfulness* as features of transcendence, although humor also shows up with other planets, as we've seen in the chapter on Jupiter. On Mercury's side, we revel in puns, humorous plot twists, and surprising punchlines when they are also clever. An ingredient of wisdom shows up from the back door.

From the cross-cultural trickster to Shakespeare's "fools" to many comedians and talk show hosts, irony and mimicry can wake us up to understand things differently, for wisdom sometimes follows wit.

Mars

The virtue of courage includes *bravery* and *persistence* that are of Mars. A solar nature for courage is evident in its word root *cor* or "heart" from Latin. It implies a will aligned with strong intention or passion. Mars brings us *bravery* or *valor* that is our ability to overcome fear and anxiety to pursue an intended course of action. Shakespeare's Falstaff was surely right that "discretion is the greater part of valor", although he was rationalizing running away from battle. Bravery is neither foolhardy nor overconfident, nor does it make excuses like the Bard's reluctant warrior. Mars provides sudden exertions of will that overpower anxiety or hesitation and allow

Virtue's Components and Its Neighbors

one to take a leap – into a public presentation, onto a battlefield, to ask somebody out on a date, or upon being taken into the operating room or going into court. *Valor* or *bravery* are also in attendance when we contemplate or directly face our own death.

We utilize courage – we "just do it." In preparation for something scary, we often need to cultivate courage deliberately. This often requires added support from others. Sometimes circumstances force a sudden response from us and we find out how brave we really are.

Eleanor Roosevelt, with Moon in Cancer in trine to her Mars in Scorpio in the twelfth house, did *not* write that every day we should do one thing that scares you. Instead, she wrote,

> "You gain strength, courage and confidence by every experience in which you really stop to look fear in the face. You are able to say to yourself, 'I have lived through this horror. I can take the next thing that comes along.' You must do the thing you think you cannot do." [155]

The internet is filled with pithy quotes like this one, testifying to the common value given to facing fear and responding straightforwardly. Roosevelt's advice, whether attributed to her or not, frequently comes up when people consult with their coaches, psychotherapists, or astrologers.

Maya Angelou excelled in a variety of roles while overcoming obstacles all along the way. Mars governs her strong Sun-Jupiter conjunction that can give ambition and enterprise. Mars is also the domicile ruler and is with the Lot of Fortune, and clearly her exertions paid off for her throughout her life. However, Mars is compromised by its opposition from Neptune and can be self-destructive. Other planets need to come to the rescue for her.

---

[155] Source from Bartlett, *Familiar Quotations (1980, p. 786)*: Roosevelt, E. *You Learn by Living* (1960)

Astrology and the Lives of People

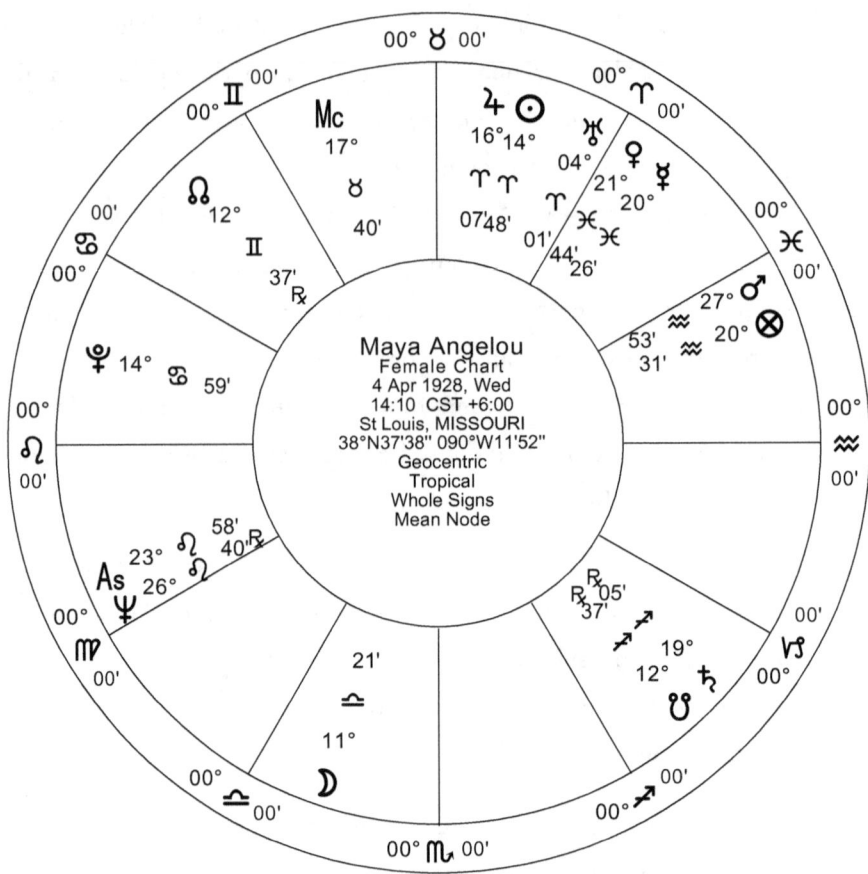

What kept Angelou striving for excellence and accomplishing so much? I look at Saturn that governs her Mars and Fortuna and is in trine to her Sun-Jupiter conjunction, adding saturnine qualities of self-discipline and toughness.

Jupiter

The virtue of justice that we associate with Jupiter contains character strengths of *fairness, citizenship,* and *leadership.* Jupiter brings us into the lives of others, into many different groupings that we humans partake of, from shared living spaces, interests, vocations, backgrounds, or just being on the same planet.

We usually equate justice with fairness, for this trait asks whether you can treat others as you would like to be treated yourself. Are you able to overcome personal biases and give everybody a decent chance? This is a high enough bar for most of us. Positive qualities of *leadership* and *citizenship* are reciprocal to each other: a leader bears responsibility for the well-being of the group and for its success, and the citizen participates and contributes to a community's achievements.

Saturn

Under the saturnine virtue of temperance is another feature of *persistence* that does not arouse itself in a Mars-like fashion but dusts itself off and continues, because there are no other good options. We may be brave enough in the moment but need persistence along the way because setbacks and self-doubts are inevitable when bringing ourselves to the limit, whatever that limit may be. When we give into discouragement and leave things incomplete, we begin to distrust our own resolve.

We continue with the saturnine strengths of *prudence* and *self-control*. Prudence weighs the consequences of what we do or not do and acts accordingly. Prudence slows down our impulses, perhaps prevents us from doing what we may later regret. Self-control (or self-regulation or self-discipline) is our ability to stay with what we are doing regardless of distractions and temptations and is a clear partner of persistence. Many of us, thinking that we lack self-control, have found that we have self-discipline when something truly important is on the line.

Venus

What character strengths go along with Venus? She clearly does not get her share in the list. Features of *appreciation of beauty* certainly qualify, as do some aspects of *social intelligence*. It is difficult to univocally classify romantic love as a character strength, although it is a critical feature of our human condition. Romantic love can spur us onto greatness or great folly, and both results are usually part of our life stories.

This fair planet that inclines us to love is also a pathway by which we can explore the different kinds of nonlunar but affectionate connections we make with others. Friendship, thought of broadly, is a sadly neglected feature of modern psychology and modern astrology, although well accounted for in the ancient world. This chapter concludes with the varieties of friendship and the variety of astrology's planets.

Friends, Colleagues, and Lovers

How often are our successes and failures related to the company we keep, by how our ambitions are supported or discouraged by others? How often do you counsel somebody that who they associate with plays a strong part in determining who they will become? We often improve quality of life first by improving our relationships – with friends, colleagues, and lovers. The five starry planets figure strongly in the nature and activities of all three kinds of personal connection.

Continuities and Discontinuities

These three categories of relationship – friends, colleagues, lovers – have connections and confusions between them: becoming friends with a colleague or developing physical intimacy with a friend can make a connection flourish or destroy it.

Our astrological houses help in our investigation of these different kinds of relating.

- The fifth house, the joy of the planet Venus, brings us to pleasure, entertainment, activity we do, to "unwind", not for gain but its own sake. This covers many activities that connect us with others.
- The seventh house, traditionally the house of marriage, includes 1:1 ties with "significant others", be they romantic or business partners, even teachers or mentors and students where the exchange benefits both parties.

- The eleventh house, the joy of Jupiter, has larger groups as its scope and signifies activity with many others, from lunchtime companions to political parties.

For our purposes I'll simply use the words "friends" and "friendship" to cover these three categories covered by the fifth, seventh, and eleventh houses. Although there are substantial differences within their scope of behavior, they all seem organized in similar ways. Our lives with friends, colleagues, and lovers – as dissimilar as they may seem – share features of *equivalence* and *reciprocity*. Equivalence (not "equality") allows for free exchanges among partners. One is neither a friend, colleague nor a lover if the interaction is not reciprocal, if there is not some meaningful exchange. If the relationship is not exactly between equals, as in between teacher and mentor and student or client, the reciprocal nature of the relationship is there to compensate.

From a lunar point of view, friends (including colleagues and lovers) provide safety, comfort, and personal and emotional support. From the solar side, these relationships allow for fuller self-disclosure and self-expression. Connections with those who are role models may inspire us to become, in some way, more than we currently are.

Emerson and The Philosopher

When we discussed Ralph Waldo Emerson in the chapter on the Sun, his democratic ideals were noteworthy when compared to those of the more aristocratic-leaning Aristotle. Both men were deeply concerned with friendship, the significant company we keep.

Most of us are not as cheerful in this arena as was Emerson. When he wrote about the foundations for friendship, he presented the viewpoint that there are no strangers but friends we haven't yet met. Here is how he opens his essay "Friendship".

> "We have a great deal more kindness than is ever spoken. Maugre [despite] all the selfishness that chills like east winds the world, the whole human family is bathed with an element of love like a fine ether. How many persons we meet in houses, whom we scarcely speak to, whom yet we honor, and who honor us! How many we see in the street, or sit with in church, whom, though silently, we warmly rejoice to be with! Read the language of these wandering eye beams. The heart knoweth."[156]

We need to include Emerson's exuberant personal presence in our assessment of him, yet it did not occur in a vacuum. He would not have become an influential thinker without the supporting network he helped create and nourish, without all the people he befriended and mentored and to whom he sometimes provided financial support. Many planets contributed to his strongly affiliative character.

Venus in the seventh house governs Emerson's Ascendant and first house; Venus also has a strong sextile to Mercury in its own sign Gemini. This brought curiosity and extraversion together. He made friends easily and believed that strangers were friends he hadn't met yet.

Walking down the streets of Concord, Ma., people sometimes crossed the street to avoid him – they didn't have his robust interpersonal energy and probably had other business to attend to. It's hard not to think of Emerson's Venus in combustible Aries.

For somebody clearly Jupiterian in his writings and personal style, it is surprising to see that Emerson's natal Jupiter is in detriment in Virgo and in the twelfth house. Planets in the twelfth house are not doomed, yet they can be sources of difficulty unless brought into the light and activated in a positive way. Noting the close square of Jupiter to Mercury in Gemini that governs Jupiter, it was Mercury's role to escort Jupiter into prominence.

---

156 Essays and Lectures p. 341

Virtue's Components and Its Neighbors

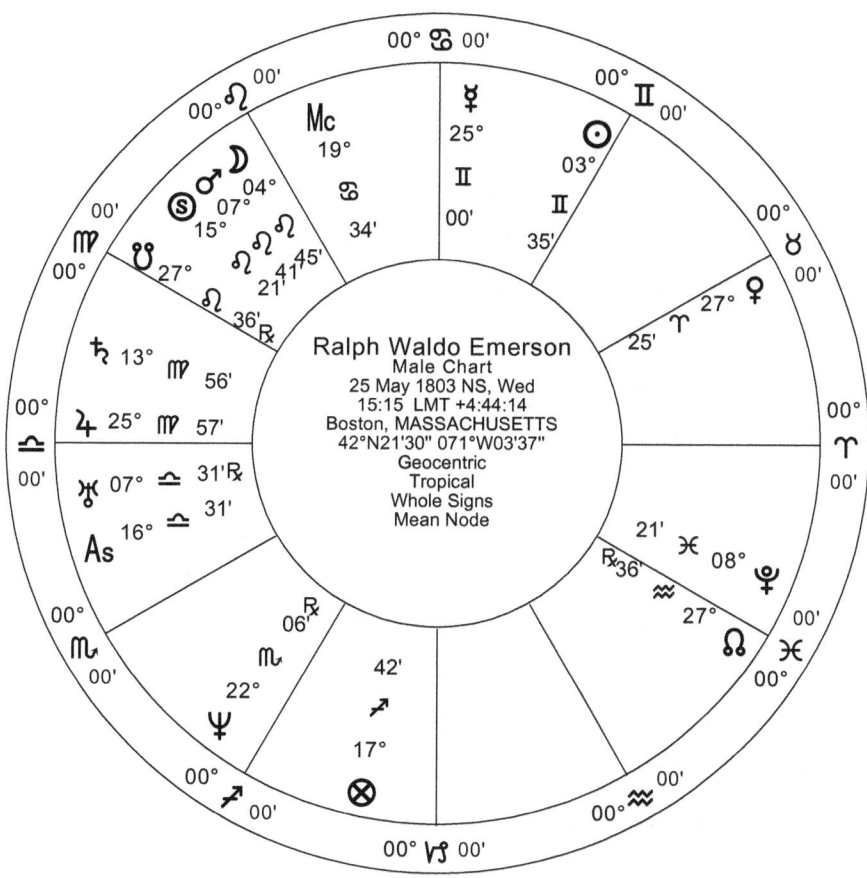

As a young man Emerson was confronted with a personal and spiritual crisis: at about the time of his Saturn return and after transiting Saturn had been in square to his natal Sun, Emerson's wife died. Also at this time, despite his background, training, and vocation, he left the Unitarian Church for which he was a minister. This left him alone and depressed, a condition he helped treat by a trip to Europe. He saw the usual sights but also met leading luminaries like John Stuart Mill, Wordsworth, Coleridge, and Carlyle. Emerson returned to America invigorated, began his first essay "Nature", and the rest is history.

All this was greatly helped by the alliance of the Moon and Mars in the eleventh house in Leo, governed by the Sun (in its joy in the ninth house and in Gemini). Emerson's group of Transcendentalists is impressive and includes the younger Henry David Thoreau, Margaret Fuller, and Bronson Alcott (father of Louise May). Emerson also discovered and encouraged Walt Whitman, although later he became nervous about the younger poet's exuberance of expression. The eleventh house is allied with groups and friendships, but ancient astrologers also designated this place as Good Spirit (opposite the fifth of Good Fortune) that accords well with the impact of our close ties upon our lives.

Toward the end of the *Nicomachean Ethics*, Aristotle discourses on the different kinds of friendship. Love, or *philia* is broader than our concept of romantic love and includes emotional ties between friends and between colleagues. Aristotle returns to his premise of our human nature as seeking what is good through means appropriate to our human nature: *philia* also refers to seeking these goods.

Aristotle outlines three bases for friendship: the first two kinds, for the sake of pleasure and utility, are ephemeral but more frequent.

> "Now those who love each other for their utility do not love each other for themselves but in virtue of some good which they get from each other. So too with those who love for the sake of pleasure; it is not for their character that men love ready-witted people, but because they find them pleasant. Therefore those who love for the sake of utility love for the sake of what is good for themselves, and those who love for the sake of pleasure do so for the sake of what is pleasant to themselves, and not in so far as the other is the person loved but in so far as he is useful or pleasant. And thus these friendships are only incidental; for it is not as being the man he is

that the loved person is loved, but in so far as he is useful or pleasant."[157]

Friendship based on virtue or excellence is more difficult to come by than the first two – and possibly more so in our modern culture. Whereas the first two are oriented toward what one gets from the relationship, the third benefits both parties.

> "Perfect friendship is the friendship of men who are good, and alike in virtue; for these wish well to each other qua good, and they are good in themselves. Now those who wish well to their friends for their sake are most truly friends; for they do this by reason of their own nature and not incidentally; therefore their friendship lasts as long as they are good – and goodness is an enduring thing...."[158]

Aristotle wrote for a culture less well-traveled than our own, with communication largely in person, and when one encountered fewer people during one's lifetime than we do now. Depending on our age, we may have already passed through at least a handful of lovers and romantic partners, many friendships, and a large flock of colleagues. In our modern age, friendships based on virtue or excellence, generally reserved for a few close long-standing ties, are difficult to come by.

Emerson valued friendship and association in its quantity, Aristotle was more mindful of the ingredients that make for quality of friendship. Advantage Aristotle? Not necessarily. As modern society yields a greater number of possibilities for connection, there is a broader pool through which one can find those who are good models, who we can learn from, who exemplify qualities we would like to develop. They may be in our lives for a relatively short time but they can make a difference. What is

---

[157] Nicomachean Ethics, Book VIII.3 W.D. Ross translation (*Basic Works*) 1156a10-22; H. Rackham translation (*Loeb Classical Library*), iii 1-3
[158] As above: Ross translation 1156b6-12; Ross translation iii.6

required of us? Let's call it opportunistic discernment: we sense who may have qualities that bring out the best in ourselves and we learn to distance ourselves from those who bring out our worst.

Our Connections and the Five Planets

Our planetary symbols address much of the complexity of connecting with others. They give us information about how friends, colleagues, and lovers come about, what makes these categories change when they do, and what poisons them.

Mercury, at first glance, conforms well to Aristotle's depictions of friendships that are based on usefulness. If we work together on a common project, the other person has information or skills that help us do our job. Perhaps our lover is good at home repair; our "best friend for life" has an extended family with a second home that is often empty during the summer. Mercury, amoral but intelligent, looks for its own advantage. As our needs and desires change, these ties may also change.

All our friendships require Mercury. Without some open conversation and exchange of ideas and perspectives, our friendships, collegiality, and romantic relationships all become dull. We often know that a new person in our life may be significant when respective mercurial minds connect, when conversation is easy and interesting. Romantic connections begin and flourish when the people have the "same mind" on some things – but not on everything.

Implicit is the need for reciprocity, otherwise one of the parties feels used. Is one getting from the relationship as much as one is giving to it? When there is an imbalance, we can feel we're being "played" by the other, and sooner or later we distance ourselves from that person.

Venus naturally relates to ties where pleasure is a strong component: that would be all types of relationships but in different ways. This planet is necessary for romantic relationships, yet over and above physical attraction there must be joy simply to be in the company of the other. This extends to other kinds of association that include witty chatter, pleasurable activities, entertainment, and even some physical attraction to add a little spice.

The downfalls of Venusian friendships arise when one person derives more pleasure than the other, making one feel they are solely the other's object of gratification. This can extend to social as well as romantic or sexual situations. Aristotle would add that when we change, what gives us pleasure may also change, and one may grow out of some friendships over time. If Mercury's downfall consists of manipulating to one's advantage, that of Venus is shallowness, superficiality, frivolousness.

Mars at first sight seems to have little to do with friends, colleagues, and lovers, yet some of our most fervent ties have a Mars dimension. We find this from those who engage in team sports or musical performances, are in the same military unit, or who participate in a political campaign – even when they are on opposing sides. Not only is there camaraderie with those on the same side but also respect, even admiration, for those on the other side even when they prevail over us. A "worthy opponent" – in a video game, athletic contest, dance competition, or courtship ritual, brings up your "game", whatever that game happens to be.

Even in our romantic relationships, most of us prefer good-natured feistiness, even some competitiveness, to predictable concordance. Mars-like relationships of this kind are also vulnerable: competitiveness can become nasty, feistiness can become hurtful, win-lose situations can become subject to cheating and humiliating a defeated opponent. Mars can be extreme.

Jupiter brings us into vaster regions of experience and provides larger contexts for knowledge and activity. Here are friendships, collegiality, and romance that connect with politics, spirituality, and culture – from neighborhood to planet. Passionate lovers become colleagues when they share membership in a larger field of activity. Friendships of this kind may come closer to Aristotle's depiction of friendships of virtue or excellence, for there can be a moral framework or concordance in values that connects individuals.

In the realm of friendship, there are three related downfalls that relate to Jupiter. Because of its focus on community, there is a temptation toward social status-seeking and excluding those lower in rank than us. Nowadays as always, cliques and tribes constitute circles that exclude others who are different from how that group defines itself. Jupiter also gives hypocrisy and flattery, where one stays "in the loop" by cutting corners with the truth. There's also the danger of groupthink and a tendency to go along, against our better judgment, because we want to remain included or involved.

Saturn reminds us that for every meeting there is a parting and there is no such thing as a *forever* best friend, colleague, or lover. As our needs change, those who once met our needs and desires become burdensome or we become burdensome to them as they change. Consequently, it's likely that every person we're close to will disappoint us sooner or later – and we will disappoint them.

Because Saturn is a planet of our solitary nature, downfalls result from mistrust of others and their motives. Out of cynicism or self-seeking, treacheries and betrayals happen. When betrayed in some fashion, we don't just feel used but directly harmed by the person we had been tied to.

Sometimes we feel that our reliance on friends, colleagues, and lovers stems from our fear of being alone – and we feel we should be more self-reliant, more saturnine. This cold dark planet, however, also reminds us that our close relationships with those we love are precious, fragile, and temporary. We are invited to do some of the hard work it takes to maintain them and grow them further.

Now we retrace our steps through the planets Mercury to Saturn and consider each planet on its own terms.

Chapter Fourteen

Beyond the Planets and Beneath the Stars

Ascending the Heavens

Across millennia and diverse cultures, many have longed to step beyond the limitations of their bodily and localized selves onto something more basic or universal. A spiritual journey imagined as celestial, beyond Saturn toward the eternal, has had a long history. The seven visible astrological bodies move continuously in time. From an ancient and medieval perspective, the cosmos beyond Saturn takes us beyond ordinary time and space.

Saturn, our final visible planet and a planet of contemplation, plays a critical role. Although too often allied with rigid convention, this planet can distance us from our desires for wealth, fame, and privilege, from our daily preoccupations. Saturn allows us to question our tribalism and all the collective assumptions that go along with it. This dark planet opens possibilities for transformative spiritual development if that is what we wish for.

Traditional depictions of Heaven aim to orient the viewer beyond ordinary life and beyond this world. As far back as Cicero's *Dream of Scipio*, a tale of a famous Roman being taken up to the heavens by his grandfather to look back on Earth, the heavens have given us a sense of higher reality and an understanding of what is truly important.

Recall the Christian motif of ascending into Heaven. Western art and literature, from the medieval era through the renaissance and continuing in some Christian belief, focus on this moment of transcendence, symbolic or literal. The final ten cantos of Dante's *Paradiso* contain a poetic ascension through the heavens. Dante systematically takes us beyond Saturn through the realm of fixed stars (conveniently rendered as the zodiac), the first movement of the heavens, to upper paradise and finally to a vision of God. From Saturn and the other planets to a vision of God, these cantos take us from sequential time to timelessness, from measurable space to beyond space. Dante relied on a template already in place to produce this sublime literature.

A thousand years before Dante, and unknown to the medieval poet, was the *Corpus Hermeticum*, a set of short treatises that combine philosophical and theological themes from Greek and Egyptian traditions.[159] The "Pomandres" tells of the final destinations of our souls. For those who lived evil lives, after death they are assailed with piercing fire and "such a person does not cease longing after insatiable appetites, struggling in the darkness without satisfaction. [This] tortures him and makes the fire grow upon him all the more."

For those who led virtuous lives, a heavenly journey awaits. Traveling through each planet, they shed their habits and tendencies associated with each planet. Now purified, they first come to the Ogdoad that is beyond Saturn, and beyond this realm is the highest heaven and divinity.

> "And then, stripped of the effects of the cosmic framework, the human enters the region of the ogdoad; he has his own proper power, and along with the blessed he hymns the father. Those present there rejoice together in his presence, and, having become like his companions, he also hears certain powers that exist beyond the ogdoadic region and hymn god with sweet voice. They rise up to the father in order to surrender themselves to the powers, and, having become powers, they enter

---

[159] These writings, once thought to be contemporary with Moses, were first translated by Marsilio Ficino into Latin – as were the other writings we'll take note of here. Later the writings of the *Corpus Hermeticum* were ascertained to be from the second or third centuries of the common era.

into god. This is the final good for those who have received knowledge: to be god. Why do you still delay? Having learned all this, should you not become guide to the worthy so that through you the human race might be saved by god?"[160]

With this knowledge of the afterlife that awaits the sinful and the virtuous, one cannot help but live a less worldly life and help others aspire to live well.

Many of us are inspired when reading about the lives of renunciants and spiritual pilgrims. As worldly beings, our minds and inspirations move upwards toward sublimity, but also downwards, conditioned by our corporeal nature within a material world. Like many of us, Plato's philosopher, the friend or lover of wisdom, longs to ascend (or re-ascend) toward divinity. Plato's dialogue *Phaedrus* contains an eloquent account of these descending and ascending motions and the tensions between them.

Astrology and Spiritual Development

On matters of religion, astrology's traditions are straightforward. Jupiter plays a role, but other planets also have their functions. Hellenistic astrology looked at the ninth and third houses for spiritual gifts like divination and dream interpretation or for vocations of priest or priestess. Medieval astrology mostly focused on the ninth house: benefics either residing in or governing this house can point to religious piety; a poorly tenanted or afflicted ninth house may incline one toward heresy or even unbelief.

Although these delineations reflect cultures less pluralistic than ours, they continue to be relevant for many of us. Belonging to a particular religion or mode of spirituality continues to be part of our cultural or personal identity. Although most of us have spiritual aspirations and some of us have dedicated parts of our lives to religious or spiritual development, this area is often just one life concern among others.

---

160 *Hermetica*, translated and edited by Brian P. Copenhaver (1992) "Poimandres", p. 6

Astrology and the Lives of People

Some have made spiritual development the firm centerpiece of their lives and in modern times astrologers have expanded the range of astrology to include our immortal longings. Following the worldwide theosophical movement of the nineteenth century, many prominent astrologers have expanded astrology's range to account for spiritual transformation. Some have used the symbolism or allegory of celestial hierarchy that tapped into the traditional allegory or belief in ascension into the heavens.

Early in the twentieth century, Alan Leo's *Esoteric Astrology* applied astrology to theosophy's teachings on our different "bodies", from material to spiritual or immaterial. Decades later, in another text entitled *Esoteric Astrology* written down by Alice Bailey, esoteric and hierarchical rulers and the seven rays applied astrological symbolism to spiritual accomplishment and world redemption. Interestingly, the origin of the seven rays was attributed to a godlike "solar logos" that moved through fixed stars through planets to manifest in our material and spiritual lives.

Partly influenced by Bailey, Dane Rudhyar in the mid-twentieth century added spiritual dimensions to astrology's traditional symbolism. Since it is natural to symbolize higher consciousness cosmologically, many have depicted the modern planets Uranus, Neptune, and Pluto as pertaining to spiritual crises and evolution. Rudhyar cited these planets as "ambassadors of the galaxy", the galaxy symbolizing a spiritual core not substantially different from Dante's rendition of the highest heaven. Closer to our time, Stephen Arroyo and many others have applied outer planets in this fashion but without the cosmologies.[161]

These approaches have their critics. Most people are not spiritual pilgrims but are more concerned with the vicissitudes of worldly life. As with many other traditions, their formulations may also be vulnerable to unconscious spiritual materialism and spiritual bypassing. Spiritual materialism is our shadow desire to appropriate spirituality as a special

---

161 See Dane Rudhyar, *The Sun is Also A Star: The Galactic Dimension of Astrology* and Stephen Arroyo, *Astrology, Karma, and Transformation*.

identity; spiritual bypassing desires to skip over our ordinary and humbling situations and focus on matters seemingly more special. In both cases the personal ego has become a subtle and sneaky obstacle to spiritual growth.[162] Extended to groups, the result of either can be a spiritual elitism that is harmful to everybody.

Virtues: Worldly and Beyond Worldly

Plato's *Dialogues* provide different perspectives on spiritual longing. Aside from its aspirational and inspirational qualities, Plato's writings are also realistic. You may recall Raphael's famous painting *The School of Athens* that depicts an older Plato with his finger pointing upwards and a middle-aged Aristotle with his palm down toward earth. This seems unfair to the older philosopher who also pondered our limitations and how we can develop wisdom while we are living, breathing, and passionately subjective beings. We can begin by trying our best to live righteously, for here is where we begin from, where we show our "true spirit".

> "In the divine there is no shadow of unrighteousness, only the perfection of righteousness, and nothing is more like the divine than any one of us who becomes as righteous as possible. It is here that a man shows his true spirit and power or lack of spirit and nothingness."[163]

Plotinus lived and taught five centuries after Plato, endeavoring to systematize Platonic thought and include a contemplative approach to

---

162 Many astrologers today avoid Alice Bailey's reformulations of astrology for the spiritual life, as much of it seems opaque, complex, and grandiose. Not disputing these responses, there are some genuinely helpful qualities in this work. The daunting complexity of this material does necessitate that the follower put in some real hard work of sharpening intellect and absorbing the material on a deeper level. Secondly is the formulation of the "glamours", those tendencies along with spiritual path to let oneself be special and to impress others.

163 Plato, *Theatetus* 176b-c, trans. F.M. Cornford. Ed. Hamilton and Cairns, *The Collected Dialogues of Plato*

transcendence. Plotinus's teachings influenced a growing contemporary Christian tradition and were rediscovered along with Plato during the Renaissance. They were brought into the twentieth century theosophical movement and fascinate many astrologers today.

Plotinus depicts the soul's movements from the One or Absolute, toward combining with matter to dwell in a human body and conditioned existence. On this Earth, the Absolute in our souls calls us to contemplation and instills revulsion at the world's distractions. Plotinus's student Porphyry began a biography of his teacher by noting that Plotinus seemed ashamed of his body and even having a personal life. Plotinus rebuked one artist who had wanted to capture his likeness, stating that this physical form is a temporary and unimportant image compared to what is truly lasting.

Although there is no more other-worldly western philosopher, Plotinus was not naïve about our obstacles and limitations, nor was he a pessimist about our chances. His discussion of the virtues acknowledges our ordinary worldly virtues but also add a transcendent dimension to them.

Porphyry, who compiled his teacher's work into the massive *Enneads*, begins Book I with "What Is The Living Being"[164]. How is it that an immortal and unitary soul is affected by sense perceptions, passions, fleeting physical pleasures, discomforts, and pain? His response is to posit an aspect of soul that is composite and containing soul and body, a "joint entity" (Armstrong) or "couplement" (McKenna). This combination is distinct from the soul or intellect that is unitary and beyond change. We are both this composite soul and that which transcends being composite. Our ordinary virtues and vices relate solely to the composite.

---

164 Using the translation by A. H. Armstrong (1966), Loeb Classical Library. Another translation, from Stephen McKenna (1872-1934) helped introduce Neoplatonism to the modern world and influenced many modern astrologers. I will confine myself to the Armstrong translation, however, for its relative clarity and closeness to the original. McKenna translates the title of the first chapter of *Ennead 1* as "The Animate and the Man"

> "The virtues that result not from thought but habit and training belong to the joint entity; for the vices belong to this, since envy and jealousy and emotional sympathy are located there...While we are children the powers of the compound are active, and only a few gleams come to it from the higher principles. But when these are inactive as regards us, their activity is directed upwards: it is directed toward us when they reach the middle region." [165]

The last sentence captures the upwards-seeming pull from the Absolute that becomes stronger in the "middle regions" of the spiritual journey. In this middle region we begin to be carried upward and less effort is required from us.

What of those virtues from "habit and training" that, in my mind, correlate to the seven visible planets that adorn our lives? Plotinus posits a distinction between the earthbound cardinal or "civic" virtues that we have already discussed and those on a higher form of existence, the "purificatory" virtues.

In the second chapter of Book I, "On Virtues", Plotinus reminds us that the ordinary cardinal virtues "genuinely set in order and make us better by giving limit and measure to our desires and putting measure into all our experience." [166] We develop these qualities through habit and training.

These ordinary virtues, however, do not apply to divine existence: in that realm there are no temptations that necessitate temperance, no fears to stimulate bravery, and so on. The unitary soul's virtues that apply to a more divine existence separate us from our bodily concerns. Plotinus reformulates the cardinal virtues and applies them to the soul's immortal nature.

---

165 Ennead 1:10:10-11
166 Ennead 2.2.2

> "So the higher justice in the soul is its activity towards intellect (nous), its self-control is its inward turning to intellect, its courage is its freedom from affections....this freedom from affections in the soul comes from virtue, to prevent its sharing in the affections of its inferior companion....for intuitive thought there is knowledge and wisdom, self-concentration is self-control, its own proper activity is 'minding its own business'; its equivalent to courage is immateriality and abiding pure in itself." [167]

Although the cardinal virtues require cultivation, those of the soul are there already and are disclosed, not developed. This corresponds to some Buddhist traditions: our inherent nature manifests its enlightened qualities as we are freed from what covers them over. I am also reminded of the medieval doctrine of "infused virtues" that Dante employed for *Paradiso*. Thomas Aquinas made the distinction between the *natural or cardinal* virtues that we develop through effort, *theological* virtues of grace, hope, and love that are given by God, and the *"infused"* virtues that are the cardinal virtues but strengthened by God to apply to the spiritual life.

In his (somewhat unfair) critique of his contemporary Gnostics in *Ennead* Book II, Plotinus warned about the arrogance of the spiritual seeker, counseling that we can go only as far as our nature allows us to go. Nor does the spiritual seeker have exclusive rights to a divine nature. "This is like flying in our dreams and will deprive him of becoming a god, even as far as the human soul can. It can go as far as intellect leads it; but to set oneself above intellect is immediately to fall outside it"[168]. This may have applied to his own students and applies to other spiritual pilgrims, past and present.

---

167 Ennead 1.2.6-7
168 *Ennead* 2.9.9

Separating the ordinary worldly life from our spiritual possibilities is important for setting out on such a journey – we all may need to move away from some things that get us stuck. As one enters Plotinus's "middle region", a split may widen between the humbleness of what is common and the specialness of what is spiritual: these are the traps of spiritual materialism and spiritual bypassing cited above. Although the aspiration to ascend "beyond the planets" is relevant to beginning a spiritual journey, astrology's visible and moving planets and their applications or ordinary life are indispensable for all parts of this journey. They keep us honest.

I have supplied many examples of people who led exemplary lives, some more overtly spiritual than others, who have used their potential to move above small-mindedness to make strong contributions to the world. Some have found different ways to fuse the active and contemplative life.

Upwards toward divinity and down here among the ordinary, the five starry planets indicate action and involvement that can result in great achievement *and* provide a good foundation for the spiritual life.

Our seven visible bodies all have powerful roles to play. Without leaving behind our ordinary needs with all their details, the Moon brings commonality that becomes compassion extending everywhere. The Sun drops our predictable mechanics of self-identification and self-absorption and discloses the brilliance of who we already are and the world in which we already live.

It is not necessary to use astrology to make assumptions about past and future lifetimes: in the words speculatively attributed to Padmasambhava who was a founder of Buddhism in Tibet: if you want to know about past lives, note the conditions of your life now; if you want to know about future lifetimes, consider what you are *doing* now. Astrology, it appears, helps people on both fronts.

Contemporary with Padmasambhava was the Venerable Bede, of a different religious persuasion and a different part of the world. Advocating for the "good news" of Christianity, Bede likened our lifetimes to the flight of a sparrow who arrives from the dark into the warm hall for the king and nobles, soon to depart on the other side, back into the darkness and cold, perhaps the storm of winter. We are all sparrows flying above the warm hall of the king.

Bibliography

Angelou, Maya	*I Know Why the Caged Bird Sings*. New York: Random House, 2009
Arendt, Hannah	*The Human Condition*. Chicago: University of Chicago Press, 1958
	Eichmann in Jerusalem. New York, Penguin, 1966
Aristotle	*Basic Works of Aristotle*, ed. Richard McKeon. New York: Random House, 1941
	Nicomachean Ethics, translated H. Rackham. Cambridge, Ma.: Loeb Classical Library, 1994
Arroyo, Stephen	*Astrology, Karma, and Transformation*. Reno, Nv.: CRCS Publications, 1978
Augustine of Hippo	*Confessions*, translated Maria Boulding. Hyde Park, NY.: New City Press, 2012
Aurelius, Marcus	*Marcus Aurelius and his Times*, translated Long. G. Roslyn, Walter Black/Classics Club, 1945
Bartlett, John	*Familiar Quotations*. Boston, Ma.: Little & Brown, 1980
Biruni, Al	*Book of Instructions in the Elements of the Art of Astrology*, translated Ramsay Wright. London: Luzac, 1934
Bonatti, Guido	*Book of Astronomy*, translated Benjamin Dykes. Golden Valley, Mn.: Cazimi Press, 2007
Brady, Bernadette	*Brady's Book of Fixed Stars,* York Beach, Me.: Samuel Weiser, 1998
Bradberry, T. & Greaves, J.	*Emotional Intelligence 2.0*. Talentsmart, 2009
Camus, Albert	*The Rebel*. New York: Vintage Books, 1984

Castiglione, Baldesar — *Book of the* Courtier, Norton Critical Edition. New York, W.W. Norton, 2002

Chan, Wing-Tsit (ed.) — *A Source Book in Chinese Philosophy*. Princeton, NJ.: Princetown University Press, 1973

Chaucer, Geoffrey — *The Canterbury Tales*, translated Burton Raffel. New York, Modern Library, 2008

Confucius — *Analects*, translated Slingerland, E. Indianapolis, In.: Hackett, 2003

Copenhaver, Brian (ed.) — *Hermetica*. Cambridge, UK: Cambridge University Press, 1992

Crane, Joseph — *Astrological Roots: The Hellenistic Legacy*. The Wessex Astrologer, 2007

Between Fortune and Providence: Astrology and the Universe in Dante's Divine Comedy. The Wessex Astrologer, 2012

Davidson, Richard — *The Emotional Life of Your Brain*. London: Penguin, 2012

Du Plessix Gray, Francine — *At Home with the Marquis de Sade*. New York: Simon & Schuster, 1998

Simone Weil. New York: Viking, 2001

Duckworth, Angela — *Grit: The Power of Passion and Perseverance*. New York, Simon & Schuster, 2016

Dykes, Ben — *Introductions to Traditional Astrology: Abu Ma'shar & al-Qabisi*. Minneapolis, Mn.: Cazimi Press, 2010

Emerson, Ralph Waldo — *Essays and Lectures* New York: Penguin/Library of America, 1983

Epictetus — *Discourses II*, translated Oldfather, W. Cambridge. Ma.: Harvard University Press/Loeb Classical Library, 2000

Ficino, Marsilio — *Meditations on the Soul: Selected Letters of Marsilio Ficino*. Rochester, Vt. Inner Traditions, 1996

Foster, Benjamin — *Epic of Gilgamesh* Norton Critical Edition. New York: Norton, 2019

Bibliography

Freud, Sigmund	*New Introductory Lectures on* Psychoanalysis, translated J. Strachey. New York: Norton, 1964
Holoka, James P.	*Simone Weil's The Iliad or the Poem of Force: A Critical Edition.* New York: Peter Lang Publishing, 2008
Ibn Ezra	*Book of Reasons,* Translated Meira Epstein. Berkeley Springs, WV.: Golden Hind Press, 1994
	The Book of Nativities and Revolutions. translated Meira Epstein. Arhat Publications, 2008
James, William.	*Varieties of Religious Experience,* New York, Penguin, 1982
Joyce, James	*Finnegans Wake.* New York, Viking, 1955
	Ulysses, edited H. Gabler, Hans. New York, Vintage, 1984
King, Maxwell	*The Good Neighbor: The Life and Work of Fred Rogers.* Solon, Ohio: Findaway World, 2018
Leo, Alan	*Esoteric Astrology.* New York, Astrologer's Library, 1978
Lilly, William	*Christian Astrology,* facsimile edition. Exeter, U.K.: Regulus, 1985
Meade, Marion	*Dorothy Parker: What Fresh Hell is This?* New York: Villard Books, 1988
Orwell, George	"The Art of Donald McGill," in *The Collected Essays, Journalism and Letters of George Orwell*, ed. Sonia Orwell and Ian Angus, vol. 2: My Country Right or Left 1940-1943. Middlesex: Penguin Books,1968
	The Orwell Reader. New York: Harcourt, Brace, 1961
Plato	*Collected Dialogues*, ed. Hamilton, E. & Cairns, H. Princeton, NJ.: Princeton University Press, 1989
Plotinus	*Porphyry on Plotinus, Ennead* I, translated A. Armstrong. Cambridge, Ma.: Loeb Classical Library, 1989

Astrology and the Lives of People

Ptolemy, Claudius	*Tetrabiblos* Book III, translated R. Schmidt. Cumberland, Md. Golden Hind Press, 1996
Rudhyar, Dane	*The Sun is Also A Star: The Galactic Dimension of Astrology.* New York, Aurora, 1975
Schoener, Johannes	*Opusculum Astrologicum,* translated R. Hand. Berkeley Springs, WV.: Golden Hind Press, 1994
Seligman, Martin	*Flourish.* New York: Simon and Schuster, 2011
Smith, Denis	*Modern Italy: A Political History.* Ann Arbor, Mi.: University of Michigan Press, 1997
Tatar, Maria	*Heroine with 1,000 Faces.* New York: WW Norton, 2021
Tobyn, Graeme	*Culpepper's Medicine.* London: Element Press, 1997
Valens, Vettius	*Anthology Book II and Book III,* translated R. Schmidt, Berkeley Springs, WV.: Golden Hind Press, 1994
Weil, Simone	*On the Abolition of All Political Parties*, translated S. Leys. New York, New York Review of Books, 2013

Chart Data List

Angelou, Maya 4 April 1928, 14:10 CST, St. Louis, MO. AA

Arendt, Hannah 14 October 1906 21;15 CET, Hanover, Germany AA

Atlas, Charles (Angelo Siciliano) 22 November 1892 3;00 LMT. Acri, Italy AA

Austen, Jane. 16 December 1775 23;45 LMT Steventon, England A

Bailey, Alice 16 June 1880 7:42 GMT Manchester, England C

Berlusconi, Silvio 29 September 1936 5:40 CET B, 6:30 AA Milan, Italy

Bernhardt, Sarah 23 October 1844 20:00 LMT Paris France AA

Blake, William 28 November 1757 19:45 LMT London, England A

Casals, Pablo 29 December 1876 20:00 LMT Vendrell, Spain A

Clinton, Bill 12 August 1946 8:51 CST Hope, AK. AA

Day, Dorothy 8 November 1897 11:30 LMT Bath Beach, NY A

Einstein, Albert 14 March 1879 11:30 LMT Ulm, Germany AA

Eliot, George (Marianne Evans) 22 November 1819 5:00 LMT Nuneaton, England AA

Emerson, Ralph Waldo 25 May 1803 15:15 LMT Boston, MA AA

Ficino, Marsilio 19 October 1433 13:26 LMT Florence, Italy A

Fischer, Bobby 9 March 1943 14:36 CWT Chicago, IL. B

Franco, Francisco 4 December 1892 00:30 El Ferrol, Spain AA

Freud, Sigmund 6 May 1856 18:30 UT Freiburg, Czech Republic AA

Hoover, J. Edgar 1 Jan 1895 7:30 EST Washington, DC XX

Joyce, James 2 February 1882 6:00 AM LMT Dublin, Ireland A

Luther, Martin 10 November 1483 22:26 LMT Eisleben, Germany AA

Madoff, Bernard 29 April 1938 13:50 EDT New York, NY AA

Astrology and the Lives of People

Mercury, Freddie 5 September 1946 5:50 BAT Zanzibar, Tanzania X

Mussolini, Benito 29 July 1883 14:00 Predappio, Italy AA

Lincoln, Abraham 12 February 1809 6:57 LMT B

Machiavelli, Niccolo 2 May 1469 23:07 LMT Florence, Italy AA

Merton, Thomas 31 January 1915 9:00 GMT Prades, France AA

O'Neil, Thomas "Tip" 9 December 1912 5:00 AM, Cambridge, MA. A

Orwell, George 25 June 1903 11:30 LMT, Motitari, India B

Parker, Dorothy 22 August 1893 21:50 ESR West End, NJ B

Robinson, Jackie 31 January 1919 18:30 CST Cairo, GA. B

Rogers, Fred 20 March 1928 8:20 Latrobe, PA. B

Roosevelt, Eleanor 11 October 1884 11:00 EST New York, NY AA

de Sade, Marquis 2 June 1740 21:13 LMT Paris, France AA

St. Exupéry, Antoine 29 June 1900 6:15 LMT Lyon, France AA

Sanger, Margaret 14 September 1879 2:30 LMT C

Savonarola, Girolamo 21 September 1452 17:30 Ferrera, Italy C

Shostakovich, Dmitri 25 September 1906 17:00 PM St. Petersburg, Russia B

Taylor, Elizabeth 27 February 1932 2:30 UT London, England AA

Twain, Mark 30 November 1835 4:45 LMT Florida, MO. C

Trump, Donald 14 June 1946 10:54 EDT Queens, NY AA

Van Gogh, Vincent 30 March 1853 11:00 LMT Zundert, Netherlands AA

Weil, Simone 3 February 1909 5:00 LMT Paris, France AA

Whitman, Walt 31 May, 1819 1:45 LMT Huntington, NY A

Wilson, Bill 26 November 1893 3:00 AM EST East Dorset, VT. B

X, Malcolm (Malcolm Little) 19 May 1925, 22:29 Omaha, NB. AA

www.ingramcontent.com/pod-product-compliance
Lightning Source LLC
Chambersburg PA
CBHW051109230426
43667CB00014B/2498